River of Hope

Published in cooperation with the William P. Clements Center for Southwest Studies, Southern Methodist University.

River of Hope

Forging Identity and Nation in the Rio Grande Borderlands

OMAR S. VALERIO-JIMÉNEZ

Duke University Press   *Durham and London*   2013

Designed by C. H. Westmoreland
Typeset in Whitman by Keystone Typesetting, Inc.
Library of Congress Cataloging-in-Publication Data
appear on the last printed page of this book.

Earlier versions of chapters 3 and 5 appeared
in *Estudios Mexicanos/Mexican Studies* and
the *Journal of Women's History*.

Duke University Press gratefully acknowledges the
support of the Office of the Vice President for
Research at the University of Iowa, which provided
funds toward the publication of this book.

Para mis padres,
Edelmira Jiménez Flores y Raúl Valerio Sánchez

Contents

Maps, Figures, and Tables

TABLES

Maps, Figures, and Tables

TABLES

Acknowledgments

This book began as a way of understanding the Tamaulipas-Texas border region where I grew up. While living on both sides of this international boundary, I did not appreciate the region's distinctiveness until I left for college. From afar, I realized that I took many of the border's characteristics for granted, and knew very little of its history. My intellectual journey from engineer to historian began in a literature course taught by Margery Resnick. Subsequent courses offered by Martin Diskin, Noam Chomsky, Elizabeth Garrels, John Womack, and Peter Smith confirmed that my interests were gradually shifting. Listening to wonderful talks by Rolando Hinojosa-Smith and David Abalos at Thanksgiving "Pachanga" celebrations, I began to consider a career as a professor. While working as an engineer and wondering what field to study in graduate school, I benefited from the advice and work of two Chicana/o historians: David Montejano, through his first book, provided inspiration and convinced me to study history, while Emma Pérez offered encouragement and wisely suggested that I attend graduate school at the University of California, Los Angeles (UCLA).

I began exploring some of the ideas for this book in research seminars at UCLA. I thank George J. Sánchez for his instruction, advice, and most importantly, for creating a stimulating intellectual environment for a wonderful cohort of graduate students. Norris Hundley Jr., with much patience, provided detailed suggestions to improve the writing and organization of this study. He set high standards that challenged me to become a better writer and scholar. The ideas and suggestions of George J. Sánchez, Sonia Saldívar-Hull, David G. Gutiérrez, and James Lockhart also shaped this manuscript. Beyond their mentorship, George, Dave, and Sonia became models of scholars who sought to transform the university curriculum and diversify its scholars. While in graduate school, I enjoyed the friendship and collegiality of Ernesto Chávez, Linda Nueva España Maram, Jeffrey Rangel, Miroslava Chávez-García, Jaime Cárdenas, Monica Russel y Rodríguez, Tony Iaccarino, Stephanie Bower, Justin Wolfe, Zeus Leonardo, and Ned Blackhawk.

I would like to thank the principal readers at the manuscript workshop at Southern Methodist University (SMU)—Neil Foley, Vicki L. Ruiz, and Eric Van Young—as well as the late David J. Weber, John Chávez, Roberto Calderón, Pekka Hämäläinen, Martina Will de Chaparro, and Francis Galán for their constructive criticisms and encouraging insights. Over the years, I have received helpful suggestions and encouraging advice from many scholars, including Louis Mendoza, Ben Olguín, Ramón Gutiérrez, Beth Haas, Susan Johnson, Arnoldo De León, Deena González, Martín Salinas, Octavio Herrera Pérez, Juan Mora-Torres, David Montejano, Raúl Ramos, Toni Nelson-Herrera, Dennis Medina, Emilio Zamora, Valerie Matsumoto, Nancy Mirabal, Richard T. Rodríguez, Samuel Truett, Michelle Habell-Pallan, Stephen Pitti, Elliott Young, Andrés Reséndez, Juliana Barr, and Benjamin Johnson. I would also like to thank Giovanni Hortúa, Tim Garvin, Brianna Rodríguez, Matine Spence, and Jacob Altman for their research assistance. I appreciate the efforts of Valerie Millholland, Miriam Angress, and Gisela Fosado in guiding this manuscript through the editorial process at Duke University Press. I am also very grateful for the comments and suggestions from the anonymous reviewers of the manuscript.

I am honored to have received the University of California's President's fellowship and UCLA's Cota-Robles fellowship to begin my graduate studies, and subsequently to obtain graduate teaching appointments from the History Department and the César E. Chávez Department of Chicana/o Studies. Funding from UCLA's Institute of American Cultures enabled me to begin my research. I also received research support from the Newberry Library, the University of Houston's Recovering the U.S. Hispanic Literary Heritage Project, the National Hispanic Scholarship Fund, the Inter-University Program for Latino Research, and the Smithsonian Institution. A fellowship from the University of California, San Diego's Center for U.S.-Mexican Studies, and a postdoctoral fellowship at SMU's Clements Center for Southwest Studies gave me time to write while refining my ideas. I thank the History Department and the Office of the Provost at the University of Iowa for providing critical funding to complete the last stage of research and writing.

Numerous staff at various libraries and archives facilitated my research. For their patience and assistance, I thank the staff at the Newberry Library; the Center for American History and Benson Latin American Library, both at the University of Texas at Austin; the Texas State Archives; the Catholic Archives of Texas; Special Collections at St. Mary's Library; Bancroft Library; Amon Carter Museum; the Archivo Municipal de Reynosa; the Archivo General de las Indias, Seville; the Archivo Histórico Diplomático in the Secretaría de Relaciones Exteriores, and the Archivo General de la Nación, both in Mexico City. I am especially grateful for the guidance and advice from George Gause, at the Special Collections Library, University of Texas–Pan American, and Andrés Cuellar, at the Archivo Histórico de Matamoros. Finally, I would like to thank the staff at the interlibrary loan departments of UCLA's University Research Library; California State University, Long Beach; and the University of Iowa.

In 2006, I had the pleasure of joining a welcoming community at the University of Iowa. I thank my colleagues in the History Department, especially Leslie Schwalm and Malcolm Rohrbough, for their generosity and friendliness. My colleagues' insightful comments have improved this manuscript. Aminta Pérez and Michelle Armstrong-Partida made my transition to Iowa easier, as did colleagues in the departments of American Studies, Spanish and Portuguese, and English.

From the beginning of this project, my family has been understanding and supportive. Although they often wondered why this project took so long to complete, they trusted that I knew what I was doing. I am especially grateful to *mis tías* (Jiménez), who opened their home and kept me well nourished during an extended research period in Matamoros, Tamaulipas. My Tío Mario was always eager to learn about my latest research discoveries, while my tías Linda and Irma shared family stories and a great sense of humor. Although they did not live to see this book in print, the interest of my tíos and tías in my research helped sustain me. I miss Anita, Emma, Armandina, Beto, Efraín, and Mario. I also remember several Valerio aunts and uncles (Antonio, Panchita, Esperanza, and Esther) who shared the region's history. During my weekly trips between my father's house in Alamo, Texas, and my tías' house in Matamoros, I was constantly reminded that nation-states use international borders to divide populations, while culture and social relations often keep them united. My father, sister, and brother provided a haven from academia. Raúl Valerio Sánchez has been a wonderful role model as a loving father, generous grandfather, skilled carpenter, and cantankerous nonagenarian. Bety, Josué, and their families have nurtured and supported me unconditionally. I learned a great deal from Edelmira Jiménez Flores during her brief life. She encouraged me to excel academically and to follow her spiritual journey. I miss her deeply.

I am forever indebted to Cathy for her constant support and encouragement. By sharing her love of language, travel, and food, she expanded my
horizons. I cherish her intellectual curiosity, storytelling abilities, and commitment to justice. She is a great companion and best friend. Though our
lives became more complicated and exhausting when our son, Samuel
Moisés, was born, he is the joy of our lives. I look forward to every moment
with him.

Introduction

This story takes place in the delta region of the Río Bravo (Rio Grande), a borderlands once located on the periphery of European colonial power and subsequently on a newly created international border. It is a story of violence resulting from multiple conquests, of resistance and accommodation to state power, and of changing ethnic and political identities. The redrawing of borders, however, neither began nor ended the region's long history of unequal power relations. Nor did it lead residents to adopt singular colonial or national identities. Instead, distant governments were part of multiple influences on local residents, whose regionalism, cultural practices, and kinship ties continually subverted state attempts to control and divide the population.[1]

The river delta, or lower Rio Grande region (an area that extends some two hundred miles in a northwesterly direction from the river's mouth), was a homeland to at least forty-nine distinct indigenous groups before European contact. In 1749, Spanish colonists arrived to establish settlements on behalf of New Spain (colonial Mexico), which sought to consolidate claims to its northern borderlands in advance of rival European colonial powers. The Spanish colonists invaded this indigenous homeland and transformed the society of its inhabitants by introducing a different language, religion, and government. They also forcibly incorporated the region's indigenous people into their racially stratified society. By the mid-nineteenth century, Mexico and the United States had replaced European colonial powers in competing for control of these borderlands. The region became a center of conflict once again as foreigners arrived, beginning in the 1820s, seeking land and clashed with Mexicans. The Anglo American newcomers would introduce an additional language, various religions, and a different government. Like the previous Spanish colonists, Anglo Americans sought to integrate the conquered population as subordinates into their racially divided society.[2]

   This book explores how three nations—Spain, Mexico, and the United States—competed for control of the lower Rio Grande region and, in the process, helped shape the social and political identities of its inhabitants. It traces the changes in identity of borderland residents through three processes of state formation: Spanish colonial (1749–1821), Mexican national (1821–48), and American national (1848–1900). State formation is a type of cultural revolution in which governments define acceptable social categories and discourage alternative modes of identification that challenge their rule. The process can be interpreted as a gradual transformation in citizens' cultural practices. National laws, civic institutions, and municipal governments cooperate to enforce and legitimate the nation-state's rule and, in part, to shape its citizenry. Federal holidays reinforce patriotism; a myriad of regulations control the population by defining socially acceptable categories, such as citizen or immigrant. Governments delegitimized alternative models of identification, both individual and collective, in order to prevent adoption of those models. Spain and Mexico earlier and the United States later, though differing in their strategies, shared a desire to legitimate their rule and to shape the citizenry's loyalty. Through rituals, social categories, and the media, they sought to control behavior with laws that encouraged a disciplined people to identify with national goals while minimizing their affinity with their ethnicity, religion, or region.[3]

   This study's period and geographic setting allow for a detailed examination of the disjuncture between the goals of three state formation processes and their social outcomes. These processes included attempts on the part of colonial and national governments to administer their territories and regulate the activities of residents through institutions and bureaucracies. In the lower Rio Grande region, the government's goal of incorporating Indians through missions fell short because of disputes between missionaries and military leaders. Likewise, New Spain's attempt to regulate commerce achieved mixed success; borderland communities engaged in smuggling to offset the dearth of merchandise and supplies available through official trade routes. Later, Mexico's efforts to promote nationalism were frustrated by regionalist sentiments and its inability to protect the northern borderlands from Indian incursions. The United States subsequently fought a war of conquest with the avowed goal of promoting democracy—a contradiction that few Americans acknowledged. Despite lofty goals, American newcomers failed to establish democratic practices, as most conquered Mexicans did not exercise full citizenship rights.

Borderland residents adapted to multiple processes of conquest while their interests developed apart and in response to their central governments' goals. Native groups along the Rio Grande bore the brunt of the first conquest, as many died from wars of extermination and the introduction of epidemic disease. Nevertheless, some indigenous groups survived by establishing alliances with colonists, while others were absorbed into Spanish colonial society. The interests of colonists and of their central government initially coincided, but a schism developed gradually as residents grew frustrated with their government's neglect. When Mexico failed to provide military protection but continued collecting taxes, Mexicans began ignoring government requests and prohibitions against trading with Anglo Americans. After the takeover by the United States, the newly incorporated Mexicans became marginalized but adapted to American political and legal changes. They became politically engaged and filed lawsuits in attempts to protect themselves. Despite the new government's disciplining effects, residents subverted the structure imposed from above by carving out spaces of opposition. They resisted through a strategic use of citizenship and by employing the international boundary. By appropriating the discourse of citizenship, border residents alternately professed membership in Mexico or the United States according to the benefits they could obtain from such claims. Although each nation's government intended that the border would separate and control the region's population, local inhabitants in both countries subverted it by moving back and forth across the river to obtain political refuge, safety from legal prosecution, and economic opportunity.

This book describes the transformation of privileged Spanish subjects into neglected Mexican citizens and, ultimately, into unwanted American citizens. As colonists claiming land for the Spanish crown, they became both agents and privileged subjects of the colonial state. They established municipal governments and complied with royal orders; in return, the colonial government rewarded them with land and tax breaks. Mexican independence introduced a change in the residents' political identity; former Spanish subjects became Mexican citizens, albeit holding weak national allegiances. Mexico's government was unable to provide adequate military protection while it repeatedly imposed demands for money and army volunteers. Predictably, the colonists grew resentful of a central government that neglected their concerns. At midcentury, the Treaty of

Guadalupe Hidalgo, which ended the U.S.-Mexican War, transformed Mexican nationals living in the annexed lands into Mexican Americans (with American citizenship). Yet, Mexican Americans confronted numerous obstacles in exercising their citizenship rights. Their civil rights were circumscribed by difficulties in defending their property and obtaining justice in criminal courts. Although able to vote and run for office, they faced Anglo politicians who were more invested in managing voters than in sharing power. In the border counties along the lower Rio Grande, Mexican Americans comprised a majority of the population, but they exercised limited social rights because *americanos* (American citizens) failed to accept them as community members. The promises of American democracy remained unfulfilled: their political and legal exclusion confirmed that although the United States coveted Mexico's territory it did not want Mexican Americans "either as citizens or subjects."[4]

In this study, I explore the transformation of citizenship, ethnicity, and marital relations—these factors shaped the cultural identity that subsequently separated Mexican Americans in Texas (*tejanos*, or Mexican Texans) from Mexican nationals. The imposition of an international boundary at the Rio Grande meant that tejanos thereafter lived in a different social, economic, and political space than Mexican nationals across the Rio Grande. American laws altered class relations for residents on the U.S. side of the boundary because elite Mexican Texans began losing their land (through legal and extralegal means), while laborers were no longer legally tied to debts as they had been in Mexico. Anglo American newcomers further transformed class relations by marrying into elite tejano families to obtain land and social status, or by becoming the new political brokers through their knowledge of U.S. laws and politics. American jurisdiction also introduced liberal marriage and divorce laws that allowed more permissive marital relations than in Mexico. Like their Spanish Mexican ancestors who had constructed their ethnic identity in contrast to Indians, tejanos in the border region shaped their ethnic identity in relation to Anglo Americans and Mexican nationals.[5]

The lower Rio Grande region might seem an unusual place to explore these issues, since it has long been located far from the centers of political and economic power. However, the area became a crucial laboratory for state formation and competing national identities during the nineteenth century because it witnessed the convergence of several nation-building processes that produced widespread political and social change. As jurisdiction over this region changed from Spanish to Mexican rule, and ultimately to American control, residents experienced corresponding calls for allegiance and the imposition of diverse local governments to enforce control. By fashioning shifting and multiple identities, border residents followed patterns common to people situated along international boundaries, "where the twin processes of state centralisation and national homogenisation are disrupted."[6]

Throughout these jurisdictional transformations, the river remained central to the residents' hopes. Indians were the first settlers attracted to the Rio Grande, and the first to place their aspirations on its abundance for sustaining a homeland. As they gathered plants and hunted animals along its banks, a diverse Indian population sought to remain undisturbed by European expansion that threatened groups elsewhere in the borderlands. Their isolation was broken by the arrival of Spanish colonists in the mid-eighteenth century. New Spain expected that its communities along the Rio Grande would secure its claims to the territory ahead of European rivals. Subsequently, Mexico intended the river towns to become bulwarks against Anglo American expansion. The Rio Grande also became an avenue through which Mexico's government sought to liberalize trade. The last arrivals, the americanos, also linked the river to their ambitions. They expected the Rio Grande to increase their commerce into northern Mexico, and to establish a territorial boundary with its vanquished neighbor. Along with each nation-state's goals for the river were local residents' creative uses of the Rio Grande to undermine government aspirations. They too invested their hopes in the river. It came to represent the residents' goals of political autonomy, economic opportunity, and freedom from government control. This book's title, *River of Hope*, refers to the goals of multiple actors in these borderlands.

Political Transformation of the Borderlands

The border region's contentious political situation did not emerge abruptly in the nineteenth century; rather, it was part of a longer process with earlier roots. Beginning in the sixteenth century, New Spain sought to enlarge its wealth and territory by expanding northward. The discovery of silver mines in the late 1540s was the initial impetus for the northern movement of Spanish colonists. Livestock production and limited agriculture supplemented the northern mining operations. As mining towns grew, the market for cattle products expanded and stock raisers moved farther north. Beyond the mining towns, however, the lack of easily accessible wealth from minerals or from the labor of the region's nonsedentary Indians created an obstacle for the Spanish colonial government, which had difficulty attracting colonists to the region.[7]

Facing encroaching French and English settlements, New Spain sought to increase its sparse northeastern population to defend its borderlands. To substantiate its territorial claims, the colonial government encouraged several settlements in the Far North during the mid-eighteenth century. As part of this defensive strategy, it sponsored a massive migration into the territory known as the Seno Mexicano (Mexican Gulf), located south of Texas, and east of Nuevo León. The resulting Spanish conquest of the Seno Mexicano (renamed Nuevo Santander in 1748) established several borderland towns, including the *villas del norte* (northern towns), which provided colonists in neighboring mining communities with protection from Indian attacks. Such settlement efforts launched the first sustained nonindigenous conquest of the lower Rio Grande region.[8]

The villas del norte endured trade restrictions, inadequate military protection, and political neglect from the Spanish colonial and the Mexican national governments. Like other inhabitants of Mexico's Far North who resented their decreasing local autonomy after Mexican independence (1821), the villas' residents gradually developed local and regional sentiments stronger than any form of national allegiance. Residents held some loyalty to their state or province beyond their immediate towns, but a broad political identity encompassing the entire northern borderlands did not exist. Besides sharing a similar ethnic heritage, the northern colonists' strongest common identity was Catholicism. The river towns grew increasingly alienated from the nation in the mid-1830s as the central government continued to demand more contributions and military volunteers to suppress the Texas rebellion. Throughout the nine years of the Texas Republic (1836–45), the villas del norte remained within Mexico's jurisdiction while its residents repeatedly expressed regional autonomy. On the eve of the U.S.-Mexican War (known to Mexicans as the War of North American Invasion), the fissures between the villas and the national government were daunting. Attempts by centralists and federalists to achieve national unity had failed. By the mid-nineteenth century, northern borderland residents had ambivalent loyalties to the Mexican nation, strong bonds to a local region, and growing economic ties to the United States. These conflicting sentiments would shape how annexed Mexicans adapted to rule by the United States.[9]

The U.S.-Mexican War embodied the clash of competing nation-building

[handwritten margin note: local + regional sentiments > national allegiance]

efforts, and its outcome introduced significant consequences for both nations. By the mid-nineteenth century, the United States had enjoyed seventy years of a postindependence stable government. It was experiencing an expanding population, the beginnings of industrialization, and increased trade. Relatively successful in promoting nationalism, the United States was in the midst of a territorial expansion onto indigenous lands and territory formerly held by Spain and Mexico. In contrast, Mexico had not yet recovered from its devastating war for independence (1810–21), which had left the country bankrupt, its infrastructure devastated, and its population demoralized. In the twenty-five years since its independence, Mexico had experienced great political instability, the presidency having changed hands over twenty-two times. Beginning in the 1830s, the Comanches, Apaches, and Navajos increased their raids on Mexico's Far North, crippling the region's economy, devastating its population, and consuming its military resources. These problems prevented Mexico from maintaining control over its northern borderlands. After losing Texas in an 1836 secessionist revolt, Mexico had repeatedly sought to regain control over the wayward republic but had only succeeded in antagonizing residents there. Moreover, Mexico witnessed mixed results in forging nationalism. Its precarious situation contributed to its loss in the war with the United States. Its devastating defeat added to its turbulent dilemmas at midcentury. In contrast, victory transformed the United States into a continental nation with critical ports in the Gulf of Mexico and the Pacific Coast.[10]

The war led to the marginalization of Mexican Americans, who lost political, economic, and social power to Anglo American newcomers. This marginalization emerged from the contradiction between the democratic ideals of the United States and the racial ideology of its citizens. The doctrine of Manifest Destiny illustrated this inherent disagreement: on the one hand, it maintained that the United States was destined to spread freedom and self-government through conquest; on the other hand, it promoted the superiority of Anglo American society. How could subordinate people establish self-government? The nation's long history of politically excluding non-white racial groups resolved this apparent contradiction. Adapting their previous racial ideology to the annexed territories, Anglos assigned Mexican Americans a racial status based on the existing class structure of Mexican society. Although the new construction of racial meaning, or racialization, varied within the American Southwest and even within Texas, Anglos generally viewed wealthy Mexican Americans as "white" and their poor counterparts as racial "others." This racialization determined the degree to which Mexican Americans were incorporated into the local and national communities. While this perception granted elite men limited citizenship rights, it placed the majority in an ambiguous position. Their rights as citizens were respected when they advanced white supremacy but were denied when they threatened the status quo.[11]

Mexicans and Americans held different conceptions of the meaning of citizenship in the nineteenth century. Each group's distinct historical experience shaped their conception of the link between race and citizenship. Under Mexican law all males were theoretically considered citizens, but in practice only the elite exercised the vote and held elected office. In Mexico's northern borderlands, the elite claimed pure Spanish blood, though in reality they were quite racially mixed. Class rather than race remained the determining factor for obtaining citizenship rights in northern Mexico. In contrast, Americans absorbed their ideas about citizenship from a very different political tradition. Some believed in the Jeffersonian ideal of a republic of educated, yeoman white farmers. As urbanization increased, the Jeffersonians promoted westward expansion, justifying the displacement of Indians and continued enslavement of African Americans as necessary for the good of the republic. Later, the Jacksonian Democrats strengthened the link between whiteness and citizenship. In their view, Mexicans joined Indians as the main obstacles to a republic whose citizens believed in "white supremacy and slavery, Protestant hegemony, patriarchy, and Anglo Saxon predominance." The Whigs, the political rivals of the Jacksonian Democrats, opposed westward expansion because they feared the spread of slavery and the inclusion of more nonwhite people within the nation. The incorporation of an "incongruous mass of Spaniards, Indians, and mongrel Mexicans" threatened the Whigs' ideal nation of Anglo Saxon Protestants. Some of these ideologies were deeply ingrained in the minds of Anglo Americans when they arrived in south Texas and assumed positions of power.[12]

Contributions and Origins of Study

Recent studies illustrate the limited power that colonizing peoples had in New Spain's northern borderlands, and highlight the agency of indigenous groups. Far from homogenous, relations between Europeans and Indians varied by region and time period, as well as by the peculiarities of Spanish communities and indigenous nations. Indians and Europeans transformed one another through conflict, negotiation, and accommodation in isolated and distant communities where the Spanish colonial state's reach was circumscribed. According to James Brooks, the mutual interdependence between Indians and Spaniards in New Mexico led to a rough equality in power relations, and to hybrid identities and communities. Elsewhere, the borderlands' contested nature meant that European powers often failed to exert control over Native populations. For the Texas borderlands, Pekka Hämäläinen and Juliana Barr describe indigenous populations who asserted control over Europeans. The Comanches established an indigenous empire, according to Hämäläinen, by adapting horses and European weaponry, and successfully playing European powers against each other. Barr argues that Spaniards in eighteenth-century Texas lacked the population and resources to subjugate indigenous nations, and thus had to accommodate to the Indians' power.[13]

My study of the lower Rio Grande region provides another example of interactions between Indians and Europeans; in this case, the Spanish colonial state's goals fell short but for different reasons than in central Texas. A lack of adequate military support, failing missions, and economic restrictions led to fissures between the villas del norte and the colonial state. As elsewhere in the northern borderlands, the colonists enslaved Indians, waged wars of extermination, and forcibly integrated indigenous servants into their society. But unlike colonists in New Mexico and elsewhere in Texas, local Spanish settlers did not engage in reciprocal taking of captives with the region's Native groups. Lacking the resources and population to exert power over Spanish colonists, local Indian nations did not seize Spanish settlers, incorporate them into Native societies, or exchange them for Indian captives. While there was a mutual "interpenetration of cultures," this exchange appeared to be mostly in the colonists' favor. Nevertheless, local Indians did not simply react to the Spanish intrusion, but rather "created the conditions," to use the apt phrase of Pekka Hämäläinen and Samuel Truett, for the development of a borderlands society. Without the region's Indians, Spanish settlers would have lacked a critical labor force and strategic allies in struggles against larger indigenous nations. As they became incorporated into Spanish society, local Indians also increased its ethnic diversity and overall population. Subject to both European and indigenous empires, the lower Rio Grande region became another contested borderlands whose development depended on various Indian and European nations.[14]

In the nineteenth century, when fixed national boundaries replaced fluid borderlands in the region, the United States and Mexico each attempted but failed to obtain hegemonic power. The international border remained porous, primarily through the daily practices and concerted efforts of the region's inhabitants. Residents did not give up local control easily or immediately assume national identities; instead, they continued transnational practices, subverted national directives, and assumed strategic identities. Nevertheless, each nation-state did influence borderland residents as both the United States and Mexico, according to Andrés Reséndez, "attempted to build the nation at the frontier." State and market forces became significant in bringing about change, and consequently shaped the identity of borderland residents. Inhabitants of the lower Rio Grande region also selectively appealed to (and claimed membership in) each nation to advance local agendas. Such actions support the contention of Benjamin Johnson and Andrew Graybill that "the state ended up as much an invited guest in the borderlands as it did an armed stranger." In his study of Béxar (San Antonio), Raúl Ramos confirms Reséndez's arguments by demonstrating that *bexareños* (Béxar residents) welcomed trade with Anglo Americans while remaining deeply involved in Mexico's political debates. Ramos also finds that residents' family lineage and their concepts of honor influenced identity formation. As Texas came under control of the United States, the roles of bexareños shifted from cultural brokers to ethnic minorities, revealing that tejano identity varied by region and political context. Building on these scholars' findings about the contextual nature of tejano identity, I argue that geography, class, and citizenship were additional influences. When the new international border divided their communities, residents of the lower Rio Grande region directly experienced the transformation that Jeremy Adelman and Stephen Aron describe as a shift from a borderlands region to a "bordered land." Their geographic location allowed the region's tejanos to continue daily transnational relationships with Mexican nationals, while interacting—as a subordinate group—with Anglo American newcomers. Class and gender divisions affected Mexican Texans' responses to the U.S. takeover as did cross-border kinship networks, both ultimately shaping their culturally hybrid identities. While the hardening of borders often leaves less room for political maneuvering, it also offers new opportunities. As Peter Sahlins argues, residents on both sides of a border can find commonalities and grow closer after the imposition of an international boundary. Like Sahlins's subjects in the Cerdanya (along the Spanish-French border), the residents on both sides of the Rio Grande used the border to subvert national control, ultimately restricting and destabilizing both nations' power in the region.[15]

As a study of the U.S.-Mexican border, *River of Hope* engages with scholarship on the history of Mexico and the American West. As elsewhere in New Spain's Far North, Spanish colonists in the villas del norte became privileged subjects and agents for the colonial government by receiving economic and political support in return for establishing settlements. Residents shared the ambivalence of early nineteenth-century inhabitants of Texas and New Mexico, characterized by Andrés Reséndez as embracing contradictory views of nationalism because of their economic and cultural ties to the United States. To understand how the nation-state attempted to obtain their allegiance, I examine state formation at the local level because, as Peter Guardino argues for early nineteenth-century Mexico, "most people came into contact with state power at the municipal level of government, and the state built new means of collective and individual identification at this level." My study also illustrates larger patterns of conquest and race relations in the American West. Recent scholarship has shown that while Mexican Americans were legally considered white, their acceptance as American citizens was often dependent on their racialization by Anglo American residents. In addition to regional variations, local class relations and ideological sentiments influenced racial views. This held true along the U.S.-Mexican border, where transnational events shaped racialization and increased the importance of residents' loyalties and identities. Their experience illustrates what Samuel Truett describes as the "contingencies and messiness of transnational relations."[16]

This book benefits from Chicana/o history's focus on conquest, internal divisions, and identity. While earlier scholarship emphasized declension after the U.S. takeover, newer studies have offered a more complicated interpretation by examining Spanish Mexican society before the arrival of Anglo Americans. For New Mexico and California, Ramón Gutiérrez and Antonia Castañeda describe the role of Spanish colonists, missionaries, and soldiers in subjugating Indians and altering Native society. In the lower Rio Grande region, colonists and soldiers led the conquest of indigenous nations through wars and enslavement, while missionaries played a minor role. For California, Miroslava Chávez-García and Douglas Monroy analyze the transformation of Mexicans from conquerors to conquered peoples, and explain the impact of American laws and institutions. These studies describe internal class and gender divisions, as well as regional variations, to explain the disparate effects on communities and the population's varied responses. *River of Hope* builds on such scholarship by exploring inequality within Mexican society before annexation by the United States, and describing how class and gender differences shaped Mexicans' response to American rule. Like studies by Lisbeth Haas and Raúl Ramos, it traces identity transformations as a result of changes in ethnic relations and regional loyalties. It also complicates David Montejano's interpretation of Anglo Americans' influence on tejano patriarchal society by exploring the gendered nature of governmental power, women's adaptation to jurisdictional changes, and the central role of citizenship in border residents' struggles.[17]

By focusing on the generations of Mexican Americans that were "instantaneously rendered an ethnic minority of a much larger society" by the U.S.-Mexican War, this book examines the construction of an ethnic identity in a region that experienced what Américo Paredes refers to as the "dismemberment of Mexico in a very immediate way." As the largest group of Mexican communities bisected by the imposition of the international boundary, the lower Rio Grande is a critical region in which to examine identity transformations through multiple stages of conquest. The communities' location along the border led to daily encounters among Mexican and American citizens (of various ethnicities) that highlighted the distinct ways that each nation's laws shaped their ethnicity, gender, and citizenship. Such everyday experiences—along with transnational political events, migration, and trade—I argue, led border residents to construct strategic identities that countered each nation-state's disciplining efforts. Their creative use of the river to resist nation-state control, and their construction of hybrid identities established social and cultural precedents for future generations. As Ramón Gutiérrez and Elliott Young remind us, such hybridity developed from the experience of "border crossers, individuals who experience the dominant culture from the margins and from the outside, persons who were members of multiple communities, [and] intercultural translators." While most scholarship on Mexican American identity and citizenship struggles focuses on the twentieth century, *River of Hope* joins recent studies by Katherine Benton-Cohen, Eric Meeks, and Anthony Mora, which trace the roots of these issues to the nineteenth century.[18]

My family's history along the United States–Mexico border partly explains the origins of this book. My ancestors hail from the borderlands of Coahuila, Tamaulipas, and Texas. By 1914, my paternal grandparents had crossed into the United States to escape the Mexican Revolution's political turmoil. My father and his parents made the opposite trip into Mexico to flee the racial animosity in Texas during the Great Depression. My grand-parents had children born in both nations; some were Mexican citizens, others American citizens. In 1969, I accompanied my family as they crossed from Tamaulipas back into Texas, seeking better economic opportunities. My mother's relatives remained in Mexico while most of my father's kin eventually moved back to the United States. The international border re-mained prominent in my bicultural and binational youth, which was marked by frequent trips across the river to visit family and friends. Yet, I did not learn about this region's history from either Mexican or American text-books. It was missing from both nations' official historical narratives. The dissonance between my own family's experience and the history curricula used in my public-school and university education informs this book. My research began as a personal effort to understand the region's history. I hope that this book will help others learn about earlier generations of borderland residents.[19]

Sources and Terminology

The Spanish-language and English-language primary sources for this study are found in archives in Spain, Mexico, and the United States. To tell the story of how the region's residents experienced conquest, I have relied extensively on municipal archives. These include local government docu-ments that reveal details about the impact of political developments, and civil and criminal court records that contain information on social and economic life, as well as ecclesiastical documents that provide a window into family and social relations. There are substantial differences between the court documents based on the Spanish Mexican legal system, which include extensive details, and the American legal system, which offer sparse particulars. A significant consequence of this difference is that the gap in detailed information does not permit the same level of analysis. I also exam-ined newspapers in Spanish and English, which contain mainly the views of Mexican government officials and American journalists, respectively. The voice of Mexicans became increasingly absent from English-language docu-ments during the American period. With a few exceptions (e.g., diaries by Anglo American women) for the American period, elite men wrote most of the documents. Yet, state formation influences society beyond the elite. By highlighting the testimony and actions of Indians, African Americans, Mex-icans, women, and the poor, I examine their distinct, and often unexplored, reactions to the efforts by nation-states to enforce rule. As the majority of the population, nonelite people played a central role in shaping the border-lands and determining the significance of that region. Using aggregate data on baptisms, marriages, and divorces, I describe broad patterns that illumi-nate how residents' actions complicated their government's daily tasks.

My use of ethnic categories combines the terms that my subjects em-ployed during the period with the categories in current use. The Spanish colonists referred to themselves as *vecinos* (literally "neighbors" but more specifically "community members") and to local indigenous nations as *indios* (Indians). After Mexico's independence, the vecinos began identify-ing as *mexicanos* (Mexicans), while referring to *foraneos* (foreigners) as *norteamericanos* (American citizens) or americanos and *europeos* (Euro-peans). These terms primarily denoted nationality. I have used *American* as an adjective and noun when the use of *United States* would be inelegant with the understanding that many Latin Americans object to the appropria-tion of this term by norteamericanos. I do not capitalize Spanish-language terms such as *mexicanos* (following standard practice in Spanish) but do capitalize English-language labels such as Mexicans (as is standard practice in English). Racial categories (e.g., the terms *mestizo, indio, mulato*) in Spanish are not capitalized, but I have chosen to capitalize the names of Indian nations (e.g., Comanche, Apache, Mulato) because many of these are the same in English. Following the custom in Texas history, I refer to European Americans in Texas as Anglos, Anglo Americans, and Anglo Tex-ans, although the term "Anglo" does not correctly account for the ethnic diversity of the European American population. After the U.S.-Mexican War, residents began using the term *mexicano* to refer to ethnicity as well as to nationality. To distinguish between Mexicans with different citizenship, I use *Mexican nationals* for Mexican citizens and *Mexican Americans* for American citizens. When the records fail to note citizenship, I use *mex-icanos* or *Mexicans* to refer to people of Mexican descent regardless of nationality. After 1848, Mexicans in Texas border counties gradually ac-cepted the regional identity of fellow tejanos, so I use this term for the postwar period.[20]

Organization

This book is divided into two parts with the U.S.-Mexican War as the dividing line: the first describes the Spanish and Mexican periods, followed by an examination of the American period. The chapters are arranged topically, but overlap chronologically.

Chapter 1 describes the initial Spanish colonization of this region, which began in the late 1740s with the founding of the villas del norte. In settling and defending these river towns, the colonists interacted with Indian workers, slaves, consorts, enemies, and allies. Through these interactions with Indians, the vecinos created their own distinct ethnic and regional identity. In chapter 2, I describe the internal divisions within vecino society. The colonial government's benefits fell disproportionately on elite men, who used their control of local government to perpetuate their rule and regulate social relations. While the vecinos shared common ethnic origins, distinct class and gender identities divided them internally. The 1823 opening of a legal port at Matamoros increased trade while accentuating class divisions within vecino society and fortifying links between the villas del norte and American trade centers. Chapter 3 examines the effects of political transformations, which introduced representative government in Mexico, on the villas del norte. The Mexican government began promoting nationalism through patriotic celebrations, forced military service and obligations, and the discourse of citizenship. Although somewhat receptive to nationalist sentiments, northern borderland residents also sought regional autonomy. Schisms that had developed between the villas del norte and the colonial state trade restrictions, political neglect, and social isolation continued to grow during the national period.

The book's second part focuses on residents of the river's left bank, who were incorporated into the United States. Chapter 4 examines the impact and aftermath of the U.S.-Mexican War, which split the river communities and made its residents citizens of different nations. As agents of the United States, Anglo Americans furthered its state formation by administering local governments and enacting laws to regulate the cultural practices of Mexicans (especially the poor). The newcomers gained political and legal power through their familiarity with the conquering nation's politics, laws, and language, while most Mexican Americans became subordinate. Chapter 5 describes the changes in class and gender relations that American conquest introduced through new social norms and legislation. Anglos used their political and legal offices to gain economic power, while Mexican Americans gradually began losing land and concentrating in lower socioeconomic positions. Elite tejanos' control over society decreased as American laws gave workers and women more rights and opportunities than they had enjoyed in Mexico. Nevertheless, border society remained unequal among all the groups as elite men exercised more legal rights and held all political and legal positions.

In chapter 6, I describe the contested meanings of citizenship by examining various armed struggles, Americanization efforts, and the porous nature of the border. Economic and political issues encouraged the region's Mexican Americans to begin distinguishing themselves from Mexican nationals during the second half of the nineteenth century, and increasingly identify with other Mexicans in Texas as tejanos. Dispossession of land and police brutality led to an uprising in which citizenship demands became prominent. Cattle theft created a rift between Mexican Texans and Mexican nationals as tejano landowners allied themselves with Anglo American ranchers, charging that thieves from Mexico stole their cattle. In turn, livestock owners in Mexico accused poor Mexican Texans of theft. Higher-paying jobs attracted Mexican itinerant workers, but their presence complicated tejanos' electoral struggles because americanos accused Mexican nationals of voter fraud. Unlike most tejanos, who became politically subordinated to Anglos, Mexican citizens in Mexico retained their social and political power. Mexican Texans were not only politically marginalized in the United States, but also excluded from citizenship in Mexico. As a result of their political and legal subordination in the United States as well as their interactions with Mexican nationals, tejano border residents gradually developed a separate ethnic identity.

By the end of the nineteenth century, the inhabitants of the lower Rio Grande region had fashioned multiple identities throughout several decades in response to various nation-building processes. The social construction of new ethnic and national identities along the border illustrates that identity formation is a dynamic process subject to multiple interconnecting influences. As they adapted to each government's attempts to impose control, Mexicans created social spaces that subverted the formal institutional structures of each country. In their struggle to adapt and resist government control, they developed fluid, and often contradictory, identities within the volatile and ever-changing political atmosphere of the borderlands.

1

Constructing *Vecinos*, Constructing *Indios*
Complex Interdependence

One day in June 1804, José Ignacio de la Garza rode on horseback to Don Calletano Medrano's house and challenged Don José Francisco Capistrán to fight. At a *fandango* (dance) in Refugio the previous night, Capistrán had hit de la Garza with the side of his sword while another man restrained him. De la Garza now sought revenge, challenging Capistrán to leave the safety of Medrano's house and use the same sword to fight "if he was a man." Capistrán did not respond to the provocation and challenge to his masculinity, but Medrano filed charges of *injurias* (insults) against de la Garza, landing him in jail and prompting legal proceedings.

The *vecinos* (community members) who testified against de la Garza represented a cross section of the *villas del norte*'s (northern towns) elite men. They included Medrano, a merchant; Capistrán, a soldier and farmer; several more farmers; a judge; and a military officer. Two of the witnesses had previously been de la Garza's employers. Everyone called to testify, with the exception of de la Garza himself, identified themselves as *españoles* (Spaniards). Most of the witnesses referred to de la Garza as "el indio Ignacio" (the Indian Ignacio). His full name was not revealed until he himself stated it in court.

The witnesses described de la Garza as a thief, a troublesome servant, and a *baladrón* (braggart). They accused him of stealing items ranging from small articles of clothing and dishes to cattle and horses. His former employers characterized him as intolerable, citing bad service, thefts, and lack of courtesy. Witnesses claimed that he provoked fights often. Medrano maintained that de la Garza would continue to threaten vecinos until he was punished for his transgressions. De la Garza's lawyer argued that his client should be judged by different laws than those that applied to colonists and "conquered" Indians; he stated that his client was like a child who lacked "civilized" manners, including respect for religion and the law.

De la Garza's own statement was at sharp odds with the vecinos' testimony. He identified himself as an honest and hardworking thirty-two-year-old unmarried Indian *vaquero* (cowboy). His first imprisonment resulted from an attempt to free his sister, a *criada* (domestic servant), from the "power of Doña Francisca Cavazos" in the nearby town of Camargo. Subsequent incarcerations had been for alleged thefts that he dismissed as resulting from misunderstandings. Authorities had jailed him for stealing from a previous employer, he explained, after he took ten hides as payment for uncompensated work as a vaquero. Similarly, he responded to a former employer's accusations of disloyalty by arguing that he had left his job as a servant after ten years because his boss had provided less clothing for him than for other workers. As for the fight with Capistrán, he was merely retaliating against the vecino's disrespect.[1]

This incident provides a telling glimpse into nineteenth-century power relations and social interactions between *indios* (Indians) and vecinos in the villas del norte and the larger geographic region of the Seno Mexicano. De la Garza was typical of the area's Indian workers, who occupied a subordinate social position among colonists. The vecinos' attitudes of superiority were characteristic of a people who traced their ancestors to the eighteenth-century conquerors of the region. These ancestors had bequeathed to the settlers their privileged position in the community, their self-image as paternalistic providers, and their expectation that Indians defer to them.

New Spain's state formation brought colonization and conquest to the Seno Mexicano, which extended the colonial government's administrative control and devastated the region's indigenous populations. Spanish colonists arrived in the region to claim the land for New Spain, create vecino communities, and establish municipal governments. The colonial government provided the colonists with military assistance and the legal justifications for controlling an indigenous labor force. For Indians, the arrival of Spanish colonists meant conquest by extermination, subjugation, or exclusion. Indigenous nations faced a cultural and demographic catastrophe. Targeted by unrelenting Spanish violence, Indians had few viable choices. By resisting the colonists' intrusions, indigenous nations risked annihilation. Accepting Spanish rule meant that Indians became subordinate workers or slaves and probably lost their indigenous identities. The third alternative was to move beyond Spanish control and leave their homelands. Regardless of their choice, indigenous nations experienced widespread disruption of their societies. Spanish colonization brought newcomers who forcibly appropriated indigenous land, enslaved Indian women and children, and introduced devastating diseases. New Spain's colonial state formation in the Seno Mexicano was a cultural revolution, but a disastrous one for Indians who lost autonomy, territory, and sometimes identity.

The colonists' perceptions of Indians arose from various social interactions. Indian workers lived in towns as subordinate members, occupying the lowest rung of vecino society, like the *genízaros* (detribalized Indians) of New Mexico. Their origins were commonly among local indigenous groups whom the settlers had conquered and incorporated into their community as slaves. Some of these Indian workers were also the colonists' potential consorts; their progeny increased the vecino population and its ethnic diversity. Those hostile to the colonists, who were identified as *indios bárbaros* (barbarous Indians), often attacked towns in search of cattle and horses. The danger posed by these enemies encouraged the settlers to develop alliances with local autonomous Native peoples, some of whom occasionally assumed subordinate positions within vecino society while maintaining residence in nearby villages. These Indian allies inhabited a space between the subservient indigenous workers and the independent enemy Indians.[2]

The settlers' views not only served to categorize Indians; they also helped shape the settlers' own identities. By feminizing Indian workers, the vecinos asserted their own masculinity. They characterized indigenous laborers as dependent, childlike, and untrustworthy, while describing themselves as independent, mature, and responsible. Their violent conquest of local Indians, and their unrelenting war against enemy Indians, shaped the colonists' masculine ethos, which privileged strength, valor, and fighting skills. Similarly, their perception of enemy Indians as cruel, barbarous, and lawless encouraged their view of themselves as humane, civilized, and law abiding. Although race, class, and gender divisions fragmented vecino society, characterizing some Indians as the "other" permitted colonists to construct a shared "non-Indian" ethnic identity. Yet, their dependence on and continued incorporation of Indians as slaves, workers, and consorts complicated vecinos' identity.[3]

Colonization of Nuevo Santander

The vecinos' views of themselves, and those around them, gradually developed over several centuries as they and their forebears pushed into northeastern New Spain. Royal authorities had encouraged their settlement in the Seno Mexicano during the mid-eighteenth century to anchor the crown's penultimate province in Mexico. The economic and strategic concerns fueling the eighteenth-century expansion into the Gulf of Mexico coastal region were similar to the motivations for colonizing the northern territories during the sixteenth century. Whereas the possibility of discovering rich mineral deposits had sparked the initial push northward from central Mexico, growth of the livestock industry provided the motivation for expansion in the eighteenth century. Likewise, the strategic need to claim land for the crown led to colonization efforts in the northern borderlands.[4]

The establishment of the Nuevo Reino de León (Nuevo León) and Nueva Extremadura (Coahuila) preceded the colonization of the Seno Mexicano. Spanish settlers moved into these northern provinces in search of precious metals during the late sixteenth century. As mining communities expanded throughout New Spain's northern periphery, the livestock industry grew to provide food and clothing for the residents. During the cattle boom in the seventeenth and eighteenth centuries, colonists from Coahuila and Nuevo León moved their livestock into the Seno Mexicano, planting the seeds for future settlement. Attracting the cattlemen to the territory was its water supply, fertile pasturage, and the prospect of obtaining title to large portions of land and avoiding the rents in the neighboring provinces. Other settlers arrived to mine its extensive salt deposits that the vecinos of Nuevo León had been intermittently exploiting since 1650. Encouraging these efforts were merchants in Nuevo León who believed that settlements and roads in the territory would facilitate access to coastal markets. Thus, the ranchers' need for new grazing lands, as well as their desire to enlarge their markets for livestock products, created the motivation to colonize the Seno Mexicano.[5]

Rival European powers provided the external pressure for a large-scale expansion from Nuevo León and Coahuila toward the coast. Royal administrators promoted northern settlements as a defensive measure against territorial encroachments by European powers and the United States (after 1789). Colonial authorities grew increasingly worried during the first part of the eighteenth century, when the French encroachment suddenly appeared more menacing. English advances into Florida and the wars between Spanish and English military forces in the 1730s and 1740s further alarmed officials in New Spain. By the mid-eighteenth century, these territorial threats were serious enough that Spanish officials approved the massive colonization of the Gulf Coast.[6]

Until then, Spanish colonists sparsely populated the Seno Mexicano. Because of its location, the Gulf Coast region was a vital link in Spain's defenses along the northern border of its New World empire. To the north was Texas; on the west were Coahuila, Nuevo León, and Charcas; and on the south were Valles and Pánuco (see map 1). Along the Seno Mexicano's western edge, the Sierra Madre Oriental ran in a north-south direction, while the smaller Tamaulipa Oriental and Tamaulipa Occidental lay parallel to the Gulf Coast in the region's center. Access came from the rivers and streams that descended from the mountains in an eastward or southeastward direction before emptying into the Gulf of Mexico. The major rivers of the Seno Mexicano included the Nueces along its northern edge; the Rio Grande, the Conchos, the Soto la Marina in the region's center; and the Guayalejo on its southern periphery.[7]

The rivers and streams produced fertile areas of vegetation and wildlife that attracted at least seventy-two indigenous groups who lived in the Seno Mexicano prior to Spanish settlement and who spoke a variety of languages, including Coahuilteco, Cotoname, and Solano. Concentrated along the territory's waterways, the Apemapem, Borrados, Masa Cuajulam, Sarnosos, and others subsisted mainly by hunting, fishing, and gathering. They moved frequently in search of the region's seasonal wild plants, such as mesquite bean pods, prickly pear fruit, maguey root crowns, pecans, acorns, and a variety of tubers and roots. Supplementing their diet were game, including deer; armadillos; rabbits; and various species of birds, fish, and snakes. A group of indigenous horticulturists lived in the southern part of the territory, where they cultivated corn, beans, squash, chile peppers, and melons. The diversity of the indigenous population became even richer in the sixteenth century with the arrival of the Malaguitas, Pamoranos, Cacalotes, and other nations displaced from Nuevo León by advancing Spanish villages. Some of the surviving names of indigenous nations are self-referential Native-language labels, while others are the colonists' creation.[8]

Continuous hostilities between Indians and Spanish immigrants on the northeastern frontier led colonial administrators to devise several methods of conquest. Unlike other areas of New Spain's northern periphery, such as Coahuila and Alta California, the "pacification" of Indians in Nuevo León and the Seno Mexicano did not rely principally on missions and presidios, due to the officials' concern about expenses. Instead, royal authorities turned to civilian settlements to subdue and "civilize" the indigenous populations. Missionaries worked concurrently with civilians, and engaged in spiritual conquest only after other methods had failed. While evangeliza-

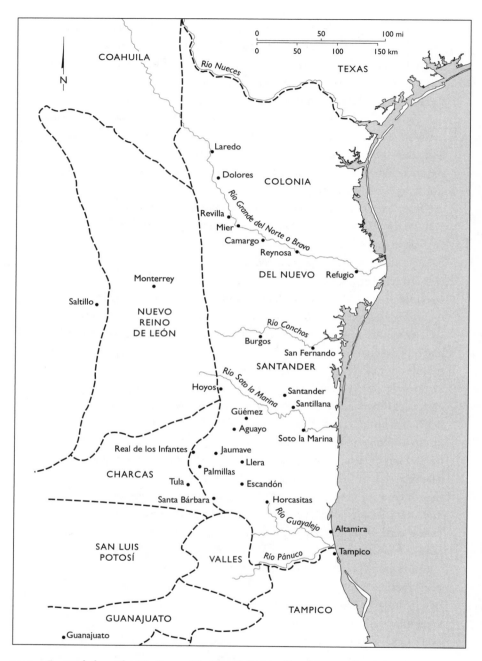

MAP 1. Located along the Río Bravo (Rio Grande), the villas del norte formed the northernmost group of towns in Nuevo Santander. Circa 1750s to 1820s. Map adapted by William L. Nelson.

tion efforts met the crown's moral goal, they were subordinate to economic and strategic concerns. Missions, therefore, often competed with civilian settlements for coveted land and indigenous labor. The already weak colonization role of missionaries was made more tenuous because of their dependence on civilians for protection from Indian attacks.[9]

In Nuevo León, the encounter between colonists and indigenous groups began violently with the initial Spanish arrival in 1577. Confronted with early setbacks in mining, colonists turned to Indian slavery for profit. In establishing the towns of Monterrey and Cerralvo, they captured Indians to sell as slaves for the mines in Zacatecas. The colonists' arrival in the late sixteenth century displaced indigenous groups. The settlers struggled to secure workers because Nuevo León's Indians—nonsedentary hunters and gatherers—were unaccustomed to the tributary labor common in central New Spain. Unable to compel Indians to work through peaceful means, the colonists resorted to armed force. During the seventeenth century, Nuevo León's vecinos obtained the colonial state's support in requiring Indians to work through *encomiendas* (legal title to the labor of Indian groups). Colonists with encomiendas forced Indian men to work and captured women and children for use as hostages and domestic servants. After colonial officials abolished the encomienda system in 1698 because of widespread abuses, they instituted a policy of gathering Indians into *congregas* (towns), as a way of "protecting" and controlling them. This change did not stop the abuse, for settlers transformed the congregas into encomiendas in all but name.[10]

The colonists' encroachments onto Indian land, use of forced labor, and outright enslavement created widespread resentment. During the early eighteenth century, the Indians struck back by attacking Spanish towns, deserting the missions, and forming alliances that strengthened their resistance. The colonists retaliated by intensifying their efforts at securing forced laborers and hostages, thereby causing the Indians to withdraw east into the Gulf Coast, from which they sent raiding parties to attack vecino settlements. Spanish slaving expeditions from Nuevo León escalated the conflict. By the mid-eighteenth century, royal authorities decided to end indigenous resistance once and for all with rapid and massive immigration into the Gulf Coast that would permit unimpeded travel between the province of Texas and other regions of New Spain. Before the mid-eighteenth century, travelers from Coahuila and Nuevo León to the Bahia del Espíritu Santo in Texas had needed to circumvent the Gulf Coast in order to avoid independent Indians.[11]

Colonial authorities selected José de Escandón to lead the settlement effort because they had favored his policies as captain general of the Sierra Gorda in Nuevo León. There he had given land to soldiers so they could sustain themselves instead of drawing money from the colonial treasury. Escandón proposed a similar strategy of soldier-settlers for the colonization of the Seno Mexicano, which he renamed Nuevo Santander after his province of birth in Spain. His plan solved the financial problems facing royal administrators, whose past experience underscored the heavy cost of the presidios and missions and their inadequacy in "pacifying" Indians. It also assumed that soldier-settlers and their families could provide Indians with an example of the behavior expected of them. Escandón's economic plan influenced colonial officials' view of Nuevo Santander as a "colony" that would not only bring savings but also rapid economic development.[12]

Escandón recruited families from nearby Nuevo León and Coahuila for the twenty-three towns he established along Nuevo Santander's rivers between 1748 and 1755. He grouped the towns into four sectors to simplify communication among the villas and to provide an effective defense against Indian attacks and a feared foreign invasion (see map 1). The villas' location facilitated their commercial exchange with external markets. The southernmost group of towns was located in an area that was easily accessible from neighboring settlements and already had a small population of colonists. Another cluster of towns was established in the narrowest portion of Nuevo Santander to facilitate communication between Nuevo León and the Gulf Coast. Escandón placed a third group between the Tamaulipas Vieja and Tamaulipas Nueva mountain ranges in hope of exerting control over the area's indigenous inhabitants. The final settlement cluster, known as the villas del norte, lay along the Rio Grande and consisted of Reynosa, Camargo, Mier, Revilla, and Laredo (see map 1).[13]

While Escandón relied principally on civilians and soldiers for the conquest of the Seno Mexicano, he also worked with clerics to establish missions throughout Nuevo Santander. Attempting to subdue the Indians through conversion to Christianity lent religious legitimacy to his colonization program and nominally fulfilled the requirements of Spanish law. As noted earlier, the founding of missions in Nuevo Santander did not precede the creation of towns as in other northern territories, but rather, occurred concurrently. From the outset, however, the "spiritual conquest" suffered because of conflicts with civilian authorities over land. The Franciscan missionaries from the Colegio de Propaganda Fiel de San Fernando de México complained that Escandón stalled in granting land to the missions,

instead favoring the towns. They also objected to his cost-savings suggestions to place only one cleric at each mission and for each priest to minister
to both Indians and Spanish colonists. In response to Escandón's cost-saving
proposals and meddling in their evangelization efforts, the missionaries
argued that spiritual conquest and efficiency would suffer in the hands of
one cleric. "What can be done with two priests in eight years," the missionaries claimed, "could not be accomplished in eighty years by one." In one of
their most searing criticisms, the Franciscans accused Escandón of exag-
gerating his discoveries of bountiful lakes and lands in the Seno Mexicano
and of lying about the Indians' willingness to congregate in missions. Because of constant disputes and recriminations with civilian authorities, the
missionaries from the Colegio de San Fernando eventually asked to be
released from the work of evangelizing Indians in Nuevo Santander. "Escandón had very little hope [for the success of evangelization]," they argued,
"and believed in the necessity of exterminating them." This accusation was
well grounded since Escandón preferred military subjugation to the missionaries' patient and deliberate attempts to attract the Indians to the missions with gifts.[14]

Despite continuous bickering with civilian authorities, the missionaries
of the Colegio Apostólico de Nuestra Señora de Guadalupe de Zacatecas
(who replaced the previous clerics) had established sixteen missions in
Nuevo Santander by 1755. The spiritual conquest, however, proved illusory.
The priests claimed to have gathered 2,755 Indians initially, but afterward
witnessed rapidly declining numbers. Two years later, only 1,926 Indians
remained in the missions. The friars stood at a disadvantage in disagreements between civil and religious authorities because Escandón doubted
the usefulness of their program and placed a higher priority on granting
land to civilians. Eventually, Nuevo Santander's missions failed miserably, a
result exacerbated by administrative problems and inadequate food supplies that drove Indians away. Several planned missions were never established, while others had occupants for only a few months. The Pintos,
Cueros Quemados, Tareguanos, Garzas, and others cultivated crops, fished,
or raised livestock at missions in Camargo, Mier, and Reynosa. However,
agricultural production lagged because of insufficient water for irrigation
in some locales and flooding in others. Disease and malnutrition ravaged
the small number of Indians who had remained with the priests. Unwilling
to wait for the Franciscans' slower (and apparently failing) "pacification"
strategy, and faced with strong resistance from the Janabres in the mountains of Nuevo Santander, colonists waged frequent wars of extermination.

Carrizos.

Carrizos: peuplade très-réduite a demi civilisée vivant autour des habitations sur les bords du Rio Grande.

1. Western Carrizo Indians of the Lower Rio Grande. Mexico's Comisión de Límites, including Jean Louis Berlandier and José María Sánchez y Tapia, probably encountered them south of Laredo in Villaldama, Nuevo León. Watercolor by Lino Sánchez y Tapia from original by Jean Louis Berlandier. Circa 1828 to 1834. Courtesy of Gilcrease Museum, Tulsa, Oklahoma.

Along the Rio Grande, the vecinos faced less resistance, but nevertheless used violence against local indigenous groups.[15]

By the early nineteenth century, the Spanish conquest had created a population catastrophe among Nuevo Santander's indigenous nations. Hunger, disease, and warfare devastated the Indians near the northern villas. Numbering approximately 15,000 when Spanish colonists arrived in 1749, the region's Indians suffered disastrous losses that left 650 survivors by 1798. Epidemics of smallpox, measles, and cholera introduced by the colonists, as well as repeated wars, inflicted widespread trauma and death. Malnutrition, starvation, and venereal diseases intensified the devastation. As Indian workers became part of vecino society, indigenous communities suffered additional losses. The censuses for the northern villas chart the population collapse. In 1789, 15 percent of Laredo's population of 718 consisted of Carrizo Indians (see figure 1). Subsequently, the number of indigenous inhabitants hovered between 2 and 5 percent of the villa's population until their existence disappeared from official records altogether in the 1830s. In Reynosa, site of a former mission, only fifty-one Indians appeared in the census of 1792. Thereafter, their numbers plummeted in response to droughts, attacks by colonists, and economic decline, before they dropped from the census completely in the 1820s. Refugio's indigenous population experienced a similar fate. By 1784, when vecinos established Refugio, the Spanish extermination of indigenous nations in its environs was almost complete. From two hundred people in 1814, the number dropped to fifty-two in 1820. New Spain's state formation in the northern villas ultimately fostered genocide and cultural eradication among the region's Indians.[16]

Indian Slaves

In the early nineteenth century, the vecinos exercised unchallenged authority over the surviving Native inhabitants, who no longer posed a threat. By then, the colonists had also developed an extensive livestock industry that would shape the region's future. The Indians, though few in number and landless, played an integral role in that industry as laborers and as servants for town residents. Raids on indigenous groups of the Rio Grande delta had begun as early as 1708, when colonists from Nuevo León captured and enslaved Western Carrizo Indians. The local indigenous population became the workforce that vecinos otherwise lacked. Although the labor demands of livestock production were not as great as those of mining or agriculture, the colonists needed ranch hands and domestic servants to give them a respite from their daily tasks. They recruited laborers from resident Indians in the villas and from nearby *rancherías* (hunter-gatherer communities).[17]

The Spanish conquest had transformed local indigenous peoples from formidable enemies into subordinate workers who performed menial tasks and lived among vecinos. Indian children worked as household servants for colonists, who referred to them as *criados* (from the verb *criar*, to rear; a criado was a servant reared in a colonial home). Because colonial laws prohibited Indian slavery, colonists used *criados* as a euphemism for slaves, and to imply magnanimous intentions for vecinos who raised and "educated" Indians to be proper subordinate members of Spanish society. Indigenous women usually worked within colonial homes as domestic servants, cooks, or corn millers. Some Indian men also worked as household servants but most labored as shepherds, cowboys, errand runners, cartmen, and even musicians. Additionally, colonists recruited temporary workers from nearby Indian groups. The Carrizos and Cotonames labored seasonally as salt miners and shepherds. Others responded to the needs of the moment, for instance, in 1814, when Refugio's officials secured the help of Indians to move the town's buildings, which were threatened by the river's floodwaters. Such use of Indian labor, forced or temporary, followed the pattern established earlier in Nuevo León, Nuevo México, and Tejas.[18]

Especially traumatic and a frequent cause of violence was the separation of Indian children from their families. A typical case was that of an Indian boy stolen by Reynosa colonists in 1777 from the Mulato Indians. The incident began with the colonist José Toro asking his in-law José Ábito Cantú to obtain an *indita* (young Indian girl) for him. As he had previously done with various indigenous groups, Cantú arranged to "purchase" the young daughter of an Indian leader in exchange for animals, clothing, and jewelry. The leader agreed, or so Cantú argued, but afterward the leader's relatives opposed the exchange. On the day that Cantú and three companions arrived at the Mulato ranchería, the Indians fled. Finding the camp deserted except for a sick elderly woman and a five-year-old boy, Cantú kidnapped the boy and sent him to Toro in lieu of the Indian girl. Upon discovering the missing boy, the Mulatos approached Reynosa authorities with trepidation to ask for his return. Their misgivings about entering the town suggest that the Mulatos did not consider their interactions with Cantú's party to be friendly. Reynosa authorities jailed Cantú and his companions, including two of his servants and a Christianized Indian because their actions blatantly broke colonial laws prohibiting indigenous enslavement. Most importantly, by returning the captured child to his Indian nation, officials prevented the Mulatos' retaliatory violence. This sequence of events demonstrates the trauma experienced by local Indians from the colonists' practice of stealing indigenous children to serve as criados.[19]

To justify their power over Indian captives, the colonists claimed to provide for the captives' material needs. They had constructed this identity as providers earlier, to justify their violation of the crown's prohibition against Indian slavery. Royal directives were clear that Indians should be incorporated into Spanish society, not enslaved. The vecinos, however, believed their investment in the captives' room and board entitled them to benefit from their labor. Like other residents of New Spain's Far North, the colonists in the villas del norte used the term *criados* partly to circumvent laws prohibiting slavery, but also to allude to the adoptive kinship created by raising and providing for Indian children. In the late eighteenth century, the Texas governor accused Nuevo Santander's vecinos of stealing Indian children to sell as slaves and of raping Indian women. In response, the viceroy launched an investigation that uncovered the rampant practice of enslaving Indians. According to a visiting priest, the settlers in the northern villas captured local Indians, "traded" goods for indigenous babies, and sold captives to residents of Nuevo León for forty to fifty pesos. Numerous colonists denied this charge, while asserting that indigenous parents had "given" them the children to raise and educate. Others claimed to have exchanged livestock and jewelry with willing parents for Indian children. The vecinos sanitized the cruelty and trauma of the forced enslavement of children by arguing that they were providing sustenance for the Indians. Refugio's officials characteristically described the town's indigenous population as "subsisting from the generosity of the vecinos."[20]

The colonists' experience with their indigenous labor force helped shape their identity as conquerors. The widespread practice of raising young Indian captives to be domestic servants demonstrates the vast power difference between the vecinos and the "conquered" indigenous inhabitants. Criados occupied an ambiguous place in colonial society. According to the historian David Weber, they were "involuntary members of Mexican households," who "performed domestic chores in exchange for their board and education." Since colonists acquired most Indian criados at a young age in order to "raise and educate" them, some vecinos argued that the children were "adopted." Numerous wills belie this claim, as "adopted" servants were rarely given any inheritance. While some criados might have developed adoptive kinship ties with their vecino family, others experienced slavery. Indeed, the colonists bought, sold, and traded criados as property. The will of Doña María Nicolasa Longoria in 1822 describes her son's inheritance as consisting of an Indian criada (unnamed) along with land and cattle. Similarly, litigants in Laredo listed an indita among the possessions in a property dispute. Notwithstanding their stated good intentions, the vecinos employed the euphemism *criados* to disguise their power over Indian slaves.[21]   1 8OOs

Throughout the early nineteenth century, the colonists continued enslaving Indian servants. Baptismal records demonstrate that vecinos captured criados at an early age. Most Indians were under a month old when baptized, and the rest were usually under ten years old. Some Indian parents, who lived in the villas del norte and presumably worked as servants, baptized their own children. Several babies were born to criadas who lived in the colonists' homes. Vecino *padrinos* (godparents) baptized the majority of Indian newborns, indicating each baby's Indian nation and noting that the child was born to either *padres infieles* (non-Christian parents) or *padres desconocidos* (unknown parents) without listing the parents' names. Priests often indicated that a colonist had acquired an infant from gentile Indians and that the padrinos were raising the infant. In 1791, Reynosa's priest identified Joseph María Ballí as the vecino who "acquired from the gentiles" a three-year-old Campacuase girl, who was christened María del Refugio. References to the children's parents and their Indian nation demonstrate that the *amos* (masters) or padrinos had acquired these babies through theft, purchase, or trade from the respective Indian groups or from rival Indians who knew the children's ethnic background.[22]

Colonists argued that they supplied the indigenous workers' material needs and religious instruction. The first step in converting Indians to Christianity was to give them a Catholic baptism, performed as soon as the colonists captured Indian children. Although the vecinos claimed to be interested solely in the Indians' religious needs, the colonists' role in obtaining the criados refutes their assertions. Some vecinos transferred captured Indians to friends and served as padrinos in their baptisms, while others became these children's masters. Don Juan Longoria y Serna and his wife, María Rafaela de la Garza, served as padrinos for a ten-year-old Indian girl, María Trinquilina, in 1819 after Don Juan stole her from parents, who had been identified as padres infieles. A similar pattern occurred in Camargo, where Captain Blas María de la Garza Falcón served as the padrino of several Indian criados. The use of war captives as criados became one of the fringe benefits of military service. Responding to questions about Indian slavery in the northern villas, an interim government official argued that it was impossible to substantiate such accusations. Nevertheless, he added, captured Indians "obtained the benefit of escaping from paganism and becoming Christians." Camargo's clerics baptized at least 226 Indians between 1764 and 1786; Refugio's priests baptized some 155 Indians between 1800 and 1822. Of those baptized in Camargo, most Native peoples were from the Cueros Quemados, Tejones, and Carrizos, while in Refugio, they were from the Negros, Mulatos, and Anda en Camino (see table 1). The number of Indian baptisms would likely have been higher had authorities not omitted the *casta* (racial category) in some entries.[23]

By the early nineteenth century, time and regional considerations had blurred the distinctions of New Spain's *régimen de castas* (racial classification system). Although the law permitted over fifty categories, officials usually employed far fewer labels, primarily español, *mestizo* (Spaniard and Indian offspring), indio, *mulato* (Spaniard and African offspring), *negro* (African), and castas (a generic term to refer to individuals of mixed ancestry). A person's ascribed casta determined her or his social status and legal rights. Throughout Latin America, this "pigmentocracy" had begun disintegrating during the late colonial period under the weight of proliferating categories and the increasing difficulty of determining a person's racial heritage because of widespread exogamy. The demographic reality of Mexico's northern borderlands further weakened the casta system. With few suitable mates from the same racial category, colonists frequently married outside their casta and subsequently produced additional mixed offspring.[24]

As occurred in central Mexico, the colonists of the villas del norte gave their charges specific Spanish-language names for indigenous people. The priest and Spanish godparents gave most criados double first names such as José Antonio, Juana María, and Juan José without any formal surname. The vecinos occasionally followed the practice of designating successive offspring as first or second, as in José Antonio Segundo. When colonists baptized Indians, they chose religious surnames—such as de los Santos, de Dios, and de Jesús—or gave them their padrinos' surnames. Camargo's vecinos followed such a practice between 1764 and 1786, when their priests performed 1,408 baptisms, which included 29 *indios de laborío* (indigenous workers), 61 mission Indians, and 136 individuals from local indigenous groups (see table 2).[25]

While Indian slaves provided vecinos with a needed labor force, the practice of enslavement inflicted widespread trauma and destroyed indigenous families. The colonists believed that they "rescued" Indians from barbarism

TABLE 1. Baptisms in Refugio by Indian Nation or Casta, 1800–1822

Year	Negros	Mulatos	Indios Anda en Camino	Indios Unspecified nation	Indios Other nations[a]	Other castas[b]	Unknown[c]	Total[d]
1800	3	1	0	3	0	48	6	61
1801	2	0	0	4	1	48	1	56
1802	3	1	0	2	0	64	3	73
1803	1	1	0	2	0	56	0	60
1804	3	4	1	4	1	93	6	112
1805	2	2	2	2	0	75	1	84
1806	4	2	1	3	0	85	2	97
1807	1	0	1	1	0	82	7	92
1808	1	0	1	5	0	71	13	91
1809	2	3	1	0	1	88	2	97
1810	2	0	0	4	0	87	5	98
1811	0	3	1	2	2	95	5	108
1812	0	0	1	1	0	64	4	70
1813	0	0	0	3	2	76	3	84
1814	0	0	2	7	1	78	2	90
1815	1	0	0	7	0	63	0	71
1816	0	0	0	1	1	46	0	48
1817	2	0	0	6	0	125	9	142
1818	5	0	0	5	0	117	0	127
1819	0	0	1	4	0	140	0	145
1820	2	0	3	4	0	105	0	114
1821	1	0	0	4	0	121	0	126
1822	4	0	0	1		41	116	162
Totals	39	17	15	75	9	1868	185	2208

Source: AEM, Libros de Bautismos 1 and 2.

[a] The indigenous nations included under "other nations" are Como se Llaman, Campacuases, Salapaquemes, Teaquiampemes, Tampacuases, Teniacapenes, and Carrizos.

[b] The "other castas" included mestizos, mulatos, españoles, and coyotes (see table 5).

[c] Some baptisms without an identified casta (under the "unknown" column) were likely indigenous, so the total number of baptized Indians was likely higher than 155 (total for the first five columns). Mexican law prohibited the use of casta categories beginning in 1822.

[d] Baptismal records do not include all births in a given year. Obstacles to baptism included infant mortality, expense, distance from the church, refusal by Indians, and unavailability of priests.

and paganism while providing for their material and religious needs. To justify the kidnapping and enslavement of Indian children, the vecinos characterized Indians as "uncivilized." For indigenous nations, the theft of their children instilled widespread terror, fueled an internal population decline, and led to the disintegration of their cultures. Instead of rescuing them from heathenism, enslavement generated a gradual genocide.

TABLE 2. Baptisms in Camargo by Indian Nation or Casta, 1764–1786

| Year | Indios | | | | | | | | | |
	Indios de misión[a]	Cueros Quemados	Carrizos	Tejones	Cotonames	Other nations[b]	Indios de laborío	Otras castas[c]	Unknown	Total
1764	5	1	1	–	–	2	0	15	9	33
1765	7	8	5	12	1	8	0	18	33	92
1766	2	20	1	28	4	4	0	2	70	131
1767	15	0	0	0	0	0	0	26	10	51
1768	13	2	0	0	0	0	0	42	9	66
1769	17	0	0	0	0	5	0	33	2	57
1770	2	2	0	0	0	0	0	44	6	54
1771	0	0	0	0	0	0	0	30	0	30
1772	0	0	0	0	0	0	6	47	0	53
1773	0	0	0	0	0	0	4	41	0	45
1774	0	0	0	0	1	4	0	65	2	72
1775	0	0	2	0	0	1	5	49	2	59
1776	0	0	1	0	0	1	0	47	0	49*
1777	0	0	0	0	0	2	0	29	0	31*
1778	0	0	0	0	0	1	0	39	3	43
1779	0	0	0	0	0	2	0	52	2	56
1780	0	0	0	0	0	1	0	45	4	50
1781	0	0	0	0	2	3	3	69	1	78
1782	0	0	0	0	0	2	3	51	0	56
1783	0	0	1	0	0	2	3	64	2	72
1784	0	0	0	0	0	3	0	83	1	87
1785	0	0	1	0	0	2	0	64	4	71
1786	0	0	0	0	0	0	5	67	0	72
Totals	61	33	12	40	8	43	29	1022	160	1408

Source: LBC.

[a] Clerics did not identify the indigenous nation of the individuals when they were baptized as "indios de misión."

[b] Under "other nations" were the following indigenous nations: Venados, Paxaritos, Tareguanos, Mulatos, Malaguitas, Como se Llaman, Guapes, Tortugas, and Pauraques.

[c] The "other castas" included *mestizos, mulatos, españoles, coyotes, moriscos, lobos,* and *castizos* (see table 6).

* Baptismal records for 1776 and 1777 were incomplete.

Godchildren and Consorts

Indian criados gradually became integrated into colonial society through *compadrazgo* (godparenthood) and intermarriage. As described earlier, the vecinos' first step was to baptize captive Indian children. The amos, however, did not necessarily serve as padrinos when baptizing the children, because the amos' material responsibilities were contradictory to the padrinos' spiritual obligations. Ideological tensions surfaced in baptizing slaves. Baptism signified humanity, equality with other Christians, and freedom from sin. In contrast, slavery represented a denial of humanity, a severe inequality, and a lack of physical freedom. The church expected padrinos to ensure that their *ahijado* (godchild) received a proper spiritual education. Not surprisingly, few amos served as padrinos for their own slaves, because the masters could not fulfill their spiritual obligations while also enforcing their power. Don Vicente de Hinojosa skirted such spiritual obligations in 1791, when he chose nonrelatives as padrinos for María Josepha, a child from the Como se Llaman nation. At her baptism, the priest identified Hinojosa as the vecino who "had acquired and removed her from barbarism" and who was raising the infant at his house, but identified two other colonists as the godparents. These practices follow patterns found elsewhere in New Spain's northern borderlands.[26]

Intermarriage also served to forge kinship ties between Indian servants and vecinos. Marriage allowed Indian servants to leave their employment and establish an independent household. Criadas who married colonists secured their freedom automatically, as was the custom throughout New Spain's Far North. For Indians who worked as indebted servants, marriage allowed them to pay off their debt through their spouse's earnings. Other indebted servants simply ran away and never repaid their debts. Not surprisingly, employers often discouraged romantic liaisons. It was common for employers to sue prospective suitors to keep them from visiting their homes, and occasionally to secure judgments that banished men from the community. Despite such intimidation, some Indian servants succeeded in marrying other Indian workers, local vecinos, or visiting soldiers, according to marriage registers from the northern villas.[27]

Unfortunately, not all criadas were able to secure official marriages and some were victims of the colonists' sexual abuse. Baptismal registers document a high rate of out-of-wedlock births to Indian women, who are identified by name while the fathers are not. Instead, parish priests recorded *padre desconocido* (father unknown) or simply left the entry blank, and designated the child as an *hijo natural* (out-of-wedlock child). Undoubtedly, officials knew the child's father in some cases but did not disclose it out of political convenience. Some Indian women likely refused to identify their lovers, fearing that an employer might take retaliatory steps against men who might be servants or indebted laborers themselves. Failing to identify the father also shielded prominent vecinos (including the amos), who fathered the children, from paternity obligations. Since such children would

amos = masters

social hierarchy

undoubtedly follow their mothers into domestic service, amos had an additional incentive to keep Indian servants from marrying.[28]

The sexual unions between Indian servants and colonists altered indigenous and colonial societies. As occurred elsewhere in the northern borderlands, the vecinos' sexual relations with criadas likely transformed these servants and their offspring into outcasts within indigenous communities. No evidence from the villas del norte suggests that criadas who were rape victims or offspring born of vecino-indigenous unions rejoined Indian communities. The birth of these mixed offspring led to a decrease in the indigenous population and a corresponding increase in the colonists' population. This demographic growth was vital because of the region's labor scarcity. Moreover, sexual unions increased the number of children with interracial backgrounds among a vecino population that was already racially and ethnically diverse. Unfortunately, the servants' indigenous heritage was lost in subsequent records, when officials neglected to identify their nation and instead labeled offspring as mestizo, mulato, or coyote (mestizo and Indian offspring). Elsewhere in New Spain's borderlands, the exchange of captives transformed indigenous and vecino societies: captives were not only integrated into their captors' kinship networks but also served as cultural negotiators. In the northern villas, no records exist to suggest that local indigenous nations took colonists as captives. Those indigenous nations that did capture vecinos in order to integrate them into Indian society or exchange them for Indian captives were enemy Indians making forays into the villas del norte; they were not local to the region.[29]

From Slavery to Indentured Servitude

The Indian slavery practiced in the northern villas did not lead to lifelong status. As Indian criados grew into adults, they became indebted servants who paid off their debts through labor. For Indian servants, the debt was usually the cost of food and shelter incurred during their upbringing, or the ransom paid by the vecinos to acquire them. The youths of Indian criados, many of whom had been separated from their parents and siblings as babies, enabled colonists to easily retain children as slaves. Growing up among the vecinos, Indian children lost their Native languages and tribal identities, and therefore were unlikely to rejoin their nations when they became free. As adults, these Indians gained their freedom either by working to pay off their debts, or when their owners stipulated in their wills that criados be released.

Still others, according to church records, changed their status through marriage to vecinos. Criados also gained freedom by fleeing. The ease by which adult criados could escape was a major reason for the transformation of slaves into indebted servants as criados grew older.[30]

Indian laborers obtained several advantages when they became indebted servants. Unlike criados—whose compensation for their labor was limited to food, shelter, and meager clothing—indebted servants also received wages. Moreover, employers often found it necessary to advance loans to servants in order to secure their service. The most important gain was the relative ease with which laborers could switch employers. The value of a worker's skills and the shortage of labor in the villas allowed runaway servants to obtain work easily. Indebted servants could escape from an abusive boss by finding another vecino willing to assume the debt owed to the former employer. Ultimately, the freedom of increasingly large numbers of adult Indian laborers forced colonists to identify themselves as employers rather than owners.

Two disputes involving servants demonstrate the relative freedom that adult Indians obtained by becoming indebted servants. While visiting Laredo in 1815, a government official threatened to remove Juliana, an Indian cook, from her employer Doña Petra González because of physical abuse. If they continued to mistreat their Indian servants, the official warned González and the other Laredo residents, they would forfeit the debts and service of their workers, who would be allowed to return to their parents or seek another employer. This was not an idle threat. In disputes between servants and employers that did not involve physical force but in which personal conflicts prevented both parties from agreeing, Laredo's officials had previously permitted the laborer to seek employment elsewhere. The *alcalde* (mayor) of Revilla offered such an option to Alexandra Rodríguez, a runaway Indian servant, who was recaptured in Laredo in October 1818. Rodríguez had fled from Doña Francisca Gutiérrez's house with the assistance of Bernardo, a criado who worked for another amo in Revilla. The alcalde indicated that Rodríguez could either return to her employer, Doña Francisca, to work off her debt, or receive her debt papers in order to find work with another employer willing to pay her obligation. The common practice among Indian servants of changing employers was replicated elsewhere in the northern borderlands.[31]

Despite the vecinos' loss of authority as their criados became indebted servants, they nonetheless continued to exercise considerable control over Indian laborers. Regulations notwithstanding, the colonists frequently hit and otherwise threatened Indian laborers in order to compel them to work. In 1814, for instance, Refugio's *ayuntamiento* (town council) planned to force a group of Indians living nearby to work as shepherds and laborers. Force was necessary, they believed, because the Indians were accustomed to "idleness and plundering" and would only be persuaded by a "respect for firearms." Residents also punished indigenous laborers who refused to work or follow orders, by restraining them with leather leashes, depriving them of necessary clothing, or withholding their pay.[32]

Indian servants transformed slavery into paid work because of the villas' labor shortage. Despite occupying a subordinate position within vecino society, criados negotiated the terms of their service. Court records demonstrate this agency in criados' ability to become indebted laborers and switch employers. Indigenous workers also challenged their employers' control by stealing household items or livestock and selling these goods to traveling merchants. Ultimately, Indians responded to the vecinos' abuse by refusing to work or by fleeing.[33]

Indian Workers

Indigenous indebted workers were marginalized within colonial society. They, along with criados, had the lowest social and economic standing in the villas. Unlike the vecinos, Indian servants owned no land and held no political posts. The colonists feminized these laborers by treating them as dependents, who were legally subsumed under their masters. Their inferior status was reflected in the colonists' lack of interest in recording their surnames, occupations, or significant details about their lives. Witnesses in legal cases commonly referred to indigenous workers as "el indio Sanchón" or "una criada Lucía." Vecinos often submerged the criados' identity altogether by recording them under their amos' name. This "language of ownership," according to the historian Ramón Gutiérrez, illustrates that Indian slaves "had social and legal personalities primarily through their masters." Wills refer to Indian workers in a similar fashion while clearly noting their subordinate position. According to the will of Don Antonio Gutiérrez, he was responsible for raising María Guadalupe, María Isidora, Lina, and José Domingo, but the testament omitted their surnames and occupations. By contrast, Gutiérrez's will identified his infant daughter, who died at twenty months of age, as Doña María Josefa Gutiérrez. By not recording significant details of servants' lives, the vecinos failed to acknowledge the workers' valuable skills, creating invisibility and lack of apparent agency in the historical record. Over time, clerics began omitting the indigenous nations of baptized Indians but noted that their parents were criados, indios de laborío, *padres gentiles* (unbaptized parents), or padres desconocidos.[34]

The colonists believed that part of their role in "conquering" Indians was to "civilize" them. Imparting civilization meant instructing Indians in vecino manners, including clothing, language, and religion. They expected Indians to become acculturated, respectful of the law, and obedient in the process of learning to be "civilized." The arguments made in the court case of José Ignacio de la Garza, referenced earlier, illustrate the colonists' expectations of "conquered" Indians. Don José de Jesús Solís, de la Garza's attorney, argued that besides becoming Christian converts, former indios bárbaros were supposed to learn how to be proper subjects by becoming obedient workers and acculturating into vecino society. Although de la Garza had been baptized and raised as a criado, Solís maintained that he was not "conquered" as were other Indians of his nation who were properly indoctrinated, catechized, and instructed in how to be subordinate subjects and *ladinos* (acculturated Indians).[35]

Colonists continued to hold these paternalistic views after Mexican independence (1821). In 1831, Reynosa officials distributed fifty-three indigenous adults among the vecinos. The municipal officers did not indicate the reason for assigning adult Indians to labor for colonists, but it is probable that the indigenous workers were war captives. The Indians came from the Comecrudo, Cotoname, Campacuase, Casas Chiquitas, Como se Llaman, and Tampacuaje nations. Indicatively, the officials asserted that the Indian laborers "chose to be" with particular amos who were responsible for the servants' conduct and education.[36]

The vecinos assumed the role of imparting "civilization" and religious instruction to indigenous peoples not only to fulfill the colonial government's expectations, but also to reinforce their identity as superiors and conquerors. Like others in New Spain's borderlands, the colonists identified themselves as *gente de razón* (people with reason) and considered Indians to be *gente sin razón* (people without reason). In the vecinos' view, religion and "civilization" separated gente de razón from gente sin razón. Commenting on this distinction, the historian Lizbeth Haas notes that "although the identities of de razón and sin razón originated out of religious discourse, they were used interchangeably with the ethnic and national categories español and indio, and implied an insurmountable divide between civilization and savagery." Despite converting to Christianity and acculturating to vecino society, some Indians still struggled to gain recognition as gente de razón. Indians entered colonial society as criados and indebted laborers; some eventually established kinship relationships with vecinos. Nevertheless, their prescribed identity as Indians was precisely what kept them from being accepted as equals.[37]

Insubordination and Resistance

This chapter's initial story highlighted the colonists' views of Indian workers as inferior members of society. The vecinos taught Indian criados to be subordinate, grateful, and deferential. Not surprisingly, the colonists believed that José Ignacio de la Garza should have appreciated their largess, but from his perspective there was little for which to be thankful. De la Garza was representative of Indian workers in several ways. Colonists had physically separated him from his family at a very young age and raised him as a criado. They had also forcibly taken his sister, who worked as a criada and likely experienced physical abuse and sexual violence. As an adult, de la Garza ran away from his master and obtained several jobs as a wage laborer. His skills and the shortage of labor allowed him to obtain work relatively easily. His use of Spanish, attendance at dances, and participation in *monte* (a card game) revealed his acculturation. De la Garza's story is unique only because extensive documentation exists that verifies his insubordination and resistance. Not only did he resist the effects of conquest by stealing from the vecinos and running away from abusive employers; he also publicly challenged the colonists' authority. By challenging Capistrán to fight if "he was a man," de la Garza not only insulted Capistrán's masculinity, but also transgressed the prescribed subordinate (and feminine) role that colonists had assigned indigenous laborers.

In 1807, de la Garza became involved in another dispute with Refugio's vecinos while playing monte. After de la Garza refused the homeowner's request to leave, the other monte players forced him outside. He then fought his way back only to be dragged out, beaten, and stabbed. As in the 1804 incident, de la Garza overstepped the social boundaries prescribed for Indian workers. Again, he refused to accept the subordinate feminine role assigned to indigenous laborers by disobeying orders to leave the house, and by speaking back to the vecinos.

The colonists permitted Indian workers the freedom to engage in popular cultural practices, such as fandangos and monte, but only as subordinate participants. Unlike the 1804 dispute, during which de la Garza clashed with prominent vecinos, this latter conflict was with rough muleteers and farmworkers insensitive to the finer points of law and decorum. Displaying the same disdain for de la Garza as the elite colonists had expressed three years earlier, the workers referred to him simply as "el Indio Ignacio" and omitted his occupation. The upper-class men had filed charges against de la Garza because they characterized him as an "incorrigible and malicious" Indian. Subsequently, the workers physically assaulted him and justified their actions by describing him as a "provocative, presumptuous, and disrespectful" person who required discipline in order to "remove his vanity." Although their tactics differed, both elite and poor colonists agreed that de la Garza did not act according to his place in society.[38]

Refugio's vecinos ultimately succeeded in punishing José Ignacio de la Garza for his transgressions against social propriety. The 1804 attempt to discipline him failed when the court dismissed the charges because of multiple legal procedure violations. The 1807 dispute ended differently. De la Garza died as a result of the injuries he received during the fight with the two workers. One assailant escaped from the Refugio jail and eluded capture. Authorities subsequently cleared the other attacker of all charges. By pardoning one of de la Garza's murderers, the legal authorities justified the views of Refugio vecinos toward Indian workers. The judge's ruling reinforced the colonists' belief that Indian laborers should remain subordinate and obey their social superiors.

José Ignacio de la Garza's story illustrates the relationships created by conquest and helps reveal important differences among the interactions with Indians. His life serves as an example of the obstacles faced by Indian workers and the inferior positions in which the vecinos placed them. Unlike the Indian allies, who had some autonomy, indigenous workers were constantly subject to social and economic dominion by colonists. This level of control permitted the vecinos to punish Indian laborers without risking the severe retaliation that they would incur if they attempted to discipline Indian enemies or allies. The circumstances of de la Garza's death and the minor consequences for his murderers demonstrate the residents' political control and, more importantly, provide an example of their perception of Indian workers. The confluence of his assailants' views with those of government officials illustrates how the colonists' identities as conquerors, providers, and social superiors were widely shared.

Enemy Indians

The colonists came to view some Indian nations as innately incorrigible, permanent enemies who would remain apart from their communities. Throughout New Spain's Far North, several indigenous groups successfully resisted Spanish efforts to subjugate them. The vecinos labeled these Indians *indios bárbaros*, and characterized them as fierce and completely independent, owing no allegiance to the colonists. The settlers saw them as unconquerable because of their large populations, excellent weaponry skills, and mobility as superior horsemen. Among the most formidable enemies were the Lipán Apaches and Comanches (see figures 2 and 3), who began attacking the villas in the 1770s. These Indian nations had originated in central and northwestern Texas and gradually moved southward as Anglo Americans colonized Texas. Caught between Mexican and American territorial ambitions, these Native groups nevertheless controlled vast borderland regions, provoked regional crises within Mexico, and ultimately shaped the outcome of the U.S.-Mexican War. Enemy Indians lived far removed from vecino settlements, but launched occasional forays to steal livestock or to respond to the provocations by colonists. Well-coordinated Indian attacks forced residents to abandon local ranches, retreat to towns for safety, and place their cattle and horses in secure locations.[39]

Unlike those Indian workers who reduced the financial resources of individual masters through theft, enemy Indians seriously endangered entire villas through their raids. The large numbers of cattle, mules, and horses that they stole undermined the colonists' livelihood. Beginning in the late eighteenth century, the threat posed by these Indian attacks tempted vecinos to consider abandoning the northern villas on numerous occasions. The incursions increased dramatically after the Comanches and Lipán Apaches established an alliance in 1816. The colonists consistently feared losing property and loved ones. An Indian attack in 1818, for example, resulted in the theft of more than ten thousand horses and mules; the slaughter of other horses, cattle, sheep, and goats; and the killing of several residents and capturing of others. More than a thousand Indians participated in the attack. Such actions led the colonists to characterize the Lipanes and Comanches as "vile scum," "savages," and "inhumans," who existed outside the bounds of their society and "lacked all knowledge." Although enemy Indians displayed several masculine qualities (weaponry skills, superior horsemanship, and courage), the vecinos despised these indigenous nations as "uncivilized" and without "reason." The vilification of enemy Indians allowed

Pl. V.

Lipanes.

Lipans

2. Originally from an area about 250 miles northwest of present-day Austin, the Lipán Apaches moved southward in response to Comanche incursions. This image might have been made during 1828, when Berlandier and Sánchez y Tapia witnessed a group of Lipán Apaches visiting Laredo. Watercolor by Lino Sánchez y Tapia from original by José María Sánchez y Tapia. Courtesy of Gilcrease Museum, Tulsa, Oklahoma.

Comanches.

Comanches du Texas Occidental: vêtement lorsqu'ils vont à la guerre.

3. The vecinos of the villas del norte considered the Comanche Indians, shown here in war dress, as unconquerable enemy Indians. Circa 1828 to 1834. Watercolor by Lino Sánchez y Tapia from original by Jean Louis Berlandier. Courtesy of Gilcrease Museum, Tulsa, Oklahoma.

the colonists to pursue an "unrelenting war" against these nations and justified indiscriminate violence. In waging a "live war" against Lipanes and Comanches, the colonists constructed a frontier masculinity that valued the punishment, subjugation, and extermination of enemy Indians. In retaliation against the "insolence" and "daring" of Indian raids, the colonists engaged in brutality to instill "terror and warning" in their enemies. After a battle in 1804, Laredo's soldiers scalped Comanche warriors and then traded their human skins with other Indians. The mutual reprisals shaped the vecinos' masculine identity of themselves as the "defenders of this land and all the frontier against the repeated incursions of the indios bárbaros." Like colonists elsewhere in the northern borderlands, the vecinos developed a strong warrior ethic based on their struggle against enemy Indians. This ethic privileged military prowess and valor, characteristics that embodied the colonists' notion of frontier masculinity.[40]

Repeated clashes with the Comanches and Lipanes gradually led the residents of the villas del norte to distinguish themselves from other borderland residents who favored peaceful dealings with Indians. The state and local governments had entered into various peace treaties with enemy Indians. By the end of the colonial period, however, the vecinos had grown suspicious of any treaty with enemy Indians, claiming that the Indians consistently broke the peace. This became evident in 1821, when the villas rejected the state governor's suggestion to negotiate a peace treaty with the enemy Indians. Refugio's town council argued adamantly that peace would not result from "soft means" but rather through armed reprisals. The council reminded the governor of the devastating 1818 attack on the villas in which enemy Indians took several residents captive. Such actions produced widespread distrust in the villas. According to the council, their policy differed from the approach taken by the Texas settlements of Bahía and Béxar, which succumbed to the misguided practice of negotiating with enemy nations. Their bellicose stance was possible because enemy Indians did not raid the northern villas as consistently as they attacked Béxar and Bahía.[41]

The sense of regional identity among the villas intensified because of the national government's failure to aid them in their defense against Indian and Anglo American incursions. After Mexican independence, Mexico's government encouraged the colonization of Texas as a defensive measure against American expansionist efforts and Indian attacks, but the policy failed. The raids by Comanches and Lipán Apaches on Mexican towns became more frequent, as these Indian nations lost land to Anglo Americans in the central part of Texas and as the game on which they depended declined. During the 1830s, enemy Indians attacked the villas del norte more frequently and caused greater damage than previously. In 1837, a newspaper described the destruction of the "once abundant livestock" of nearby ranchos and accused Anglo Texans of aiding the Indians. Increasing contact with Anglo American traders led the Comanches and Lipán Apaches to obtain firearms and carry out more aggressive raids. Appeals to the national government for help went unanswered, leaving the villas to fend for themselves.[42]

The attacks prompted local officials to coordinate joint responses among the river towns. Municipal officials throughout the villas urged one another to pressure the state and central governments for military aid. When these appeals went unanswered, the villas became adept at fending for themselves. The towns kept each other informed about enemy movements and supplied firearms and volunteers to settlements under attack. Officials in Matamoros (formerly known as Refugio) responded to an 1830 request from Mier by sending troops to repel a Comanche incursion. The coordinated actions included armed patrols and anticipatory strikes. Laredo officials devised just such a punitive campaign in 1837, urging the other settlements to join them because only through such a strategy could they save the "villas from the evils that they frequently received from the savages."[43]

Political turmoil during the 1830s prevented the state and national governments from supplying the northern villas with adequate military protection. Tamaulipas (known as Nuevo Santander until 1824) became embroiled in internal political disputes between federalists and centralists, while Mexico remained preoccupied with the Texas rebels. Indeed, the central government increased the vulnerability of the villas by asking them to provide military aid for the Texas campaign. Angered by such requests, municipal officials from Laredo to Matamoros protested that the villas had contributed so many horses, carts, steers, and servants for the campaign that their daily chores went unfulfilled. To make matters worse, federal officials acknowledged their failure to provide protection and encouraged the towns to furnish their own defenses. The vecinos were the best suited to fight the Indians, argued military and government officials, because they were familiar with the terrain and with the enemy's methods. National authorities appealed to the "patriotism" of the colonists, urging them to patrol their own towns and thereby free the military to continue its campaign against the rebels. Such indifference on the part of the central government reaffirmed the colonists' growing sense of alienation from the national government.[44]

The intensity of Indian raids, coupled with the lack of military protection, had devastated the villas del norte by the 1840s, while simultaneously strengthening their sense of regional identity. Previously, the villas had provided a defensive barrier between the enemy Indians to the north of the Rio Grande and the towns in the interior of Tamaulipas. Laredo's alcalde, Basilio Benavides, expressed the common sentiment throughout the river towns when he wrote that the vecinos "do enough with continuing to live here and taking a heroic stand against the savages in order to protect those that live in the interior." The northern towns had succumbed to a "sad and disgraceful condition" after enemy Indians eliminated their livestock and began attacking interior towns. Although state newspapers recognized the river towns' defensive role, state officials did not. In 1841, a representative from the northern villas sought to persuade the Tamaulipas legislature to grant them an exemption from military duty because they had provided "a powerful fort against which the ferocity of the Indian savages had crashed." Although the colonial government had previously granted this exemption because it recognized that the northern towns supplied all the presidial forces, Mexico's national government forced them to provide additional volunteers and denied all requests for aid.[45]

While the colonists' social contact with Indian *workers* shaped their identity as conquerors and superiors, their interaction with Indian *enemies* fostered a sense of regional identity across the villas del norte. This regional identity united residents with the common goal of defending their settlements. The vecinos came to believe their villas were unique because of their constant struggle against enemy Indians. Consequently, they gradually became distant from Spanish authority. Far from unique, the vecinos' alienation from the central government was a common experience for colonists in the northern borderlands. In turn, the colonists' susceptibility to enemy Indian attacks encouraged them to seek alliances with other Indian nations that might come to their defense. For local indigenous groups, their motivation to ally with the vecinos was their nation's inability to challenge formidable foes.[46]

Indian Allies

The northern villas had begun establishing alliances with local indigenous nations shortly after Spanish colonists first arrived in the area. In order to counter sporadic forays from Comanches and Lipán Apaches in the late eighteenth century, the villas allied with several indigenous nations, among them groups of Carrizos—who had been living on the outskirts of Laredo since 1788—and several nations who had migrated to the area after being displaced by colonists in eastern Nuevo León. Over several decades, the Cotonames and Carrizos had fostered friendly relations with the vecinos of Laredo, Revilla, and Reynosa, as servants, shepherds, vaqueros, and salt miners. By the nineteenth century, the settlers considered these local indigenous nations to be *indios mansos* (tame Indians) who subsisted by hunting deer and working occasionally as domestic laborers for the colonists. Carrizos also accompanied the vecinos in their offensives against enemy Indians and served as scouts, informing the officials when enemy Indians were in the vicinity.[47]

Indian alliances became crucial for the northern towns as raids by enemy Indians increased. In the 1820s and 1830s, Texas colonists displaced the Comanches and Lipán Apaches, who moved southward and became embroiled in conflicts with smaller Indian nations such as the Carrizos, Carancahues (Karankawas), Garzas, and Tancahues (Tonkawas; see figure 4). The Garzas and Carrizos were from the Rio Grande area, whereas the Carancahues and Tancahues were newcomers from the gulf and central region of Texas. Since these nations were not large enough to combat the Comanches or Lipanes alone, they responded favorably to overtures for alliances with the villas. Indian allies eagerly sought the firearms supplied by the vecinos, while the colonists profited from the additional Indian warriors and their knowledge of the countryside.[48]

While some alliances developed out of earlier friendly relations between the colonists and local indigenous nations, others were created out of expediency during the turbulent 1820s and 1830s. The Tancahues and Lipanes had previously participated in attacks against the villas del norte, but occasionally they cooperated with the vecinos. Their cooperation was motivated by their desire to punish Indian rivals. The Tancahues gained the confidence of colonists by providing them with information concerning threats to their lives and property. In May 1837, for example, the Tancahues notified Reynosa authorities about numerous Anglo Texans stealing horses and cattle near Camargo. The Lipanes continuously battled the Comanches, so

Pl. IX

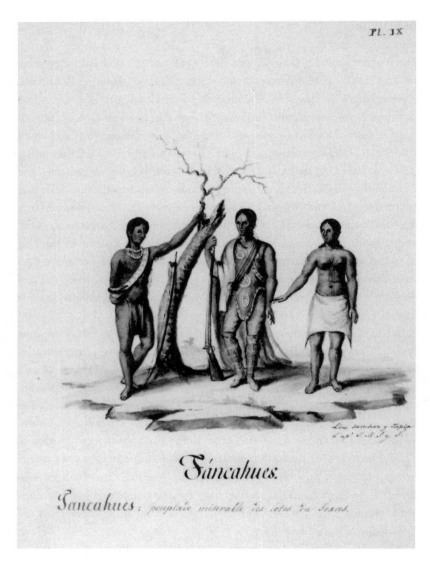

Táncahues.

Tancahues: peuplade misérable des côtes du Texas.

4. Tancahues (Tonkawa Indians) originally lived west of present-day Austin. Incursions by Comanches and Lipán Apaches pushed the Tancahues southeastward, and some as far south as the Rio Grande delta. Circa 1828 to 1834. Watercolor by Lino Sánchez y Tapia from original by José María Sánchez y Tapia. Courtesy of Gilcrease Museum, Tulsa, Oklahoma.

their alliance with the colonists was a strategy to gather support to fight a much larger Indian nation. In 1825, the vecinos accused the Comanches of breaking a peace treaty by attacking the villas, stealing horses, and taking captives. In response, a group of fifty Lipanes accompanied sixty soldiers from Laredo in an attack against the Comanches. These alliances benefited the Tancahues and Lipanes because they sought to punish Anglo Texans and the Comanches but needed the vecinos' assistance to do so. In both cases, the colonists rewarded the Tancahues and Lipanes with horses, saddles, and other goods. The vecinos, in turn, valued the cooperation of the allied Indians, who alerted them to stealing and raiding expeditions.[49]

The mutual benefits of such alliances were demonstrated in 1837 when the Tancahues and the vecinos of Matamoros joined in a successful attack against the Comanches. As town residents were preparing to launch an offensive attack against enemy Indians, the Tancahues approached them to offer assistance. They cooperated as equals, with each commander responsible for his own followers, sometimes disagreeing on tactics. Nicolás Chapatón, the Tancahue leader, provided critical advice by predicting the movements of the enemy so that a successful ambush could be set. The vecino commander acknowledged the Tancahues' valuable service, and identified them as a *nación amiga* (friendly nation) determined to fight the enemy. Likewise, the Tancahues demonstrated their satisfaction with the joint action by volunteering more armed men whenever enemy Indians attacked next.[50]

Another joint foray in the same year proved equally successful. A group of Eastern Carrizos, living near Reynosa, requested firearms from the region's military commander, who asked Matamoros's alcalde for advice on responding to the request. The alcalde assured the commander that the Carrizos were peaceful "mission Indians" who were willing to "provide all types of service that they are asked to perform." Unlike the enemy Indians who raided for livestock, the Carrizos subsisted by hunting and gathering or by working for the colonists. Besides assisting the residents with domestic chores, the official noted, the Carrizos had been the first to defend Reynosa from attacks by Comanches and other enemy nations. As a result, the alcalde recommended that the Carrizos' request for firearms be granted.[51]

The alliances between the northern villas and their Indian cohorts reinforced a sense of regional identity among the river towns. The coalitions emerged as Indian nations faced displacement by Anglo American colonization and clashed with rival Indians. Smaller Indian nations allied themselves with the villas because they did not have sufficient members to protect themselves. In turn, the colonists joined these alliances, recognizing that the southward movement of enemy Indian nations threatened their towns as much as it threatened the allied Indians. As in other parts of Mexico's northern frontier, these unions were based on fighting a common enemy. This cooperation also served to reinforce a regional pride among the residents of the villas by demonstrating their ability to repel enemy Indian attacks without assistance from the state and national governments.[52]

The colonists' perception of themselves varied over time depending upon the particular group of Indians with whom they were interacting. In their relationship with Indian workers, vecinos identified as conquerors, civilizers, and providers. These roles reinforced their identity as "non-Indians." Central to their identity as gente de razón was their belief in their own superiority and in Indian workers' subordination. Even when colonists established kinship ties with indios who became ahijados or consorts, the vecinos continued to hold power over the Indians. In contrast, the colonists generally sought to exclude enemy Indians from their society. The settlers also created alliances with local indigenous nations and, on occasion, with smaller enemy Indian groups in order to fight the powerful Comanches. These alliances were mutually beneficial, with neither party exercising control over the other. Although the colonists often alluded to a vecino-indio divide, their relationship with indigenous nations was more complicated than a simple ethnic binary. Vecino-indio relations existed along a continuum from intimate ones with consorts to distant or nonexistent ones with enemy Indians. These relationships were based on various differentials of power, which could change over time, as criados became indebted workers, servants became consorts, and enemies became allies. The colonists' experience with various Indians demonstrated their interdependence with workers, criados, ahijados, consorts, and allies. Without these Indian partners, the vecinos would have struggled even more to develop the villas del norte.[53]

2

Fragmented Communities
Class and Gender Hierarchies

From the beginning of Spanish colonization, community relations were
complex and fragmented in the *villas del norte* (northern towns). Colonists
banded together when confronted by enemy Indians, but such unity reflected a shared ethnic and regional identity that masked sharp internal
class and gender divisions. Wealthy residents wielded greater power than
the poor, and men not only possessed more social influence than did women,
but also exercised all political and judicial authority. That control rested in a
small group of upper-class men who used their power to shape and perpetuate the northern settlements' intricate and unequal social structure.

The policies and laws of the colonial and national states gave these men
their power. As agents of the state, they extended government rule to the
northern borderlands, and in exchange received powerful positions. The
colonial state reinforced patriarchal power through land policies that favored men and through organization of municipal governments that rewarded military service. The Catholic Church was instrumental in the
states' regulation of acceptable behavior by its enforcing of policies on
racial classifications, sexual relations, and marriage. Accompanying the
political transformation brought about by Mexican independence were
social and economic changes, but these reforms reinforced existing inequalities. Civic and religious institutions, thus, cooperated to encourage
specific activities, while suppressing alternative behaviors. Through institutions, rituals, and routines, the state reached the northern borderlands and
structured its society. Yet, the state's influence was not absolute. Local
conditions and the lived experiences of residents provided additional contingencies from which the *vecinos* (community members) socially constructed their class and gender identities.[1]

Foundations of Inequality

Class and gender divisions expanded as the region's population increased and its ties to international markets grew. Ranchers from Camargo and Reynosa established Refugio in 1794, downriver and twenty miles from the Gulf of Mexico. The town's economy, political structure, and social relations mirrored those of the other villas. By discarding Spain's rigid mercantilist economy, Mexico's national government liberalized trade and linked the region to international commerce through an official port at Refugio. Eclipsing the other towns in population, Refugio became a vanguard of cultural, economic, and demographic change that reverberated throughout the river settlements. However, the town's complex society did not appear suddenly; rather, it developed gradually from the inception of settlements in the mid-eighteenth century.

Like others in the Far North of New Spain, the first vecinos of the villas del norte had humble origins. They formed part of a large stream of colonists from nearby provinces who established twenty-four settlements in the colony of Nuevo Santander between 1748 and 1756. Royal authorities had to offer incentives to entice them to an inhospitable region with few known mineral deposits. The attractions consisted of land grants, transportation subsidies, and tax exemptions. Accompanying landless families were criminals promised pardons for theft, murder, and nonpayment of debts if they joined the venture. Attracted by the opportunity for economic advancement, an escape from criminal pasts, or the possibility to start anew, the colonists shared motivations with settlers elsewhere in the northern borderlands. Contemporary observers described the colonists as "unsettled families who had sought shelter on haciendas, paid rent for land or worked for the owners, and would have left for other provinces if they had not arrived here." Harsher in his assessment was a visiting government inspector, who described them as "vagabonds and malefactors."[2]

Drawing on their stock-raising experiences and the favorable geographic conditions, the colonists devoted their energies to cattle production. It required small monetary outlays, minimal tools, and few workers, so even those of moderate means could own herds. The main requirements were what they now possessed: grasslands and water. They obtained large yields from the livestock that they introduced from Nuevo León and Coahuila. By 1757, the population of the colony's twenty-four towns had increased to 8,869, while their livestock numbered 83,443 head of *ganado mayor* (cattle, horses, and mules) and 285,854 of *ganado menor* (sheep and goats). The

TABLE 3. Population and Livestock in the Villas del Norte, 1757

	Camargo	Dolores	Laredo	Mier	Revilla	Reynosa	Villas del norte	Nuevo Santander
Population	638	123	85	274	357	290	1,767	8,869
Ganado Menor	71,770	0	9,080	38,659	44,850	12,700	177,059	285,854
Ganado Mayor	10,426	9,050	1,133	4,385	6,374	4,116	35,484	83,443

Source: Osante, *Orígenes del Nuevo Santander*, 143, 179.

villas del norte became the most productive livestock region among Nuevo Santander's four sectors of towns. Although the six villas accounted for only 20 percent of the colony's total population, their inhabitants owned over 60 percent of Nuevo Santander's ganado menor and more than 40 percent of its ganado mayor (see table 3).[3]

In distributing land, the colonial state reinforced inequality. The need for large tracts of pasture, as well as dissension between colonists and missionaries, led royal officials to abandon the initial eighteen-year experiment in communal landholding. In 1767, authorities fulfilled one of the promises used to attract settlers by appointing a commission to survey and divide property among individuals and missions throughout Nuevo Santander. This marked the first major distribution of private land in the Rio Grande gulf region. The major beneficiaries were the military and political leaders, who were rewarded according to their service and length of residence in the colony. Those with the longest residency—so-called primitive settlers who had lived in the villas for over six years—received two *sitios* (leagues; 8,856 acres) of land for pasture and twelve *caballerías* (1,500 acres) of agriculture land. Colonists whose residency was from two to six years, "old settlers," obtained two leagues for grazing and six caballerías (750 acres). The newest settlers, those arriving within the last two years, received only two leagues for pasture. Authorities rewarded a captain (the highest authority in each villa) with twice as much land as a primitive settler. The land commission made the grants to the heads of families, mostly men but also some widows. Thus, the state's land distribution policy in the northern towns institutionalized class divisions, and promoted patriarchal control.[4]

The land commissioners followed distribution guidelines designed to minimize potential conflicts. Most grants bordered the rivers (Nueces, Grande, and Conchos) to give the owners access to water (see map 2). These *porciónes* (portions) were quadrangles with nine-thirteenths of a mile of riverfront that extended eleven to sixteen miles away from the river.

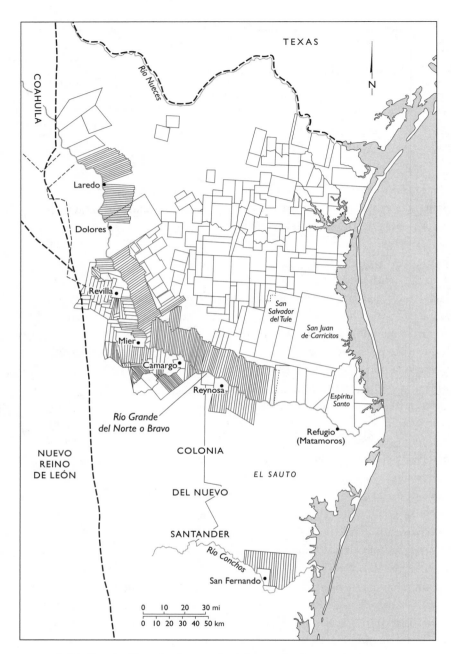

MAP 2. Political and military leaders received the vast land grants, such as
Espíritu Santo and El Sauto, while original settlers obtained *porciónes*
(narrow strips of land bordering rivers). Circa 1750s to 1820s.
Map adapted by William L. Nelson.

Individuals who had earlier made improvements on land assigned to others received compensation. The commissioners assumed responsibility for ferreting out those who misrepresented their years of residency and, additionally, required new arrivals to register with royal officials before receiving grants. To resolve future land disputes, they established a mechanism and regulations for settling disagreements locally before sending appeals to distant superior courts.[5]

Subsequent land assignments further skewed the distribution of property and wealth. These grants tended to be larger, most over two leagues, and were given to socially prominent vecinos. Military and political leaders of Reynosa and Camargo received vast grants, such as the Llano Grande in 1778 (twenty-five leagues) and the Espíritu Santo in 1781 (fifty-nine leagues and eleven caballerías). Both bordered the Rio Grande on the north between Reynosa and the Gulf of Mexico. In 1781, an absentee owner and Mexico City resident, Antonio de Urízar, obtained 658 leagues (2,913,624 acres), the largest grant in Nuevo Santander. His vast hacienda, known as El Sauto, covered the territory between the Rio Grande and the Río Conchos and stretched from Nuevo León to the Gulf of Mexico. These large grants notwithstanding, the typical landholding was less than five square leagues. In 1794 Nuevo Santander boasted 437 ranchos but only seventeen haciendas.[6]

The ranchos remained predominantly devoted to livestock throughout the eighteenth century (see figure 5). In southern Nuevo Santander some colonists engaged in mining, but the scarcity of mineral deposits limited the development of this industry. Others obtained moderate profits from salt mining along the coast. In the mid-eighteenth century, Nuevo Santander's colonists were trading with merchants in northeastern and central Mexico. They exported salt, livestock, and hides while importing corn and other food. Some trade extended as far as New Mexico, where, in 1775, merchants bought horses when a drought severely reduced their stock. By the end of the eighteenth century, most of the trade was with nearby Nuevo León, Coahuila, and Texas. The colony's exports remained primarily livestock, and its herds had increased to approximately 800,000 by 1794. The annual income from cattle and other livestock was close to two-thirds of the province's total annual revenue. Those earnings were also approximately three times greater than the total return from silver, copper, lead, and salt mining.[7]

The livestock industry's growth sparked the late eighteenth-century territorial expansion into the gulf region as cattle owners sought additional pasturage. After illegally establishing ranches along the coast, vecinos from

Pl. XXXIV.

Ranchero de N. Leon y Tamaulipas.

Habitant de la campagne des états de Nuveau Leon et de Tamaulipas

5. Ranchero from Nuevo León and Tamaulipas. Circa 1828 to 1834. Watercolor by Lino Sánchez y Tapia. Courtesy of Gilcrease Museum, Tulsa, Oklahoma.

Camargo and Reynosa undertook two organized expansions. They secured most property north of the Rio Grande through royal grants, while they obtained land south of the river through purchases. In 1784, thirteen families bought 113 sitios (500,364 acres) of ganado mayor from the hacienda El Sauto, on part of which they subsequently founded Refugio (see map 2). The newly acquired pasturage allowed livestock to flourish and the villas del norte to remain the colony's most productive group of towns. In 1794, the river towns accounted for one-sixth of Nuevo Santander's population, but their inhabitants owned over 26 percent of all livestock and over 50 percent of all sheep in the colony.[8]

Stock production in the villas was influenced by climactic restrictions on alternative enterprises. Insufficient rainfall and inadequate irrigation resulted in small yields of corn, cane, and beans. Grown near the river bottoms, these crops could not meet subsistence needs. Agriculture also fell prey to cycles of drought and flooding made worse by unpredictable overflows and changes of course of the Rio Grande. Under these conditions and with impressive, easier-to-generate profits from stock raising, the villas turned to importing corn, wheat, and other farm products from nearby states in exchange for salt and livestock.[9]

Administrative obstacles to commerce limited legal trade. The area boasted an abundance of salt, ebony, and fish, as well as a natural harbor near Refugio, but colonial authorities prohibited the creation of a port there. Without an official avenue for exports, the vecinos could not exploit their natural resources for commercial gain. Like others settlements in New Spain, the northern villas suffered from the colonial government's mercantilist policy, "which limited trade to Spanish goods, handled by Spanish merchants, and carried on Spanish vessels." By discouraging manufacturing in New Spain and limiting commerce through the official port at Veracruz, the colonial government created scarcity and drove up prices. The villas' distance from Veracruz exacerbated these problems by making trade costly and time-consuming, which in turn encouraged smuggling. The widespread contraband trade illustrated the limits of Spanish colonial state formation. European immigrants and *americanos* (American citizens) soon joined local smugglers to control the black market in foreign-made goods. These foreign merchants found a racially diverse society that had been that way from the earliest days of settlement.[10]

Race and Class Divisions

Most of Nuevo Santander's initial settlers had a mixed racial heritage. Even among the political leaders, *peninsulares* (Spaniards born in Spain) were scarce because of their unwillingness to leave adjoining provinces for borderland posts. Thus, Escandón selected his captains mainly from among *criollos* (American-born Spaniards) and mestizos. In 1788, peninsulares and criollos made up only 22 percent of Nuevo Santander's total population of 23,514. Most settlers were mestizos, *mulatos* (Spaniard and African offspring), *castas* (generic term for mixed-race offspring), *lobos* (Indian and mulato offspring), *negros* (Africans), and *indios* (Indians).[11]

Casta assignations in the villas del norte reflected the narrowing of categories in the late colonial period. The difficulty of determining purported racial heritage for an increasing intermixed population led officials to use far fewer labels than the 56 casta categories allowed in Mexico. Over a thirty-one-year period, officials employed inconsistent racial categories and, in time, classified most residents as *españoles* (Spaniards) and castas (see table 4). The absence of the mestizo category in Reynosa and the mulato label in Refugio reveal inconsistency and the tendency to reduce the number of classifications. The large number of españoles in these towns (over 41 percent in Laredo and Reynosa, and over 64 percent in Refugio) is suspect, considering the diverse origins of these residents' eighteenth-century forebears. In 1819, Laredo officials further reduced the categories to "español" and "other castas."[12]

Baptismal records confirm the inconsistency and subjectivity of racial classifications. In Refugio, between 1800 and 1822 four priests chose one of six categories for each child baptized. Clerics classified few babies as mulato, and did so only during a five-year period in which two priests baptized most newborns (see table 5). Between 1804 and 1806, priests classified most infants as español, then as mulato, and finally as mestizo. Similarly, clerics in Camargo chose mulato between 1774 and 1779 and *coyote* (mestizo and indio offspring) between 1781 and 1786 as popular castas (see table 6). Such random assignments suggest that the friars had difficulty in determining a person's casta. Don Calletano Medrano and Doña María Teresa Gutiérrez, who conceived four children over a five-year period, witnessed this quandary. A priest baptized their first child as española and their next as mestiza. A different cleric classified their third daughter as española, but a year later baptized the couple's son as mulato.[13]

Social status also influenced racial designations. Individual examples

TABLE 4. Population Statistics with Casta Classifications for Laredo, Reynosa, and Refugio, 1789–1820

Town	Español	Mulato	Mestizo	Indio	Casta	Europeo	Indios, castas, y mestizos de origen africano	Total
Laredo 1789	334	188	178	110	0	0	0	*810*
Laredo 1819	620	0	0	0	0	0	798	*1,418*
Reynosa 1792	490	78	0	51	482	2	0	*1,103*
Refugio 1820	1,489	0	33	52	746	0	0	*2,320*

Sources: Herrera Pérez, *Monografía de Reynosa*, 126; AHM-COL 1:18; DG 6, 21.

TABLE 5. Baptisms in Refugio by Casta, 1800–1822

Year	Indios	Mestizos	Mulatos	Españoles	Coyotes	Unknown	Total
1800	7	15	2	31	0	6	*61*
1801	7	19	0	29	0	1	*56*
1802	6	29	0	34	1	3	*73*
1803	4	26	0	30	0	0	*60*
1804	**13**	**33**	**10**	**50**	0	6	*112*
1805	8	**13**	**28**	**34**	0	1	*84*
1806	10	**6**	**39**	**39**	1	2	*97*
1807	3	46	0	34	2	7	*92*
1808	7	44	0	24	3	13	*91*
1809	7	49	0	34	5	2	*97*
1810	6	52	0	32	3	5	*98*
1811	8	52	0	38	5	5	*108*
1812	2	23	1	39	1	4	*70*
1813	5	25	0	51	0	3	*84*
1814	10	24	0	53	1	2	*90*
1815	8	11	0	52	0	0	*71*
1816	2	14	0	32	0	0	*48*
1817	8	63	0	62	0	9	*142*
1818	10	78	0	39	0	0	*127*
1819	5	75	0	63	2	0	*145*
1820	9	56	0	49	0	0	*114*
1821	5	60	0	61	0	0	*126*
1822	5	27	0	14	0	116	*162*
Totals	*155*	*840*	*80*	*924*	*24*	*185*	*2,208*

Source: AEM-BAU 1 and 2.
Note: Items in boldface correspond with discussion in chapter 2.

TABLE 6. Baptisms in Camargo by Casta, 1764–1786

Year	Indios	Mestizos	Mulatos	Españoles	Coyotes	Other castas[a]	Unknown	Total
1764	9	1	4	10	0	0	9	33
1765	41	2	8	6	2	0	33	92
1766	59	0	1	1	0	0	70	131
1767	15	2	9	15	0	0	10	51
1768	15	0	7	34	1	0	9	66
1769	22	1	6	23	2	1	2	57
1770	4	11	6	23	3	1	6	54
1771	0	6	5	19	0	0	0	30
1772	6	5	9	29	3	1	0	53
1773	4	12	2	26	0	1	0	45
1774	5	9	**22**	31	3	0	2	72
1775	8	5	**21**	23	0	0	2	59
1776	2	2	**27**	18	0	0	0	49*
1777	2	0	**13**	16	0	0	0	31*
1778	1	8	**13**	16	0	5	0	43
1779	2	13	**11**	25	1	2	2	56
1780	1	7	4	32	0	2	4	50
1781	8	6	3	42	**17**	1	1	78
1782	5	4	5	36	**4**	2	0	56
1783	6	7	4	41	**5**	7	2	72
1784	3	14	9	43	**15**	2	1	87
1785	3	2	2	46	**14**	0	4	71
1786	5	5	7	45	**10**	0	0	72
Totals	226	122	198	600	80	25	157	1,408

Source: LBC.

Note: Items in boldface correspond with discussion in chapter 2.

[a] Under "other castas" were *moriscos* (offspring of español and mulato), *lobos*, and *castizos* (offspring of español and mestizo).

* Baptismal records for 1776 and 1777 were incomplete.

abound of vecinos in the northern borderlands "whitening" their casta as their wealth increased. Colonists sought to be classified as españoles because the colonial state had a long history of bestowing certain privileges on españoles and discriminating against castas and indios. Demographic and baptismal records from the villas del norte suggest that casta corresponded to class status. Officials increasingly grouped a disproportionate number of residents as españoles, strongly hinting that this label connoted the elite and middling classes, while the other casta designations referred to the poor. As the use of numerous castas declined in favor of a few select terms, colonial authorities implicitly acknowledged the impossibility of maintaining multiple categories. In 1810, they divided Nuevo Santander's population into only three groups: españoles, castas, and indios. In 1821, Mexico's newly independent government prohibited the use of racial labels.[14]

Unlike the fluctuating racial divisions, socioeconomic classes had become more distinct by the beginning of the nineteenth century. The landowning elite ruled over a large laboring class, and a small middling class. The upper class were mostly *criadores* (stock raisers), whose wealth was in real estate and livestock. A few—such as José María Ballí and Rosa María de Hinojosa—controlled vast amounts of property. The couple's hacienda, La Feria, stretched over twelve-and-a-half leagues; held horses, donkeys, and cattle; and had a total worth that exceeded twenty-eight thousand pesos in 1788. The majority of criadores, however, held less property. With only two leagues of land, Antonio Capistrán had accumulated an extensive array of horses, cattle, sheep, lambs, and oxen that were valued at more than thirty-four hundred pesos in 1806. Over time, merchants from northeastern Mexican capitals arrived and joined the elite through their purchase of land and herds, or by acquiring property as payment for previously extended loans. Attracted by the contraband trade, newly arrived americanos and Europeans contributed to the diversity of the elite.[15]

The elite exercised considerable economic power in the community. They financed loans of money and livestock to workers and other criadores, hired numerous laborers, and owned Indian *criados* (servants reared in a colonial home) and African slaves. Landowners capitalized on their extensive real estate by renting portions of their unused property for pasturage. They incurred debts in a complex credit system that involved residents throughout the northern villas and merchants in distant capitals. In 1806 Antonio Capistrán held over five hundred pesos in loans of cattle and money to seventeen criadores and merchants, while he also owed some two hundred pesos to six landowners. His considerable economic influence included loans to local military officials and laborers as well as to stock raisers in neighboring Nuevo León. The material wealth of the elite became their legacy by their bequeathal of property to their offspring and to local institutions. In 1804, José María Ballí and Rosa María de Hinojosa exercised their influence by giving an endowment of four thousand pesos to the Catholic Church.[16]

Despite their wealth, the elite did not live in opulence, largely because of the borderlands' privation. The manufactured items they owned were limited to such necessities as farm tools, kitchen utensils, and rustic furniture.

Though inexpensive in major metropolitan areas, these basic goods were scarce and valuable along Mexico's northern borderlands. Beyond land and livestock, inheritances consisted of scarce manufactured goods and few luxury items; only a handful of women bestowed jewelry or fine clothing while elite men willed firearms or fancy saddles. While the elite owned several houses, most dwellings were primitive one-room *jacales* (huts of mud and straw); only a few were multiple-room structures made of stone or adobe.[17]

Various workers assisted the elite. Indian criados toiled as domestic servants under the strictest conditions, receiving food, clothing, and housing in exchange for their labor. Others earned wages from diverse employers, worked as indebted laborers, or sold the products of their labor. Women found employment as cooks, corn millers, and domestic servants. Men worked as cowboys, shepherds, muleteers (see figure 6), and day laborers. Earning two pesos per month, day laborers were the lowest paid. Domestic servants secured a fraction more, at three to four pesos per month. Cowboys and shepherds garnered the best wages, which averaged five pesos per month but could be substantially higher during cattle drives.[18]

Accumulated financial obligations temporarily bound indebted workers to their *amos* (masters). Initial debts began with *avíos* (monetary advances) that employers provided to obtain laborers' services. Workers negotiated work contracts directly with employers, new arrivals made arrangements through town officials, and others became indebted laborers for friends or families. Indigent parents established contracts for children, who worked as domestic servants or apprentices. Wages were often insufficient for subsistence, so workers borrowed from their employers, who enumerated the accrued charges for housing, clothing, and food in a *papel de cuentas* (account document). Indebted servants' obligations were not perpetually binding, because they could switch jobs by finding other amos willing to assume their outstanding debts. Most workers possessed few material goods besides clothing and essential household items. To secure housing and food, indebted laborers forfeited a portion of their wages to employers. Other workers lived independently but owned little besides their jacales. Some inherited a few cattle, furniture, or modest dwellings from their employers, who occasionally rewarded them for years of service.[19]

Prior to the 1820s, a handful of artisans and professionals lived in the northern villas. In addition to blacksmiths and butchers, some shoemakers and tailors migrated to the region but their numbers remained small. Reynosa, the largest town, had only ten artisans in 1792, whereas Refugio had

Arriero Mexicano.
Muletier Mexicain

6. Mexican *arrieros* (muleteers), who worked throughout the villas del norte, began facing increasing competition from steamboats as foreign trade expanded. Circa 1828 to 1834. Watercolor by Lino Sánchez y Tapia. Courtesy of Gilcrease Museum, Tulsa, Oklahoma.

four in 1814. Decreases in population and economic depressions occasionally forced artisans to find alternate work or move elsewhere. As the urban population grew, carpenters and bricklayers arrived, and housing subsequently improved. Schoolteachers were among the first professionals to arrive. Refugio hired its first teacher in 1814 at a salary of 294 pesos; Laredo hired a long-term schoolteacher in 1821. In addition to receiving higher incomes, artisans and professionals fared better than most workers because they were able to purchase houses or build them on modest vacant plots acquired from the local government.[20]

The colonial state's land policies and casta categorization shaped the class and racial divisions of the vecinos. The state's social categories, however, were not static. Nor did residents accept their imposition uncritically and without resistance. As elsewhere in the northern borderlands, the vecinos could alter their casta as their wealth changed. The enforcement of official casta categories, and the laws that afforded their privileges, became impossible within the daily practices and demographic realities of the villas. Independence would accelerate these changes. Although the national state liberalized trade and eliminated casta distinctions, its policies perpetuated inequality because the elite were best able to capitalize on economic changes, and civic categories became inscribed with status distinctions. Subsequently, economic changes would alter the villas' class and racial compositions; improve job opportunities for merchants, artisans, and laborers; and increase the availability of goods.

The Emergence of Foreign Trade

Class divisions became more complex during the early nineteenth century. The population increased through natural growth, migration from neighboring provinces, and foreign immigration. People displaced by the independence struggle and deteriorating economic conditions in central Mexico, as well as others attracted by the contraband trade, further augmented the population. Refugio became the third-largest river town by 1821 (see table 7). Discarding the rigid mercantilist system of the Spanish crown, Mexico's national government liberalized trade and opened a new port at Refugio in 1823. In addition to fueling economic expansion, the harbor drew many newcomers, including residents of neighboring villas, foreign merchants, and government workers. Federal employees consisted of officials who staffed the maritime customhouse and soldiers who guarded its

TABLE 7. Population of the Villas del Norte, 1757–1837

Town	1757	1794	1821	1828	1837
Camargo	678	1,174	2,956	2,587	4,017
Laredo	85	636	1,417	2,053	1,736
Mier	274	973	2,228	2,831	4,399
Refugio	—	100	2,461	6,700	16,372
Revilla	357	1,079	1,693	3,167	2,710
Reynosa	290	1,191	3,201	4,060	5,346
Totals	*1,684*	*5,153*	*13,956*	*21,398*	*34,580*

Sources: Prieto, *Historia, geografía y estadística del Estado de Tamaulipas*, 195; Hinojosa, *A Border-lands Town in Transition*, 123; Vigness, "Nuevo Santander in 1795," 475n27; De la Torre, *Historia general de Tamaulipas*, 108–9, 207–9; Berlandier, *Journey to Mexico during the Years 1826 to 1834*, 2:426–31; Herrera Pérez, *Monografía de Reynosa*, 127; Zavaleta, "The Twin Cities," 134.

revenue and patrolled Matamoros' strategic port (Refugio became Mata-moros in 1826). By 1837, Matamoros' population almost equaled the com-bined size of the other river towns.[21]

The port's opening transformed Mexico's northeastern states by redirect-ing the economy away from ranching and toward commerce. Laredo's wool exports and Reynosa's lime production surged with the heightened demand from the expanding trade. In exchange for foreign-manufactured imports, merchants exported livestock products, gold, and silver. According to the historian Juan Mora-Torres, the new port "liberated the frontier from the center's commercial domination, forever altering center-periphery trade relations by reversing commercial roles." Trade with the United States remained dominant even as commerce with the Caribbean and Europe increased. Goods arrived from New York, Philadelphia, and New Orleans en route to Monterrey, the principal distribution center for Mexico's North-east. Matamoros facilitated two-thirds of all imports for the region north of Guadalajara to Querétaro, and supplied four of the nation's nine-largest trade fairs.[22]

The growing economy and population complicated local government and increased its size. Matamoros officials feuded with national political leaders vying to control the customhouse and with custom authorities over the collection of funds. Altercations between soldiers and civilians further heightened administrative problems. Its *ayuntamiento* (town council) faced new burdens from the increasing number of foreign immigrants, many of whom were transitory and did not speak Spanish. With approximately three hundred foreigners by the mid-1830s, Matamoros became a commercial center dominated by transients and foreign merchants. Litigation rose as local creditors called on magistrates to salvage property from defaulting merchants, while translators and foreign consuls helped immigrants file lawsuits. As communications with foreign ports expanded, the ayuntamiento was forced to impose quarantines to limit the spread of contagious diseases, including cholera and yellow fever.[23]

Despite these problems, the newcomers provided much-needed services to a booming population with few native professionals and artisans. Of Matamoros's twelve established merchants in 1826, only two were native born. Foreign businessmen boosted chain migration by bringing their own clerks and encouraging other traders to immigrate. The newcomers included newspaper editors, doctors, teachers, and lawyers. Immigrant carpenters, silversmiths, and shoemakers augmented Matamoros's population of craftsmen, which reached sixty in 1826. By contrast, only one merchant and twenty-eight artisans worked in Laredo in 1829. The population of craftsmen increased as soldiers remained in the villas to assume skilled occupations after their discharge. Americanos predominated, but Irish, French, and Italian immigrants also arrived, as well as businessmen and professionals from the Mexican interior and Guatemala.[24]

Foreigners adapted to vecino society to different degrees. Some immigrants, especially unmarried americanos, remained aloof by living in foreign-owned boardinghouses and socializing exclusively with immigrants. Others established commercial links with elite vecinos by purchasing houses in Matamoros or near the port at Brazos Santiago. Gaining acceptance through their professional skills as doctors, pharmacists, and surveyors, foreigners acculturated to local customs by speaking Spanish and creating economic ties to the native-born elite. The vecinos, in turn, acknowledged the foreigners' valuable community service by naming them as expert witnesses in local tribunals. Some unwed immigrant men also forged social ties with the elite through intermarriage.[25]

Locals responded unevenly to the foreigners' arrival. The elite generally welcomed the newcomers, who purchased houses and property from vecinos. Families whose daughters married immigrants embraced the newcomers. Joint-trade ventures with foreign merchants benefited vecino businessmen. Workers, however, had a mixed response. On the one hand, the increase in foreigners benefited some workers by producing more demand for washerwomen, cooks, and domestic servants. On the other hand, some immigrants' business ventures threatened the livelihood of muleteers and cartmen, who successfully protested their possible displacement by steamers on the Rio Grande.[26]

Matamoros's growth provided urban workers with more jobs and greater autonomy than their rural counterparts. The influx of people created demand for service jobs—bakers, barbers, pawnbrokers, postmen, laundresses, and *tortilleras* (tortilla makers). As commerce increased, craft jobs opened for store clerks, coopers, coachmen, painters, and *coheteros* (makers of fireworks and gunpowder). Surging transportation needs fueled the need for freight carriers, muleteers, and stevedores. Attracted by the burgeoning economy, artisans arrived from interior cities. Men left indebted work on ranches to become urban laborers or artisans. Women gained more independence and better pay by leaving domestic service to work as seamstresses or *planchadoras* (ironing women). Laborers' autonomy increased; some became property owners and petty entrepreneurs. By 1831, several tortilleras and planchadoras operated businesses from their homes, which doubled as boardinghouses for numerous soldiers and unwed men.[27]

Trade liberalization increased the northern villas' ties to world markets, and decreased their isolation. Their economic transformation fueled rapid population growth from foreign immigration and internal migration. While the increased trade brought more food and manufactured items into the northern villas, it also sharpened class disparities because the elite were better able than the poor to capitalize on new commercial activities. The opening of the port also began the process of tying Mexico's economy to that of the United States, and of laying the groundwork for the northern borderlands' subsequent capitalist development.[28]

Escalating Fragmentation
and Foreign Cultural Influence

The economic boom increased distinctions in housing. During the late eighteenth century, the villas lacked government buildings, jails, and inns. Most residents lived in jacales, and only a few resided in sturdier houses. Laredo had four stone structures, two adobe houses, and numerous jacales, while Refugio was limited to mud, straw, and adobe houses as late as 1816. By 1826, Matamoros boasted 589 houses, which consisted of three brick structures amidst many jacales. Matamoros's housing stock surpassed the other villas by 1837, with 164 brick houses in the municipal center and

1,729 jacales located along the city's outer edges. Foreign architectural influences began to appear in the city's brick houses, which attracted merchants who sought structures with multiple rooms and floors. As improved construction and luxurious furnishings raised the value of real estate, some houses sold for as much as twenty thousand pesos. Workers continued to reside in humble *chozas* (huts) and jacales made of reeds that were valued at less than fifty pesos and located in areas prone to flooding.[29]

Cultural practices also reflected increasing foreign influences and evident class divisions by the mid-1830s. This change was most evident in Matamoros. All levels of society participated in the dances, horse races, and bullfights that accompanied the religious celebrations honoring the city's patron saint. The rich attended the theater, visited immigrant-owned pool halls, and authored poems and editorials that were published in local newspapers. Foreign influences permeated material culture of the elite, who acquired clothing, fine jewelry, and furniture manufactured abroad as well as food, spices, and fine wines from the United States and Europe. Such luxuries were out of reach for most workers, whose recreational activities were strictly regulated. The villas selectively controlled gambling by taxing playing cards and prohibiting games of roulette and dominoes. Laredo officials established curfews, required licenses for holding dances, and instituted fees for liquor vendors. Other villas penalized billiard-hall owners for admitting domestic servants, while employers prevented laborers from attending city celebrations.[30]

Accompanying the increasing class divisions was a reconfiguration of status categories introduced by Mexican independence and national state formation. During the 1820s the vecinos changed their language to acknowledge class identity. Throughout the colonial period, they had used the honorifics "Don" and "Doña" to refer to elite residents, and greeted the poor by name (often without their surname), by occupation, or by their amo's name. In 1821, the Mexican government introduced civic categories which residents adopted to highlight class distinctions. Vecinos appended the term *ciudadano* (citizen) to the names of the elite and *paisano* (countryman) to those of the poor. Juan de la Rumbe, a ciudadano, made such a distinction in an 1827 lawsuit against a local politician accused of carrying an illegal firearm, when he argued, "all the paisanos carry such firearms at night, I do not mean the honest ciudadanos, but even the plebe use them." Henceforth, the vecinos reserved the appellatives "Don" and "Doña" for elite foreigners. Acknowledging their higher educational attainment, the rich also boastfully self-identified as the nation's "thinking class."[31]

These condescending attitudes partly resulted from and were reinforced by the elite's control of local politics. The colonial state had reinforced community divisions through the unequal distribution of political power, initially concentrated in military captains who ruled each villa. Colonial authorities subsequently allowed elections for local officials but permitted only male landowners to vote and hold municipal office. The change increased political participation, but excluded the majority of colonists: women and the landless. In the national period, Mexico's 1824 constitution made all men equal citizens in theory, yet in practice social distinctions persisted. The elite retained political power because land ownership remained a requirement for voting and holding elected office. Despite the rhetoric of equality, national state formation continued to privilege wealthy men.[32]

Mexico reinforced patriarchal power by granting upper-class men control of local tribunals. As judges in the courts of first and second instance, the *alcaldes* (mayors) oversaw both criminal and civil proceedings. Lawyers or prominent men with some legal training occasionally represented each party in criminal cases. Although solely responsible for criminal judgments, magistrates obtained assistance from arbitrators in civil proceedings. For civil disputes, litigants chose an arbitrator, called an *hombre bueno* (reputable man), who was usually a wealthy landowner or merchant, occasionally a professional or artisan, but never a worker. The arbitrators recommended judgment and attempted to convince the parties to accept the sentence. If either party rejected the tribunal's recommendation, the case could be resubmitted to a higher court.[33]

Elite men's literacy, political connections, and wealth strengthened their legal advantages. Literacy helped them understand laws and pursue litigation. Wealthy families gained legal knowledge from relatives and friends who served as judges or hombres buenos. Unlike most residents, the affluent could hire lawyers, and pay for the transportation and litigation costs necessary to pursue appeals in distant cities. Their financial and political clout resulted in preferential treatment. In 1837, a Matamoros magistrate instructed a fellow judge to visit wealthy women's homes to record their declarations rather than force them to appear in court. He justified this special treatment by arguing that "the law has always had certain considerations for the prudent women of good conduct that it does not concede to those of other classes."[34]

Through municipal tribunals, local officials enforced the laws of the Spanish colonial and Mexican national states. These courts also allowed wealthy men to protect their property and maintain control of society. The exclusion of women from political and judicial offices further reinforced male dominance. Women actively used the courts, but their success varied according to the type of lawsuits they filed. They defended their property as well as men, but faced considerable obstacles in lawsuits over sexual transgressions. As administrators of justice, elite men engaged in moral regulation by punishing those who did not follow permissible modes of behavior. Workers were expected to show deference to the affluent, and women were required to be submissive to men. An analysis of the use of courts by vecinos demonstrates their differential access to power based on their class, ethnicity, and gender.[35]

Wealthy Vecinos

Elite vecinos protected their wealth by drafting wills to bequeath property and by suing over livestock sales, private land demarcations, and inheritance distributions. Property owners exerted extensive economic influence through rental contracts with stock raisers and merchants. Landlords flexed their legal power by suing to collect overdue rent or to evict the occupants. After the port opened, contract disputes over manufactured items began to outnumber suits over cattle and land. While livestock owners remained influential, the merchants' control of import-export commerce reflected its expanding power.[36]

Local tribunals also helped the elite regulate labor relations. Officials upheld the transfer of property and settling of debts in the testaments of elites, even when this involved transferring the services of criados and indebted servants to the inheritors. Landowners petitioned provincial or state officials for help in punishing workers, and also capitalized on vagrancy laws. In 1814, the villas received a governor's edict to submit a monthly report enumerating each town's idle population. Thereafter, authorities required vagrants to report to local tribunals for job assignments or provide proof of employment. If the unemployed did not find jobs within a week, the ayuntamientos could legally punish men with eight years of military service and place women as domestic servants in "virtuous homes." Subsequent laws authorized municipal officials to detain persons who appeared suspicious and to send vagabonds to frontier military service against the Indians. Municipal officials also relied on vagrancy laws to compel vagabonds and criminals to construct local schools, make bricks, and work at municipal factories.[37]

To maintain a disciplined labor force, employers punished recalcitrant workers. Some employers beat or whipped their workers to enforce their authority, as did Ignacio Dávila. After striking his sister-in-law, who worked as his domestic servant, Dávila claimed "a right to reprimand her because she was his servant." However, abusive employers risked prosecution under colonial and national laws that prohibited the use of indiscriminate punishment. Because of these legal protections, the wealthy appealed to local courts to chastise errant workers. Judges prosecuted workers who disobeyed orders, failed to show proper respect, or stole from their employers, resulting in fines (which increased their indebtedness) or in forced labor on public works.[38]

Employers sought to control workers' personal lives by suing to prevent suitors from courting female domestic servants. Judges imposed fines, warned the men to stop, and banished undeterred wooers from town. Employers feared that suitors would help indebted workers to flee, especially if the men and servants married or eloped. Of particular concern were those female workers who might leave when their soldier admirers were transferred or discharged from the army. To discourage such liaisons, military authorities often imprisoned soldiers who were courting female servants, while civil officials placed the women in shackles.[39]

The upper class used municipal courts as an instrument to maintain class inequalities and control the labor force. By regulating workers' behavior, officials fulfilled a local need for compliant workers and satisfied the colonial state's goal of developing productive civil communities in the northern borderlands. Moreover, vagrancy legislation gave employers a critical tool for regulating workers in a region with chronic labor shortages. The sentences for unruly workers reinforced gendered norms: recalcitrant men earned punishments of military service while disobedient women received sentences of forced labor as domestic servants. Employers' attempts to control the courtship of workers underscored the power given to them by the colonial and national governments. By exercising this power, the villas' elite became the local conduits for moral regulation on behalf of the colonial and national states.

Foreign Merchants and Artisans

Foreigners relied on their wealth and political connections to protect their property and defend themselves in criminal proceedings. However, they faced several disadvantages. Some were ignorant of Mexican laws, others did not speak Spanish, and several believed that Mexican judges favored citizens over immigrants. Furthermore, they accused the national and local governments of imposing additional restrictions on foreigners and interfering with their businesses. Non–Spanish speakers overcame language difficulties in court proceedings by selecting native-born or foreign interpreters from among their business contacts. Others chose vecino merchants to advocate on their behalf as hombres buenos. Immigrants who intermarried with the native elite relied on their in-laws to provide legal assistance. A few foreigners became proficient in Spanish and sufficiently knowledgeable of Mexican tribunals to serve as hombres buenos for fellow immigrants. Foreign businessmen hired lawyers, while most immigrants called on consular officials for legal assistance. Several foreign powers established consular offices in Matamoros soon after the port opened. These foreign representatives were usually businessmen who also served as consuls for their native countries—United States, Prussia, Spain, and so on. Along with extensive trade experience, they possessed knowledge of the Mexican legal system. Immigrants routinely called on consuls to resolve disagreements over business contracts, property sales, and criminal charges.[40]

The U.S. consul Daniel Smith was among the most active. A local merchant, he often appeared in court to defend himself against contraband charges and lawsuits over sales contracts. He assisted local authorities in settling the estates of U.S. citizens who died in their jurisdictions, and intervened to resolve criminal charges against americanos. In 1835, he successfully obtained the release of Chester Starks, who had been arrested for attempting to prevent the authorities from jailing his drunken friends. Smith created the most controversy by defending americanos detained for transporting contraband tobacco, clothing, and liquor. He exacerbated long-standing tensions with blanket accusations against local officials, charging them with corruption, legal ignorance, and selective prosecution of foreign merchants. In his zeal to protect his countrymen's interests, he occasionally asked armed U.S. vessels to appear off the port as an unsubtle threat to customhouse officials. His forceful actions alienated fellow U.S. merchants, who accused him of providing more assistance to smugglers than to legal businessmen.[41]

Among the foreigners were craftsmen and unskilled workers, who had immigrated with their employers or arrived on their own. They found work as independent artisans or as clerks in trade houses; only a few were domestic servants. Immigrant laborers hailed mostly from the United States, Spain, Ireland, or France. Although they had fewer resources than the foreign merchants and limited social ties to the native elite, immigrant workers' option to appeal to their consul gave them an advantage over native laborers. In 1832, Enrique Viudy, an immigrant barber from New York, benefited more from his ties to the United States than from his social networks among Mexican workers. Authorities charged Viudy with shooting and killing José Jorge Orr, his brother-in-law; both were African Americans married to nonelite *mexicanas* (Mexican women). According to several witnesses, Orr had a pattern of hitting María de Jesús Franco, his wife, who had separated from him several times. Orr accused Viudy of hiding Franco during a recent separation, cursing at Viudy in French, and threatening to drive a knife into Viudy's stomach. In Viudy's defense, Smith characterized Orr as "a provocative drunk who loved engaging in disagreements and fights," while portraying Viudy as someone "who always has a moderate and peaceful conduct, and is dedicated mainly to his job and family." Smith successfully defended Viudy by affirming his moral character, presenting fellow merchants as supportive witnesses, and arguing that the shooting occurred in self-defense.[42]

The arrival of foreigners altered the villas' ethnic composition and introduced cultural changes. Matamoros, in particular, became more cosmopolitan as newcomers arrived who were speakers of French, English, and German. Some immigrants intermarried with local vecinas of the same class status. These social ties helped the newcomers acculturate to vecino society, while commercial links opened doors for foreign merchants. Although they faced some disadvantages as foreigners in Mexican society, the newcomers overcame some obstacles through their social connections and assistance from consuls.

Vecino Craftspeople and Unskilled Workers

While vecino artisans and unskilled laborers had less wealth, access to officials, and legal knowledge than their elite counterparts, they were resourceful in using their social networks. Their class status barred them from political or judicial positions, and their minimal literacy hindered their legal understanding. Most could not afford to pay for lawyers or appeals. Occasionally they became embroiled in disputes over job contracts, petty property, or criminal charges, in which their resourcefulness was their sole advantage. Trinidad Salmerón faced considerable obstacles when the landowner Cesario Martines charged the bricklayer and two fellow workers, a shoemaker and day laborer, with theft. With a lawyer's assistance and his servants' supporting testimony, Martines persuaded the judge to imprison the workers, deny them bail, and confiscate their tools and supplies. The defendants appealed to relatives, previous employers, and the town's priest to testify on their behalf, and asked a military captain friend to defend them. Their tactics succeeded; the captain won their freedom and obtained monetary damages for lost wages and their families' subsistence.[43]

By relying on employers, friends, and families, unskilled laborers overcame formidable obstacles of limited literacy and lower status. In 1824, José María Olguín, an illiterate twenty-four-year-old cowboy and foreman, defended himself against criminal charges for injuring the ranch owner José Antonio Sánchez. Nicolás Ballí, a Matamoros priest and his employer, defended Olguín because the altercation occurred when the servant, following the priest's orders, attempted to prevent the ranch owner from trespassing on Ballí's property. More common were employers' numerous lawsuits charging their workers with theft of money, household goods, or livestock. Stock raisers also sued shepherds and cowboys for livestock that died or was lost under their supervision. Workers faced steep odds, but occasionally won lawsuits if the losses were accidental.[44]

Relatives occasionally intervened on behalf of underage indebted laborers. To ensure the education of children, ayuntamientos passed laws to limit underage servitude, but poverty forced families to ignore these stipulations. Families filed charges against employers who mistreated child workers, or who refused to pay or failed to release their children after an obligation had been fulfilled. Paulina Álvares successfully charged Espiridión Villarreal, an employer, with failing to guard her sister, who was "susceptible to the ruin of youth," and won her sister's release from her work obligation. Parents also sued on their daughters' behalf when coworkers or employers forced female workers to have sexual relations. The poor children who were domestic servants or apprentices included orphans. Without relatives to intervene, orphans and Indian criados rarely had a similar recourse to prevent their exploitation.[45]

Adult workers challenged their mistreatment by appealing to local tribunals. Although the extent of their knowledge of protective labor legislation is unclear, several workers did use colonial and national laws to stop employers from administering corporal punishment. Some litigants convinced magistrates to absolve their debt, jail their amos, or grant them damages for court costs and medical expenses. Not all lawsuits were successful, but enough laborers won their cases that in 1823 several employers petitioned the governor for a legal change to permit whippings. The employers argued that workers were provoking foremen to hit them in order to file charges and obtain their release from indebted servitude. Refusing the request, the governor argued that laws were passed precisely to prevent the excessive punishments that these employers wanted to inflict on their servants.[46]

Despite protective legislation, numerous employers escaped repercussions after physically mistreating workers. In 1835, Manuel Puentes, an illiterate laborer, accused Ramón de Urresti and his son of beating Puentes's oldest nephew to death. The nephew, an orphan, had worked as a shepherd for Urresti, a Reynosa livestock producer. Believing Urresti's claim that the nine-year-old shepherd had run away after a whipping, a local tribunal ordered Puentes to return his nephew's avío. Reynosa authorities refused to reconsider the case despite repeated requests. Appealing the case in Matamoros, Puentes argued that there had "not been equality in administering justice nor much less the impartiality required of judges" in the Reynosa tribunal. Despite the testimony of municipal employees that verified Puentes's moral character, he lost the case. Commenting on Urresti's acquittal, Puentes accused authorities of failing to administer the law without regard to "status, class, or condition."[47]

Some indebted servants changed employers to escape mistreatment. Occasionally they obtained the assistance of potential employers who rescued them from abusive amos. In most cases, workers filed lawsuits independently after suffering excessive punishment or encountering irreconcilable differences with their amos. New employers were required to pay the workers' debts. Lorenza Garza exercised this prerogative in 1838 after she fled from the service of the Camargo priest and was apprehended in Matamoros. She refused to return to the priest's service, so the alcalde found another resident to employ Garza and pay her outstanding debt.[48]

To undermine their amos' power, indebted workers fled without repaying their obligations. Such unpaid debts could exceed 180 pesos, which was between four and five years' salary for a domestic servant. These substantial financial losses motivated employers and municipal authorities to pursue and discipline runaways. Alcaldes distributed detailed notices to nearby towns to help identify and capture fugitives. Officials could legally discipline runaways with twenty-five lashes for the first offense and fifty for the second, and file criminal charges for any subsequent escapes. Some men were sentenced to labor on public works while women were disciplined by detention in their amos' homes. Judges punished servants by ordering them back to work in shackles until they repaid their debts through their labor. If workers had stolen from their employer when they fled, magistrates imposed additional fines or jailed them. However, authorities seldom apprehended runaways, who easily secured new jobs because of the constant labor scarcity. Female servants often fled with the assistance of male runaways with whom they had romantic relationships. Even if runaways were captured, authorities usually placed them with different employers who were willing to assume their debts, as opposed to following the letter of the law. Moreover, female servants left jobs by marrying men who repaid their debts, while male workers escaped indebted servitude by joining the military. Despite protests from employers, military officials protected these workers' right to enlist and allowed them to gradually repay their debts from their surplus earnings.[49]

Craftspeople and laborers occupied subordinate positions within vecino society that subjected them to physical and sexual abuse. Their limited power came from their lower-class status, limited literacy, and exclusion from elected offices. Yet, workers were not powerless. They challenged elite control by pressing their claims within the villas' existing social and political framework. Despite numerous disadvantages, laborers were resourceful in obtaining legal help from relatives, former employers, and friends. They also took advantage of the northern villas' remoteness and scarcity of labor to switch jobs or escape. Thus, regional conditions influenced workers' resistance to domination.

Structured Gender Inequality

The Spanish colonial and Mexican national governments structured gender relations by enacting restrictive and protective provisions that dictated women's inequality. Restrictive measures prevented women from holding positions of political and legal power over men. The law excluded women from voting, holding elected office, and serving as lawyers or judges. It also prevented them from being witnesses for legal transactions or representing another individual in court. Protective measures safeguarded women from becoming victims of economic or social destitution, since they were considered weaker than men in all aspects of life. Inheritance laws ensured that daughters and sons received equal amounts and that widows obtained a portion of their spouse's estate. To prevent economic ruin to married women if their husbands died or encountered financial difficulties, legislation allowed married women to maintain legal ownership of their dowries and *arras* (wedding gifts from their husband). Women had the right to prosecute men for broken marriage promises or sexual assault. Safeguards for women's sexual virtue were considered necessary to preserve their ability to marry and their family's social standing.[50]

Women exercised these rights with varying degrees of independence determined by their age and marital status. Young women and men shared similar legal rights as minors, but their rights differed considerably when they reached the age of maturity (twenty-five). As minors under their father's authority, girls and unmarried women could neither enter into contracts nor litigate without permission. Adult women were limited by restrictive legislation, whereas men were free to pursue independent legal action. Marriage transferred women from the control of their father to the dominion of their husband and imposed additional restrictions. To appear in court, wives needed their husband's permission. Only adult single women and adult widows could litigate independently. Most women were further restricted from pursuing litigation by their illiteracy. Landowning women fought over property and engaged in labor disputes with their workers. Poor vecinas disputed petty property and labor arrangements. Wealth and political connections enabled elite vecinas to enjoy a greater degree of authority and judicial familiarity than that exercised by working women. Yet, regardless of class, female residents filed the overwhelming number of cases concerning sexual assault, premarital and domestic disputes, child custody, and divorce. Women had less access to the courts than men of the same social class. Consequently, they were often forced to rely on men—sons, brothers, or husbands—as intermediaries. In the villas del norte, as elsewhere in the borderlands, female litigants with male allies were more successful then women who lacked such support.[51]

While relatively rare in the existing documents for the villas del norte, sexual assault lawsuits include accusations of rape, attempted rape, and incest. Feeling shame or fearing retribution, some victims did not report sexual assaults, while others were silenced by threats. Among twelve victims who sued between 1827 and 1846 were eight girls, and four married women. Four girls were victims of incest by a father or stepfather. Three cases involved attempted rapes. Five victims were elite or middling class, and seven were poor. All twelve victims were vecinas and most identified the perpetrators as their neighbors, coworkers, or relatives. The twelve arrested assailants were mostly poor workers, but also included several newcomers and one americano. Few confessed to committing sexual assault. Instead, they denied the charges or argued that the victim had consented to sexual relations.[52]

Male power and privilege were evident in the obstacles that women faced pursuing litigation. Convictions were difficult to obtain. The burden of proof fell on the accuser, creating several obstacles for poor victims. Some were intimidated by the court proceedings, as was María Manuela Gudiño, who refused to testify unless a priest was present. A trial made the violation public and increased the community pressure on some victims to drop their charges. The court's insistence on medical examinations, performed by midwives or doctors, for rape and incest victims added to their trauma. Convictions were more likely when wives accused their husbands of incest. Without a third-party witness, however, the male perpetrator had an advantage because the all-male court valued his testimony over that of his female victim. In 1846, Martina García accused Florentino Peña of attempting to rape her while she washed clothes at the river. Despite the supporting testimonies of three men, including García's husband, Peña escaped a conviction because no third party witnessed the attack.[53]

The lengthy process of interviewing witnesses and performing medical exams prolonged most trials, and hindered successful convictions by increasing the possibility of legal irregularities, which were likely due to the dearth of trained legal personnel. For appeals, higher courts often overturned sentences on technicalities. Long proceedings increased the likelihood that the accused would escape from prison or receive a pardon. To escape punishment for breaking a marriage promise, single men might agree to marry their lovers or give them financial reparations. Married men accused of incest occasionally gained pardons if their imprisonment caused their family's impoverishment, which could force their wives or daughters to drop the charges. After accusing Francisco Botello of raping her fourteen-year-old daughter (his stepdaughter), María Guadalupe Quintero eventually dropped the charges because Botello's lengthy detention was economically devastating to the family. The judge dismissed the case and ordered Botello to confess to ecclesiastical authorities before resuming his married life.[54]

Few assailants were punished beyond their imprisonment during the trial, although possible sentences included whippings, exile, mandatory service on public works, or years of presidio service. The victim's family had a legal right to kill an accused rapist, but this result rarely, if ever, occurred in the villas. Several men escaped from prison during their trials; others were released after charges were dropped. Local courts successfully prosecuted and punished only two of twelve men. Both had attacked wealthy victims with abundant resources to litigate and a strong interest in protecting their family's honor. The courts sentenced one man convicted of attempted rape to serve two months in shackles. Another guilty of incest received four years of presidio service, but gained his release on appeal after serving less than one year.[55]

Despite limited success in punishing attackers, some females stopped abuse by pursuing litigation. Because victims of incest were vulnerable to continued attacks, judicial authorities removed them from their family's residence and placed them in a *depósito* (safe house) with vecinos who could assure their safety during the trial. If the father was convicted of incest, the court stripped him of legal custody and assigned the victim another guardian. Relatives, friends, and church authorities assisted most victims in filing suit, although a few adult women independently sued their attackers. The involvement of a variety of community members afforded a measure of safety and often led to attacker's public shunning.[56]

Women's lawsuits over sexual attacks demonstrated the inherent inequality in protective legislation, and the numerous obstacles that victims faced in availing themselves of such laws. The colonial and national states not only placed women in a subordinate legal position to men, but also barred them from the judicial positions from which legislation was enforced. Such limited power forced most victims to obtain male allies to pursue litigation. Moreover, women's success in punishing their attackers often hinged on their class status. Regional conditions, such as a shortage of trained legal representatives and inefficient courts, further impeded women's claims. The lax punishments meted out to offenders meant, in effect, that local tribunals condoned their actions as part of male privilege; men could attack women (especially the poor) with little fear of repercussions. While the colonial and national states structured gender inequality through legislation, women's litigation in the northern villas shows that municipal courts enforced this inequality. Lawsuits over courtship provide further evidence of local tribunals' power to shape appropriate gender norms.

Courtship

An unmarried female exercised limited legal rights under Spanish and Mexican law, which upheld the principle of *patria potestas* (paternal authority), giving a father exclusive authority over his children. He controlled her property, education, and legal transactions and was solely responsible for granting parental consent to marry. Nevertheless, unmarried women claimed legal rights bestowed on them by protective legislation, including provisions to safeguard them from insults, inappropriate courting, and broken marriage promises. A blemish on an unmarried woman's sexual reputation could jeopardize her marriage plans, limit her social mobility, and lower her family's honor. Officials in the villas usually imposed jail sentences, banishment from the community, and fines on unwelcome suitors. In 1837 a Laredo judge sentenced Albino Bustamante to eight days in the barracks and warned him about the "full force of the law" if he continued pursuing an unwelcome romantic relationship with his stepsister, Carmen.[57]

Despite legal deterrents, some men imperiled women's plans for matrimony through inappropriate courtship and spurious claims. Josefa Salinas's wedding plans were temporarily derailed because a spurned suitor alleged that she had previously accepted his *palabra de casamiento* (promise of marriage) during an illicit affair. After her fiancé canceled their wedding, Salinas's father charged the spurned wooer with defaming his daughter's honor. Because a previous palabra de casamiento was a religious impediment to marriage, a priest conducted an investigation. Ultimately, Salinas convinced the priest that she had spurned the suitor's advances. Although she succeeded in marrying her fiancé, Salinas had to endure lengthy litigation in civil and ecclesiastical courts to defend her virtue.[58]

An unmarried woman was beholden to her parents or guardian, who might object to a suitor's class background, inappropriate behavior, or inability to make a marriage commitment. Guardians pursued litigation to preserve a family's honor when a daughter's virtue was questioned. If fines or jail sentences did not deter unwanted suitors, magistrates banished them from the northern villas. Several parents (usually fathers) complained about wooers who had "insulted" their home with late night visits or unescorted walks with daughters. Others tired of lengthy courtships if suitors were slow to propose marriage. Additionally, some women welcomed litigation to pressure admirers to advance beyond courtship to marriage.[59]

Unmarried women found ways to circumvent parental authority. Those who faced parental opposition to marriage occasionally ran way from home. Judges returned captured runaways unless they were victims of physical abuse, in which case magistrates assigned a different guardian. Suitors who helped young women escape faced kidnapping charges and received warnings, fines, or jail sentences. If a runaway couple eluded capture and married, the Catholic Church would not reverse the marriage if the bride was at least twelve and the groom was older than fourteen. María

Antonia García took advantage of this religious provision to marry against her father's wishes. García deceived a priest in a distant town by claiming that her father was dead, so the clergyman allowed her mother to grant the permission to marry. An unwed woman could also marry without her father's permission if she was an adult. In 1833, Juana Rosales's fiancé successfully sued to remove Rosales from her father's custody. After determining that Rosales was an adult, the judge placed her in a depósito while her fiancé made marriage arrangements. These judicial actions supported a key purpose of the depósito: to allow adult women to decide on marital plans without interference either from their families or suitors.[60]

Single women also subverted parental authority by engaging in premarital sexual relations. Unmarried couples sometimes consummated their relationship after men gave their palabra de casamiento because this promise was widely considered to initiate the marriage process. According to the law of *esponsales* (engagements), a suitor's verbal promise was binding even without a third-party witness. If a suitor subsequently spurned a young woman, her parents could press charges. After subverting parental authority, some young women subsequently asked parents to pressure lovers to comply with betrothals. Pregnancy made this goal more important for fathers such as Norato Vela. He accused Rafael Villarreal of impregnating his daughter after offering his palabra de casamiento. After facing a lawsuit and the intervention of public officials, a priest, and the girl's parents, Villarreal eventually agreed to wed Antonia Vela.[61]

Young women did not always succeed in pressuring their lovers to marry them. Authorities could not legally force people to marry against their will, so the law allowed men to make financial reparations in place of marriage. The financial settlement, or dowry, paid for child rearing and increased a woman's economic standing after her loss of virginity, potentially enabling her to find a husband. Some men paid the reparations to avoid marrying beneath their social status. In 1841 Jesús Godoy, a clerk, refused to marry Benito Rodríguez's daughter, an indebted domestic servant, claiming that he was not the first to have sexual relations with her. A judge ordered Godoy to pay a ten-peso dowry and forbade him from speaking publicly about the affair. The small dowry was not surprising because it was typically scaled to the woman's class status.[62]

The outcome of lawsuits over marriage promises depended on the reputation of the women. Men commonly defended themselves by maligning the women's moral character. They acknowledged having sexual relations but denied responsibility for the loss of the women's virginity. This tactic proved successful for Nepomuceno Treviño, who had a premarital affair with María Teresa Moya. Her mother sued Treviño, who acknowledged the affair and initially agreed to marry. However, he changed his mind after several witnesses, including Treviño's parents, characterized Moya as a loose woman who had borne two children. Because of her alleged reputation, Moya failed to marry her lover and obtain a dowry. The judge punished Treviño with fifteen days of labor on public works, and permitted him to marry another woman. The law contained a double standard that authorized judges to consider the past sexual practices of women but not of men.[63]

Local tribunals' child support verdicts depended on women's class and alleged reputation. An unmarried mother could sue for financial support if the child's father refused to marry, but only if both parents were unmarried and no marriage impediment existed. Fathers did not always have power over children born out of wedlock. Typically, the mother maintained control over offspring born as result of a premarital affair, but she also bore the financial brunt of raising the children. In the villas, several grandparents sued for child support on behalf of their grandchildren. Unfortunately, their class background influenced subsequent rulings. To obtain financial support for his granddaughter, Dionicio López sued Joaquín López Duque de Estrada in 1842. By the time the litigation was filed, however, both birth parents had married others, so a clear impediment to matrimony existed. López Duque de Estrada escaped punishment and won custody by arguing that López could not provide for the child as a handicapped widower of the "poorer class" who lacked any reliable means of financial support.[64]

Although all-male tribunals considered a woman's alleged character, they neglected the reputation of the man when they determined child support. Several protective legal provisions were reserved for "honest" and "decent" women who had not committed any sexual transgressions. The law stripped prostitutes and "vile women" of the right to sue for sexual assault and for child support. In contrast, men did not lose any legal rights for previous affairs unless they were convicted of rape or adultery. This bias defined women foremost as sexual beings by conditioning legal protection on their sexual behavior. For prostitutes without a stable means of financial support, the legal restrictions on child support forced some to place their children into temporary or permanent adoption. The women's alleged sexual behavior became an issue if they subsequently attempted to regain child custody. In the villas del norte, judges permitted prostitutes to retain custody of sons, but not of daughters, whom they feared would engage in prostitution under their mothers' influence. The courts' double standard was evident in that officials failed to remove sons from philandering fathers.[65]

In adoption rulings, magistrates favored birth parents and the wealthy. Child-custody litigation sometimes pitted adoptive mothers against the birth parents or relatives. Some families allowed others to raise their children because they could not afford food or education, often after the death of one or both parents. While some arrangements were legal adoptions, many were simple oral agreements, because women were normally not legally permitted to adopt children or the birth mother considered the adoption temporary. Adoptive mothers inevitably sued if the birth mother attempted to regain custody of the child. Judges in the villas commonly resolved child-custody lawsuits in favor of the birth parents. If the birth mother had died, the court awarded custody to the wealthier litigant under the assumption that she or he could better provide for the child. Upon losing custody, several adoptive mothers countersued the birth mother for child-rearing expenses during the adoption period.[66]

Men's authority to determine child custody did not go unchallenged in the villas. Not surprisingly, some adoptive mothers became outraged after losing custody. Several affluent women traveled to the state capital to appeal custody judgments. The experience of one elite adoptive mother provides insights into a woman's frustration with the male-dominated legal system. In 1827 Doña María Guadalupe Treviño lost custody of a baby boy to the birth mother, Guadalupe Bermea, and subsequently sued for child-care expenses. Treviño claimed expenses for a wet nurse, clothes, and laundry for a seven-month period. Not satisfied with the money awarded, she challenged the lower court's decision, calling the judgment an act of "despotism" that "lacked justice." In her appeal, Treviño expressed her devastation over the lower court's failure to consider her emotional attachment to the baby. More importantly, she questioned men's ability to pass judgment by accusing the magistrate and hombres buenos of "not being able to know and conceive of the immense work that a woman has in raising a child and less of being able to place a value on it." Although the outcome is unknown, Treviño's case exemplifies her determination to seek justice, and the stinging criticism raised suggests that some women believed that men should not pass judgment on issues of which they knew little.[67]

Courtship lawsuits reveal the extent to which tribunals in the villas del norte contributed to the moral regulation of sexuality by the colonial and Mexican states. Through their rulings, local magistrates defined acceptable sexual behavior for men and women, and reinforced gender inequality.

Such rulings reinforced discourses of gender honor that civil and religious officials used to construct and regulate sexual subjectivities and social reproduction. Local officials supported fathers' control of their daughters' courtship practices. Moreover, they considered women's class status and sexual reputation in monetary value rulings for their loss of virtue. Such practices confirmed that men ultimately had control over women's honor. Some women did challenge patriarchal authority (either their father's or the court's), but their uneven success illustrated the limits of their legal rights and power. Women who strayed from accepted sexual norms faced greater consequences than did men. Judges reinforced a double standard in which women's sexual reputation determined their legal rights, but men's sexual transgressions had little effect on their legal standing. Child support and adoption litigation further confirmed elite men's power over social reproduction by determining custody and financial support for households.[68]

Marital Rights and Divorce

Marriage in the northern villas followed patterns elsewhere in Mexico in which civil law structured conjugal bonds. The law curtailed women's rights further after their nuptials. Husbands controlled children, most of their wives' property and earnings, and the majority of their wives' legal transactions. Women retained ownership, but not legal control, of their personal property. They only controlled the *bienes parafernales* (the goods that a wife brought to the marriage beyond the dowry). Men could dispose of community property or profits from the dowry (but not the principal) without their wives' consent. To initiate litigation, married women needed their husbands' permission, although the law allowed for exceptions. Women could sue their husbands if the men sold their property without permission, failed to provide financial support, or mistreated them. Women in the villas maneuvered within these limitations, and outside of them, to improve their position in marriage. Domestic-dispute lawsuits serve as windows into both the vecinos' fulfillment of nuptial vows and their views on gendered marital roles.[69]

When facing marital problems, women often employed extralegal means by asking male relatives, priests, or employers to intervene—a strategy that the historian Steve Stern identifies as "pluralization of patriarchs." Resentful of this interference, husbands sued vecinos for meddling in their marriage. However, judicial officials were generally sympathetic when relatives intervened, as did Antonio Castillo in Laredo. Castillo brought charges against his son-in-law, Andrés García, for striking his daughter in 1834. The court sided with Castillo, reprimanded García for easily resorting to violence, and suggested that García "correct his wife's faults by scolding or advice rather than [by] blows."[70]

If marital discord continued, women in the villas frequently left home. Most were suffering from physical abuse, but others abandoned husbands unable to provide financial support. These wives sometimes faced lawsuits from husbands demanding their return. Men initiated far fewer domestic-dispute lawsuits than did women, but the majority of husbands' complaints concerned abandonment. Local courts typically detained wives who abandoned their husbands or forced the wives to go home. Some judges compelled poor wives who refused to join their spouses to work as domestic servants until they agreed to reunite with their husbands. Women rarely succeeded in petitioning to live apart from their husbands. Yet, women's actions occasionally led to court and community pressure on wayward husbands. María Reducinda Gutiérrez became embroiled in a lawsuit after refusing to accompany her husband to a new job, because he had failed to provide financial support. The judge pressured Gutiérrez to rejoin her spouse, but also encouraged her to appeal to her husband's employer or to the court to resolve future marital disagreements. The court also ordered her husband to meet his family obligations or risk legal punishment. However, most wives who left home never returned; rather, they unofficially separated or filed for an ecclesiastical divorce (a legal separation of bed and board).[71]

When extralegal attempts failed, women sued their husbands in *juicios de conciliación* (trials of conciliation) for mistreatment, financial neglect, physical attacks, and adultery. The courts sought to reconcile couples through mutual compromise and by social pressure from the arbitrators, judge, and community. In the villas, judges used this strategy to obtain eighteen reconciliations in thirty domestic-dispute cases. Officials usually threatened couples to obtain these agreements, as occurred in the juicio between Josefa de Luna and Domingo Siprián in Laredo. De Luna accused her husband of striking her in the face because she had demanded to know his whereabouts during an absence. She asked for permission to live apart from Siprián, but the arbitrators pressured the couple to reconcile after threatening the husband with a monetary fine and the wife with whatever punishment her husband requested should she "provoke" a future altercation. A successful reconciliation often involved a husband's promise to stop his mistreatment, a judge's threat of future punishments should problems persist, and a couple's promise to adhere to their marital obligations.[72]

Civilian officials cooperated with ecclesiastical authorities to enforce the Catholic Church's view of marriage as a binding sacrament. In their rulings, magistrates reminded spouses of marital obligations and the Catholic doctrine on marriage, which stipulated, "those whom God united under the bond of matrimony cannot and should not be parted." Among the successful reconciliations was the dispute between Miguel Balleto and Guadalupe Robles, who accused one another of adultery and requested the dissolution of their marriage in 1833. The judge banished the couple's respective lovers from Matamoros, and the arbitrators urged the couple to "forgive one another, reminding them of the obligations that, in their [marital] state, we have as Catholics."[73]

Spouses often accused one another of failing to meet gendered marital expectations. In 1835, Eulogio Peres charged his wife with forsaking her domestic duties and of being inattentive to his needs, while his wife accused Peres of failing to provide financial support. Husbands usually neglected their families when they began extramarital affairs, and indeed, Peres was having an affair with his sister-in-law. Countercharges of infidelity were common in disputes involving adultery accusations. When both spouses had been unfaithful, judges ordered each spouse's lover exiled from the community, and threatened both spouses with imprisonment and fines if they continued their respective affairs. Officials were similarly vigilant if an adulterous couple fled, by instructing the adjacent towns' authorities to apprehend them. While reconciliation might be impossible in these cases, aggrieved spouses nevertheless sought a court hearing, possibly to file for a legal separation.[74]

A spouse could pursue an ecclesiastical divorce only after enduring a long process in which civil authorities pressured for reconciliation. Before they could file for a legal separation, a couple had to attempt mediation through a juicio de conciliación. If reconciliation failed, the court required a waiting period before another mediation bid. Magistrates quickly dismissed frivolous separation petitions. Benito Bon learned that he could not divorce for believing that his wife's "behavior and defects were unbearable." Manuela Núñez argued that their marriage lifted Bon from abject poverty to financial security, and his subsequent divorce attempt was for convenience. Because of the lengthy mediation process and the aggressive attempts of civil authorities to reunite bickering couples, few spouses obtained permission from civilian tribunals to file for a legal separation in ecclesiastical courts. Officials in the northern villas failed to reconcile only twelve out of thirty domestic-dispute cases; significantly, the wife had sought divorce in each of the nonreconciled cases. After obtaining permission to file for an ecclesiastical divorce, women usually sued to determine child custody and temporary living arrangements.[75]

Until the late 1850s, the Catholic Church was the only institution authorized to grant an ecclesiastical divorce in Mexico. Ecclesiastical divorces were difficult, while annulments were practically impossible. By securing an ecclesiastical divorce, a couple could legally separate but not remarry while both ex-spouses lived. Officials allowed temporary legal separations if an individual physically mistreated a spouse, contracted a contagious disease, attempted to persuade a spouse to engage in crime, or practiced heresy or paganism. The habitual neglect of gendered marital obligations— a husband's failure to financially support his family or a wife's disdain of domestic responsibilities—was considered valid grounds. The separation was supposed to be temporary, since the church expected the couple to reunite after overcoming marital difficulties. Religious authorities would not grant a divorce for convenience or because of incompatibility. For marital disputes involving drunkenness, insanity, or relentless hatred, the litigant had to prove her or his spouse's incorrigibility and the danger of a continued union. The church granted a permanent ecclesiastical divorce only if either spouse (but not both) committed adultery, and witnesses corroborated the transgression. Absolute divorce was not permitted under civil law in Mexico until 1917.[76]

Spouses who lost ecclesiastical divorce proceedings incurred severe economic and personal penalties. Judges required guilty men to support their families and stripped them of child custody, dowries, and community property. Guilty women lost custody of children older than three and forfeited the right to their husbands' financial support. Wives convicted of adultery lost ownership of dowries and community property. Additionally, courts required guilty parties to pay court costs. These punitive consequences made the *threat* of divorce an effective tool to pressure spouses to reform. In 1842, Cecilia Figueroa threatened to divorce Francisco Leal because she could no longer stand to live a *mala vida* (bad life) with her husband, who failed to provide financial support and treated her with contempt. The couple agreed to reconcile but only after Leal promised to change his behavior and his employer, acting as his surety, promised to punish any future infractions. These punitive results encouraged husbands to do their utmost to dissuade wives from filing for legal separations. Ecclesiastical divorce was typically the final option for women whose previous pleas were ignored.[77]

Women gained more than men from legal separations. Ecclesiastical divorce freed them from bad marriages and granted wives legal rights previously held by their husbands. In the twelve nonreconciled juicios de conciliación from the villas, women sought divorce by claiming their husbands failed to provide financial support, inflicted physical abuse, committed adultery, or some combination of these. By the time they filed for divorce, most women had left their husbands to live with their parents or relatives. The legal right to live apart from their husbands was critically important for women who suffered from domestic violence. Once legally separated, women gained the right to litigate independently, to live separately, and to receive husbands' financial support. Women also recovered control of their dowries, their share of community property, and child custody. According to several vecinas who filed for divorce, economic independence proved critical because husbands' lack of support had brought misery upon families and forced wives to work for wages.[78]

Divorce petitions fueled further acrimony. The depósito was designed to protect wives from their husbands' influence and possible physical assaults while they pursued separation litigation. It also protected their family's honor as the safe house's residents were entrusted with ensuring the wives' faithfulness; the courts did not make similar arrangements to confirm the husbands' fidelity, reflecting a double standard of honor and sexual purity. Because courts forced husbands to pay for depósito, they frequently insisted on choosing which safe house. When wives chose the house, husbands usually argued that their spouse enjoyed too much freedom and urged the court to enforce their seclusion. Wives preferred living with parents or relatives, and often complained that their seclusion was a punishment. Not surprisingly, every case involving depósito in the northern villas was accompanied by threats of violence and bitter disputes over the choice of safe house.[79]

During divorce proceedings, husbands maintained considerable financial advantages over their wives by controlling the couple's property. This economic control allowed elite men to live comfortably, hire attorneys, and punish their wives by refusing to pay for their depósito expenses. Feuding spouses further aggravated bitter disagreements with child-custody disputes. María Concepción Solís obtained custody of her seven-year-old daughter while the ecclesiastical court considered her petition to separate from Sabas Olivares. The proceedings included adultery charges and mutual accusations of moral degeneracy. Officials permitted Solís to leave the original depósito for her parents' house, but reversed this decision upon Olivares's complaint. He argued that Solís lived extravagantly with her parents, who provided minimal supervision. Describing her disadvantaged economic position, Solís argued that she "did not have the resources to hire an attorney as had her husband (despite declaring himself insolvent)."[80]

The acrimony of separation proceedings increased the possibility of violence. Some wives feared their husbands' pattern of violent behavior. Others were aware that local men had badly beaten, and occasionally killed, their wives over domestic disputes and escaped punishment by fleeing. Those women who lived far away from relatives were especially vulnerable and in need of protection. Because of this danger, officials chose the depósito carefully. In 1832, a priest informed civil authorities that Doña Mónica Carriaga feared that her husband might harm or kill her for initiating divorce proceedings. The same priest testified about the danger faced by María Concepción Flores. While walking past her residence, the priest and a parishioner came to her aid when they observed Flores running away from her knife-wielding husband. Subsequently, the priest placed Flores in depósito at his own residence while she sought a divorce to escape a fifteen-year marriage plagued by domestic violence. Although they pressured feuding couples to reconcile, Catholic clergy supported legal separations for marriages beset by physical abuse.[81]

Domestic violence victims were the most likely to persevere through numerous legal obstacles to press for ecclesiastical divorces. While women gave multiple reasons for seeking separations, the most common reason in the villas del norte, as elsewhere in Latin America, was to escape physical abuse. For the twelve vecinas who rejected reconciliation, the danger posed by their violent husbands outweighed any social stigma attached to divorce. Some women who had unofficially separated sought ecclesiastical divorces only in response to their abusive husbands' legal attempts to force them to come home.[82]

Another common reason for divorce was husbands' lack of financial support. Negligence by husbands often forced women to transcend prescribed gender roles as subordinate partners to become the family's main wage earner. One woman complained about enduring fifteen years of mala vida characterized by her husband's financial neglect and physical abuse. During this time, she had provided for her family's economic needs and even loaned her husband money from her sales of handmade clothes. Similarly, Marta de Ávila employed vivid language to describe her increasing role as her family's financial provider. Her husband, Jesús Guadalupe Olvera, had repeatedly threatened to kill her, and he had never provided for the family's maintenance, so Ávila refused to live with him. Ávila had toiled at physically demanding jobs to support her children and husband. Making clear her desire to end the marriage, Ávila stated, "[I] no longer wanted to be in his company because I know that it would be not as his wife but rather as his slave."[83]

The women who filed domestic-dispute and separation lawsuits had varied backgrounds. Most had Spanish-language surnames and were born in Mexico. Two cases involved interethnic couples: one vecina married to an Anglo American man and another mexicana married to an African American man. Divorce litigants represented various classes, but wealthier vecinas filed more suits. The financial and legal independence gained from an ecclesiastical divorce was important to propertied women, who were more likely to seek legal separations than were poor women. Control of dowries and community property were rarely relevant for indigent women, so they avoided the costly and lengthy divorce proceedings by pursuing nonsanctioned separations. While recovering financial and legal control through a legal separation was appealing to some wives, ending physical abuse or mistreatment was the overriding factor for most.[84]

Juicios de conciliación and divorce petitions provide a window into marital expectations in the villas. Women who filed for legal separation often contrasted their husband's violent behavior and other failings with their own fulfillment of domestic responsibilities. Shaped by the law, their arguments strategically employed their society's prescribed gender roles, including an acknowledgment of a wife's subordination. In 1835, a husband accused his wife of forsaking her domestic duties and of being inattentive to his needs, while his wife charged him with failing to provide financial support. Another woman described herself as an ideal wife who offered the "caress of a woman who is tender, friendly, and docile." Women argued that they fulfilled domestic duties by assisting husbands, raising children, and preparing food. In return, they expected husbands to provide for and protect their families. María Concepción Flores accused Francisco Quintanilla of abusing the power entrusted to him in marriage. The canonical teachings that assigned "men as head of the home," she observed, did not have the desired legal effect when men "forgot their obligations and abused that superiority." These findings support the historian Silvia Arrom's conclusion that Mexicans accepted women's submissiveness to their husbands, but disagreed on its degree. Women who filed for legal separations were not claiming equality with men. Rather, they disagreed about the extent of their subordination or believed husbands had abused their "superior position."[85]

The northern villas were communities rife with internal conflict in which upper-class men held several advantages. They controlled the reins of power at the local level and personified what the sociologists Philip Corrigan and Derek Sayer, in a different context, describe as the "pervasive masculinity of the State." Through legislation and local courts, the colonial and national states accentuated class and gender divisions by favoring elite men in distributing political and economic power. Municipal courts reinforced a vecino view of masculinity associated with power, control, and independence, while prescribing weakness, dependency, and lack of control as feminine characteristics. Although women and nonelite residents faced obstacles in pursuing litigation, they found legal and extralegal ways to occasionally overcome disadvantageous situations. They exercised some agency in socially constructing their social identities, which were contingent on regional and temporal factors. Yet they remained subordinate members of a society in which class, gender, and race determined power, and where laws and judicial rulings shaped their daily social interactions. Civil and ecclesiastical courts enforced laws that determined acceptable behavior and social categories. Ultimately, through local authorities, the Spanish colonial and Mexican national states, in cooperation with the Catholic Church, shaped social identities in the villas del norte, a group of communities located far from the centers of political power.[86]

3

Opposing Forces
Political Loyalty and Trade

Visitors to the *villas del norte* (northern towns) in the eighteenth century discovered these towns to be isolated and geographically distant from central New Spain. With relatively few Spanish colonists and with minimal commerce, these communities along the Rio Grande seemed unimportant to imperial goals. Yet, these fledgling towns became significant for the crown's strategic interests of claiming the territory ahead of competing European powers. To secure the Seno Mexicano, the colonial government needed Spanish settlers to conquer indigenous populations and colonize the region with loyal subjects. The *vecinos* (community members) fulfilled a critical role as agents for the colonial government by establishing Spanish towns and developing a livestock industry. Moreover, the northern villas remained strategically important for distant central governments. Replacing European colonial powers were two nations, Mexico and the United States, eager to assert their power by establishing jurisdiction over the Rio Grande borderlands.

The Spanish colonial and Mexican national governments sought to obtain the villas' loyalty by shaping their society through political and economic policies. The vecinos, however, resisted certain aspects of state formation considered detrimental to their interests. Economic and political disagreements fostered schisms between the northern villas and Mexico's central government. The rift emerged in the Spanish colonial era and grew larger during the turbulent period of the nascent Mexican nation. The disagreements centered on the vecinos' perception of central government officials as unresponsive to their needs. The villas' residents felt removed from the concerns of government leaders, physical distance being one of many obstacles they faced. Differences between the economic goals of the residents and those of government officials constituted another hurdle. The colonial and national states needed civilian support for their military, so they attempted to obtain compliance by fostering allegiance among the populace without truly understanding the social and economic realities of the villas del norte. The outbreak of the Texas rebellion (1835–36) strained the northern villas' ties to the Mexican nation because federal officials ignored the vecinos' request for military protection from enemy Indians while repeatedly asking them to assist soldiers en route to Texas. Although the villas del norte remained within Mexico's jurisdiction during the period of the Texas Republic, this separatist revolt alongside the increased Indian hostilities left the vecinos alienated from the nation. The financial and personnel costs of a military presence in the North ultimately proved too burdensome for the settlers, intensified their unhappiness, and frayed the weak links with the central governments.

Agents and Privileged Subjects

During the eighteenth century the goals of the colonial state coincided with the aspirations of the colonists who founded Nuevo Santander's towns, including the villas del norte. The colonists sought economic opportunity, land, and the colonial state's support and protection to establish their towns, while royal authorities needed the colonists to settle the land on behalf of the crown and secure its claim. The confluence and interdependence of these goals placed northern settlers in a favored position. Like others in New Spain's northern borderlands, those living in Nuevo Santander were both agents and privileged subjects of the colonial state.[1]

As the crown's agents, the vecinos claimed the Seno Mexicano for Spain. In addition to founding towns and establishing municipal governments, they sought to "pacify" or "reduce" the region's indigenous populations. Their actions advanced the crown's goal to convert "barbarous" Indians who threatened settlements into proper "conquered" subjects who contributed economically to Spanish society. Through provincial volunteer militias under the leadership of town captains, the vecinos conquered and decimated the region's Native inhabitants. Although the military conquest was predominantly a masculine undertaking, female and male colonists cooperated to integrate Native people into vecino society. All colonists ultimately benefited from incorporating conquered Indians into vecino society as indigenous workers, consorts, and allies, who helped transform Nuevo Santander into communities of Spanish towns.[2]

The colonial state granted several benefits to the vecinos as privileged subjects, including crucial military protection from Indian attacks. Three *compañías volantes* ("flying squadrons") were placed in strategic locations throughout Nuevo Santander. Troops stationed in Laredo were responsible for guarding the northern villas. The state also assisted the settlers by giving them monetary compensation, supplies, and land, as a reward for moving into the region and claiming it for the crown. As an additional inducement, the colonial administration exempted the settlers from tax payments during the first years of colonization and again in 1774.[3]

As elsewhere in the Far North, the establishment of Nuevo Santander developed from New Spain's strategic interests. However, its colonization, unlike the Spanish settlement of Chihuahua and California, was heavily dependent on civilians. Instead of relying principally on presidial soldiers, who were expensive to maintain, the government depended on colonists who doubled as livestock producers and volunteer soldiers. The vecinos also filled the gap left by the missionaries who failed to convert the region's indigenous peoples in sufficient numbers. As long as colonial authorities continued to provide land, supplies, tax exemptions, and supplementary military assistance, Nuevo Santander's residents remained loyal subjects, willing to comply with royal directives.

The military's control of Nuevo Santander facilitated this political allegiance. Throughout the colonial era, Nuevo Santander's government was an independent entity except for brief periods (1788–92 and 1813–21), when it fell under the jurisdiction of the Comandancia General de Provincias Internas. The Intendancy of San Luis Potosí exercised some control on various fiscal matters. From initial settlement in the mid-eighteenth century, the colonizer José de Escandón instituted a municipal system of government in which he selected military captains, who were usually elite landowners, as each town's political leaders. These captains and their fellow officers reported to Escandón who, in turn, answered directly to the viceroy, the crown's top administrator in New Spain. Through this system of governance, royal authorities sought to maintain rigid political control and ensure disciplined residents.[4]

After the viceroy removed Escandón from the governorship in 1767, Nuevo Santander's residents enjoyed a brief period during which they exercised some choice over their leaders. For some twenty-seven years, colonial authorities allowed male landowners to elect town governments organized as *medios cabildos* (modified *ayuntamientos*, or town councils). The medio cabildo consisted of a *justicia mayor* (chief justice) or an *alcalde*, a *síndico procurador* (public attorney), and two *regidores* (aldermen) elected each year. Despite this reform, military captains and their subordinates captured most elected positions because of their social and political influence. Military men benefited from past leadership experience, political connections to royal authorities, and social prominence resulting from their large land holdings.[5]

In 1794, the colonial state imposed a more direct form of military rule in Nuevo Santander by eliminating the elective municipal offices in favor of a governor-appointed military captain as justicia mayor, a sergeant as the síndico procurador, and *tenientes* or *alferezes* (first or second lieutenants) as regidores. As towns grew in population, more officers were added to the ayuntamiento. Refugio's town council grew to include a second alcalde by 1814. To maintain control, Félix Calleja, Nuevo Santander's governor, asked alcaldes to submit a list of "the subjects of distinction who lived in [each] villa" from which to select town officials for the next year. The standing ayuntamientos chose the following year's councilmen, and thereafter the alcaldes forwarded the list to the governor. The town councils inevitably selected other prominent landowners, including family members and friends, for these posts.[6]

By maintaining control of municipal government, elite male landowners determined each town's political loyalties. The selection process ensured a small circle of landowners, self-described as the *vecinos más principales* (most prominent community members), for multiple ayuntamiento positions year after year. Predictably, these beneficiaries of leadership positions, monetary assistance, and large land grants proclaimed their town's allegiance to the Spanish king, referring to him as "our dear monarch." In official communications, they identified one another as a *buen vasallo* (good subject) to show their loyalty to the crown. Unlike the municipal leaders, nonelite vecinos had few opportunities to express loyalty to the crown. Far more common for them was regionally based political identification. Their attachment to neighboring villas was based on social ties to family and friends in those locales and to their continuous cooperation with other towns to defend against Indian attacks. By sharing livelihoods and experiencing the same hardships as fellow residents, they strengthened these bonds. Yet, for eighteenth-century residents of the villas del norte, the strongest sense of political attachment was their town. According to the historian David Weber, the political identity of the vecinos of New Spain's

Far North was primarily "loyalty to one's locality, one's *patria chica*, [which] frequently took precedence over loyalty to the patria, or nation as a whole." The historian Peter Sahlins describes a similar parochialism and gradual territorial identification of European rural society with a concentric circle model—where the innermost circle symbolizes the village and the outermost circle represents the nation. Residents' political attachment to a geographic area diminished as the spatial distance between the area and their hometown increased. A resident of Camargo, for instance, identified most strongly with Camargo, and then with the villas del norte, Nuevo Santander, the northern provinces, and ultimately with New Spain.[7]

When the vecinos constructed their corporate identity in relation to foreigners, however, they were engaging in a process not easily explained by the concentric circle model. As Sahlins argues, this image of encompassing circles fails to consider the oppositional and dynamic characteristics of identities. Relying on models of segmentary organization advanced by anthropologists, Sahlins posits an alternative model of "counter-identities" in which "the social and political expression of loyalties and affiliations is also an expression of difference and distinction." Accordingly, people construct their identities in opposition to others. Applied to political loyalties, this model explains how people can identify as members of their town in relation to, and in opposition to, nonmembers or residents of another town. Residents used the term *vecinos* to refer to members of the villa, and a variety of terms—including *foráneos* (strangers) and *extranjeros* (foreigners)—to identify those who were not members. The distinction between vecinos (insiders) and extranjeros (outsiders) provides the best example of counteridentities during the colonial period.[8]

The counteridentity model also explains how the vecinos gradually expressed an attachment to the villas del norte in opposition to other regions of New Spain and to the colonial government. During the early nineteenth century, they constructed a regional identity (as did others in New Spain's Far North), based in part on their geographic isolation and on colonial authorities' administrative failures. The large distances between the villas and other settlements contributed significantly to the vecinos' feeling of detachment from other towns and from the colonial state. Such geographic isolation made communication between the Nuevo Santander's northern towns and its capital difficult and infrequent. Contact with colonial authorities in Mexico City was even more sporadic.[9]

This lack of communication kept the colony's authorities uninformed about the needs of the Rio Grande settlements. The mail service, established during the late eighteenth century, remained slow because of the harsh conditions of the roads connecting the villas with the interior states. Most trade between the villas and the nation's commercial capitals depended on itinerant merchants traveling on mules. This rudimentary means of communication impeded the development of commerce, and limited the colonial government's state formation. A geographic divide further hampered communications, making the threat of Indian attacks more serious because the vecinos were often without government military aid. The necessity of providing their own defenses against Indians shaped the vecinos' expressions of masculinity. Alluding to their masculine characteristics, historians characterize the residents as people who were "strong in spirit," not excitable in nature, and "bulwarks of liberal principles" owing to their experience living along a frontier. Ultimately, a desire for local autonomy emerged from the vecinos' "relative self-sufficiency."[10]

Isolated Spanish Borderlands

The economic policies of New Spain's government created one of the first schisms between the colonial state and the communities along the Rio Grande. The mercantile system restricted trade with foreign countries to protect manufactured goods produced within the Spanish Empire. In the late eighteenth century, the Bourbon reforms expanded commerce, but royal officials continued to require goods to pass through the official port at Veracruz and to impose import duties. Tariffs added significantly to the royal treasury. While benefiting large merchants in trade capitals, restricted commerce hurt towns located along New Spain's periphery. The villas del norte, along with other borderland communities, became "an internal colony of merchants farther south." The northern towns were forced to use Veracruz despite the possibility of reducing transportation costs by establishing a legal port near Refugio. This trade requirement made imports expensive and limited the local economy's development. Also limiting trade were the lack of currency, poor communications, and the insecurity of travel throughout the region.[11]

In the 1790s, a visiting royal inspector succinctly described the villas del norte's main obstacles to economic development. Indian raids and the lack of additional ports, noted Félix Calleja, hindered the colony's ability to trade. Calleja maintained that the solutions to both obstacles were interrelated because increasing the economic development of the colony would attract more people, who would then enlarge its industries and serve to diminish the Indian threat. He offered several concrete recommendations to overcome these obstacles, beginning with the government's adoption of a tougher Indian policy. A local port in the northern villas and two auxiliaries, he added, would substantially improve trade by increasing the number of exported cattle and livestock products such as meats, waxes, soaps, and hides. Commerce with new Caribbean markets would triple the vecinos' income from cattle. The lack of sufficient export revenue also prevented the vecinos from importing necessary goods for their subsistence. Colonial officials, however, ignored Calleja's sound recommendations, reflecting their lack of concern for the economic welfare of the northern borderlands.[12]

In the mid-1810s, the villas continued facing the same obstacles that Calleja had outlined two decades earlier. The vecinos complained that trade languished due to the high cost of transporting livestock and other products to distant ports. Although overland commerce was expensive and time-consuming, it was necessary because all maritime trade had to pass through Veracruz. Alternative potential sources of revenue were salt from mines near Reynosa, fish from small lakes and the gulf, and the region's abundant ebony. The salt mines accounted for substantial trade, but fish and ebony met only local needs. Echoing Calleja's earlier suggestions, local officials recommended opening a nearby port but the appeal, like Calleja's years earlier, fell on deaf ears. The villas would have to wait several years before increased export revenues would stimulate trade with the colony's other regions and pay for necessary imports.[13]

Enduring trade obstacles stimulated smuggling's growth. Illegal trafficking along the sheltered coastline north of Refugio became popular among vecinos and immigrants. Contraband emerged shortly after the establishment of the first towns in the mid-eighteenth century. Contributing to the increase in smuggling were *alcabalas* (excise taxes), the limited variety of manufactured goods, and the state's monopoly on certain crops including tobacco. By the 1770s, smuggling had become a way of life for residents, who built homes along the Gulf Coast and at the river's mouth, locations later known as Bagdad and Punta Isabel. Prominent vecinos lived alongside newly arrived foreign merchants. Joining them were town officials who became complicit in the clandestine trade by neglecting to enforce trade restrictions and by actively smuggling. Northern borderland officials tolerated contraband, as a California governor observed, because "necessity makes licit what is not licit by law."[14]

The viceregal government actively sought to discourage contraband. Officials jailed smugglers caught by the crown's soldiers, and confiscated their merchandise. In 1805, colonial authorities jailed Juan José Ballí, Reynosa's military captain, and three prominent vecinos for smuggling. Despite such punishments, the contraband trade became widespread, causing the governor to complain in 1816 about its impact on revenue. Such groaning indicated that the economic interests of the villas were sharply diverging from the economic policies of the colonial state. Accompanying the towns' increasing distance from the royal government were their growing economic ties to the United States. Ironically, the government's strict trade regulation drove the vecinos closer to Anglo American merchants.[15]

The economic goals of the vecinos and of colonial authorities began to diverge by the end of the eighteenth century. After developing a vibrant livestock industry, the vecinos faced multiple trade obstacles from colonial economic policies. Moreover, the government began imposing the alcabalas in 1768, resulting in loud protests and an increase in subversive practices designed to avoid commercial restrictions. Underpaid and ill trained, customhouse officials readily accepted bribes to allow contraband through. In the early 1800s, the economic problems grew worse as merchants stopped shipping manufactured goods to the villas, authorities failed to pay soldiers and priests, and cash, in general, stopped flowing throughout the northern borderlands. During the remaining years of colonial rule, the vecinos failed to comply with several royal orders designed to collect money for the treasury. They began behaving like those living elsewhere in New Spain who passively disobeyed orders that did not advance their interests.[16]

Prelude to Mexico's Independence

In 1810, rebels launched an armed struggle to gain independence from Spain. The eleven-year insurgency took place mostly outside of Nuevo Santander, but the residents of the northern villas felt the war's impact and witnessed a few skirmishes between rebels and royalist soldiers. Colonists were financially affected by the insurgency, when the state intensified attempts to collect money and supplies to support its soldiers. These efforts further taxed the northern towns' resources and magnified their political distance from the central government. Moreover, the vecinos continued to suffer from neglect as viceregal officials ignored their pleas for assistance to combat Indians.[17]

The widespread dissatisfaction with royal policies contributed to the rapid spread of insurrectionary activity by inhabitants of Nuevo Santander. Although the villas del norte's cabildos remained loyal, the rebellion gained popular support during the final months of 1810 and the first half of 1811. Among the prominent local men who supported the independence movement was José Bernardo Gutiérrez de Lara, a landowner, blacksmith, and native of Revilla. In addition to organizing rebels in the northern villas, Gutiérrez de Lara contributed money and served as a liaison between Mexican insurrectionary leaders and the U.S. government. Upon the arrival of the royalist commander Joaquín de Arredondo in the villas in mid-1811, however, rebel activities began to diminish. Arredondo imposed strict controls and brought in large numbers of royalist troops. Gutiérrez de Lara's unsuccessful attempt to obtain support for the Mexican rebel forces from the U.S. government nevertheless brought him into contact with American politicians and helped him recruit Texan volunteers.[18]

Local indigenous groups added to the villas' insurgent activities. In April 1812, Carrizo and Garza Indians temporarily took over Camargo. Julián Canales, the Carrizo *capitán* (leader) from Camargo's mission, along with Eusebio Solís, the Garza capitán from Mier, led the uprising, and issued a proclamation denouncing the authorities' mistreatment of criollos and Indians. Resembling the initial call for independence issued by insurgents in Dolores, Guanajuato, in September 1810, the statement endorsed the king, New Spain, and Catholicism and denounced bad government. The indigenous uprising seems to have been provoked by a combination of local grievances against municipal authorities and by the influence of Manuel Salgado, an Indian from Dolores, where the independence movement began. Less than two months later, a joint force of royalist soldiers, provincial militia units (from Laredo and Reynosa), and allied Indians defeated the indigenous rebels and forced them to flee into the interior of Nuevo Santander.[19]

The brutal repression unleashed in the aftermath of this rebellion spurred another indigenous revolt in the villas. Several residents, including José García Salinas and Felipe Garibay, supported Gutiérrez de Lara's rebellion and later traveled to Nuevo León. After suffering a defeat in Monterrey, Garibay and others fled to the northern villas to recruit local Indians. In Refugio, they obtained the support of the Garza, Ayagua, and Carrizo Indians. Within a month of the rebel mobilization, a large contingent of royalist soldiers decisively defeated the insurgents. Garibay fled for safety across the Rio Grande, abandoning his indigenous allies. At least thirty-three local Indians lost their lives in the battle (including the Carrizo Indians' leader), over forty were captured, and several were executed. Thereafter, the villas did not experience any significant armed rebellion for the duration of the independence struggle.[20]

The impact of the independence struggle was evident in the central government's decrees. Throughout the colonial period, royal authorities sent town officials a variety of instructions—from periodic reminders to submit tax and census information to orders forbidding card games and liquor sales. They also ordered residents to celebrate the inauguration of a new monarch or the royal family's birthdays and weddings. After 1810, the decrees continued to instruct town officials on mundane government operations, but their content carried a new sense of urgency to maintain control. Faced with widespread insurrection, colonial communications stressed allegiance to Spain. They ordered local officials to encourage public displays of support for the crown and to honor the martyrs of Spanish liberty. Royal decrees urged the vecinos to defend their towns against attacks by insurgents and encouraged priests to instruct mission Indians to remain loyal to the crown. In 1814, Nuevo Santander's governor sent communiqués praising the Spanish king, denouncing the liberal 1812 Cádiz Constitution, and ordering the erection of a monument in each town's principal plaza to celebrate the "joyous" period under the monarchy's rule. Additionally, colonial officials encouraged schools to instill loyalty through the teaching of civic responsibility so that children could be "useful to the state." Royal decrees instructed local officials to control the population by restricting travel, prohibiting the carrying of firearms, and discouraging alcohol sales. While colonial authorities diligently sought allegiance in remote borderland municipalities, the degree of overall compliance is unclear.[21]

The colonial government endeavored to instill a sense of obligation to the Spanish crown by attempting to persuade the villas to help the royalist forces. It was an audacious plea, to be sure, because New Spain's officials had begun decreasing military spending for the northern frontier's defense. On several occasions, colonial authorities appealed to the vecinos' "patriotism" when urging them to pay taxes or provide the military with supplies. To contain the insurrection, officials required all travelers to carry passports, imposed curfews, prohibited the vecinos from housing strangers, and banned all communication and trade with the rebels. In Laredo the alcalde, José Gonzales, threatened to impose the death penalty on anyone who harbored insurgents or communicated with the rebels or their Indian allies.[22]

The financial and material support from regions such as the northern villas was crucial for the central government. In 1810, New Spain was saddled with mounting debts incurred from Spain's war effort in Europe during the previous two decades, and because regional treasuries stopped remitting tax revenue in order to pay for costly local military expenditures. The central government, in an effort to generate needed funds, levied new *arbitrios de milicias* (duties) on manufactures, food, and commercial transactions. It also increased taxes on property and on individual wealth throughout New Spain, the latter called *contribuciones militares*. These financial burdens affected all classes and persuaded some to side with the insurgency. Although few armed conflicts occurred after Arredondo occupied the villas in 1811, many residents passively resisted the crown through noncompliance with government orders (especially tax collection), while others angrily voiced their displeasure at the tactics used to siphon their resources.[23]

Throughout the independence struggle, Nuevo Santander's governor and military officials asked the northern towns for a wide range of supplies, volunteers, and monetary contributions. The most frequently requested supplies were horses and mules, but occasionally firearms and canoes were needed. Local officials submitted mandatory lists of the number of cattle and horses owned by each vecino to enable the governor's staff to calculate the proportional amount of each community's contributions. Although cattle contributions depleted the vecinos' livestock reserve and carved into their profits, they were not as detrimental to the population's food supply as were the corn donations. Unlike the plentiful livestock, corn did not grow locally in sufficient quantities so military donations were drawn from the stores of imported grains. These contributions exacerbated existing shortages resulting from the insurgency's disruptions. In September 1811, Laredo's residents complained about lacking food, tobacco, and soap. Moreover, military leaders threatened forced conscription should the towns not provide enough volunteers. The villas were already supplying muleteers and laborers to accompany their cattle and horse donations. Additionally, the viceregal government asked for monetary contributions by imposing a 10 percent tax on houses and forced loans to support the army.[24]

The economic strain on the vecinos was intense. Mier's residents housed and fed some of the soldiers, provided volunteers and muleteers, loaned firearms and tools, and even repaired the military's firearms. Refugio's population donated cattle, horses, mules, sheep, goats, corn, salt, and wood. These contributions exhausted the towns' resources, leading to food shortages. The cancellation of regional trade fairs in 1811 dimmed the prospects of restoring reserves. To justify Laredo's inaction regarding a request for additional volunteers in 1812, its alcalde explained that residents were already staffing the local garrison, serving sentry duty, and patrolling the mail to Béxar. In addition to livestock and monetary contributions, Reynosa's vecinos supplied the military with salt from its nearby mines and numerous *fanegas de bizcochos* (bushels of corn biscuits). As the requests mounted, the vecinos began to chafe under the weight of the financial burden and to refuse requests.[25]

The vecinos complained to the governor and military authorities not only about the mandatory contributions, but also about the military's theft of their property. In Laredo, a stopping point for royal troops headed for Béxar, one regiment "borrowed" (but never repaid) 723 pesos from its church. In March 1814, Refugio's ayuntamiento protested "the excesses that some soldiers committed by arbitrarily taking the possessions of the vecinos." Its letter was part of a chorus of complaints from other northern towns accusing the military of using force to extract horses, supplies, and volunteers. Several months later, the secretary of the provincial deputation informed the villas that they would be exempt from further contributions; he had confirmed their fulfillment of requests and payment of taxes, as well as the military's arbitrary confiscation of goods and forced enlistment of recruits. Nevertheless, problems persisted because colonial officials failed to provide the villas with adequate military protection. Subsequently, rancheros stopped rounding up their livestock for fear of Indian attacks. Widespread cattle theft (some carried out by the military) aggravated the already dire situation, according to complaints from Laredo, Revilla, and Palafox.[26]

Municipal leaders became further embroiled in conflicts over the soldiers' excesses and the military's continuous aid requests. Laredo's presidial captain accused the vecinos of failing to protect shipments to Béxar and of refusing to provide the military with livestock donations. In a sharp critique, Refugio's ayuntamiento rebuked a military commander for not controlling his troops, who were killing the vecinos' cows. According to local officials, soldiers looked on the town as a desolate region, where their actions would have no repercussions. The military should follow proper procedures and make formal requests, argued the ayuntamiento, before taking private property. A few of these actions displayed flagrant arrogance. One military commander had ordered his troops to forcibly appropriate horses and to punish physically any local official who interfered. Another military leader did not appreciate the vecinos' sacrifices to supply his troops with corn. He had ordered the alcalde to instruct the town's women to cook the donated corn into *vastimientos* (provisions) and threatened the women with punishment if they did not prepare the meals properly.[27]

Compounding the pressures on the northern towns was the economic devastation from drought, Indian attacks, and depopulation. Residents endured widespread hunger in 1814, after a drought caused low agricultural yields, leading to inflated food prices. Refugio's ayuntamiento warned state officials about a possible food shortage if vecinos continued paying for goods bought from traveling merchants with livestock. Preoccupied with the insurrection, the colonial government repeatedly failed to respond to requests for military assistance. In Laredo, frequent Comanche and Lipán Apache incursions kept rancheros from rounding up their livestock, and farmers from visiting distant cornfields. Residents continued to depend on muleteers to bring in corn and other grains because local farmers could not supply the towns' needs. By 1819, the protracted Indian raids had forced Laredo's residents to abandon thirty-seven of forty-four ranches. Many left Laredo for the safety of towns in Nuevo Santander's interior. Others felt trapped in their towns, unprotected by the military from Indian incursions that left several vecinos dead and families grieving children taken captive. The livestock and agriculture losses depleted residents' cash reserves for trade goods, so local merchants decreased their inventory. Also affected by the economic depression were artisans, who abandoned their shops to work the agricultural fields. Informed of the economic devastation and kidnappings resulting from Indian attacks, Viceroy José María de Echeagaray admitted the colonial government's neglect by responding "you tell me you informed my predecessor who in turn informed the higher authorities who did not respond, and consequently nothing has been done."[28]

Responding to the military's abuses and the colonial government's neglect, the vecinos defied orders for additional contributions. Residents veiled their noncompliance by arguing that they lacked materials and finances. A dearth of supplies and dire economic straits, alcalde José María Girón argued, prevented Refugio from complying with a military request for a canoe. However, the probable reason lay elsewhere. The vecinos seemed unwilling to construct another canoe due to a military leader having appropriated and then destroyed their boats on a previous occasion. Municipal officials subsequently refused to provide additional horses because the military had misused the town's earlier donations. After other villas refused to comply with the military's repeated requests, a royal official reprimanded the river towns in 1816 for failing to collect taxes levied on houses and wagons. If these actions of noncompliance to specific requests irritated royal officials, the vecinos' daily acts of subversion probably gave them greater cause for concern.[29]

The vecinos engaged in various acts of subterfuge to avoid making contributions. After Nuevo Santander's governor discovered residents hiding from census takers, he instructed Refugio's alcalde to assure them of the census's innocuousness. The colonial state's use of population statistics to demand material contributions and volunteers, however, belied the governor's reassurances. Predictably, some vecinos attempted to avoid forced contributions by failing to report the livestock they owned or by claiming property tax exemptions. Laredo's residents ignored regulations against the unsupervised slaughtering of cattle, to avoid livestock taxes. Others violated royal decrees by smuggling tobacco into the interior to avoid colonial duties.[30]

Colonial authorities blamed the villas for depleting Nuevo Santander's treasury through their failure to cooperate with customhouse and tax officials. Refugio's officials hid behind a technicality to avoid remitting taxes. Their population was exempt from a 10 percent tax on stone and brick houses, they argued, because most residents' straw jacales were of little value. The villas were not alone in neglecting their duties to the crown, but they figured prominently on the list of delinquent towns. In 1816 Nuevo Santander's governor reprimanded fourteen towns for failing to submit yearly lists of alcabalas over a period of four years. Five of the fourteen towns were among the villas del norte. By this time, the vecinos' dissatisfaction with colonial authorities had become abundantly clear and revealed an unmistakable weakening in their political identification with the colonial state.[31]

Mexico's independence struggle tested the limits of the villas del norte's loyalty to the colonial government. No longer privileged subjects, they enjoyed few benefits from the crown; instead, they felt overburdened by its monetary and material demands. Although they did not fight directly against royalist forces after 1813, the vecinos contributed to the opposition by failing to aid royal soldiers and authorities. Noncompliance, widespread rebellion, and faltering colonial support eventually proved too great. After an eleven-year war that left thousands dead and widespread devastation, Mexico won its independence in 1821. The vecinos expected better relations with the new nation's leaders, so Mexico's independence period began with great promise.

Subjects into Citizens

Mexico's leaders introduced a new political language and promoted novel cultural practices to foster a national identification among the country's disparate regions. Such actions were necessary because Mexico was "not yet a nation," according to the historian Enrique Krauze, but rather "an assemblage of villages, settlements, and provinces isolated from one another, without any conception of politics, even less of nationality, and controlled by the strong men of each locality." In their attempts to "forge a nation," the political elite used newspapers, education, rituals, and symbols to spread nationalist sentiment among a dispersed population. Throughout Mexico, dailies and political broadsides blossomed from the mid-nineteenth century onward as government officials sought to create a national imagined community. In Tamaulipas (formerly Nuevo Santander), newspapers began appearing in the 1820s; in Matamoros (formerly Refugio) alone, at least twelve gazettes appeared during the 1830s and 1840s. Most newspapers focused on political issues in play as factions sought to gain adherents during the turbulent period after independence. The ideal of nationalism, however, succumbed to regionalist realities.[32]

Education became a means for the political elite to spread their nationalist messages to a wide (albeit male) audience. Tamaulipas state officials began establishing public schools in 1828, but political instability and a lack of funds hindered the development of these institutions there and elsewhere. Consequently, large portions of the population remained illiterate. Throughout the villas del norte, teachers struggled to establish schools, persuade parents to enroll their children, and cajole the community into paying teachers' salaries. Several teachers attempted to maintain regular school attendance but struggled to persuade parents who objected to the teachers' discipline and the school's costs. Only boys attended Laredo's schools, so girls were left to be educated at home. Facing widespread illiteracy, politicians turned to symbols and rituals as more effective channels to communicate the budding nationalism.[33]

Language emerged as an important medium for the transmission of nationalist symbols. The new administration changed the place-names of provinces and towns to reflect the transformation from a colonial to a national state. The word *imperial* gave way to *national*, according to the historian Andrés Reséndez, and the "crowns that had embellished public buildings and carriages were mercilessly erased." The Republic of Mexico replaced New Spain. The colony of Nuevo Santander, named after a region in Spain, became the state of Tamaulipas, a name derived from the Huasteca word for two local mountain ranges. To underscore the nation's independence, officials referred to the "estado libre de" (free state of) Tamaulipas in communications. Similarly, in 1826 the town of Refugio became Matamoros, the name of a fallen hero of Mexican independence.[34]

The political transformation affected daily language used throughout Mexico. Newspapers and political directives used such terms as *patria* (nation) instead of *provincias* (provinces) and *ciudadano* (citizen) in place of *súbditos* (subjects). These terms spread even to remote regions such as the villas del norte. Soon after independence, these towns' alcaldes began referring to themselves and their constituents as ciudadanos in official documents, and they no longer addressed high government officials as "your majesty" but rather as fellow ciudadanos. Local leaders joined national and state politicians in attaching special significance to a new nationalist calendar that, in official documents, identified the year 1824, for example, as the "third year of our independence."[35]

New days of celebration spread throughout the country. Rather than commemorating Spain's royal family and heroes, towns began honoring the heroes of Mexican independence. From Laredo to Matamoros, municipal and military authorities established "patriotic juntas" to coordinate elaborate celebrations. To commemorate the 1824 Constitution, Reynosa officials organized three days of celebration that included a military gun salute, the ringing of church bells, and a mass. Other rituals reminded citizens of their national allegiance. In taking possession of land, citizens shouted, "Long live the president and the Mexican nation." The government also affixed the emblem of the new nation (an eagle atop a cactus eating a snake) on official items sent to local municipalities. Other reminders included coins, flags, and holidays commemorating the deaths and birthdays of independence heroes.[36]

The new national discourse imparted status distinctions and individual political identities. In 1821 the Mexican government eliminated racial categories from official documents. The 1824 Constitution further eliminated distinctions, in theory, by removing property and literacy requirements for citizenship. In practice, however, the previous racial designations became civic classifications. In the villas del norte, a resident's social class determined her or his civic status. The colonial era's multiple racial labels were replaced with two civic categories: ciudadano and *paisano* (countryman). Thereafter, vecinos referred to upper-class men as ciudadanos and to the poor as paisanos. Legal documents and political directives illustrated the change as *ciudadano* replaced the honorific title *don*. In 1819, for example, a letter to Refugio's mayor was addressed to "Señor Alcalde Don José María

Girón," while an 1832 letter addressed the same man, who was again mayor, as "Señor Alcalde primero Ciudadano José María Girón." The new terms reflected a shared identity as equal citizens and conveyed a more intimate association among fellow residents than the meaning derived from the term *royal subjects.*[37]

Despite the egalitarian intentions of the new Constitution, residents in the northern villas, as elsewhere, continued to observe status distinctions. Community membership remained an important local identity. Town residents weighed several factors, including length of residence and community service, to determine if an individual was a community member. By separating insiders, or vecinos, from outsiders, they defined a community identity. However, only the elite male members of the community exercised full rights of local citizenship. Residents also began using nationalist language and referring to the ideals of the independence movement in their litigation. José Francisco García, Macedonio Capistrán, and ten other vecinos employed nationalist imagery in an 1825 petition. Referring to themselves as ciudadanos first and vecinos second, they asked Matamoros's alcalde and the state government to approve their claim to land owned by the absentee proprietors of the hacienda La Sauteña. The petitioners needed the additional land for pasturage and water for their livestock. The owners of La Sauteña, they argued, were violating laws requiring landowners to populate and cultivate their property. Instead, the owners were charging "feudal" rents to poor residents who settled on the land. In their claim, the group compared the hacienda owners to "an orchard owner's dog, which neither eats nor allows others to eat the food he guards." The hacienda's vast holdings were surprising, according to the group, especially when compared to the previous disparities in wealth which existed in the colonial era, when "the powerful oppressed and subjugated the poor." They asked officials to comply with the independence movement's ideals that had "eliminated oppression, slavery, and tyranny as well as stripped the cancerous roots of the old government, which allowed the rich to imprison the poor."[38]

The petition revealed the residents' view of local citizenship. The petitioners were, in effect, giving their definition: community members were those persons who developed and defended the land, while outsiders were those who had failed to uphold community obligations. The owners of La Sauteña were outsiders because they were absentee property holders and, most importantly, because they were not active participants in Matamoros's community of landowners. The absentee owners neglected to comply with their civic responsibility to provide watering holes for travelers and to assist in the defense of the villas. In contrast, the vecinos identified themselves as having "acquired the merit of being the defenders of this land, and of the entire frontier against the repeated incursions of the barbarous Indians." To punctuate their accusations, they asked, "Has the Hacienda Sauteña assisted in this defense? Of course not because only this community of vecinos . . . undertook the defense." Matamoros's ayuntamiento concurred with their accusations and appended a letter of support to the petition. A note in the following year's census confirmed these views. Long-term residence, the alcalde observed, was a requirement for community members. The census totals did not include soldiers, military families, or foreigners, he noted; they were transient residents and therefore "not included in the number of legitimate vecinos."[39]

National legislation, which was inscribed with class and gender distinctions, influenced local citizenship practices as well. Not all men were considered equal citizens in daily practice, since land ownership was a requirement for ciudadano status. Only male ciudadanos enjoyed full participation in a community's political and legal life. Holding all political and judicial positions, they alone voted for elected office. Local officials excluded paisanos from political participation (they could neither vote nor hold elective office) but allowed the indigent to freely use the courts, own property, and enter into contracts. Thus, ciudadanos in the villas exercised political and civil rights, while paisanos retained only civil rights. Non–community members, such as immigrants and Indian residents, held limited civil rights and very restricted political rights. Additionally, the new Constitution conferred citizenship only on men (although gender equality was not a constitutional goal), as women were not allowed to vote or hold office.[40]

Citizenship rights also depended on an individual's ethnicity. The "conquered" Indians who lived among the Spanish Mexican population were too poor to own land, which prevented them from voting and holding office. The vecinos viewed enemy Indians as "uncivilized" people who lived outside their communities. Elsewhere this issue was frequently subject to debate. "Should they [Indians] be considered as children of the great Mexican family, or as enemies to be driven beyond the boundaries of this state?" asked a Chihuahua military commander, echoing questions from California politicians. Mexico City authorities, such as President Antonio López de Santa Anna, believed enemy Indians were Mexican citizens so long as they had been born and lived in the republic. Other administrators and politicians shared the vecinos' view of enemy Indians as noncitizens. A visiting inspector from Mexico City characterized the "barbarian" Indians as part of "the extended Mexican family," who might qualify for citizenship, but only if they pledged allegiance to the government, adopted Catholicism, and joined settled communities. In Mexico's Far North, groups such as the Comanches and Lipán Apaches were generally not accorded political rights. In 1838, *El Ancla*, a Matamoros newspaper, identified the Comanches as a people who could not claim citizenship: "Not all who have been born within the territory of the republic are Mexicans, but only those who live under its pact. Neither the Comanche barbarians, nor the traitors, who have violated the faith that they owe this pact and government, violating the national honor, deserve this name."[41] National authorities specifically singled out Spanish immigrants for exclusion and expulsion during the 1820s. Suspicion of peninsular Spaniards, who swelled the ranks of the royal government and militias, was at a high following independence. The discovery of an 1827 Spanish plot to reconquer Mexico, and of a failed invasion of Tamaulipas in 1829 by royalist supporters living in Cuba, increased this distrust. Subsequently, the national government ordered local officials and military commanders to monitor peninsular Spaniards and to require immigrants arriving in ports to carry proper passports. National legislation ultimately expelled peninsular Spaniards from the country in 1828 and 1829.[42]

Despite this general distrust, the vecinos accepted some foreigners as community members. A lengthy residence or intermarriage with a native-born person helped immigrants gain acceptance. Several peninsular Spaniards with deep roots in the northern villas obtained "insider" community membership. In 1828, the Matamoros alcalde asked the governor not to enforce the expulsion law against six peninsular Spanish residents, because several had married *hijas de México* (daughters of Mexico), had lived within the republic for ten to thirty years, were considered citizens, and had held several local political posts, including that of alcalde.[43]

A few long-term foreign merchants received political privileges, such as serving as *hombres buenos* (reputable men) in trials involving fellow immigrants, but most foreigners could not hold judicial office or participate in the political system. Only a few immigrants obtained minor positions in local governments after years of providing some service to the community. Jean Berlandier became an exceptional foreigner who managed to hold a lower-level public office. The Swiss scientist settled in Matamoros after working as a botanist and zoologist on the Mexican Boundary Commission in 1827 and 1828. Married to a Mexican woman, Berlandier worked as a pharmacist, physician, and surveyor until his death in 1851. He held the post of síndico procurador and served numerous times as an *hombre bueno*. His community service and marriage allowed Berlandier to become an insider after a long residence in Matamoros.[44]

Mexico's independence transformed colonial subjects into national citizens. Facing strong regionalism throughout the nation, Mexico's new leaders attempted to spread nationalism through education, rituals, and language. Their efforts at state formation reached the villas del norte, where nationalist language and rituals became part of daily life. While officially eliminating racial classifications, the new nation continued to impose status distinctions by making landownership and maleness requisites for voting and holding elected office. The national state thus continued to shape local society by regulating civic categories. As the nation adopted more liberal trade policies, elite foreigners (especially merchants and professionals) gained increasing acceptance as community members. Reflecting national patterns, the villas' political elite (including foreigners) continued to exclude the poor, women, and Indians from power.

Port of Matamoros

Accompanying the changes in the residents' political identity and the region's demography was an economic transformation that increasingly tied the villas del norte to the United States. Following the trend initiated by the royal authorities during the Bourbon reforms, the national government further relaxed trade restrictions. The most direct impact was the long-awaited establishment of a port at Matamoros in 1823 (see figure 7). This action legalized direct trade between New Orleans, already the main trading partner for the region's smugglers, and Mexico's Northeast. The consumption trends in the villas and nearby northeastern commercial capitals stimulated a surge in American manufactured imports, formerly acquired as contraband. The legalization of this previously underground trade greatly expanded commercial ties with the United States and the Caribbean, creating a timely economic boost after eleven years of turmoil during the war for independence.[45]

To regulate the port trade and collect tariffs, the national government established an *aduana* (customhouse) at Matamoros. This income was critical because the national government had assumed debts incurred by Spanish colonial authorities, and because the independence struggle devastated

Carretero del puerto de Matamoros.   *Charretier du port de Matamoros*

7. Cart driver from the port of Matamoros, when foreign trade increased dramatically with the official opening of the port. Circa 1828 to 1834. Watercolor by Lino Sánchez y Tapia. Courtesy of Gilcrease Museum, Tulsa, Oklahoma.

the economy. The duties on the voluminous trade through Matamoros became a significant part of the national treasury. The national government could finance the daily needs of its military in northeastern Mexico by combining the revenues from customhouses in Matamoros and Tampico. For fifty years after Mexican independence, the federal government obtained an estimated 80 to 90 percent of its income from import and export duties. The majority of the aduana revenue came from import duties, which the national government kept high to pay for its debts.[46]

The vecinos pursued smuggling to avoid import taxes and to introduce prohibited items into the country. Contraband consisted mostly of imports, having higher tariffs than exports. Smuggled items were manufactured goods and raw materials. Among the most popular manufactured imports were clothing, shoes, liquor, and tiles acquired from American merchants. Following the colonial government's practice, the national government prohibited the introduction of foreign manufactures as a way to promote their local production. Yet, smuggling continued to flourish because Mexico's industries could not meet the vast needs of the nation's residents.[47]

Smuggled raw materials included corn, rice, flour, coffee, sugar, tobacco, and cotton. The government's monopoly on tobacco (from harvesting to finished product) and the availability of better-quality tobacco on the black market encouraged smuggling. Tobacco became one of the most profitable contraband imports because of the large disparity between its foreign and domestic value. Purchasing tobacco in New Orleans for $1.00 to $1.50 cwt (hundredweight), smugglers sold the contraband in Mexico for $50 to $75 cwt. They paid for smuggled imports with silver bullion, the predominant contraband export, which allowed merchants to avoid export duties. Contraband exports included hides, wool, and other animal byproducts, but in smaller shipments because of their bulk and low cost relative to silver.[48]

Merchants employed a variety of means to transport contraband items. Some were stashed underneath legal trade goods on which they paid taxes. Customhouse officials found contraband items below ships' hulls, in secret compartments, and disguised as legitimate goods. By transferring goods from cargo boats to lighter craft that could dock in secluded regions of the gulf or navigate undetected along the Rio Grande, smugglers evaded officials. They also avoided the customhouse by docking at unofficial ports, bringing in contraband through Corpus Christi, approximately 120 miles north of Brazos Santiago (the harbor at the mouth of the Rio Grande), and then transporting it overland to Matamoros. Smugglers increasingly used Corpus Christi after 1828, when the Mexican Congress decreed that only Mexican-owned vessels could transport goods into the country's ports. Since most Mexican ships traveled between New Orleans and the nation's ports, the law led to a shortage of legal transportation vessels and effectively ended legal trade between Texas and Mexico.[49]

The lucrative contraband trade attracted both foreigners and Mexican nationals. Many smugglers were immigrants with long-standing ties to New Orleans merchants. Foreigners also worked as the captains and crews of the contraband ships owned by American and European smugglers. Some, like Ramón Lafon (Raimond La Fou) for instance, had established residence in Matamoros during the colonial era when they began smuggling. Others married into prominent local families. Relationships with local citizens became an advantage to smugglers when they were arrested. Few remained in prison, because they were skilled at convincing authorities of their innocence. Other smugglers bribed customhouse officials to avoid confiscation of their contraband. As graft and smuggling increased, a Mexican politician estimated what many suspected: approximately two-thirds of the nation's imports were contraband. Through direct participation and refusal to disapprove of the practice, the vecinos became complicit in smuggling. Several owned boats used in the contraband trade. They also served as captains and crew of large oceangoing ships and riverboats carrying smuggled goods while others worked as muleteers transporting contraband. Landowning vecinos cooperated with smugglers by hiding the contraband on their ranches. As distributors and consumers of the smuggled goods, local citizens profited from the illicit trade. Far from being scorned as an occupation, smuggling became respectable in the villas, as it was along other international borders.[50]

The national government failed to stop the clandestine trade, because profits were too lucrative. Faced with the overwhelming task of patrolling its extensive northern border with relatively few underpaid troops, the government instituted a woefully inadequate enforcement. While compensating citizens with smuggled goods for assisting authorities became a successful government incentive, it paled in comparison to the generous profits that smugglers collected. Contraband became so widespread that the national government repeatedly threatened to close the Matamoros port. The closure never materialized, however, because the government depended heavily on the revenue from legal trade. By the mid-1840s, the villas had become dependent on American supplies and trade. In the course of two decades, these river towns (along with communities in California and New Mexico), had "broken loose from the grasp of Spanish mercantilism," according to the historian David Weber, "only to be embraced by American capitalism."[51]

In addition to increasing the government's revenues, the port enhanced communication and lessened the region's isolation. In 1821, the region still lacked the variety of institutions, such as schools and hospitals, found in the nation's capital. Visitors often complained about the villas' lack of "culture"; they felt that the towns remained socially isolated from other regions. Few nonregional newspapers reached the area and popular cultural activities were limited to local productions. Professionals avoided the villas because of their geographic isolation. Furthermore, the region's economy remained predominantly based on husbandry, and luxury items remained scarce. The port's opening in 1823 not only reduced the region's social and cultural isolation but also transformed its economy: trade blossomed and livestock production declined in relative financial value. The burgeoning economy attracted newcomers—doctors, lawyers, teachers, and traveling entertainment groups—who, in turn, altered the social and cultural life and invigorated the community.[52]

The Matamoros port strengthened ties between the villas and the state and national governments as communications increased and the harbor assumed a larger role in the governments' financial and military plans. Indications of the port's growing importance became evident in the dramatic rise in the number of newspapers and official pronouncements received there. By the mid-1830s, city residents could choose among eight or more local, state, and national newspapers to keep abreast of current events. State and national officials, in turn, became more interested in the port's economy because their governments grew dependent on the tariffs collected at the aduana. Financial reports and official orders exchanged between the customhouse staff and government authorities figured significantly in the increase in communication. Also contributing were the edicts and letters sent to military commanders and soldiers guarding the customhouse. The expulsion of Spanish loyalists in 1828, for example, led to a flurry of government correspondence with Matamoros.[53]

The national government spurred international trade and demographic growth, and improved communications by opening the Matamoros port, but its economic policies retained elements that antagonized the villas del norte. The vecinos' tastes for foreign, especially American, products overrode the government's efforts to promote nationalism. Responding to its high import duties and the scarcity of manufactured items, the vecinos continued smuggling. By subverting its trade policies, they distanced themselves from the national government and forged ties with American merchants. Their reactions to the increasing military presence in the villas would further hamper national goals.[54]

Mexico's Taxing Requests

Despite improved communications and less isolation, the vecinos continued to complain about the central authorities' neglect of their economic and military needs. While the national government had liberalized trade and increased communications, these reforms were accompanied by financial and military demands that harkened to the colonial period. As the region's economy surged, the government's incessant requests for contributions continued, the insurgency having left the nation's economy in ruins.

Additionally, the government experienced a period of instability after 1821, which exacerbated economic problems. As the centralists and federalists battled over power, this "period of anarchy" witnessed frequent changes in the presidency and several revolts. The vecinos' experience during two rebellions, the struggle of Texas for independence (1835–36), and the federalist uprising in the villas del norte (1838–40), further alienated them from the national state. Moreover, the government's attempt to suppress these rebellions and the persistent need to defend the northern towns against Indian attacks made financial support for the military crucial.[55]

Like its colonial predecessor, the Mexican government appealed to loyalty in its requests for contributions. Nationalist pleas replaced exhortations about loyalty to the crown. "The fatherland is always deserving of our sacrifices," the governor wrote in an 1825 communiqué to the villas del norte, "[and] to defend [the fatherland] all citizens are obligated to lend their help." According to the governor, male vecinos could express their patriotism by volunteering for military duty. Infantry companies became "voluntarios de la Patria" (volunteers of the fatherland) to reinforce the obligations of citizenship. The government urged citizens to provide the "best service to the fatherland" by complying with requests for supplies and helping apprehend army deserters. The river towns, as noted earlier, witnessed an increased military presence after the port's opening to protect the money collected at the aduana and to stem the flow of contraband. Additional troops arrived to guard against a feared Spanish invasion between 1827 and 1829, to fight the insurgents in central Texas in the mid-1830s, and to suppress the federalist rebels in 1838.[56]

Although the central government appealed to nationalism in order to obtain allegiance, its efforts, like those of the colonial government, failed for similar reasons. Residents tired of the frequency of the requests; the contributions taxed their resources; and, most importantly, they had little motivation to honor the government's pleas because few benefits resulted from their contributions. Admittedly, the military supplied some services to towns, such as providing doctors and medicine for the indigent, but the disadvantages of the troops' presence far outweighed the advantages.[57]

Between 1821 and 1836, the military requested mostly volunteers and livestock from the villas. Calls for volunteers to join the regular army increased tensions with municipal officials who needed able-bodied men for civilian militias to protect the villas from Indian attacks. Moreover, military commanders repeatedly asked the vecinos to furnish horses and cattle for their troops. Although residents grumbled about fulfilling the military's requests, they usually complied in part. As the petitions mounted and became more frequent, however, the vecinos began complaining about the quantity of livestock required of them. In response to citizens' complaints, municipal officials wrote angry letters to military commanders accusing the army of "extortion."[58]

An 1823 response to a governor's request was typical of the vecinos' disgruntled obedience. Although they had fulfilled all previous military requests, the assistance had become a heavy burden, and the vecinos refused to comply with future petitions. Their resistance resulted from deteriorating relations with the military and government bureaucrats. In one glaring example, the chief customhouse official (a nonresident appointed by Mexico City administrators) appropriated horses, jailed residents without the consent of civil authorities, and forced the alcalde to sign indictments against suspected smugglers. In Laredo, tensions between municipal and military officials surfaced, when the town council attempted to recover contraband belonging to a foreign merchant. Likewise friction between the military and civilians in Matamoros increased after troops appropriated the residents' canoes and boats to transport personnel. Because the soldiers were paid professional troops and the military had been abusive, the vecinos argued, the armed forces should supply their own horses. The residents, stated the alcalde, "in essence refused to provide [the aid] and the few who help do so with great animosity."[59]

Municipal officials initially complied with the military's petition for recruits. According to the governor, the state needed additional volunteers to patrol the port for contraband, to defend the villas against Indian raids, and to fill the ranks of the national army. A draft would not be needed to obtain soldiers for the provincial militias, the Matamoros alcalde claimed in response, because the town's inhabitants were "pleased" to volunteer. The military's dearth of supplies forced the state government to ask recruits to provide their own firearms and horses. Officials in Camargo, Mier, and Laredo received similar appeals for self-equipped volunteers. As the government's demands for volunteers continued unabated, residents grew weary. They grudgingly complied with an 1825 request, but the Matamoros City Council sent the governor a letter strongly protesting the quantity of required recruits. Matamoros had been asked to contribute more men than had other towns with similar populations. The ayuntamiento pledged the city's allegiance and reiterated its willingness to sacrifice for the nation. But its contributions, the ayuntamiento argued, should be proportional to the city's population.[60]

As they had done during the colonial era, civilians responded to this abuse by subverting the government's efforts to collect taxes for support of the military. State authorities insistently pressed the river towns for tax remissions. Town officials, however, sided with the population by passively disobeying government instructions. The northern villas were not alone in their insubordination; the practice of ignoring laws which were not beneficial to local interests occurred throughout Mexico's northern borderlands. Municipal authorities repeatedly failed to remit demographic and property statistics in order to prevent the Tamaulipas state government from using these figures to calculate each city's tax contributions.[61]

The problems arising from the military presence in the villas gradually increased their political rift with the national government. The outbreak of hostilities between rebels in Texas and the national government further intensified the weight of this burden. While the vecinos complied with the national government's orders not to aid the rebels, other requests proved more difficult to fulfill. The military used the port at Matamoros to land troops recruited in Veracruz and Tampico before sending them overland to Texas. Thus, Matamoros and Laredo became way stations for battalions. The increased army presence, along with the proximity of the conflict, created an explosive situation. As the military's calls for assistance increased and its abuse reached greater levels, the citizens' complaints grew louder and further distanced the towns from the national government at a time when the nation most needed popular support to quell the Texas rebellion.

The military solicited livestock, volunteers, money, and food, as well as personnel, to transport supplies. Initially, several river towns fulfilled government requests for aid to battle the rebels. Municipal officials grudgingly complied while asking for payment for supplies, but eventually refused aid requests. Laredo's ayuntamiento often clashed with military authorities, who demanded more provisions but neglected to consider the vecino food needs. The military's disrespect for residents was evident when Colonel Domingo Ugartechea took possession of their best horses on his march to San Antonio. To make matters worse, Ugartechea left his troops' old horses with Laredo's military commander instead of replenishing the civilians' contributions. Alcalde Ildefonso Ramón complained about the military's usurpation and lack of payment, but state officials ignored his plea. Rather than sending payment for the supplies, state officials forwarded additional requests.[62]

Physical confrontations between soldiers and vecinos further exacerbated military-civilian tensions. Because the army had difficulty filling its ranks, officers often conscripted less-than-exemplary individuals. Vagabonds and criminals were more likely to join peasants in the military's ranks than elite vecinos, who often purchased exemptions. Compounding the problem was the central government's inability to feed, clothe, and equip the soldiers, whose morale dropped significantly. According to municipal officials, soldiers engaged in "excesses" during public games and entertainment. As troops robbed local residents, fought with civilians and foreign merchants, or became unruly while intoxicated, daily conflicts arose. Vecinos engaged in physical confrontations with soldiers over the affections of women and over barroom disagreements. Civil disputes raised tensions even further, with residents suing soldiers over stolen property and unpaid rent on land and houses. Tensions heightened when civil magistrates failed to prosecute crimes committed by soldiers who claimed their *fuero* (privilege) to be tried in military courts. In rare instances, officers permitted civilian authorities to prosecute army members. Wives and children of soldiers, as well as muleteers and gunsmiths who worked for the army, could also claim exemption under the military's fuero. Further aggravating the conflict over jurisdiction were physical disputes between city constables and soldiers resisting arrest.[63]

Despite the widespread tension between the population and the army, the antagonism was not uniform. Class and gender differences explain some alternative views. Indebted workers occasionally joined the military to escape from disadvantageous employment. Military service provided workers with economic opportunities to repay debts and avoid mistreatment by employers. Female domestic servants used a similar avenue, establishing romantic liaisons with visiting soldiers and accompanying their partners when the army withdrew. Fearing this possibility, employers frequently sought legal means to prevent soldiers from courting or marrying their domestic servants. Losing workers to the army added to the resentment of elite vecinos, already angry about the burden of taxes and forced military contributions.[64]

Disputes increased as the concentration of soldiers in the villas grew rapidly during Texas's separatist revolt. Interpersonal conflicts were negligible compared to the army's organized institutional mistreatment. In February 1836, the military engaged in widespread theft despite receiving civilian donations of horses, mules, oxen, muleteers, and carts to carry their provisions. Troops stole horses and livestock, complained the vecinos, and committed "thousands of disorders and violent actions" as they traveled

through the area, leaving disgruntled residents in their wake. After enduring several months of theft, Laredo's stock raisers were on the verge of
giving up. "The only substantial work that the inhabitants here did was
cattle raising," reported Laredo's mayor, Bacilio Benavides, "and now in the
desolate fields are left only a few horses and cows that for lack of care will
soon die also."[65]

Local officials' responses to calls for contributions during the Texas rebellion were more brazen, and their resistance more damaging to the national
government's cause, than previous replies. Matamoros's ayuntamiento fired
off a critical letter to the governor strongly condemning soldiers as "military
despots" who did not consider the vecinos' sacrifices, and asking for indem-
nification for the "harms suffered by its citizens." Aware of the possibility for
abuse, the national army's leaders had ordered towns to obtain payment
before handing over supplies to the military. These instructions were impossible to follow, the ayuntamiento observed, because military commanders routinely ignored complaints, forcefully appropriated supplies, and de-
fiantly justified their actions by citing the exigencies of war. Moreover, the
Texas rebellion had cut off supply ships to Matamoros. The military's outrages had suspended trade, the alcalde vociferously complained in a subsequent letter; residents were too frightened of the military to travel, creating
shortages of basic staples throughout the villas.[66]

The military's rationale for requests lost its sway with the vecinos. In
1836, pushed to their limits, they expressed their grievances more forcefully
and in larger numbers. Matamoros's ayuntamiento complained that its
inhabitants "had been reduced to misery because everyone had contributed" all they possibly could. Other villas also protested continued levies.
Alcalde Benavides asked for a tax exemption for Laredo's residents, who
suffered miserably from the burden of contributions and Indian raids. Describing the desperation in the town, Benavides wrote, "The larger part of
the town has only meat to eat, as flour and corn have to be brought from
other towns and it is very dangerous to travel; besides, there are not enough
horses left to hitch to the wagons. . . . If something is not done right away to
help them, I believe that they will start looking for other places to live and
abandon this village."[67]

Municipal leaders asserted the northern villas' separate identity from
other towns in the state's interior by citing the sacrifices undergone by their
communities. They were not alone in resenting militia service and obliga-
tory contributions to the army; these were unpopular throughout Mexico.
The reluctance to join the army was understandable because enlistees had

to abandon their families and remain absent during harvests, plantings, and brandings. Armed defense figured prominently in shaping the river towns' community identity. When enemy Indians had threatened the villas in the past, residents had cooperated willingly with inhabitants in other river towns. As the exigencies of war increased, the vecinos forged a collective identity "counter" to the interests and needs of the towns in the state's interior.[68]

When their sharp criticism failed to sway national leaders, the vecinos actively sought to hinder the army's recruiting and its requests for aid. Their daily acts of resistance indirectly helped Texas rebels repel the Mexican government's efforts to reestablish control. In 1836, municipal officials attempted to persuade the governor to reduce the number of recruits required of Matamoros. Despite a population of some ten to twelve thousand inhabitants, the ayuntamiento argued, many residents were transient merchants and thus ineligible for military service; others were too elderly or too critically needed as workers. After towns across the country failed to meet their quotas, the national government instituted a compulsory draft. In response, some vecinos in the villas emigrated while others hid in the countryside to avoid forced conscription. Part of their motivation for hiding, according to local officials, was to avoid serving in the infantry. In a decision exemplifying the army's lack of concern, federal officers ignored municipal officials' suggestions to capitalize on the vecinos' equestrian skills by placing recruits in the cavalry. Feeling no obligation to serve in a military that constantly mistreated them further spurred the residents to hide.[69]

Often, entire towns and groups of municipalities refused to comply with orders. Laredo's alcaldes neglected to acknowledge military requests for assistance and troops. Concerned with Indian raids and the failure of the central government to remit military salaries, local officials paid the local garrison's soldiers instead. Matamoros declined outright to help the army on several occasions and began to ignore government orders to donate money, horses, and other supplies. Their refusal was not surprising: the military had not repaid civilians for multiple loans. Only after complaining to the governor did some citizens obtain payment for items taken by the army. Because the military repeatedly took advantage of the population's hospitality, vecinos began to refuse housing for visiting army commanders and troops. Several elite residents had rented residences to the military, but they soon grew weary of their tenants. Soldiers refused to vacate houses after their leases expired, and others neglected to pay rent. In response to an army's request for a house to place a temporary hospital, an alcalde described the residents' negative mood. "The best houses of the population are occupied by the military," Juan Nepomuceno Molano argued, so it is "impossible to remove" the citizens who live in the few remaining structures, who refuse to lose additional money.[70]

Ignoring the military's orders to capture deserters, the vecinos instead gave aid to the runaways. The gravity of the desertion problem was evident in the numerous circulars sent to the villas by military commanders and state officials. In addition to threatening punishments for helping fleeing soldiers, these notices offered monetary rewards for their capture. Nonetheless, individuals and ayuntamientos continued to aid runaway soldiers. Undoubtedly, local residents—like others in Mexico's Far North—sympathized with deserters, aware that the troops were constantly underpaid and chronically suffered from shortages of weapons, food, and clothing. Like the vecinos, the deserters had become victims of the military's abuse and neglect.[71]

Local residents' immediate concern was not the distant rebellion, but rather Indian attacks on the villas del norte. Their regional concerns and identity were stronger than their national identity, the more so because enemy Indians took advantage of the military's preoccupation with Texas rebels to renew their raids on the river towns. When the army removed Laredo's military garrison during the winter of 1835–36, the villas were left vulnerable to attacks from Comanches and Lipán Apaches. The Indian incursions devastated the region's livestock and forced stock raisers to abandon their land on the river's left bank for safety on the right bank. The villas organized their own defense, but these patrols were poorly equipped; the military had taken many of the residents' firearms and horses. Municipal authorities throughout the northern villas gradually realized that Laredo's alcalde, Ildefonso Ramón, had been correct to suggest that the central government did not care about their safety. Complaining to the governor about the state's inability to protect his town from Indian attacks, Ramón argued that "if this town be considered as an integral part of the Mexican Republic," then it should receive aid. The government's continued neglect of the villas suggested otherwise.[72]

Residents were further disillusioned because the increased Indian raids and the army's efforts to suppress the Texas rebellion hampered the local economy. Trade profits were flourishing prior to the outbreak of the Texas insurrection, but Indian incursions greatly curtailed inland commerce beginning in 1836. The lack of military protection permitted robbers to prey upon overland caravans. Moreover, Texas rebels began seizing Mexican ships early the same year and threatened to confiscate American vessels engaged in trade with Mexico. After securing independence from Mexico in April 1836, Texas enforced a blockade of Matamoros. As a result, local antagonism toward American merchants increased and ultimately drove them away. By the end of 1836, the villas were in financial ruin. Maritime trade resumed, but at lower levels than previously because of the departure of most American merchants and the loss of confidence in secure commerce among the remaining traders.[73]

Even with the rebellion over, government officials continued to request supplies and recruits while the army continued its mistreatment of civilians. Not surprisingly, the vecinos refused to obey the government's prohibitions against pursuing commercial relations with Texas colonists. By this time, the vecinos had become dependent on smuggled American goods, official trade channels failing to satisfy local demand. Laredo's residents ignored the military's threats and traveled to Texas to exchange their cattle for supplies. Military commanders angrily accused residents of treason: "forgetting the label of mexicanos, they continued trading with the enemies of the nation, protecting them with clandestine commerce . . . and in fact, recognizing the independence of Texas."[74]

The villas del norte emerged from the Texas Revolution politically and emotionally distant from Mexico's national government, under whose jurisdiction they had lived for more than fifteen years. During that period, legal and illegal trade flourished, but the national government's repeated petitions for assistance curtailed the villas' economic prosperity. As the region emerged from the economic devastation of war, its inhabitants continued ignoring the orders of the centralist government, which demanded their support but did little for their benefit. The vecinos followed the pattern of other frontier people, whose "ambivalent loyalties" led them to "inevitably set up their own nexus of social contact and joint interest" with other frontier dwellers (who are not necessarily fellow citizens). The sinologist Owen Lattimore's description of a frontier dweller, as one whose "political loyalty to his own country may in this way be emphatically modified by his economic self-interest," fit the typical resident of the villas. The vecinos certainly had "ambivalent loyalties," as did others living in Mexico's northern borderlands whose wavering sentiments were intensified by "the neglect of the central government, extreme distance from the nation's core, and by virulent regionalism."[75]

Regionalist Uprisings and Independent Indians

The northern villas' discontent was part of a larger pattern of dissatisfaction with the central government throughout the northern borderlands that inspired several regionalist uprisings. A political shift in the national government during the mid-1830s combined with long-standing problems to increase the disaffection of *fronterizos* (borderland residents). In 1835, the centralists had returned to national power, and undercut the federalist Constitution of 1824. They converted states into departments without political or fiscal autonomy, substituted juntas for state assemblies, and replaced elected governors with appointed ones. Opposition to the centralists' reorganization led to rebellions in various states, including Zacatecas, Yucatán, and Guerrero. Regional and demographic differences shaped the goals of these rebellions, from demands for more local autonomy in Zacatecas, to separatism in Yucatán and Texas. In the northern borderlands, anticentralist opposition was also fueled by the fronterizos' dismay at the national government's failure to provide military protection from independent Indians. Aggravating their resentment was the centralist government's decision to impose new taxes and request more military contributions. Growing anticentralist sentiment led to the Chimayó Rebellion in New Mexico in 1837, and to a federalist uprising in neighboring Sonora the same year. State and municipal leaders from northern states had repeatedly called on the federal government to adequately supply presidios in the northern borderlands, but Mexico City ignored their pleas. The national government's indifference to protecting borderland communities from Indian attacks was among the principal complaints of rebels in both regions. Similar grievances would inspire rebels in Tamaulipas.[76]

The uprising in Tamaulipas expressed the vecinos' long-standing discontent with Mexico City, but was sparked by centralist actions to consolidate power and restrict state autonomy. In 1835, the national government attempted to close the Matamoros port, ostensibly to stop contraband trade, but in reality it was to reinstall the trade monopoly that Veracruz had enjoyed during the colonial period. The government's bid failed under strong opposition from local and state officials, who believed that closing Matamoros's port would bring economic ruin to the region. The vecinos' perception of government neglect was strengthened when centralists replaced customhouse officials at various ports (including Matamoros) and removed state and local politicians allied with the federalists, who soon began plotting their return to power. In October 1838, federalists in Tampico, who were removed from office by the national government, launched a rebellion that spread throughout the state and to neighboring Coahuila and Nuevo León. The insurgent leaders sought to expel the government-appointed centralist officials and to restore the 1824 Constitution. The rebels quickly gained supporters in the northern villas, when Antonio Canales issued a *pronunciamento* (proclamation) in favor of federalism and began recruiting vecinos. Providing additional motivation for the insurgents in the villas del norte was their perception that the national government was "deaf" to their grievances, and had aggravated their circumstances by passing an "ominous contribution law." Moreover, old tensions with the military had worsened. After its defeat in Texas in 1836, the Mexican Army had returned to the northern villas and resumed mistreating residents. The rebellion gained both popular support and the approval of the region's cabildos, resulting in the creation of a provisional government initially based in Laredo and later moved to Guerrero (formerly Revilla).[77]

The vecinos' interactions with Indians figured prominently in their support for the federalist rebellion. One of their recurrent grievances with the national government was its inattention to their protection from enemy Indians. Comanche raids in 1837 elicited a blistering newspaper letter from "Unos Adoloridos" (Some Sufferers) that sarcastically criticized federal soldiers and clearly identified fronterizos as citizens deserving protection. The raids, according to the letter, had "not aroused the courage that the Mexican soldier is said to possess, when he sees the property and security of his fellow citizens insulted, those for whom he takes up arms, and at whose cost he is maintained." Not surprisingly, among the insurgents were several men, including Antonio Zapata, who were well respected for having served in civilian militias that protected the river towns from Indian incursions. Their previous roles as Indian fighters, and their promises to protect the river towns from future attack, helped the rebels garner popular support. In their campaigns against the Apaches and Comanches, the vecinos had repeatedly allied with local Indians against common enemies. Not surprisingly, the rebels called on some indigenous allies, the Carrizos, to join them in the 1838 uprising. The centralists, however, used this alliance to turn public opinion against the federalists. According to the historian Brian DeLay, the centralists purposefully mischaracterized the Indian allies as barbarous nations in order to accuse the rebels of treason. A government military officer argued, "Those that the traitor Canales leads are not federalists. They are thieves! They are barbarian Indians!" Such accusations aroused the villas' most pressing fears. Moreover, the government spread rumors that the federalists were disarming towns, which made them more vulnerable to attacks by independent Indians. Contributing to the erosion of support was the rebels' practice of extracting contributions from local communities. Centralists newspapers reported that Zapata's troops not only demanded supplies and money from local residents, but also killed and raided for livestock. Although federal troops frequently engaged in such practices, centralist newspapers emphasized that the federalists' "iniquities and depredations" were more akin to that of independent Indians. Ultimately, the government's propaganda campaign (to equate the rebels with "barbarous savages") succeeded in diminishing the support for federalists in the northern towns.[78]

Anglo Texan involvement in the uprising further undermined the federalist cause. Although the federalists were split about allying with Texans, a rebel faction led by Canales actively sought the support of the Texas government in return for recognizing the republic's independence from Mexico. Texas provided assistance because it believed that the rebels sought to establish a separatist state, labeled the "Republic of the Rio Grande" by the Texan press, which could serve as a buffer against Mexico's attempts to reclaim Texas. Although Texas never formally recognized the provisional government, it did allow the insurgents to travel freely throughout the state, gather armaments, and recruit volunteers. Within the rebel ranks, the unruly activities of Anglo Texans led to increasing weariness about their intentions. Furthermore, federalist support waned when residents discovered that Anglo Texans, whom they identified as "vandals" and "adventurers," were helping the rebels. The centralists exploited local suspicions of Anglo involvement to accuse the rebels of treason for allying with the "bloodthirsty enemies of our country." Ultimately, the insurgents also grew alarmed at the Texas government's expansionist claims to the land between the Nueces River and the Rio Grande. Such fears led the rebel federalists to surrender in November 1840, but the popularity of their insurrection enabled them to negotiate favorable terms for their return to power. The Mexican government accepted the federalist insurgents' reintegration into the regional political and military leadership because it too feared the loss of additional land. Faced with Texan expansionist designs, the central government protected its national borders and acceded to federalist demands. Thus, the rebels and centralists agreed on the importance of the nation's territorial integrity. Unlike the fronterizos' calls for protection, which the government ignored, the rebellion did succeed in garnering the government's attention.[79]

The federalist rebellion was a regionalist expression, but it also voiced the rebels' vision of the nation and their place within it. The uprising in the villas del norte was shaped by the vecinos' pressing concerns: desire for more autonomy, protection from independent Indians, and an end to onerous military contributions. Yet, these regional goals had national implications. The call for more autonomy was linked to the restoration of the 1824 Constitution, a goal that fronterizos shared with other federalists across the country. In various letters and proclamations, the insurgents argued that the nation had a responsibility of protecting them as citizens from enemies, whether these were "barbarous" Indians or foreigners. In their complaints about the national government's failures, the historian Brian DeLay argues, northern Mexicans (including those in the villas del norte), "returned to the same rhetoric of nationalism they had encountered over the previous decade and turned it to their own purposes." By faulting the government for failing to provide protection while insisting on contributions, the vecinos underscored their own role in protecting the nation's territorial periphery. Faced with Texan claims to Mexico's land on the right bank of the Nueces River, and with a threatened takeover of Laredo, Canales stated: "I will have to avail myself of centralist troops. This is the only reason for which I can stop being a federalist, because the territory and national honor comes before all." Precisely because they lived along the nation's northern periphery, the rebels were most concerned about protecting Mexico's territorial integrity. By choosing to defend the nation's borders over advancing their regional goals, the rebels engaged in the debate about the meaning of national citizenship. Their actions clearly articulated a cogent view of membership in the national imaginary.[80]

During the early nineteenth century, Mexico's War of Independence transformed the vecinos from Spanish subjects into Mexican citizens. Through economic and political changes, the national government sought to incorporate the northern borderlands into the nation. Its goals were partially frustrated because the villas del norte did not develop a strong national allegiance. Rather, they held onto a regional identity that had developed gradually during the Spanish colonial period. The vecinos failed to embrace nationalism; they were familiar with the concept, but the federal government could not fulfill its responsibilities to them as citizens. Their critiques of the Mexican government were clearly informed by their views of the nation and citizenship. Physically isolated from the nation's administrative center, they grew increasingly frustrated with, and alienated by, the government's failure to address the region's economic concerns, protect the towns from Indian raids, and stop the military's mistreatment of civilians.

Through various acts of noncompliance, the villas del norte resisted Mexico's efforts at nation building. Although they adopted the new discourse of nationalism, their political identification with their region remained strong, and intensified as the national government continued its colonial predecessor's habit of neglecting the interests of those living on the northern periphery. Caught between the territorial goals of Texas and Mexico, the vecinos reluctantly chose Mexico but their sense of regional identity and alienation from the national government persisted. As the middle of the nineteenth century approached, the vecinos remained neglected citizens of Mexico and willing trade partners of the United States.

4

Bandidos or Citizens?
Everyday Forms of Resistance to Political and Legal Changes

American westward expansion in the mid-nineteenth century ushered in the third state-building effort (after Spain and Mexico) for the *villas del norte* (northern towns). In some ways, it paralleled New Spain's earlier northward thrust. New Spain and the United States, under weak—but ambitious—central governments, engaged in territorial expansion as a means of increasing power at the center and promoting state building. A strong central government, however, never fully emerged in New Spain or in Mexico, because each power had trouble controlling its northern borderlands. Poor communications with distant territories and sparse populations of Spanish colonists in those areas hampered the colonial state's efforts. The Mexican government similarly failed to establish control; it was hampered by internal political crises and a devastated economy after independence. In contrast, the American government grew in size and power as the nation's territory expanded. Yet, internal disunity, especially sectional disagreements over slavery, also grew. While Spain and Mexico strove to maintain control over their northern borderlands as a defensive measure against other imperial powers, the United States expanded westward as a solution to its political and economic problems. The additional lands, according to the expansionists, would lessen the conflict over slavery and help the nation emerge from its economic depression of the 1830s.[1]

Each expanding power's colonists also shared similarities. They regarded the people already living on the coveted land with disdain; only the subjects of their contempt differed. Spanish Mexican colonists claimed their conquest brought civilization and religion to indigenous nations. Anglo Americans justified their acquisition on the grounds that they were better guardians of the land than were Indians or Mexicans. Like their Spanish Mexican predecessors, Anglo Americans were critically important to their nation's state-building efforts. They migrated in search of economic opportunities, which they realized by acquiring land and establishing trading ventures, and depended on their government for military protection. The American government, in turn, needed the settlers to enforce its jurisdiction on a conquered population, to establish local governments, and to defend its territory. Such interdependence transformed the arrivistes into agents and privileged citizens of the United States.[2]

The villas del norte were at the center of the binational contest over territory. The U.S.-Mexican War began in the northern villas, and its outcome would not only change national boundaries; it would also transform the river towns. The Rio Grande, the new international boundary after the war, divided the *vecinos'* (community members') community since they owned land on both sides of the river. Residents who stayed on the left bank became U.S. citizens, while those on the right bank remained Mexican citizens. This chapter traces the social and political consequences of this jurisdictional change for the residents of the left bank.

Agents and Privileged Citizens

As agents, Anglo Americans initiated American civilian rule by establishing municipal and county governments. They advanced state building by introducing new judicial and political processes to former Mexican citizens. Moreover, their celebrations of national holidays and cultural traditions stamped an American imprint on the region. Using English-language newspapers, schools, and Protestant churches, the newcomers disseminated the conquering nation's ideologies and beliefs among the native-born, Spanish-speaking population. Ultimately, they helped U.S. efforts at nation building by seeking to cultivate allegiance among the conquered Mexicans.[3]

The newcomers enjoyed many privileges as American citizens. The U.S. government built and staffed several garrisons along the international boundary to protect the region's inhabitants from possible Mexican counterattacks and Indian incursions. The military presence also served as a deterrent against armed uprisings by the conquered population. National authorities expected the arrivistes to create republican forms of government and to adhere to the nation's laws. But the U.S. government lacked the strength to impose its will in such a remote area, so civilians—like others throughout the American West—enjoyed wide latitude to administer municipal and county governments. The federal government also failed to enforce trade laws along the international boundary, partly for lack of means and partly to avoid angering border merchants, many of whom profited handsomely from smuggling.[4]

American migrants were part of a larger westward movement that had begun earlier in the nineteenth century. Mimicking American ideologues, westward settlers relied on common beliefs to justify territorial expansion: the superiority of American institutions and the backwardness of nonwhite people. Some believed in the nation's "Manifest Destiny" to spread what they perceived as liberty and self-government throughout the continent. According to this ideology, God supported the nation's mission of inevitable territorial expansion to extend its superior culture and institutions to other lands. Ultimately, acquiring "all of Mexico" became the principal goal for some of Manifest Destiny's most fervent supporters.[5]

Yet, sectional differences and nativist opposition interfered with the nation's "divine mission." Northerners became alarmed at the prospect of slavery's continued expansion into the nation's western lands. Others opposed expansion because they objected to the inclusion of more nonwhite people. They feared that incorporating Mexico's racially mixed and culturally distinct population into the United States would cause a race problem. This unresolved issue formed the primary dispute in the annexation debate; politicians wondered what to do with the conquered Mexicans. Nativists were further alarmed about incorporating another predominantly Catholic population in the aftermath of a large Irish immigration.[6]

Expansionists overcame sectional and ideological differences by using nationalism to forge a temporary alliance. Acquiring Mexico's northern borderlands, they argued, would provide the nation's growing population with farmlands needed to preserve the Jeffersonian ideal of a republic of independent white yeoman farmers. To obtain support from the North, expansionists manipulated the region's racial fears, convincing slavery's northern opponents of the advantage of westward expansion—preventing free blacks and escaped slaves from migrating to northern cities. Rather, they argued, blacks would move to western states because of their warmer climate. A partial annexation ultimately proved more agreeable to a majority of political leaders, who believed the northern borderlands' sparsely settled population would either disappear or eventually identify with U.S. institutions.[7]

The American plan to acquire Mexico's territory began to unfold after rebels in Texas launched a separatist revolt against Mexico. By establishing the independent Republic of Texas in 1836, the insurgents brought the United States and Mexico closer to war. While the United States and several European nations officially recognized Texas's independence, Mexico refused. The dispute erupted into armed conflict on several occasions, including Mexican plots to regain the wayward republic as well as Texan counterplots to obtain additional lands from Mexico. These confrontations worsened ethnic relations as Anglo Texans increasingly transferred their animosity toward Mexico onto Mexicans in Texas.[8]

The international hostilities and resulting ethnic conflict eventually spread to the villas del norte. Before the 1840s, the villas had enjoyed friendly relations with independent Texas, with which they had carried on trade despite the Mexican government's prohibitions. Ironically, the vecinos had experienced more confrontations with the Mexican military than with Anglo Texans. The towns' relative isolation ended in 1842, when Texas launched a counteroffensive in response to the Mexican military's two attacks on San Antonio. Anglo Texan soldiers captured Laredo and Guerrero. Ignoring orders to return to San Antonio, a majority of the soldiers launched the Mier Expedition in which they attacked additional villas but were forced to surrender at Mier. Despite promising to spare the Texans' lives if they surrendered, the Mexican Army forced the Mier Expedition prisoners into a lottery and shot the losers. The army marched the remaining prisoners to Mexico City, where they obtained their freedom. This confrontation not only soured relations between the villas and Texas, but also fueled the American public's anger toward Mexico. Survivors' written accounts popularized the Texans' suffering, disseminated fears about the Mexican government's alleged cruelty and corruption, and increased public support for the American annexation of Texas and for the U.S.-Mexican War.[9]

The villas remained in the middle of the conflict as tensions grew. Responding to increasing hostilities with Mexico, Texas renewed its efforts to join the United States. The election of James Polk, a supporter of annexation, as the nation's president in 1844 buoyed the republic's hopes. In quick succession, Texans voted to join the United States, Congress accepted the state's new Constitution, and Polk signed the act admitting Texas into the Union. While pursuing diplomatic talks about Texas and the possible purchase of California and New Mexico, Polk ordered military troops to southern Texas and naval vessels to Mexico's Gulf Coast. Talks were unsuccessful. Among the unresolved issues were disagreements over Texas's southern boundary. The United States claimed the boundary lay at the Rio Grande, while Mexico believed the border was at the Nueces River.[10]

Far from the centers of national power, the villas again became the flashpoint for conflict. Motivated by better economic opportunities along the Rio Grande, the vecinos' ancestors had claimed the land for Spain. Subsequently, the vecinos had helped Mexico expand its international trade to recover from a devastating war of independence. Yet, this trade drew them closer to Americans and more distant from Mexico's central government. The ensuing conflict over territory offered vecinos a complex choice involving political allegiance and trade alliances. Burdened by years of neglect and onerous trade restrictions, they lacked enthusiasm for Mexico. Although the United States offered greater economic opportunities, its citizens were partially motivated by an ideology that placed Mexicans in an inferior position.[11]

Americano (American citizen) newcomers to the villas propagated this expansionist discourse of Manifest Destiny through their writings. Directed at Mexican readers, an editor's explanation of the U.S. flag as his newspaper's masthead is illustrative: "Well each of those stars represents a State —and any one of those States, with Uncle Sam to back her, could withstand your whole vain-glorious Republic, in deadly conflict. . . . The only way in which you will ever become 'a People' is to 'camp' beneath its folds. Do so and you will soon become free, prosperous and happy. From ignorance you will rise to intelligence—from poverty to affluence, and from degradation to respectability." Others were less strident, but equally proud of their nation's destiny. According to the newcomer Helen Chapman, who observed "athletic Americans, and puny-looking Mexican laborers," the scene conjured up strong sentiments, which she expressed in vivid prose. "It was that of an *old race* passing away—a *new race* pressing on its departing footsteps—a new scene in the *history of the Country*," she wrote, "a *possession by conquest*." Previous social interaction with Indians and African Americans had popularized racial Anglo Saxonism, and contact with Mexicans reinforced this ideology. The tone of superiority occasionally reached absurd levels. Comparing Anglo American robbers to Mexican thieves, Chapman wrote, "It is curious to see how much more energetic even in their vices our own people are than the Mexicans. The Americans will plan a bold, extensive and successful robbery; the Mexican will confine himself to petty theft."[12]

Newspapers played a prominent role in disseminating negative views of Mexicans. In the 1830s, the national press had described the Texas Revolution as both a racial struggle and a conflict concerning unjust government.

Subsequently, Americans increasingly equated the Mexican government with the Mexican people. They attributed the inefficiency and injustice in the Mexican government to the innate inferiority of "mongrel" Mexicans, which stemmed from their racial intermixture of Indian, African, and Spanish blood. These popular notions contributed to the commencement of the U.S.-Mexican War and determined the amount of territory the nation obtained. Although fervent expansionists wanted more territory, the United States acquired only the land north of the Rio Grande because of fears of incorporating too many "mongrels" and Indians. Labeled as the nation's "first foreign war," the U.S.-Mexican War was the first major conflict to be covered by the so-called penny press (inexpensive, tabloid-style newspapers), which fed the public's voracious appetite for war news while simultaneously propagating stereotypes of a corrupt government, an idolatrous "priest-ridden" society, and an inferior people.[13]

The United States Invades

The boundary dispute led to a military confrontation along the Rio Grande, igniting the war. In early February 1846, President James Polk ordered General Zachary Taylor to lead U.S. soldiers across the Nueces River and south toward the Rio Grande. The Nueces Strip, the land between these two rivers, was disputed territory. Texas had claimed the land since breaking free from Mexico in 1836, and the United States had repeated this claim after annexing Texas in 1845. However, the land was located in northeastern Tamaulipas, which was under Mexico's jurisdiction. Moving soldiers into disputed territory was designed to incite the Mexican Army to attack American troops. U.S. troops immediately began constructing Fort Texas across the river from Matamoros, occupying lands owned by the city's families. Commenting on the movement of troops into disputed territory, Lieutenant Ulysses S. Grant observed years later, "We were sent to provoke a fight, but it was essential that Mexico should commence it." Before any shots were fired, some two hundred U.S. soldiers (of Irish and German ancestry), tired of the anti-Catholic nativism prevalent in the U.S. Army, deserted and sought refuge in the northern villas. Tensions mounted as Mexico's military ordered Zachary Taylor's troops to withdraw from Mexican soil. Ultimately, the provocation worked. In April 1846, Mexican troops defeated two companies of U.S. dragoons at El Rancho de Carricitos, about twenty miles upriver from Fort Texas. This skirmish left fourteen U.S.

soldiers dead. Upon learning of the resulting American casualties, Polk issued his infamous statement claiming that Mexico "has passed the boundary of the United States, has invaded our territory and shed American blood upon American soil." This embellished rhetoric assured that Congress would support his declaration of war.[14]

After scoring decisive victories in the first two battles of the war, American troops occupied the villas del norte. The overwhelming U.S. victory ensured a cordial appearance of relations between troops and residents during the occupation's early days. Officers dined with Mexican families, soldiers took Spanish lessons while others attended their first Catholic Mass, and the military's band staged exhibitions. On the streets, soldiers conversed through grilled windows with *mexicanas* (Mexican women). Camped and quartered outside the villas, the U.S. Army reportedly paid market value for goods bought from residents. In light of the friendly relations between American forces and civilians, the occupying officers placed the villas under a light guard.[15]

Underneath the friendly veneer, the American army began establishing the instruments of social control. The interim U.S. military government placed officers in supervisory positions over elected Mexican officials, who remained nominally responsible for local government. The politics of occupation allowed Mexican politicians to govern Mexican civilians without giving them authority over American soldiers. The American quartermaster William Chapman controlled the collection of taxes and directed a provisional police force. Only under his supervision were the Matamoros City Council and mayor able to carry out their responsibilities. This political arrangement would serve as a local model for American municipal and county governments in the postwar era.[16]

Early in the occupation, the United States began a campaign to weaken Mexico's control over its citizens. The army published a bilingual newspaper, the *Republic of the Rio Grande and Friend of the People*, aimed at winning over local residents. It sought to rejuvenate the separatist idea of an independent "Republic of the Rio Grande" and criticized the Mexican government's corruption. Its stated goal was to bring "the people of the states of Tamaulipas, Nuevo León, Coahuila, and Chihuahua to an appreciation of the merits of a separate Northern Mexican federation." Failing to attract Spanish-language readers, editors underestimated their political understanding. After publishing two issues, the newspaper changed editors, dropped its Spanish-language version, became known as the *American Flag*, and abandoned its goal of reaching Mexican residents. Instead it aimed exclusively at an English-language audience and promoted Manifest Destiny. This military-backed newspaper set a precedent for the region's future English-language publications, which would continue criticizing Mexico while extolling the American government's virtues. Its publication also signaled the beginning of a new era in which local Anglo American journalists disseminated negative representations of Mexicans.[17]

Matamoros's deceptively tranquil environment changed radically with the arrival of additional troops in May 1846. These reinforcements, which included regular and volunteer troops, augmented the number of soldiers from some twenty-five hundred to approximately twelve thousand men. They easily maintained control of a population estimated at four thousand. However, the troops' needs proved too taxing for the available military supplies and accommodations. Many volunteers had no military training, lacked discipline, and were ill prepared to confront the humidity, heat, and disease that plagued the crowded river camps. Accompanying the military were sutlers, gamblers, and prostitutes who, together with the soldiers, transformed the tranquil city into a raucous and lawless setting. These hangers-on sought easy profits from naïve soldiers and unsuspecting Mexicans. Dance halls, saloons, and a vaudeville theater found an eager audience among the volunteers, who could hardly bear their three-month tour of duty. Taylor attempted to restore order by prohibiting liquor sales, but he was unsuccessful. Shootings occurred daily, the local jails bulged with American soldiers, and drunks littered the streets.[18]

The increase in disorder inflamed ethnic tensions between local Mexicans and the occupying troops. Hungry and bored with camp life, the volunteers began stealing cattle and corn, as well as tearing down houses and fences to use as firewood. They murdered civilians, terrorized local residents, and raped mexicanas. Louisiana volunteers "had driven away the inhabitants," a regular U.S. officer observed, "taken possession of their houses and were emulating each other in making beasts of themselves." After complaining unsuccessfully to U.S. Army officers, many vecinos fled. Most grew fearful of the volunteers, but a few developed strong animosities. Some residents who openly objected to the occupying army's criminal behavior were summarily shot. American wrongdoers evaded punishment by bribing or threatening Mexican officials, who, fearing recriminations, released them. The regular soldiers, who resented the army's use of volunteers, accused them of lacking discipline and of killing civilians "for no other object than their own amusement."[19]

The Texas volunteers distinguished themselves for their hatred of Mexicans and use of indiscriminate violence. Organized as Texas Rangers, they wore no official uniforms and established separate camps. The Rangers, unlike other soldiers, had experience fighting Indians and Mexicans. They also had deep-seated prejudices formed during the Texas Revolution and the Mier Expedition. The Texas volunteers "brought their old sets of enemies with them" as they sought to inflict revenge on Mexicans for past conflicts. Their violence left the countryside "strewed with the skeletons of Mexicans sacrificed by these desperadoes," according to a U.S. soldier. "Some of the volunteers and about all the Texans seem to think it perfectly right to impose upon the people of a conquered city to any extent," observed Ulysses S. Grant, "and even to murder them where the act can be covered by dark." Although dismayed at this behavior, U.S. officers hesitated to discipline the Rangers, whose knowledge of Mexico's northern frontier was indispensable.[20]

In addition to inflaming ethnic tensions, the war forced the vecinos into an uncomfortable position of choosing sides. They again became embroiled in a competition over territory. During the colonial period, they had supported the Spanish crown's goals because they benefited by wrestling land from Indians. The U.S.-Mexican War was also a territorial dispute, but the vecinos' goals were no longer aligned with those of their central government. After years of government neglect, they had become more independent and developed a closer identification with their region than with the Mexican nation. Unsurprisingly, the vecinos offered minimal support for the Mexican forces facing the invading army. Their alternatives were threefold: to resist the U.S. occupation, cooperate with the foreign troops, or remain neutral. A single strategy did not prevail in the villas. Instead, the vecinos adjusted to changing circumstances to maximize their opportunities. Their response echoed the actions of *tejanos* (Mexican Texans) during Texas's secession. Like others in similar borderlands, they kept their allegiances ambiguous precisely because they wanted to increase their opportunities for survival.[21]

Some vecinos did resist the occupying army. They gave American soldiers faulty directions or took up arms to repel the invasion. Others refused to help soldiers find food and supplies. Among the resisters were Antonio Canales, Juan Cortina, José María Carvajal, and Blas Falcón, who had fought on the Mexican Army's side at Palo Alto and Resaca de la Palma, the war's first battles. Canales, a Camargo resident who had spearheaded the 1838 regionalist rebellion and punished Anglo Texans involved in the Mier Expedition, led the most notorious band of locals in resisting the Americans.

Known as *guerrilleros* (guerrillas) by American troops, Canales's men harassed the invading army on its way from Camargo to Monterrey, and interdicted their supply and communication lines. Rumors of the guerrilleros' impending attacks became a constant distraction for American troops.[22]

Armed resistance was impractical for most vecinos. Instead, they strategically cooperated to advance their interests. Although some residents opposed Mexico's military rulers, they did not necessarily welcome the occupying American forces. One middle-class vecino described himself as a resident of an occupied city and "a republican opposed to all recent military Governments, and as a patriot opposed to the Americans." When American troops moved upriver to occupy Reynosa, Mier, and Camargo, they were pleasantly surprised to encounter no resistance. The soldiers believed they were better received because the Rangers had not repeated the Matamoros atrocities upriver. Moreover, the villas' residents, still smarting from the Mexican military's recent atrocities, were careful not to antagonize the U.S. forces.[23]

Strongly pressured by Mexican and American troops, civilians often found themselves pleasing neither side and incurring reprisals from both. Some cooperated with the guerrilleros by giving them money and supplies. Yet, many were weary of the Mexican Army's continuous aid requests and failure to protect the villas. Predictably, residents expressed only lukewarm support for the Mexican troops. Tensions also developed between local civilians and guerrilla leaders, who extracted forced loans to punish inhabitants for assisting the Americans.[24]

Most civilian officials cooperated with American forces. This support provoked criticism from Mexican guerrilleros, who accused town officials of disloyalty. After they admonished Reynosa for aiding U.S. troops, its alcalde reminded them of municipal officials' principal responsibilities—the population's safety. Civilian authorities could not refuse to cooperate without incurring the Americans' wrath. Neither could they launch an armed assault against enemy troops that far outnumbered civilians. The villas' armed defense, according to these officials, was the Mexican military's duty. Mexico's newspapers denounced the vecinos for cooperating with the invading army, but they acknowledged that the Americans were forcing residents to turn over supplies. Journalists identified the precarious position of the occupied towns, whose residents were suffering doubly from a national embargo of supplies and the demands of an invading army.[25]

Some civilians assisted the U.S. Army for economic reasons. They worked as guides, rented land for campgrounds, or sold supplies. By supplying the swelling number of U.S. soldiers with provisions, Mexican traders' business boomed. Petty entrepreneurs and laborers also profited from new opportunities. Despite the guerrilleros' threats of reprisals, men worked for the American troops and women sold them food. These laborers had previously been indebted servants, and were able to settle their arrears with higher wages from Americans. The new job opportunities created a shortage of laborers, with elite vecinos struggling to obtain servants and to match American wages. Residents also sold mesquite wood to fuel the military steamboats ferrying troops and supplies up river, while others worked as steamboat crewmen, teamsters, stevedores, and casual laborers.[26]

The war fueled ethnic tensions that were kept from exploding by a large U.S. Army presence. The vecinos acutely suffered the war's impact when the occupying army ran roughshod over their property, desecrated churches, and murdered with impunity. While some residents resisted the invaders, most were in no position to confront a more numerous and well-armed foe. Instead, they attempted to remain neutral. Alienated from years of government abuse and neglect, they offered minimal assistance to the Mexican military. Paradoxically, the U.S. Army's presence in the villas created trade and employment opportunities. These complexities hindered a uniform response from the vecinos.

Postwar Growth

The region's troubles continued directly after the war because the peace agreement introduced major jurisdictional changes. With its principal cities occupied and its economy devastated, Mexico reluctantly signed the Treaty of Guadalupe Hidalgo, ending the war and giving up half of its national territory to the United States. The estimated 100,000 Mexicans in the conquered territory were required to choose to remain Mexican citizens or become American citizens within a year of the treaty's passage. If they did not make a choice, they would automatically become American citizens. The newly incorporated Mexicans were entitled to "the enjoyment of all the rights of citizens of the United States according to the principles of the Constitution" and their "property of every kind," the treaty stipulated, "shall be inviolably respected." These rights included the right to vote, testify in American courts, own land, hold elected office, and all other political privileges of Americans. Unfortunately, events in the annexed territories revealed inconsistencies between the law and reality. The outcome of the war established the Rio Grande as the eastern part of the new international boundary, which split the villas del norte and its residents' land.[27]

The vecinos faced a complicated postwar decision. Families with property on the Mexican side of the river (right bank) chose to remain in the older villas. Since Laredo was on the U.S. side (left bank), some of its residents with land in Mexico moved across the river to establish Nuevo Laredo, opposite the older settlement. Joining them were vecinos who felt insecure under American rule. By 1849, Nuevo Laredo's population was half Laredo's size. To retain control of their land on the left bank, property owners became American citizens. Elite vecinos who held municipal political posts before the war, now faced an uncertain future with the change in governmental jurisdiction. Those who had remained loyal to Mexico by fighting to repel the U.S. invasion or by providing tactical assistance to Mexican forces faced the possibility of living amid their enemies.[28]

Attracted by better economic opportunities, many residents chose to live on the U.S. side, spurring the growth of new towns. The war devastated the villas by reducing livestock production and subjecting residents to thefts, taxes, and forced loans from both armies. Mexico's ranch owners began incurring great losses due to indebted laborers fleeing across the river with stolen cattle and other goods. These workers found higher-paying jobs in Texas, and avoided repaying debts to their former employers now that they lived outside Mexico's jurisdiction.[29]

Economic opportunities also attracted Anglos and European immigrants, who became the region's newcomers. Many who accompanied the U.S. Army, either as soldiers or civilians, remained after the war. Others arrived on ships from New Orleans and New York, the region's main trading partners. By 1850, the population of Texas's three southernmost counties had grown to 8,541, of which 13.9 percent (1,184) were not Mexicans. Excluding children and slaves, the newcomers were about equally divided between American citizens and European immigrants. Two-thirds of the adults born in the United States (591 total) came from New England, the East Coast, or the Middle Atlantic states. The remainder hailed from Louisiana and the north-central states. Most European adults (446 total) came from England, France, Germany, or Ireland, but a sizable number (43) had been born in Spain or Portugal (see figure 8). These newcomers were merchants, professionals, or craftsmen while a small number worked as laborers. Among the latter were African Americans: fifty-three slaves and twenty free people.[30]

In addition to encouraging a population shift, the new international

8. Ángel de la Vega, a Spanish immigrant, married Ángela Ballí, from a well-known family in Cameron County, and worked as a merchant in Matamoros and Brownsville. De la Vega moved to the Santa Anita Rancho in Hidalgo County to work as a ranch administrator for John McAllen, his brother-in-law. De la Vega also became a stock raiser and served as a county commissioner. Circa 1866. Pictured from left to right are Joaquina, Ángela, Sofía, Ángel, José, and Florinda. Courtesy of Museum of South Texas History, Edinburg, Texas.

boundary transformed the urban landscape. When the war ended, the villas (except Laredo) were located on the Rio Grande's right bank, while the left bank consisted mainly of ranchos. The establishment of American settlements and forts began during the war and increased rapidly after the conflict ended. Within a few years, each Mexican villa was paired with an American town across the river. Together the towns and forts (housing U.S. soldiers) transformed the geography on the river's left bank into a series of communities, which mirrored the older villas del norte (see map 3). The new border towns' built environment increasingly displayed American influences in housing, town centers, and place-names. Yet several towns retained Mexican cultural influences, such as the central plazas common in the villas.[31]

To enforce its jurisdiction, the United States established forts along the Rio Grande. The army built Fort Texas across from Matamoros and Fort Polk at Point Isabel during the war. Subsequently, it built additional forts at strategic locations to repel Indian raids and invasions from Mexico. Americanos relied on the forts' troops to control civil disturbances and to assist civilian officers in capturing cattle thieves. The number of soldiers stationed locally depended on prevailing military exigencies and on residents' ability to persuade the national government to provide additional reinforcements. Fluctuations in troops occasionally resulted in inadequate military protection, forcing state and municipal governments to reinforce depleted forces with Texas Rangers and civilian volunteers. Despite these fluctuations, the army presence remained large. From 1848 to 1860, the government distributed as many as 1,418 troops among several companies (varying from two to twenty) in the Nueces Strip.[32]

As privileged citizens, americanos were the primary beneficiaries of this military protection. Many were merchants who arrived in the villas del norte before the war, moving to the U.S. side afterward. Others were civilians and former soldiers who hoped to profit by obtaining land. Anglos became the principal lawyers, artisans, and schoolteachers in the new communities. As English-speaking residents, they provided critical assistance to American state-building efforts by establishing local governments, enforcing laws, and controlling the conquered Mexican population. Moreover, the merchants and military officers enjoyed political and economic connections with leaders in other U.S. capitals, who advised and otherwise assisted them in running the new governments.[33]

Attracted by the lucrative trade with smugglers, American merchants acquired large land tracts for their own use and to sell to future newcomers.

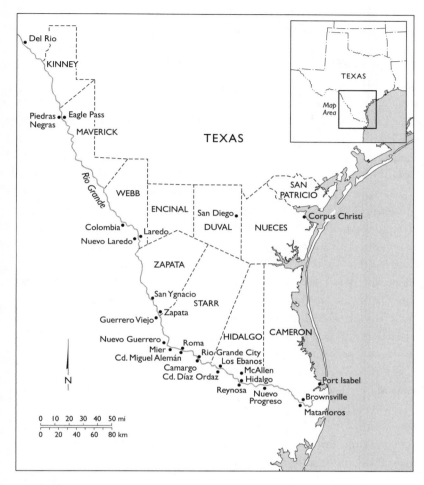

MAP 3. The twin cities along the lower Rio Grande. Circa 1850s.
Map adapted by William L. Nelson.

Among the businessmen who had arrived to pursue trade and land opportunities were Mifflin Kenedy and Richard King, steamboat entrepreneurs, as well as Charles Stillman and Samuel Belden, established Matamoros businessmen. Speculators bought property from Mexican owners during the war and at its conclusion. Fearing their inability to defend property titles in unfamiliar U.S. courts, some vecinos were eager to sell or join in partnership with americanos. Such business relations offered some security, the vecinos believed, because Anglos were knowledgeable about U.S. laws.[34]

Land developers selected new town sites to provide ready access to commerce in Mexico. Promoting real estate via newspapers and organized tours, they attracted buyers through steamboat excursions, dances, and promises of future trade bonanzas. By placing the new towns opposite the villas, they profited from commerce with the Mexican border towns, gained access to established trade routes into the Mexican interior, and allowed developers to operate ferry services between twin towns. In this manner, H. Clay Davis founded Davis' Rancho (later renamed Rio Grande City) opposite Camargo, Charles Stillman, and other merchants established Roma across the river from Mier, and John Young founded Edinburg opposite Reynosa.[35]

The developers' success depended on business connections and geographic placement. Among the most profitable land development companies was the Brownsville Town Company operated by Charles Stillman, Samuel Belden, and Simon Mussina. It flourished because Stillman, a merchant with more than twenty years of experience in Matamoros, lent the enterprise respectability, and Mussina promoted Brownsville through his newspaper, the *American Flag*. Like Rio Grande City, which benefited from the presence of Ringgold Barracks, Brownsville succeeded as a result of its proximity to Fort Brown. In addition to providing military protection, the fort's soldiers ensured Brownsville traders a steady supply of business.[36]

The postwar period reconfigured the region's physical, political, and social landscape. The outcome of the war physically divided vecino landholdings, led to the creation of new towns opposite the older villas, and spurred the arrival of Anglo Americans and European immigrants. While Mexicans remained the majority, the main beneficiaries of the U.S. government's assistance were the American newcomers. They controlled the postwar political arrangement because of their position as privileged U.S. citizens. Such power also gave them control over the towns' increasingly transnational economies.

Growth of Smuggling

The main impetus for the growth of new towns became the economic opportunity created by the international boundary. Brownsville replaced Matamoros as the lower Rio Grande region's commercial center. By transferring control of Brazos Santiago (a natural harbor, located ten miles north of the river's mouth) to the United States, the war cemented Brownsville's trading importance. Annexationists and Texas Republic leaders had long planned on acquiring the harbor because the port's location provided access to the northern Mexican trade. The harbor's potential was soon realized during the postwar boom years, when the annual trade passing through U.S. customs in Brownsville was valued at ten to fourteen million dollars. The war also introduced the quartermaster system, creating critical trade links between the military and local merchants. Aided by profits garnered by selling supplies to American troops and controlling steamboat traffic, Anglo American merchants became the undisputed commercial brokers of the northern Mexican trade.[37]

The new border fueled a boom in legal and illegal commerce. Most legal trade consisted of furniture, dry goods, lumber, liquor, and hardware. A tremendous postwar increase in unlawful goods altered this commerce. Before 1848, smugglers moved contraband from New Orleans to clandestine points along the gulf and then over long desolate land routes to reach Mexican commercial centers. Smuggling became easier after the war with the growth of the population on the river's left bank. Brownsville-based merchants imported goods through Brazos Santiago and subsequently smuggled them into Mexico from various border towns.[38]

Mexico's postwar trade policies backfired along the border. At midcentury, it was economically devastated because of its War of Independence, decades of political instability, and the U.S.-Mexican War. In an effort to replenish the treasury's coffers and pay its foreign debts, the Mexican government reintroduced high tariffs on imports. These taxes also protected Mexican industry and agriculture, but they benefited the central Mexican states while sacrificing the periphery regions' interests. Accompanying the import taxes were strict laws requiring merchants to declare their exact trade route and adhere to a schedule; these stipulations made it easier for traders to be robbed en route. Moreover, when traders failed to meet these requirements, authorities confiscated their supplies.[39]

Instead of increasing the government's revenue, the tariffs and trade requirements fueled the growth of trade in contraband. Legal commerce became a mere "camouflage for highly profitable smuggling." Few importers paid the regular tariffs. Large merchants negotiated with upper-level government officials for lower import duties, British traders obtained special agreements by offering loans to the Mexican government, and smaller merchants resorted to bribing local customhouse officials. Few goods entering through Brazos Santiago were earmarked for local consumption. In Starr County only one-twentieth of the half million dollars in trade was consumed locally in the late 1850s. The majority of imports were destined for Monterrey to supply northern Mexican markets (Saltillo, San Luis Potosí, and Zacatecas). Contraband commerce inverted the Northeast's previous economic subjugation to traders in the nation's center. The blossoming international business (legal and illegal) catapulted Monterrey into northeastern Mexico's leading trade capital and created a transnational economic space, linking northeastern Mexico and southern Texas to world markets.[40]

Smuggling into Mexico triggered a growth in contraband exports. Merchants surreptitiously slipped goods out of Mexico to avoid paying import duties at U.S. customhouses. Lead, pigs, and mules augmented the traditional exports of wool, hides, gold, and silver from northern Mexico. With the exception of mules destined for the West Indies, most goods were intended for the U.S. market. American customs officials had difficulty identifying whether livestock products were produced domestically or in Mexico. Rio Grande City traders shipped Mexican wool, hides, and other goods to Brownsville disguised as American products to avoid import duties. Moreover, merchants took advantage of debenture laws to import European goods supposedly destined for Mexican markets, but in practice sold in Texas for greater profits than they could garner in Mexico.[41]

Legal and illegal trade sparked the growth of border towns upriver from Brownsville. Rio Grande City benefited from its location between Corpus Christi and Monterrey. Situated on the gulf about 130 miles north of Brownsville, Corpus Christi had grown because of its prewar smuggling role. Its merchants began siphoning some of Brownsville's northern Mexico trade by shipping merchandise through San Antonio, Laredo, or Rio Grande City. Traders sent goods (mostly contraband) through Laredo to Coahuila and Chihuahua, and also funneled supplies to Monterrey through Rio Grande City. According to Abbé Emmanuel Domenech, a French priest stationed in the region, Rio Grande City was "a vast assemblage of American stores and Mexican huts where smuggling progresses on an extensive scale." The population of Roma and Edinburg also boomed from the ubiquitous contraband trade. Domenech believed that smuggling "was identified with the best part of the population" and became the "romance and legend of the frontier." The acceptance of smuggling was not surprising since people living along international borders have often regarded contraband as a natural part of their society.[42]

What was surprising was the widespread rule breaking pursued by the American newcomers. While previously critical of Mexico's corruption, the americanos became some of the leading smugglers and purveyors of bribes to Mexican officials. The newly created American border towns and their merchants greatly facilitated this illicit commerce. Ultimately, the imposition of the border at the Rio Grande transformed the region's illegal and legal trade. The volume of commerce reconfigured Mexico's traditional supply routes; Monterrey became a new trade capital, and American border merchants obtained considerable international economic influence. These merchants would also assert their influence locally through their control of municipal governments.

Once Were Conquerors

Accompanying the region's physical transformation were symbolic reminders of the new international boundary's significance. The names of the villas del norte honored cities in Spain and heroes of Mexican independence. Several new American settlements, in contrast, commemorated non-Spanish European cities, American heroes of the U.S.-Mexican War, and Anglo American colonists. Matamoros, Reynosa, and Camargo became paired with the new towns of Brownsville, Edinburg, and Davis Ranch. In addition to signaling a jurisdictional change, the towns' names demonstrated American officials' efforts to shape the region's culture through nationalist imagery. Fort Brown (previously known as Fort Texas), Ringgold Barracks, and Fort Polk immortalized fallen war heroes and the nation's former president. The labels also served as constant reminders of the war's victors. County names followed a similar pattern as officials chose Cameron, Starr, and Webb to honor U.S. soldiers and politicians (see map 3).[43]

When selecting place-names, American officials could not ignore the large Mexican population and its long history in the area. Joining Laredo and Dolores, were new towns such as La Feria, Ramireño, and Port Isabel, named after nearby vecino-owned ranchos or land grants. By choosing Spanish-language labels, officials hoped to gain electoral support from Mexicans. With this goal in mind, local authorities named Hidalgo and Zapata Counties after Miguel Hidalgo y Costilla, a priest and leader of Mexican independence, and Antonio Zapata, a local *mulato* (Spaniard and African offspring) known as an Indian fighter and leader of a regionalist rebellion.[44]

The influence of Anglos in naming the new settlements, forts, and counties was indicative of the region's postwar transformation in ethnic relations. The vecinos who adopted U.S. citizenship became subordinate mem-

TABLE 8. Population Estimates of Mexican Americans (MA) and Anglo Americans (AA), in Percent, by County, 1850–1900

County	1850		1860		1870		1880		1900	
	MA	AA	MA	AA	MA	AA	MA	AA	MA	AA
Cameron	80	10	77	14	77	16	87	9	91	8
Starr	—	—	86	12	88	9	86	8	91	6
Webb	—	—	86	8	79	13	86	8	90	9

Source: De León and Stewart, *Tejanos and the Numbers Game*, 12.

bers of American society. Like Mexicans in California and New Mexico, the former vecinos (thereafter known as tejanos) began losing property through legal and extralegal means. They also lost political power as americanos replaced them in county and municipal governments, law-enforcement positions, and judicial offices. The extent and speed of their loss varied by location, but overall, they were no longer the politically dominant group, as were their relatives and friends across the Rio Grande. Replacing them were Anglos who assumed privileged positions because of their service during the war and their previous experience as American citizens.[45]

Tejanos' loss of political power cannot be explained by the ethnic distribution of the region's population. Anglos continued to arrive for years after the war, but their population remained relatively small. In the 1850 census, Mexican Texans numbered 7,357, or 86.1 percent, of the total inhabitants of Cameron, Starr, and Webb Counties. Cameron County subsequently became the home to more americanos than did Starr and Webb Counties. Across the region, however, tejanos would remain the majority (usually, over 77 percent) throughout the nineteenth century (see table 8).[46]

Despite their small numbers, Anglos became the dominant politicians as a result of a postwar arrangement with the tejano elite, which permitted americanos "to maintain law and order without the constant use of force" during peacetime. For this "peace structure" to work properly, according to the sociologist David Montejano, two conditions were necessary: Mexicans became politically subordinate to Anglo Texans, and the elites of both groups reached a social accommodation. This arrangement grew out of the U.S. military's wartime occupation of the villas, when American officers supervised the elected Mexican officials who carried out daily administrative functions. The tejano elite, with few exceptions, accepted this arrangement as a means of retaining control of their land. Through their alliances with the newcomers, who became the first lawyers and judges in the new

U.S. towns, the old elite hoped to ensure the confirmation of their Spanish and Mexican land titles in American courts.[47]

Laredo's political arrangement is exemplary of the peace structure. As the seat of Webb County, the town had municipal and county officers who were critically important for enforcing American jurisdiction. Mirabeau Lamar, the military captain of the federalized Texas Rangers' occupation of Laredo during the war, organized the town's first election for county precinct offices. Despite an overwhelming tejano population, an americano won one of three elected positions. Subsequent elections followed a similar pattern; political offices were split almost evenly. Power sharing resulted in a division of political offices whereby Anglos obtained the majority of county positions while Mexican Texans captured most municipal offices. Merchants and clerks, typically former Texas Rangers, were among the americanos elected to office while the tejano officials consisted mainly of large property holders.[48]

As occurred in Arizona, California, and New Mexico, elites in the border counties forged social ties through interethnic marriages and through the newcomers' selective adaptation of Mexican cultural traditions. Elite intermarriage in the mid-nineteenth century usually occurred between Anglo American men and *tejanas* (Mexican Texan women). These unions allowed the newcomers to obtain land, and to integrate themselves into local society. For tejanas, interethnic marriages gave their families some protection in the tense atmosphere following the Texas Revolution and the U.S.-Mexican War. Intermarriage, as the historian María Raquel Casas argues for California, served as means of exchanging cultural capital for Mexicans interested in acquiring trade contacts and for Anglos seeking property. The elites were also bound together via *compadrazgo* (godparenthood), as occurred throughout the Southwest. By agreeing to serve as godparents to elite Mexican Texan children, americanos obtained critical social and political connections. Compadrazgo also bound the newcomers and poor tejanos by helping employers obtain employees' allegiance while workers protected their jobs. The arrivistes reached a social accommodation with the Mexican Texan elite by maintaining existing class relations. At the top of the social hierarchy were large landowners and merchants; followed by artisans, cowboys, and small farmers making up the middling class; while day laborers, Indians, shepherds, and domestic servants constituted the poor (see figure 9). By reproducing the old elite's social patterns, the newcomers obtained support across the tejano community.[49]

The extent of power sharing varied throughout the border region. Unlike

9. Water carriers were among the poor tejanos who were at the bottom of the social hierarchy. Throughout the second half of the nineteenth century, Brownsville's residents obtained fresh water from wells and water carriers, who transported water from the Rio Grande in barrels on carts pulled by donkeys. Circa 1880s to 1890s. Courtesy of Brownsville Historical Association, Brownsville, Texas.

Mexican Texan politicians in Webb and Hidalgo Counties, those in Cameron County did not capture many elected offices. They won only minor political posts. Tejanos failed to win the mayor's office and consistently represented a minority of the city council or were excluded altogether. Such patterns of political marginalization were common to other parts of the American Southwest. In the first decade after the war, members of the Ballí, Cortina, and Cavazos landowning families won positions as justices of the peace, county commissioners, and tax collectors. Nevertheless, tejanos remained a minority in county government. They did not capture elected positions in Cameron County's law enforcement until after Reconstruction.[50]

During the first chaotic years of American rule, local officials faced the formidable task of controlling an unruly population, including disorderly and quarrelsome immigrants. Like western towns, the border communities witnessed considerable unlawful behavior from itinerant migrants intent on making money quickly. According to a former Brownsville mayor, William Neale, the population was full of "men of desperate character, desperate fortunes, and evil propensities." Observers criticized americanos, in particular, for their behavior. Abbé Domenech commented: "The Americans of the Texian frontiers are, for the most part, the very scum of society —bankrupts, escaped criminals, old volunteers, who after the treaty of Guadalupe Hidalgo, came into a country protected by nothing that could be called a judicial authority to seek adventure and illicit gains."[51]

The establishment of local governments gradually brought some order. During the first years after the war, "lynch law was in full force" among a populace accustomed to imposing its own capital punishment. To gain control of the population, officials gradually established courts of law, created a police force, and passed local ordinances. Municipal governments passed some quaint laws—such as fining individuals for galloping wildly on horseback through city streets and regulating the number of dogs within city limits. They also enacted revenue-generating legislation, including licensing of pawnbrokers, ferry operators, billiard houses, and drinking houses. Addressing public safety, local governments placed curfews on saloons and limited the wearing of firearms in public.[52]

Tejanos lost political and economic power with the arrival of americano newcomers. However, the loss was not uniform. Those in counties with smaller Anglo populations were able to secure several municipal offices. By contrast, Mexican Texans in counties with a larger americano presence only won minor political posts. Throughout the border region, Anglo Americans held most county positions. So the political loss of tejanos, like the fortunes of *californios* (Californians), varied by region and over time. By the late nineteenth century, tejanos had made more political gains in some counties but remained subordinate to Anglo elected officials.[53]

Restrictions on Mexican Cultural Practices

The newcomers passed legislation, similar to that enacted in California, to restrict the cultural practices of Mexicans. American regulations resembled earlier Spanish legal restrictions. Influenced by Enlightenment ideas, Spanish officials had attempted to restrict or prohibit popular diversions such as bullfights and cockfights, which they considered barbaric. In the villas del norte, ayuntamientos attempted to control the popular entertainment by taxing playing cards, licensing popular dance halls, and restricting liquor sales. Ultimately, these diversions were restricted, but not eliminated, because their licensing brought in needed revenue. The postwar legislation grew out of cultural differences between Anglos in positions of power, who were trying to impose their version of social propriety on a conquered, subordinate Mexican Texan majority. Their designations of Mexican cultural practices as immoral and barbaric were comparable to Spanish officials' earlier descriptions and regulation of Indian traditions and poor vecino diversions. Both sets of legislation were elite attempts at social control. By targeting particular ethnic or racial groups, officials racialized their popular practices.[54]

In the postwar period, Anglo politicians authored laws to regulate Mexican cultural practices, including their daily use of the river. Since the Rio Grande provided drinking water, officials believed washing clothes in its waters created unsanitary conditions. For *americanas* (Anglo American women) accustomed to washing clothes by boiling them or by using soap and a washboard, Mexicans' use of the riverbank rocks seemed rudimentary. Describing this daily sight, one woman wrote, "They wash their clothes by the river bank, or in ponds of water, by throwing them and squeezing them against a smooth board . . . and never boil them at all, merely washing and rinsing in the cold water of the river." Such criticisms were significant because Anglo American women along the border, as elsewhere in the American West, assumed the role of moral arbiters. Such ethnic and class bias shaped the social regulation that ensued due to elite americanas' disapproval of poor Mexicans' cultural practices.[55]

Ideology influenced Anglo American women's disapproval. Observing the harsh conditions of Mexican women's daily chores, Helen Chapman commented, "The Mexican mother [suffers] the curse of our first mother, her labor is all hard." These sympathetic comments were accompanied by disparaging remarks. "There can be little comfort in this animal sort of existence," opined Chapman. "Mexican women can be seen at any hour of the day washing clothes [in the river's ponds and lakes]," wrote a newcomer, Teresa Vielé, "while their little naked children are splashing in the water in great glee, or lying asleep on the bare ground, under a shady bush, like so many little animals." These views were revealing, since poor mexicanas often became domestic workers in Anglo American homes. Describing her servants, Cora Montgomery made a generalization about Mexican society: "This obedient, passive race have in them the elements of good service for whoever will have the forbearance to be good masters." Influenced by Manifest Destiny, some americanas identified the onerous labor of mexicanas as justification for the American conquest. According to

Chapman, "We frown very justly on the idea of [manifest] Destiny being made the excuse for this rapacious invasion of our neighbor's rights and yet it is impossible to live among a people so morally, physically and intellectually degraded without feeling assured that a more powerful race must before long subdue them."[56]

More alarming than washing clothes was bathing in the Rio Grande. During the colonial era, poor residents had become accustomed to mixed bathing despite restrictions on such practices. Mixed bathing, however, left Anglo American travelers surprised and disgusted. Despite their apparent revulsion, men's sharp observational skills and thorough descriptions revealed more than a passing interest: "few left the scene quickly." The participants' lack of concern for the public nature of their bathing puzzled most observers. However, those who took time to understand the custom of public bathing realized the innocence of such practices. One traveler, who came across a mixed group of adults and children in a river, observed that he "never saw a merrier bathing party." Upon their invitation, he undressed to join them in the water and was soon "thoroughly enjoying the fun." Embarrassed at the public nudity, most americanos expressed stronger criticisms.[57]

What seemed conventional bathing practices to poor *mexicanos* (Mexicans), appeared as promiscuous spectacles to americanos. It also seemed— to Anglo American men—an excellent opportunity to court mexicanas. During the war, a group of soldiers, obviously misinterpreting the situation, jumped into the Rio Grande but were prevented from approaching bathing women by a Mexican guard on the opposite riverbank. Other servicemen spent hours voyeuristically staring as women bathed innocently and seemingly undisturbed. In contrast, when bathing men became the objects of feminine gazes, the soldiers jumped out of the river in embarrassment. Humiliated by women watching him bathe, a serviceman bitterly wrote, "Mexican women were no better than beasts nor half so modest." The soldier expressed the view of many americanos who believed that public bathing confirmed mexicanos' promiscuity and moral laxness. To American newcomers imbued with the ideas of Manifest Destiny, the sight of mixed bathing reinforced their image of Mexicans as socially and morally inferior.[58]

In response to these river activities, municipal governments from Laredo to Brownsville passed ordinances limiting use of the riverbanks. The restrictions imposed fines on violators and limited the areas reserved for bathing, washing clothes, and gathering drinking water. In addition to ensuring hygiene, the laws sought to uphold an Anglo Protestant version of morality. To discourage residents from viewing nude bathers, city councils prohibited bathing between five in the morning and eight in the evening. The fines discouraged public bathers in the United States, but could not stop such practices on the Mexican side. In 1851, Brownsville's exasperated city councilmen asked their counterparts in Matamoros to limit the times and location of their citizens' river baths. The practice resulted in the "annoyance of our citizens," argued Brownsville's officials, and was "contrary to all decency and morality."[59]

The zeal of municipal authorities to restrict poor tejanos' social practices is evident in ordinances limiting cockfights. To confirm their characterization of Mexicans as depraved, perfidious, and sadistic, americanos pointed to cockfights. According to a contemporary observer, "The excitement is upon the part of horror, and is improper, while the moral effect cannot be attended but with evil results." Journalists added to the criticism of this "barbaric" and "un-American activity," which municipalities soon outlawed. Yet, observers failed to note that americanos also participated as cockfight spectators and rooster owners. Contemporaries believed mexicanos generally treated animals cruelly, as did a newspaper editor who wrote: "Beyond any sort of doubt there are stronger evidences of barbarism on this border than exist anywhere else in the United States." Similarly, a visiting British soldier observed: "The [carriage] driver ill-treated his half-starved animals most cruelly." The press criticized bullfights as "brutal," although both americanos and tejanos crossed into Mexico to attend these spectacles. Motivated by nativism, americanos in California also passed legislation outlawing bullfights and cockfights, popular among poor californios.[60]

Dance restrictions were another avenue of social control. By the mid-nineteenth century, *bailes* (dances) had become staple social interactions in the villas del norte. They were part of religious festivities, weddings, and secular parties commemorating national holidays and trading fairs. In addition to providing much-needed entertainment in remote areas, dances were crucial events for courting. According to the folklorist Jovita González, love letters flowed through the rural mail for weeks, the result of young men pursuing women they had met at the bailes. Dances also served to introduce newcomers to the river towns' residents. They were held in various locales from enclosed private residences, barrooms, and dance halls to open-air events on the street, riverbanks, or on a rancho's dusty grounds. In the city, participants danced to the sounds of an orchestra with bass drums, clarinets, and violins while in the countryside a lone fiddler might provide the only musical accompaniment.[61]

After the war, the upper class organized "grand balls" for exclusive social clubs, birthday celebrations, or commemorations of American or Mexican national holidays. Regaled in their finery, participants danced to the brass band music and listened to poetry readings as well as piano and violin solos. Prominent tejano families hosted formal dances to celebrate New Year's Day, to commemorate Our Lady of Guadalupe, or to honor a visiting statesman. Formal balls expanded elite tejanos' social ties with upper-class americanos. Prominent citizens forged binational ties by hosting balls in government buildings, hotels, or aboard steamboats for their cross-river counterparts. One report described "the beautiful, the lovely, the fair of Matamoros and Browns-ville" attending a ball held on the steamboat *Camargo* in honor of a visiting government official from Mexico.[62]

A greater cross section of people attended *bailes decentes* (dignified dances). Often hosted by an elite family, bailes brought together family and friends across generations to celebrate religious feast days, holidays, or weddings. Tejanos, eager to introduce their customs to newcomers, frequently invited americanos to these formal affairs. The nuptial festivities, often lasting two to three days, began with a group of forty to fifty women and men riding on horseback to the surrounding ranches and towns to extend the *convite* (a formal wedding invitation). The baile was second in importance to the marriage ceremony. The celebrants began assembling in the late morning and danced until dawn to the strains of guitars, violins, drums, and accordions. Illuminated by kerosene lamps, the dance floor consisted of rancho's packed dirt surrounded by wooden benches. The hosts expected participants to follow traditional rules of decorum: women could attend only if chaperoned, unmarried couples could neither dance to consecutive songs nor talk while dancing, and the musicians could only play instrumental music.[63]

In contrast to staid balls and respectable bailes decentes, *fandangos* (popular dances) were boisterous events. By the mid-nineteenth century, workers throughout northern Mexico had transformed the popular dances into exuberant all-night spectacles to reclaim leisure and pleasure. This growing rowdiness concerned Mexican officials. Occurring weekly or daily, irrespective of religious or national holidays, these dances were held outdoors or in "fandango houses" (makeshift dance halls). The mostly poor participants enjoyed gambling, eating, and drinking. Accompanying fandangos were horse races, monte games, and booths where small merchants sold a variety of beverages and food including liquor, watermelons, tamales, and chiles rellenos. Liquor and card games at fandangos often led to fights and homicides. Diverse classes of men occasionally attended, but most americanas and elite tejanas avoided fandangos.[64]

During the occupation of the villas, U.S. soldiers became familiar with fandangos and bailes. While attending a fandango near Camargo, Captain Justin Smith was surprised to recognize songs and discover the Mexicans' affinity for the waltz, a dance of European origin. Smith, like other American soldiers, attended fandangos hoping to meet young mexicanas, only to be disappointed to find them "generally inaccessible." Despite their lack of luck, servicemen continued attending the popular events and marveling at the participants' joy. Other observers were intrigued with the dancers' gracefulness and endurance, when events lasted until dawn. However, some americanos expressed reservations. A soldier wrote to his wife that fandangos were "vulgar, disgusting places" at which he had picked up fleas.[65]

Worried that fandangos created public disorder and spread immorality, U.S. authorities characterized the dances as "disgraceful and demoralizing assemblages," "nothing but a heterogeneous mass of rottenness," and filthy assemblies. Their criticisms were infused with ethnic prejudices linking Mexicans with moral depravity. The dance was uncivilized and its participants lacked culture and refinement, according to a newly arrived lawyer from New York. Other americanos criticized the perceived erotic nature of the participants' movement. Many newcomers considered Mexican women's "low-cut dresses as provocative and their uncorseted figures immodest." To the lustful gaze of americanos, who often remarked on the attractiveness of voluptuous *señoritas*, the female dancers seemed particularly sensuous as they became enraptured by the fandango's sounds.[66]

Characterizing the dance halls as "licentious fandango houses," newspapers warned servicemen to avoid fandangos lest they fall prey to "Mexicans in attendance whose sole object is to decoy the unwary." Tejano attendees, according to one periodical, were likely to murder americanos for their money. The fandango came to be "identified with [the] lewd passions and lasciviousness" of Mexicans. Other observers described the dance as obscene and the participants as the lowest class of mixed-bloods—uneducated, slovenly, and poorly dressed. Protestant religious leaders throughout Texas targeted the fandango as a corrupter of morals and as an example of the Catholic Church's degenerate influence. Religious leaders were particularly disparaging of dances when they took place on the Sabbath. Even some European-born priests were critical; they organized youth groups to lobby against fandangos.[67]

As public pressure against fandangos grew, municipal governments throughout Texas sought restrictions. "All the murders and outrages" in the city since the Mexican period resulted from the toleration of fandangos, claimed San Antonio's Anglo American mayor, who supported a fandango ban. Similarly, the Austin City Council banned fandangos. Newspapers supported bans, describing the popular dances not only as sources of infamy and dishonor, but also as schools of immorality and relics of barbarism. Moreover, the press sensationalized the altercations at fandangos with banner headlines such as "murderous assault" or "cold blooded assassination." When bans failed, local governments began taxing fandangos, which proved to be a boom for municipal revenues. Laredo officials sought to control fandangos by requiring hosts to obtain dances licenses. Brownsville imposed fines of between twenty-five and fifty dollars for attending a fandango on the Sabbath, and between five and fifty dollars for frequenting a dance within the city limits. Local governments also directed their police officers to increase their vigilance of dances in the countryside. Subsequently, arrests for drunk and disorderly charges at fandangos constituted the majority of apprehensions carried out by law-enforcement officers. Poor tejanos, argued the *Daily Ranchero*, had "polluted this beautiful dance into a pandemonium, where a big drum and a cracked horn mark the time to a revelry called dancing."[68]

The fandango ordinances, however, met with organized resistance because the dances were profitable and extremely popular. Saloon and dance-hall owners found creative ways to waltz around the restrictions. Some proprietors petitioned the city council for permits, while others advertised the events as "balls" to make them appear more respectable. The Brownsville City Council discovered the ruse and passed an ordinance to fine attendees at fandangos "no matter by what name or title it may be designated." Laredo's laws prohibited minors under sixteen years old from attending public dances; participants and dance promoters incurred a fine for every violation. The popularity of fandangos led participants to repeatedly ignore restrictions, which municipal and county governments struggled to enforce. The potential profits motivated saloon and dance hall owners to pressure local municipal politicians to modify or rescind restrictions. Lobbying on behalf of their Mexican Texan constituency, aldermen occasionally succeeded in lifting fandango bans. In order to appease those citizens clamoring for an outright ban, city councils approved legislation requiring promoters to obtain fandango licenses, prohibiting gambling at the events, or stipulating that police officers oversee dance halls. By the early 1870s, Laredo and Edinburg had relaxed fandango restrictions, with municipal officers acknowledging the legislation's inability to end the popular dances.[69]

Fandango legislation ultimately failed because of tejanos' active subversion. Employing creative solutions to continue dancing and "turn their bodies into instruments of pleasure," some skirted bans on licensing requirements by organizing the popular dances in private homes. Creating alternatives to commercialized leisure, Brownsville dancers frequented more than six underground and unlicensed fandango houses. Elsewhere, dancers avoided bans within the city limits by holding fandangos in the countryside. A few resisted the legislation through physical confrontations with authorities. When law-enforcement officials arrived at private homes to enforce a ban, participants occasionally assaulted them or chased them away. The fandangos' continued popularity suggests their powerful attraction as a cultural site where poor tejanos constructed a shared community and attempted to escape American officials' efforts at social control.[70]

The postwar period introduced a significant change to restrictions on cultural practices. Unlike authorities in the villas, most American lawmakers no longer belonged to the same ethnic group as the majority of the population. Infused with the ideas of Manifest Destiny, Anglo legislators restricted those popular Mexican cultural practices that they deemed "immoral," "barbaric," or "bloodthirsty." This characterization racialized Mexican cultural practices and cast aspersions on the tejano community. While visiting americanos generalized about the entire Mexican Texan community, local Anglos mainly criticized the poor. In the postwar period, poor tejanos saw their popular practices under increasing attack, with American lawmakers imposing controls and moving one step closer to criminalizing them as a distinct group.

Criminalization

As Mexican Texans lost political power and control of the local print media, they confronted an increasingly hostile press. Anglos published four of five newspapers during the first two decades of U.S. rule in the lower Rio Grande region. Several English-language periodicals issued Spanish-language versions for brief periods, but Anglo American editors determined the content. Like Spanish-language newspapers throughout Mexico, those published in the villas del norte mostly covered political events. In contrast, English-language media reported on various local issues along with state and national news. However, this press focused almost exclusively on the activities of americanos.[71]

Notable exceptions to the news blackout of tejanos were criminal court proceedings. The periodicals sensationalized crimes involving Mexican Texans arrested for drunkenness, disorderly conduct, or fighting. A typical story, in the *Fort Brown Flag*, detailed the detention of 160 men attending several dance halls. Characterizing the prisoners as "a crowd of Mexican lazzaroni," the newsmen arbitrarily accused them of robbery and treason without corroboration. Moreover, American border journalists frequently exaggerated, as did one who claimed, "one of the most atrocious murders ever reported" had involved torture. Without substantiating his accusation, the journalist observed: "The murdered man was a Mexican, and of course the murderous mode of procedure was purely Mexican." Despite failing to locate any witnesses, the sheriff arrested several "suspicious characters." All were Mexicans, the journalist admitted, with no definite ground for suspicion. The press specifically blamed *pelados* (meaning ill-bred poor men) for most crime, while offering positive portrayals of wealthy tejanos. Journalists liberally referred to workers as "thieves" and "murderers" who lacked education, morality, and knowledge. Accompanying sharp criticisms were vast generalizations about Mexican Texan workers, including the following incendiary column (labeled "Thievery"): "Three-fourths of our population consists of Mexican *pelados*—born, bred, and matured thieves. They live in sinks, sewers, and shanties. They infest the alleys day and night. . . . Nine out of ten *jacals* [sic] are but receptacles of stolen goods, and nine out of ten families live by stealing. . . . This is the most important step to be taken. The entire and complete exclusion from our back doors of thieving greaser eyes."[72]

News items on criminal activity carried a clear bias against poor tejanos. In 1860, local editors penned a diatribe describing fandango attendees as "the outcasts of society" and as "the lowest species of humanity." The newspaper offered a sweeping generalization linking the tejano attendees to "gambling, drunkenness, robbery, theft, maiming, prostitution, and murder." While reports on Anglo criminals carried few, if any, editorial remarks, stories on tejanos were more critical. An account of an attempted crime is illustrative: "Judge Galván's Court was open yesterday for the examination of the case of that murderous looking devil, Julián Castillo, charged with attempt to assassinate Sr. Toledano. The prisoner may have been innocent of the murderous assault; but his looks would hang him on general principles." Journalists frequently labeled Mexican Texan suspects as "monsters," "greasers," and "demons." Scorn and a general disregard for the lives of tejanos became so common in news accounts that death became a subject of humor. While reporting on the death of a poor worker from an infection, a newsman wrote, "A Mexican died yesterday of lockjaw in great haste; he had stuck a nail in his foot which proved to be the nail in his coffin."[73]

The news stories' tone reflected a trend among Anglos, whose views increasingly associated Mexicans with delinquency and with a disregard for human life. When officials failed to obtain eyewitnesses or make arrests in a criminal investigation, the press often blamed Mexicans for the crimes. Using the headline "Murder by Mexicans" for a story about the killing of the Hidalgo County sheriff, a journalist admitted to some uncertainty about the assailants' identity by stating "it is generally believed" the guilty parties were Mexicans. Other stories, in the same issue, accused "concealed Mexicans" of firing on three "Americans" near Ringgold Barracks and blamed a "party of Mexicans" for attacking a Brownsville's city marshal with knives. The accused remained nameless, but clearly identified by ethnicity. Moreover, numerous local and state news stories seared the image of tejanos fighting with knives into the popular imagination—even when no weapons were used in quarrels. Reporting on a fight between two mexicano teenagers, a journalist observed, "they are called Mexicans, but might with more propriety be called Indians," before concluding "it is almost a disgrace to trouble the courts with such murderous devils." This comparison was consistent with the ideas of Manifest Destiny, which sometimes equated Mexicans and Indians. The local practice of linking Mexicans to criminality was part of a larger pattern common throughout the American West.[74]

Conventional stereotypes in the United States shaped the criminalization of Mexicans. Westward-moving Anglo Americans, who absorbed long-held negative views of Spaniards, identified as the "Black Legend," often characterized Mexicans in unflattering terms. They viewed Mexicans as "lazy, ignorant, bigoted, superstitious, cheating, thieving, gambling, cruel, sinister, cowardly half-breeds." Tellingly, the inaugural issue of the first English-language newspaper published in the villas del norte promoted the Black Legend. According to the *American Flag*, "Mexicans are too indolent to cultivate the land, or do anything else but 'hunt lice' and herd cattle. A bad character we give them, but they deserve it." Anglos believed that "swarthy" Mexican "half-breeds" had inherited their Spanish ancestors' negative characteristics and their Indian forebears' worst qualities. Jane Cazneau, a transplanted New Yorker living in Eagle Pass, voiced these prevalent views by characterizing Mexicans as "wayward as children, and

[who] have much of the singular unteachableness [*sic*] of the unconquered tribes of their race."[75]

The media's reckless accusations cast suspicion on poor tejanos and racialized their living quarters. By using terms such as *Mexican criminals* without identifying any individuals, journalists spread fear about the majority of Mexican Texans. Authorities should close a local boardinghouse run by a "dirty Mexican," opined a local daily, because its patrons slept during the day and stole at night to pay for their room and board. Reports accusing tejanos of murder were even more outlandish and denunciatory by employing terms such as "vicious-looking Mexicans," *scoundrels*, and *devils*. Other news items described knife fights between unnamed tejanos or identified the location of a crime as a "Mexican jacal." Illustrative was a description of a Mexican-owned ranch as a "most detestable place in regards to thieves, assassins, and robbers." By omitting suspected criminals' names, newspapers created the specter of widespread criminal activity among tejanos. Journalists emphasized racial signifiers while frequently omitting personal details that would allow readers to identify the individuals. Such omissions had the effect of dehumanizing the individual while, at the same time, criminalizing a large segment of the community.[76]

The negative media portrayals of Mexican Texans shaped public opinion locally and nationally. The press disseminated stereotypes among a broad audience, which bolstered Anglos' discriminatory views or nourished their nascent prejudice. G. D. Kingsbury, Brownsville's postmaster who occasionally served on juries, penned an illustrative description reminiscent of news items. "The population of the county," he wrote, "is about 7000[,] not less 6000 of which is Mexican[,] of which 5000 may be reckoned as thieves." In turn, state and national newspapers reprinted sensationalized local stories. New Orleans's *Daily Delta* reproduced a story about a murder and subsequent vigilante hanging of an accused tejano under the headline "Another Brutal Assassination and Speedy and Summary Justice." Journalists working for national periodicals readily repeated common stereotypes. According to a *Harper's Weekly* correspondent, tejanos had no regard for human life and "did not count it a grievous crime to murder either in private quarrel or public brawl."[77]

Pointed editorials were particularly detrimental for Mexican Texan defendants awaiting trial. Newspapers often suggested punishment for prisoners—a recommendation that jury members likely read. Brownsville should hang fifteen tejano prisoners, a *New Orleans Times* correspondent suggested, to set an example for "the community of 'greasers' at large."

Reprinting this correspondent's report, local editors added, "There ought to be fifty more in the military prison on a charge of murder." Acknowledging the harm created by local newspapers' unconfirmed accusations and punishment recommendations, the attorney G. W. Reynolds criticized the editors' recklessness for blaming his client of a crime before the trial. He believed the editors had "duly convicted Mucio Villareal of theft," and their unsubstantiated accusations, he said, "will render it very difficult to obtain an unbiased jury, should a new trial be granted."[78]

The criminalization of tejanos along the border replicated patterns elsewhere in the American West. As part of the westward-moving American population, local americanos espoused negative views of Mexicans that harkened back to the Black Legend beliefs (mentioned earlier) against Spaniards. Acting on these perceptions, they authored restrictive legislation and critical press coverage that criminalized poor tejanos and racialized their cultural practices and dwellings. Through this moral regulation, americanos advanced U.S. state formation by "normalizing" Anglo American traditions while "marginalizing" poor Mexicans' practices.

Drunks and Vigilantes

Widespread drinking aggravated ethnic tensions by increasing the likelihood of disputes. The visiting journalist Frederick Law Olmsted witnessed weekly physical altercations and murders in town plazas. According to Olmsted, the mingling of races on unequal terms caused such conflicts, especially when men frequented drinking establishments. Arrests for drunkenness mirrored each ethnic group's proportion of the population. Officials typically jailed and fined the drunks; those unable to pay fines were punished with time on public works projects. The elegant brick buildings housing saloons, according to a wry observer, illustrated the bars' popularity, compared to the "barns," which passed for churches. Commenting on the border population's penchant for liquor, a recent arrival was surprised to see "a great number of people drunk, sprawling asleep in the sun before the grog-shops where they get intoxicated." Trips across the border were popular among local residents, who patronized bars in Mexico. While observing a fandango in Matamoros, a visiting British soldier confirmed that ethnic tensions were a source of fights by writing "if there ever is a row, it is invariably caused by [Anglo] Texans from Brownsville."[79]

The prevalent drinking culture influenced law-enforcement and judicial practices. Residents frequently encountered Anglo policemen and politicians comfortably intoxicated. Several unprovoked shootings of civilians resulted from inebriated officers' actions. At a local tavern, a visitor expressed surprise to find a judge proposing a toast to "justice modified by circumstances." Drinking and the underlying ethnic tensions compromised the goal of administering justice, according to a French priest. In a blistering attack, Abbé Emmanuel Domenech wrote: "When drunkenness and this ignorance too is further added venality, fear of a strong hand, and party feeling, then it is only a Mexican, a simpleton, or a coward that would appeal to law for justice. The Americans and Europeans[,] who know how things stand in these still savage regions, dispense with magistrates; and the dispensers of justice never interfere in the disputes of such people, knowing well the consequences of their intermeddling." Even the local chapter of the Washingtonians, a temperance society, could not diminish the population's thirst for liquor. One observer noted, "The young men of Brownsville are drinking themselves almost to death." The temperance groups had a minimal influence, because although "members promise to abstain from wine, they nevertheless indulge in other fermented liquors."[80]

Confirming Domenech's observations, local residents often circumvented the courts to settle disputes. Vigilante mobs occasionally lynched men attempting to escape imprisonment or awaiting trial. Olmsted observed a crowd with few scruples lynch a mexicano for *attempting* to steal a horse. Some executions were carried out methodically as crowds stormed jails, demanded their victims, and reluctantly allowed clergy to administer last rites. Others resulted from rapid emotional decisions by angry mobs such as a group of americanos in Brownsville, who lynched a tejano accused of killing a justice of the peace. "While hanging but just before his pulse had ceased to beat," a witness reported, "a stranger with flowing cape and slouched hat, embraced the body and lifting his own feet from the ground so as to throw greater weight on the murderer, muttered, 'That's the way we used to do them in Californy.'" Judges and newspaper editors embraced the population's combative spirit. A chief justice became known for settling disputes with his fists, while the *Rio Grande Sentinel's* editor gained a reputation for starting duels, until his confrontational manner got him killed. The border region shared its unruliness with Texas, and the greater American West, where extrajudicial lynchings were common.[81]

Long-simmering ethnic tensions fueled lynchings, which left mostly tejano victims. One newcomer, who witnessed a crowd capture and threaten a Mexican accused of rape, expressed astonishment. Referring to the Anglo

American participants, she wrote, "It is difficult to convince these people that a Mexican is a human being. He seems to be the Texan's natural enemy; he is treated like a dog, or, perhaps, not so well." In the border region, lynchings claimed victims of various ethnic backgrounds, but mob rule appeared to have targeted more tejanos. In 1852 several altercations led a "hastily assembled and incensed multitude" to lynch one americano and nine mexicanos over a one-week period. Fueled by ethnic conflicts and cattle theft, the lynchings of Mexican Texans became rampant during the 1860s and 1870s, and continued throughout the nineteenth century.[82]

Overzealous law-enforcement officials joined vigilantes in targeting tejanos. Anglo American support for aggressive enforcement tactics emboldened sheriffs and their deputies. Reports of officers shooting unarmed Mexican Texans attempting to escape became common. Even an observer critical of the population's immorality and lawlessness justified a sheriff's shooting of a Mexican trying to elude arrest. "No one seems to blame him [the sheriff]," Helen Chapman observed, "and perhaps in these new places such acts are terrible necessities." Summarizing americanos' views, a correspondent wrote, "The community justifies the act, because [the] deceased was a bad man and a greaser." The Texas Rangers were even more aggressive than local sheriffs. As cattle stealing increased during the 1870s and 1880s, the Rangers terrorized Mexicans on both sides of the border by applying their policy of "shoot first and ask questions later." Their campaign to "pacify" the border rested on inspiring fear among mexicanos. Rather than "pacifying" the region, the Rangers inflamed ethnic conflict by breaking up fandangos, harassing Mexicans, and killing many innocent suspects.[83]

According to contemporary observers, tribunals and law-enforcement officers shared the media's bias against tejanos. "Most [homicides] were charged upon the Mexicans," Olmsted noted, because their "passionate motives are not rare." Domenech agreed, asserting that Mexican Texans appeared to be charged with crimes more often than other groups. He identified local courts' shortcomings by noting "the magistracy is far from giving adequate guarantees for the security of the public; and in criminal matters it is barefaced as it is revolting." Tejanos confronted americanos' deep-seated attitude of racial superiority, Domenech argued, and faced an anti-Catholic bias among judges and law-enforcement officials. "Let the criminal be an American," he said, "and though he were the worst ruffian in the town he is let off scot-free, with a mere promise to pay a sum of money, which of course he never pays."[84]

A murder case illustrates how ethnic bias influenced court proceedings.

A bailiff, who heard the deliberations about a Mexican Texan murder suspect, remembered the discussions of the all-Anglo jury in a border town. When a juror recommended acquittal, another quickly advocated sentencing the accused man to ten years in the penitentiary because, the juror said, "he is a dam[n] Greaser anyhow." They eventually condemned the prisoner to a two-year penitentiary term. The bailiff considered informing the judge of the jury's deliberation but was intimidated by americanos' strong feelings against tejanos. Jesse Sumpter explained his inaction: "I considered that it was better for that poor Mexican to go to the penitent[i]ary for two years, than it was for *me* to lose my life trying to defend him."[85]

The liquor habits of Anglo Americans appeared to have tempered their goal of introducing the rule of law to the border region. Despite newcomers' frequent criticisms of Mexico's corruption and their praise of American courts, they failed to administer justice impartially. In addition to alcohol, simmering ethnic tensions and firm beliefs in Manifest Destiny clouded their judgments. Americanos accepted extralegal killings, especially when the victims were tejanos, whose guilt they often assumed. In addition to facing the criminalization of their cultural practices, poor Mexican Texans had to confront unsympathetic Anglo officers and juries. If they avoided becoming lynching victims, indigent tejano suspects appeared in courts that frequently sought their long-term imprisonment.

Increasing Incarceration

Texas penitentiary statistics and court records from border tribunals support contemporary observations about the incarceration of Mexicans. Soon after the state's first penitentiary at Huntsville accepted its inaugural prisoner, mexicanos became overrepresented among the inmates. Because most criminal defendants in the United States during the nineteenth century were men, the state's adult males are the most appropriate group to consider for crime statistics. Mexicans accounted for only 3 percent of the state's adult male population by 1860, but accounted for 35 percent (70 out of 201) of convicts at Huntsville. Juries did not sentence African Americans to the penitentiary in significant numbers until the beginning of the Civil War. After Emancipation, their penitentiary numbers rose dramatically, while the number of Mexican convicts began to decline. African Americans made up 30.3 percent of Texas's adult male population in 1860, but they accounted for 46.4 percent (121 out of 261) of the inmates at Huntsville in

1866 while mexicano prisoners made up 15.7 percent. By 1867, African American inmates had climbed to 52 percent (155 out of 298), and Mexican prisoners had decreased to 11.7 percent (35). Given their overall populations in Texas, mexicanos and African Americans were significantly over-represented in the penitentiary. The disproportionate penitentiary incarceration of Mexicans in the postwar decades fit a larger pattern also found in California.[86]

Criminal convictions from Cameron and Webb Counties illustrate the judicial advantages that americanos enjoyed over mexicanos. The conviction numbers do not account for all cases, because judges dismissed or dropped criminal indictments when suspects were never apprehended or fled from custody. Courts also transferred some trials to other counties at the defendants' request. For cases with final verdicts, juries in both counties issued more "guilty" than "not guilty" decisions. They also issued a disproportionate number of guilty verdicts to mexicanos. Mexican men made up 73.6 and 75.5 percent of the adult male population in Cameron County and Webb County, respectively. However, they received 80.4 and 90.9 percent of the guilty verdicts in these counties. Accompanying guilty decisions were punishments that also fell disproportionately on mexicanos. Penalties for minor crimes (larceny and assault) included fines and short jail sentences, while major crimes (aggravated assault, murder, and cattle theft) usually elicited multiyear penitentiary sentences or the death penalty. An Anglo convict received the lightest prison term (one hour in jail), while a Mexican received the longest penitentiary sentence (life) and the most severe punishment (death by hanging). Penitentiary sentences illustrate the greatest disparity, as mexicanos received 93.8 and 90.5 percent of all penitentiary judgments in Cameron County and Webb County, respectively. County juries gave one life sentence and two death sentences to mexicanos, but no life or death sentences to americanos. The disparity in conviction rates and sentencing suggest that Anglo Americans had the best access to lawyers, and were more familiar with legal procedures than were Mexicans. Among americanos' legal strategies were transferring their cases to distant counties, asking for procedural delays, and obtaining dismissals based on technicalities.[87]

The composition of the juries administering these skewed sentences points to the significant influence of class and demography. In Webb County, tejanos were overrepresented (88.5 percent) as jurors, while in Cameron County they were severely underrepresented (17.7 percent). They were also well represented on Webb's petit and grand juries; occasionally, they filled all jury positions. Tejanos filled 55.2 percent of jury foremen in

Webb, and often presided over juries that included several americanos. As in other counties, prominent men (occasionally from the same family) repeatedly sat on juries. By contrast, Mexican Texans rarely (11.8 percent) served as jury foremen in Cameron County, especially when americanos were fellow members. This uneven representation can be partly attributed to each county's population. In 1870, Cameron County's population of 10,999 was more than four times greater than Webb County's population of 2,615. Americanos were present in larger numbers in Cameron, and therefore, contributed to a larger pool of qualified jurors than in Webb. While tejanos' underrepresentation on Cameron juries likely accounts for their high conviction rates, what explains the even higher conviction rates in Webb County, where they were overrepresented on juries? The county's postwar power-sharing arrangement offers one explanation. Unlike their Cameron counterparts, Webb's tejano elites shared political power with americanos, and were thus more closely allied with the newcomers. In contrast, Cameron's Mexican Texan elite experienced a general exclusion from political office. Since most criminal convictions fell on the poor, the willingness of Webb's elite tejanos to punish Mexicans in disproportionate numbers suggests that the Mexican community's prewar class divisions continued to matter more than shared ethnic ties. Ultimately, the conviction patterns of juries in both counties confirm the criminalization of poor mexicanos. Criminal convictions and jury service vary greatly across the American Southwest. In San Antonio, tejanos witnessed their postwar jury service plummet, much like in Cameron County. In San Miguel County, New Mexico, however, Mexicans served on juries in proportion to their adult male population. The conviction patterns for Cameron and Webb Counties run counter to those found by the legal scholar Laura Gómez for San Miguel County, where Mexicans were underrepresented as convicts during a similar period. Such contrasting outcomes can be attributed to distinct demographic patterns, power-sharing arrangements, and ethnic relations for reach region.[88]

Unrepresentative juries resulted from a flawed jury selection process. According to Texas law, eligible jurors had to be qualified electors (male citizens), between twenty-one and sixty years of age, and either owners of land in the state or a house in the county. Even though many tejanos met these requirements, few were included in Cameron County lists of possible jurors. Therefore, grand and petit juries were dominated by americanos. In Webb County, Mexican Texans served on juries in higher numbers but were still underrepresented as jury foremen. This disproportional jury representation contradicted the ideals of the United States. Throughout the nation's history, jury service has been an obligation of all citizens, and the opportunity to be tried by one's peers has been a long-established tradition. By limiting tejanos' opportunities to sit on juries, Anglos were undercutting their citizenship rights and their political engagement in the community. Unsurprisingly, poor Mexican Texan defendants received more guilty convictions and harsher sentences than americano suspects.[89]

Administering these sentences was a judiciary with a skewed ethnic representation. Through their control of politics, americanos captured most judicial positions throughout the border counties. During the first eighteen years of American rule, seven district judges and six chief justices presided over courtrooms in Cameron County; all were Anglos. Webb County's judicial officers (five district judges and eleven district attorneys) were exclusively americanos during its first twenty-eight years. Tejanos did capture some lower-level positions in the judiciary, but their numbers remained small. Among the twenty-two justices of the peace elected in Cameron County between 1848 and 1866, only two were tejanos. This imbalance persisted throughout the nineteenth century, with Mexican Texans winning only a few lower-level judgeships but no upper-level positions.[90]

The ethnic composition of the courts' attorneys and administrative staff mirrored the judges' background. Despite their extensive jury service in Webb County, tejanos did not gain entrance to the bar for some time. The first generation of Mexican Texan youth educated in American schools became lawyers after the Civil War. A tejano did not practice law in Cameron County until 1870 and in Webb County until 1882. Americanos also held a stranglehold on the district attorney position: they filled the first eleven positions in Webb County and the first fifteen positions in Cameron County. Mexican Texans in Cameron County held only minor posts, but not positions as county or district clerks, which were filled by twenty-two americanos. Tejanos filled six of twenty-four posts as bailiffs, and one of three slots as court interpreters. During the same period, Anglos secured all nineteen law-enforcement offices as constables, deputy sheriffs, and sheriffs. Occasionally, Mexican Texans were hired to assist the sheriffs but they did not serve in an elected position until the late 1880s. Such unbalanced ethnic representation resulted in a double standard of justice.[91]

An explosive situation in the border region during fall 1866 demonstrated how americanos' judicial overrepresentation could alter court sentences. The political climate across the border was very unstable; multiple military coups and rebellions brought a series of state governments to

Tamaulipas. These disturbances in Mexico attracted americano filibusters who served as hired mercenaries. Adding to the turmoil, troops allied with various *caudillos* (strongmen) in Mexico repeatedly crossed the international border to seek refuge or to launch attacks against their enemies. On the American side, the tension increased dramatically, when African American Union soldiers arrived to help establish the Reconstruction governments at the end of the Civil War. Their presence inflamed tensions, with shootings, theft, and fights among americanos, African Americans, and mexicanos becoming common. Taking advantage of the border region's turmoil were thieves, who carried out a spate of robberies and murders at various ranchos, owned mostly by Mexican Texans. The press rushed to charge mexicanos for the robberies, but scattered reports also blamed African American soldiers and Anglo American filibusters.[92]

Anglo Texans reacted in predictable fashion by blaming Mexicans for the majority of the thefts. The media portrayed mexicanos as unrepentant robbers and murderers who engaged in "guerrilla barbarism." Local courts sentenced several alleged thieves to the state penitentiary. The *Daily Ranchero*, whose editors were strongly pro-Confederate, reserved its strongest words for African American suspects. When these soldiers committed armed robberies or engaged in altercations with local residents, the newspaper sensationalized the conflict with headlines announcing "highway robbery" or "women threatened and insulted." Its harshest condemnations were directed at the Union Army for imposing its will on border communities by allowing African American soldiers to patrol the region, intimidate local politicians and law-enforcement personnel, and exert power over Anglo American civilians. Characterizing local residents as a population under siege, the press denounced attacks on tejano-owned jacales and ranches. In an unprecedented display of compassion, the editors described a peddler who was robbed by an African American soldier as "a poor industrious Mexican, who is striving to earn an honest living, out of the price of his bread." So the arrival of African American soldiers gave americanos another scapegoat to blame for local crimes. Noteworthy was the periodical's characterization of other victims as the "peaceable and unoffending portion of our Mexican population." In order to stop the altercations, the press persistently urged military authorities to punish the allegedly unruly African American soldiers.[93]

Americanos reacted very differently to the prosecution of some Anglo American thieves during the same period. After several armed encounters between americano filibusters and tejano rancheros (see figure 10), the

10. Rancheros were part of the tejano elite throughout the nineteenth century. Among the families who continued ranching on their land into the late nineteenth century were those from Hidalgo County. Circa 1889. Pictured from left to right are Salvador II and José María Cárdenas of La Noria Cardeneña Ranch, Camilo Vela of El Desierto Ranch, and Uvaldo Vela (seated) of El Veleño Ranch. Courtesy of Museum of South Texas History, Edinburg, Texas.

media identified forty-four americanos as the thieves responsible for stealing horses and firearms. The rancheros killed twenty-three thieves and
arrested sixteen, but the remaining robbers escaped. Justifying a detailed
and sympathetic account of the affair, local editors argued, "We are giving
the prisoners' version of the whole transaction . . . and our duty, and justice,
alike to all, demand their statements" be published. The conduct of judicial
officials was more astonishing still. The courts indicted sixteen americanos
on five different counts of theft, to which they pleaded guilty. Because the
accused thieves were unable to pay for legal representation, three local
lawyers (including Judge F. Cummings) volunteered as their counsel. Attorneys portrayed their defendants (whose families many court attendees
knew) as misguided youth who were "led astray, and deluded into the
commission of crime" by older men in their company. The testimony of
hardship given by one thief, a youth of sixteen years, elicited tears from
many in the courtroom, including the presiding judge, Stephen Powers,
who subsequently dismissed the sixteen-year-old's charges.[94]

Describing the remaining fifteen men's ordeal at length, their attorneys
asked the jury for consideration. The men had enlisted in the Mexican
Army as hired mercenaries, but eventually resorted to cattle theft to survive. Agreeing with the defense, the district attorney, Frank Macmanus,
recommended the minimum sentence. Judge Powers concurred, asking the
jury to be lenient. Jurors sentenced the defendants to five years in the
penitentiary on the first indictment, theft of animals, while adding two
years for the second indictment, theft from a house. In contrast, most
Mexicans found guilty of stealing horses or cattle received five to fifteen
years in the penitentiary (averaging seven years per sentence). "No one [in
the courtroom] was unmoved" during the sentencing, according to the
newspaper, and "all evinced a deep feeling of sympathy and sorrow."[95]

The sympathy of the media and of the jurors was highly unusual. Most
criminals, including other americanos, received harsher treatment. Although atypical, the case illustrates Anglo American views toward crime
and punishment. Several case details were unprecedented: the newspaper's
decision to publish the accused men's accounts, the detailed reports of the
courtroom drama, and the judicial officials' expressions of sympathy. What
was not surprising was the jury's leniency. Previous sentences demonstrate
a pattern in which Cameron County juries were more compassionate toward americanos than toward mexicanos. The bias present at various stages
of the judicial system was amply reflected in the newspapers' views, the

lawyers' remarks, and the judges' instructions to the jury on sentencing proceedings.

Neither Mexicans nor African Americans received similar leniency from the Anglo American–dominated press and legal system. The words of one of the lawyers defending the sixteen youth summed up Anglo American sentiments. According to the attorney, the youngsters "were not thieves, although by the law their acts were criminal." Ignoring the contradictions in the lawyers' reasoning, Anglos refused to consider these young offenders as criminals. They extended another extraordinary act of compassion toward the prisoners, when a heavily armed force of local deputies and American soldiers led a group of forty-three men to the state penitentiary two months later. Among the group were mexicanos, African Americans, Indians, and the fifteen americano youth. Several community members, described as "noble hearted Texan[s]," collected contributions of approximately $150 to help the americano youth pay for their expenses on their five-hundred-mile journey to the penitentiary. Tellingly, the other prisoners did not receive similar assistance.[96]

Class and ethnicity influenced jury composition and legal sentences. Underrepresentation of tejanos as legal officers and jurors led to their increasing overrepresentation in penitentiaries. The ethnic composition of juries followed the pattern of political representation for each county. In Webb County, where americanos and tejanos shared political power, Mexican Texans secured a larger percentage of juror positions than in Cameron County, where they failed to obtain key elected offices. Moreover, americanos filled most legal and law-enforcement positions in both counties despite their tejano majorities. This skewed representation had detrimental effects mainly for poor mexicanos, who received harsher sentences than Anglo defendants. In contrast, elite Mexican Texans sat on juries, enjoyed access to legal representation, and generally avoided lengthy sentences.

Everyday Forms of Resistance

Faced with dim prospects in American courts, poor suspects risked their lives to resist arrest or escape from prison. The international boundary's proximity facilitated their flight: local residents of various ethnic backgrounds avoided prosecution by crossing into Mexico. Mexican Texans benefited most from this strategy because they were familiar with Mexico's geography and language. Unlike tejano suspects, whose physical and linguistic characteristics allowed them to blend in with Mexican nationals, African Americans and Anglo Americans stood out and could be easily identified by authorities. Local Mexican Texans also benefited from friends and relatives in Mexico, who could provide shelter and shield them from authorities. The Rio Grande became a "weapon of the weak" for tejanos confronting a biased media and an Anglo American–dominated justice system.[97]

Poor Mexican Texans were not alone in fleeing across the international boundary. Thieves routinely crossed into Mexico to sell their booty, while others fled after brawls, murders, or prison escapes. Joining suspected criminals were deserters from the Mexican and American armies. Rancheros in Mexico escaped across the river to avoid conscription by local caudillos, while their tejano counterparts fled into Mexico to evade the Confederate draft during the Civil War. Political disturbances in both countries further encouraged border residents to cross the Rio Grande for protection. The river did have its dangers; the individuals who swam across braved strong currents and occasionally drowned.[98]

Flight into Mexico often followed escapes from insecure county jails, which were usually overcrowded and in disrepair. Sections of courthouses or makeshift buildings served as prisons because county governments lacked sufficient funding to build proper structures. According to a jurors' report, the prison was a "most wretched place for the keeping of human beings[;] the roof is so open that in time of rain the prisoners suffer from the water coming in upon them." A contemporary observer believed jails were of little use. "Though all the prisoners were chained down," he noted, "many broke their bonds, and escapes were of no rare occurrence." Inmates broke free by digging holes underneath or through the jail walls or by picking their cells' locks after receiving tools or logistical assistance from visitors. While visiting the Rio Grande City Jail, Vielé suggested to an Anglo American inmate the best means of breaking out, which the prisoner successfully used. Escapes involved cooperation among interethnic groups of prisoners, lax justices, and law-enforcement officials who left jails unattended.[99]

To combat the river's use to escape prosecution, American and Mexican federal authorities sought to establish an extradition treaty. Negotiating this treaty proved difficult because of the Mexican government's instability, with federalists and centralists struggling over control. During his visit to the border area in 1853, an American military surveyor described the insecurity of property and the difficulties confronting law-enforcement personnel in both nations. In a report supportive of an extradition treaty, the surveyor touched on problems resulting from nationalist sentiments, which would plague any implementation of a future agreement: "The boundary between the United States and Mexico is here only an imaginary line running down the centre of the river, and an offence can be committed on either side with impunity. A few minutes serve to place the offender over the line, where the jealousies of the law on either side step in to protect him; and where national prejudices are involved, the criminal is not infrequently extolled for his exploits." Finalized in 1861, the extradition treaty authorized officials to arrest foreign suspects and return them to the other country to face justice.[100]

The treaty, however, produced mixed results. Authorities captured and transferred fugitives across the river on various occasions. Once the municipal governments initiated cooperation, fugitives began returning to their home country to avoid arrest and extradition. However, the English-language media accused Mexican authorities of violating the trust required for prisoner exchanges. They believed that Mexican officials failed to return every prisoner requested by American authorities. "The extradition treaty is and always has been a dead letter," argued a journalist stationed in Mexico. "None but American citizens [meaning Anglo Americans] are surrendered for crimes committed on this side of the river." Although his argument was only partially true, since Mexican authorities had previously extradited tejanos, his statement supported the 1853 military surveyor's observations about "nationalist prejudices." Mexican Texan fugitives not only obtained shelter from friends and relatives in Mexico but also found sympathetic authorities, who sometimes refused to arrest and extradite them. This lack of cooperation suggests that Mexico's officials were aware that fugitive tejanos would struggle to receive a fair trial if extradited.[101]

Mexican Texans further resisted their legal prosecution through acts of sabotage and direct assaults on law-enforcement officers. During an 1859 uprising, tejano rebels intercepted and read the mail to obtain clues about Brownsville's attempts to secure additional military aid. Some cattle thieves targeted americanos who had obtained property at the expense of tejano landowners, or who strongly supported local law enforcement. Profits from stolen livestock were easy to obtain because thieves could sell their plunder to a steady supply of customers on both sides of the border. On other occasions, saboteurs cut down telegraph lines to prevent authorities from contacting state officials to request additional military forces. They were also motivated by a desire to punish the telegraph's owners, Mifflin Kenedy and

Richard King. Both were large landowners who obtained tejanos' lands in suspicious ways and received protection from the Texas Rangers. Targets of shootings and ambushes included constables, sheriffs, and judicial officers, who were responsible for incarcerating a large number of tejanos and Mexican nationals. Although infrequent, these attacks made law-enforcement officers wary and possibly limited their use of force.[102]

American annexation introduced the second conquest of the border region within a hundred years. The colonists who had dominated the region's Indians in the mid-eighteenth century became a conquered people, as Anglo American newcomers began to gain power over them. Serving as agents of the United States, americanos advanced its state formation by controlling local governments and passing legislation to regulate Mexican cultural practices. The Mexican Texan elite lost political and economic power, while the poor became increasingly criminalized. Most faced political and social exclusion from the community that emerged on the American side of the border after the U.S.-Mexican War. Instead of gaining acceptance as equals, as promised in the Treaty of Guadalupe-Hidalgo, they became second-class citizens. Ultimately, the conflict engendered by their exclusion became part of tejanos' struggle to gain full citizenship rights.

5

Divorcées, Rancheros, and Peons
Changing Class and Gender Relations

Border residents read shocking news in the *Daily Ranchero* on 13 June 1867. They learned about Señora Canute de la Paz's visit the previous day to the office of Brownsville's mayor, William Neale, to submit an affidavit accusing Julio García of raping her eight-year-old daughter. De la Paz, her daughter, and García worked and lived on Edward Dougherty's ranch. Filing the affidavit was obviously difficult because of the nature of the crime. The newspaper editors expressed their disgust with García and concluded by writing, "We expect to see the scoundrelly greaser get his deserts." The editors' wishes were unfulfilled; Cameron County officials failed to indict García. It is likely that he avoided prosecution by escaping into Mexico.[1]

This tragic story illustrates the postwar transformation in the newly annexed lands along the border. Prior to the takeover by the United States, most workers, ranch owners, and municipal officials shared a common ethnic background. In the aftermath of the war, Anglo Americans and European immigrants were among the new arrivals, increasing Brownsville's population to three thousand in its first two years, and to nearly five thousand by 1867. The effects of the demographic and jurisdictional change were apparent in the news story. Edward Dougherty and William Neale were not only the district judge and mayor, respectively, but also major landowners—prominent positions in a county whose *americano* (American citizen) population was only 16 percent. Dougherty, an Irish immigrant, served as one of Brownsville's first aldermen, and became an entrepreneur and a booster. Neale, an English immigrant, had arrived in Matamoros in the 1830s, established a stage line, and eventually bought a ranch after the war. Both officials, like other newcomers, had undergone a degree of Mexicanization by adopting various *vecino* (community member) cultural practices. Dougherty cultivated community ties after marrying María Marcela García, serving as district attorney, and legally representing several *tejano* (Mexican Texan) litigants. Neale had nurtured cross-border ties to Mexican politicians and won elected office by appealing to Mexican Texan voters. By displacing the long-established social and cultural ties between Mexican patriarchs and their ranch workers, the arrivistes created new employer-worker relationships. They also frayed the cultural and familial bonds between residents and civic leaders.[2]

Accompanying the postwar population changes was the introduction of American legislation that contributed to altering the region's class and gender relations. As agents of the American nation-state, municipal and county officials cooperated to implement the laws that transformed society. American legislation loosened elite tejano control over the local community. As elites lost economic power by forfeiting land, they struggled to defend their property in a different legal system. Moreover, employers' dominance over workers weakened, as did men's power within marriage. American laws provided women and workers with more rights and opportunities than they had enjoyed in Mexico. Yet, structural inequality remained. Men continued to hold advantages over women not only by exercising more legal rights, but also by occupying all political and judicial positions. Among the annexed population, the landed elite were best able to pursue litigation because of their literacy, wealth, and political connections. Others less privileged, such as de la Paz, also adjusted to the American legal system, and its accompanying challenges—new laws and legal procedures written in English and implemented mostly by Anglo American judicial officers.

The outcome of this rape trial illustrates the formidable obstacles that victims of violent sexual assault continued confronting in the postwar period. As in Mexico, women struggled to punish their assailants legally. They overcame some barriers through interpreters and friends with legal knowledge, and workers like de la Paz undoubtedly obtained assistance from their employers—especially from those like Dougherty who had legal expertise. American legislation gave assault victims more rights, but uneven enforcement weakened its effectiveness. Officials were slow to arrest perpetrators of sexual assaults, and the heaviest burden of the lawsuits fell on victims. Moreover, the jurisdictional change introduced a new obstacle because criminals could escape from prosecution by fleeing across the international boundary. While the tejano community was buffeted by outside forces during the postwar period, the misogyny evident in the rape of a female child demonstrates that internal inequality remained sharp and was enforced by violence.[3]

Anglo American–Dominated Courts

Anglos shaped social relations in the border region by controlling the political and judicial system. Excluded from positions of power in Mexico, their fortunes improved after the war, when they became agents of the American government. They advanced the nation's interests by establishing military and civilian control over the newly acquired territory. The relationship was mutually beneficial. The United States sought to control the area's inhabitants, while Anglos wanted to acquire land and capture political offices. The confluence of these goals placed americanos in the border counties, as elsewhere in the annexed territories, in a favored position. They passed local ordinances to maintain control of laborers and used political power to perpetuate their rule. By becoming the new elite, the newcomers also transformed class relations. As the Mexican upper class had done before them, the Anglo American arrivistes used political power for economic gains including lower taxes and ferry contracts, and to obtain state and federal military protection. They also implemented laws that transformed ethnic and gender relations.

Although both groups were theoretically entitled to the same legal rights, americanos had clear advantages over tejanos. Anglos had a greater command of English and were familiar with American legal procedures. Court interpreters assisted Spanish-speaking litigants, but these bilingual employees could not completely compensate for the language barrier. Moreover, americanos had greater access to attorneys, which increased the likelihood of appeals, venue changes, and plea bargains. Anglo American men's legal knowledge was reinforced by service on juries and through elected judicial positions, experiences that were not readily available to tejanos. Mexican Texans did not become magistrates in U.S. courts until the late nineteenth century. Further, many americanos had the advantage of presenting their lawsuits before judicial authorities and juries composed primarily of fellow Anglos. The composition of a jury was critical to a trial's outcome given the ethnic and racial antagonisms pervasive in postwar Texas.[4]

Litigation by Elite Tejanos

Elite Mexican Texans witnessed a dramatic decrease in economic power following annexation by the United States. Although the Texas legislature affirmed titles to most of the region's Spanish and Mexican land grants, tejanos gradually lost property to americano newcomers. Some loss resulted from extrajudicial means, as when squatters invaded their land, while other losses occurred after extensive litigation. Among the primary beneficiaries were well-financed land companies and lawyers.[5]

One group with the financial resources to fight a land development company was the Cavazos family, owners of the Espíritu Santo grant. Shortly after the war, Anglo American speculators began obtaining property through inglorious machinations: buying it from squatters with dubious property rights or claiming rights to *ejidos* (public land of the northern villas). To acquire properties, Charles Stillman and his colleagues from the Brownsville Town Company went to court to resolve their competing claims against the Cavazoses. In a controversial compromise, the Cavazos family gave up portions of land as payment for attorneys' fees in order to gain confirmation of the grant's remaining fifty-eight leagues. They accepted the unfavorable conditions rather than risk losing the entire tract in long, drawn-out litigation. The land grant's confirmation spurred counterlitigation by a disgruntled faction of developers. The U.S. Supreme Court ultimately upheld the lower court's decision, leaving bitter feelings between the two factions of developers and the Cavazoses.[6]

As the Cavazos family saga illustrates, tejano elites encountered formidable challenges in an unfamiliar legal system. Despite having social connections and wealth, they faced lawyers and land speculators with extensive experience in real estate litigation. Additionally, squatters created legal entanglements for landowners by fraudulently selling property titles. Some lost portions of their estates by settling lawsuits out of court instead of pursuing time-consuming litigation and court-ordered boundary surveys. Others relinquished property to their own lawyers, who charged fees in land. Landowners also forfeited property through taxation, sheriff's sales, and intimidation. Squatters moved fences, threatened the owners, and occasionally assaulted the rancheros. After enduring various lawsuits, taxation, and other obstacles, some tejanos fell prey to the "play of the market." Because they lacked capital and access to credit, they were less able than americanos to maintain land ownership during economic downturns.[7]

Partible inheritance contributed to land dispossession. The Mexican tradition of subdividing property equally among heirs created smaller plots as the population grew. In Mexico, land had been subdivided but held in common so titles remained tied to large land holdings. By contrast, Texas law required land titles to be specific and up to date, so titles began to correspond to smaller and smaller acreage. Ultimately, owners sold property because their small plots were commercially unprofitable. Sales increased as widows, minors, or disabled individuals disposed of property due to a lack of interest or an inability to manage holdings.[8]

Although land dispossession was widespread, the pattern varied by county. In Hidalgo, Starr, Webb, and Zapata Counties, Mexican Texans were the majority landowners until the 1880s. These rancheros retained ownership longer than their counterparts in adjoining counties because few americanos competed for land there. Americanos preferred the coastal counties of Cameron and Nueces, whose access to the Gulf of Mexico offered trade possibilities. In these counties, merchants acquired large tracts of land as they diversified their businesses, quickly making Mexican Texans minority property owners.[9]

The tejano elite also experienced diminished legal power over workers. The upper class had relied on Mexican officials to enforce vagrancy ordinances and control idle laborers in the *villas del norte* (northern towns). Authorities compelled vagrants to labor on municipal public projects, sent them into the military, or placed them with local employers. After the war, American officials passed similar vagrancy laws with punishments consisting of fines, jail sentences, or forced labor on municipal works projects. However, employers were no longer permitted to use vagrancy ordinances to ensnare workers to toil on their ranches or in their houses. Moreover, employers lost the ability to ask local magistrates to punish workers who were disobedient or showed disrespect.[10]

The tejano elite were no longer able to regulate workers' employment or their social life. Laborers north of the Rio Grande continued to incur debts, but unlike Mexican tribunals, U.S. judges did not enforce these obligations. The international border further weakened employers' power because workers began crossing the river to escape onerous labor conditions. The upper class also lost some control over their laborers' social life and courting practices. Absent were employers' lawsuits, common in Mexico, seeking to force suitors to stop wooing their domestic servants.[11]

The implementation of U.S. laws and policies along the border led to the decline in power of the tejano elite. They lost their monopoly on land as a growing number of Anglo Americans became property owners. The newcomers displaced tejanos from economic power, with the region's trade increasingly tied to the United States. American jurisdiction also weakened the elite's control over their workers. Ultimately, U.S. state formation loosened the Mexican Texan elite's domination over society. No longer could members of the tejano upper class view themselves as the region's sole economic and social leaders. They now had to share this power with newcomers who enjoyed several advantages over them.

Tejano Artisans and Workers

Mexican Texan artisans and petty vendors faced even greater obstacles. They had less money than the elite to hire lawyers, and fewer social contacts among the judiciary, police force, and juries. Their legal knowledge was limited because they rarely served on juries. Furthermore, their sparse English-language skills hampered their understanding of court proceedings. Nevertheless, vendors and artisans pursued litigation to protect their interests. Appealing to lower-level courts in the majority of cases, they filed charges to recover stolen merchandise, settle disputes with customers, and resolve disagreements with fellow workers. However, they filed litigation less frequently than in Mexico due to legal obstacles, language barriers, and shrinking numbers.[12]

The regions of Texas with the heaviest concentration of tejanos did not share equally in the state's economic expansion. Because most were located in isolated areas, with fewer ties to the U.S. economy, tejano communities did not attract capital and jobs. Employment in professional services, trade, and transportation increased in most parts of the state but decreased in Mexican Texan settlement regions. While jobs in manufacturing and mechanical industries decreased throughout the state, the change in tejano regions was sharper. Between 1850 and 1900, the state's agricultural workforce hovered between 24.0 and 31.3 percent. In the tejano settlement regions, however, the number of Mexican Texans engaged in agriculture decreased from 41.1 to 18.9 percent while the number of americanos in agriculture increased from 18.1 to 32.3 percent. The trade and transportation industries witnessed similar trends. The most significant increase occurred in the unskilled labor segment, which rose to 7.7 percent in the state and to 36.7 percent in Mexican Texan regions.[13]

The economic transformation pushed skilled workers from specialized occupations in trade, transportation, manufacturing, and mechanical industries into unskilled general labor. In tejano settlement regions, the number of unskilled Mexican Texan workers shot up to 54.5 percent, while the number of Anglo American unskilled workers increased only to 19.0 percent from 1850 to 1900. Several factors explain these trends. Americano employers tended to view "cotton picking, grubbing, sheep herding, working cattle, laundry work, food service, and other low-grade tasks" as "Mexican work" and hired tejanos for these low-paying positions. Migratory patterns within the state provide another explanation. After annexation by the United States, Mexican Texans rarely migrated to regions where employment opportunities were expanding because americanos made it abundantly clear that tejano laborers were not welcome. Instead, these areas relied on African Americans, migrants from northern states, and European immigrants for their labor supply.[14]

American jurisdiction over the communities on the river's left bank led to mixed results for mexicano artisans and workers. They faced declining opportunities for skilled jobs with the economic transformation of the region and the arrival of Anglo Americans. They also had to adapt to a new legal system, and had fewer resources to pursue litigation than the elite. Nevertheless, workers discovered that they enjoyed more freedom under U.S. laws than under Mexican legislation. American courts did not enforce the debt labor system practiced in Mexico, so laborers in Texas enjoyed greater liberty to change jobs. Domestic servants, agricultural hands, and common laborers no longer had to appeal to tribunals for permission to leave abusive employers. Workers simply walked away. While their job prospects became more limited in the postwar period, laborers enjoyed more mobility and therefore, more independence.

Border as a Weapon of the Weak

Another major change in the region's labor relations resulted from the shift of the international border to the Rio Grande in 1848. This created new opportunities for workers, and changed the significance of the boundary. The border became a tool for laborers on both sides of the river who needed to escape from debt, abusive employers, or enslavement. Laborers from Mexico "liquidated" their debts simply by crossing the river. In 1849, the governor of Tamaulipas complained that the state's ranch owners were suffering two types of losses: indebted laborers fled across the river without repaying their debts, and they carried stolen cattle and goods. So many workers fled into Texas that cotton production in Mexican border states almost ceased. Coahuila's governor advocated greater cooperation among municipalities to recover runaways because their flight was paralyzing agriculture. Similarly, Nuevo León's agricultural producers identified indebted laborers' escape across the Rio Grande as their greatest problem during the 1850s. Lacking an extradition treaty with the United States, Mexico could not stop the flow of workers into Texas.[15]

Indebted laborers followed the pattern established by early Mexican immigrants who worked for the U.S. Army during the war. Wages in Mexico remained relatively static throughout the nineteenth century. In response, muleteers, cowboys, and farmworkers found higher-paying jobs in Texas. In Mexico's northeastern states at midcentury, domestic servants received about four to five pesos monthly ($3.84 to $4.81) plus food, while hacienda laborers received between three and five pesos monthly ($2.88 to $4.81) and a portion of their food. In contrast, livestock herders in Maverick and Nueces Counties earned six to seven dollars per month plus a portion of food. Highly skilled ranch workers, such as horse tamers, could earn twenty dollars monthly. By the late 1860s, agricultural laborers in the border counties earned about fifteen dollars per month plus food. Cowboys could earn from eight to ten dollars monthly during the 1860s, and twelve dollars monthly by the 1880s. These wages benefited both Mexican laborers and Anglo American employers.[16]

The Civil War further increased economic opportunities. The Union and Confederate Armies recruited on both sides of the border, swelling their ranks with Mexican nationals and tejanos. Mexican-immigrant recruits received a monthly stipend of eleven to thirteen dollars. Some cart drivers earned as much as seven hundred dollars over three months hauling cotton, while others secured sizable advances in gold. Higher wages attracted so many workers that Nuevo León's merchants struggled to retain cart drivers. One wrinkle in the robust job opportunities was the wage differentials that paid americanos more than tejanos for the same jobs. Nevertheless, laborers from Mexico continued to accept jobs in Texas because they could earn considerably higher wages than in their native land.[17]

Social and economic stability in Texas also attracted Mexican laborers, escaping from Mexico's incessant armed conflicts. Beginning with the American invasion at midcentury, Mexico suffered several military conflicts, including the War of Reform (1858–61) and the period of French intervention (1861–67). In 1876, the ascendance to national power of Porfirio Díaz, with his policies favoring wealthy landowners in Mexico, increased emigration, leaving many rural residents landless and unemployed. Emigration also resulted from the demographic pressures of population growth, declining wages, and price increases of basic goods. The combination of internal taxes on Mexican goods and high import duties on American manufactures pushed prices prohibitively high in Mexican border cities. The prices of groceries and clothes in U.S. border cities were four times lower than in their Mexican counterparts.[18]

Laborers' flight across the border persisted throughout the nineteenth century. According to an 1873 Mexican investigative commission report, some 2,812 indebted laborers, accompanied by 2,572 relatives, had fled into the United States since 1848. Agricultural and ranch owners in Nuevo León and Coahuila claimed financial shortfalls of $379,116 from the workers' debts. While the erosion of capital and livestock hurt Mexico's economy, the commissioners believed that the most significant damage was the loss of a dependable workforce. By crossing the river into Texas, workers undermined labor controls and weakened indebted servitude in Mexico.[19]

On the American side, slaves had created a similar practice of crossing the international boundary to subvert labor restrictions over the course of the nineteenth century. African American slaves began escaping into New Spain's sparsely settled northern borderlands before the Adams-Onís Treaty (1819) formalized the boundary between the United States and New Spain. The flow of slaves across the border increased after Mexico outlawed slavery in 1829. Their flight into Mexico crippled slavery along the border, and motivated slave-owning Texans to launch their separatist rebellion in 1835. After Texas independence, Mexican government and military officials encouraged runaway slaves to flee to Mexico. Their collective efforts to flee, according to the historian Sean Kelley, indicate that Texas's slave communities had gradually associated Mexico with nonslavery and had invested the border with "liberationist significance." In the ensuing years, reports about runaway slaves enjoying life in Mexico confirmed this view. A prisoner in the aftermath of the ill-fated Mier Expedition encountered Tom and Esau, the former slaves of the Texas president Sam Houston. They had acculturated to Mexican society and gained wide acceptance as evident by the Mexican Army general who served as godfather at one of their weddings. Both criticized their former master and clearly appreciated the freedom they now enjoyed.[20]

Slaves also escaped into Mexico during the U.S.-Mexican War. American officers reported that slaves had fled in 1845 as the army marched toward the Rio Grande: "every inducement is offered by the enemy." Runaway slaves owned by army officers and Texans would continue to escape into Mexico throughout the war. Border residents provided the runaways with asylum, which angered slave owners according to the appraiser general, who argued: "The frequent escape of slaves from the American side of the Rio Grande into Mexico, and the folly of any attempt to recapture them— although you often met your own property in Matamoros—has been one of the excitants of bad feeling between the citizens of Mexico and those on the frontier." By 1855, over four thousand slaves had obtained their freedom by fleeing into Mexico. Like Mexican ranchers whose indebted laborers fled into Texas, slave owners complained about the lack of an extradition treaty that would return runaway slaves from Mexico. Repeated American efforts to establish a treaty failed because the Mexican government refused to return runaway slaves. Downtrodden workers from each nation "crossed paths" at the Rio Grande, as the historian Juan Mora-Torres argues, and dismantled labor controls through their flight. As the international boundary moved, workers gradually invested the border with new significances associated with freedom and opportunity. Both slaves and indebted laborers trafficked in stolen goods to sustain themselves. Such actions demonstrate that international borders unite people just as readily as they divide them. Indebted laborers and runaway slaves shared a common "weapon of the weak" (flight) and a view of the international border as a tool of freedom.[21]

Indebted Labor Reemerges

The loss of slaves forced Texas landowners to rely on Mexican laborers. Jobs in domestic service and ranching offered a measure of security and benefits —year-round employment, room, and board—while agricultural employment did not, making the procurement of labor a principal challenge for cane or cotton growers. Among the ex-peons who crossed into Texas, many were unwilling to pick crops because their jobs ended with the harvest. Without slaves or peons to employ, growers lacked a dependable labor supply, thereby hindering the development of commercial agriculture in the border counties. Another obstacle was landowners' preferences for livestock production. While tejano ranchers continued raising cattle out of custom, americanos chose livestock production and trade, pursuits that were more profitable than agriculture.[22]

Ranchers struggled to recruit and retain common laborers, sheep shearers, and teamsters, until they discovered that debt resolved their labor problem. If workers became indebted, employers believed that their labor force would be more loyal and stable. Laborers incurred debts for the same reasons they had done so in Mexico: salary advances for food, clothes, transportation, and medicine. Farmers, whose seasonal needs made them vulnerable to labor shortages, resorted to giving advances. Cotton farmers preferred laborers with families to single men because those with dependents were less likely to leave without repaying their advances. Without national or state legislation supporting indebted servitude, farmers promoted a belief in the legal authorities' right to jail those who abandoned their jobs without settling their arrears. Employers continued to offer informal debt labor contracts throughout the nineteenth century; such agreements were mutually beneficial. Promises of continuous employment were particularly important during periods of job scarcity, when necessity forced many agricultural workers to migrate in search of work. Debts also became a "certificate of character" in that workers who changed jobs became indebted, figuratively and literally, to their new employers, who assumed their old debts.[23]

In the postwar period, Anglo American employers adopted the debt contract arrangements prevalent in Mexico. Most shepherds in the late 1870s were heavily in debt. Both americano and tejano employers advanced loans to workers of various skill levels, from the lowly *peones* (who worked as shepherds, goatherds, and manual laborers) and female domestic servants to the more independent cowboys. Cowboys and shepherds "in the '60s [1860s]," recalled a tejano in Corpus Christi, "used to be in debt from $300 to $400." He remembered that one employer, "Ramírez, the Mexican rancher, wanted them in debt like slaves." Ranch owners hoped the financial obligations would bind laborers to their jobs; as the years passed, they were not disappointed. At the prevailing wages, many cowboys (earning ten dollars a month) were forced to work three years and some shepherds (earning four dollars a month) toiled for nine years or more before they could settle their financial arrears.[24]

These indebted labor arrangements assumed the character of *patrón-peón* relationships, which offered stability through reciprocal obligations and paternalism. Anglos adopted the patrón-peón relationship, which transplanted southerners might have likened to slavery's paternalism. For employers, workers' loyalty was crucial during attacks by Indians or cattle thieves, especially on isolated ranches. Laborers, in turn, considered their financial liabilities to employers as guarantees for future work. Unlike migrant workers, permanent laborers could depend on employer-provided food, medical supplies, and housing throughout the year. Indebted workers were loyal in exchange for their employer's protection in the tense postwar atmosphere where violence against tejanos was common. Additionally, elderly workers expected their bosses to provide them with housing and supplies in return for years of loyal service.[25]

Despite the mutually beneficial patrón-peón relationships, employers occasionally resorted to intimidation and physical violence to retain workers. Resentful of workers' freedom to change jobs, ranchers and farmers threatened to dismiss foremen if indebted laborers under their supervision left without repaying their loans. Employers also counseled regular workers to warn them when laborers intended to leave without settling their arrears. By forcing vagrants to work in cotton fields under armed guard, law-enforcement officials colluded with landowners. Ranchers and farmers withheld employees' pay or confiscated their property—such as clothes and small articles of furniture—to retain them. Some even intimidated a worker's family members should the head of the family seek to leave their employment.[26]

Seasonal work, created by labor shortages during harvests and busy livestock times, continued to attract workers. This labor need led Mexican nationals to join tejanos in seasonal migrations. The availability of cheap migrant labor became a selling point to attract farmers to the border counties. Land agents placed newspapers advertisements that obliquely referred to the seasonal migration of Mexican nationals as a source of labor. "This is a good point to procure Mexican labor," a journalist in Rio Grande City advised readers in 1877, "[because] good ranch hands with families may be had for eight or ten dollars per month with board." By the mid-1880s, migratory flows from Mexico were well established as evident by the number of border crossings of *tasquines* (sheep shearers), which reached numbers as high as four hundred per week at the Piedras Negras–Eagle Pass port of entry. Livestock producers needed these workers on a seasonal basis, which required tasquines to migrate to Texas twice a year.[27]

The quantity and variety of workers emigrating from Mexico increased dramatically with the arrival of the railroad in the late 1870s. Between 1865 and 1880, Texas underwent significant economic transformation by market forces, which increased the specialization and commercialization of agriculture and stock raising. The railroads dramatically increased cotton production, allowing its transport to distant markets. Trains also enabled the transportation of a cheap and abundant labor supply from Mexico to targeted agricultural regions in Texas. As the economy boomed, the number of workers migrating across the Rio Grande grew exponentially. This burgeoning stream included men who found employment as day laborers, cowboys, teamsters, and shepherds, as well as women who worked as domestic servants.[28]

Mexican workers filed fewer lawsuits than they had in Mexico, because the United States did not enforce indebted labor arrangements. Laborers in Mexico were motivated to file charges against abusive employers in order to change jobs legally. Mexican tribunals could also lower or forgive a laborer's debt. In the United States, employees no longer needed the court's consent to abandon their employment. A worker could challenge an employer's physical assaults in court, but only to pursue criminal charges. Such was the goal of a fifty-year-old Mexican ranch hand who charged his employer, Agapito Longoria, with torture in a criminal lawsuit. The laborer suffered lacerations and welts after Longoria tied him up by the heels and "kept him in that position until nearly dead."[29]

Substantial advantages accompanied the ability to file criminal charges against employers. In Mexico, magistrates resolved laborers' lawsuits for mistreatment by lowering debts or granting money to cover medical expenses. Rarely were masters jailed. By contrast, U.S. judges presiding over similar lawsuits often fined or jailed guilty employers. Families and friends assisted in filing lawsuits in both nations, especially when workers were underage. In 1866, two small boys obtained such assistance in charging their employer, Patricio Huertas, with cruelty. The court found Huertas guilty of harnessing the boys to a barrel of water, which was stuck in the mud, and whipping them with a pole until they retrieved the barrel. The mayor punished Huertas by fining him three dollars plus court costs. Other employers guilty of mistreatment were not so lucky. In 1867, Pedro Pérez faced charges of aggravated assault on an eight-year-old tejano boy after Brownsville's mayor determined that the charges warranted a criminal trial in a higher court. The judge sent Pérez to prison and imposed a bail of five hundred dollars to keep the aggressor from leaving the city before his trial.[30]

Despite their legal gains, some workers, particularly women, continued to face substantial obstacles in pursuing justice. An 1867 lawsuit illustrates a male employer's power and abuse of authority as well as a female domestic servant's marginality. Caroline Bell, a German immigrant, had begun working for Adolphe Smith, a butcher, as a live-in servant nine months before she sued him. Smith reneged on his promise to pay the agreed-upon twenty-five dollars per month in wages, and confiscated two trunks of Bell's clothes and furniture in order to retain her. When Bell decided to leave, Smith refused to return her property and attacked Bell. After sustaining multiple injuries, Bell sued the butcher in the mayor's court for assault and battery as well as for theft. Afraid of further reprisals after the mayor inexplicably released Smith from custody, Bell subsequently abandoned her lawsuit and left the area. The outcome of her litigation exemplifies the considerable impediments facing workers. Bell, like other laborers, was hard pressed to convince authorities of the severity of her employer's assaults and the seriousness of his threats. Officials gave the benefit of the doubt to the butcher—possibly because they valued the testimony of Smith, an employer, and doubted the charges of Bell, a female immigrant worker.[31]

The reemergence of indebted labor as an informal arrangement reveals that regional factors, in addition to American laws, shaped labor relations. Without legislation that enforced indebted peonage, employers created unofficial debt agreements that relied on paternalism and intimidation to retain laborers. Such extralegal arrangements were possible because indebted contracts were familiar to local workers. Regional factors could also help laborers: the change to U.S. jurisdiction directly affected seasonal employment in that immigrants attracted by higher wages easily crossed the international boundary. American laws also altered the legal recourses for workers. Those with knowledge of the law could file criminal charges against abusive employers, and thereby claim more power over their working conditions than they had enjoyed in Mexico. Yet, female workers continued facing greater obstacles than their male colleagues because the courts and law enforcement remained exclusively male. This gender inequality extended to laws meant to protect women and those that regulated marriage.

Women's Increasing Independence

Seven months after the end of the U.S.-Mexican War, Sarah García married James H. Clay before a justice of the peace on 16 September 1848 in Brownsville. This civil union illustrates two broad patterns of the postwar period: the Catholic Church's decreasing influence over marital issues, and an increase in interethnic marriage. Eight years later, García became the first tejana to file for divorce in the border counties. Her successful lawsuit charged Clay with abandoning her in 1849 and with failing to provide financial support. García's initiative to free herself from a bad marriage illustrates two additional broad patterns: tejanas' willingness to exercise new advantages in marital relations introduced by the change to rule by the United States, and their gradual adaptation to American culture.[32]

Despite new opportunities in the United States, women faced many of the same obstacles as they had in Mexico. They remained subordinate to men in political and legal arenas. They could neither vote nor hold elected office. Nor could they serve as judges, lawyers, legal witnesses, or jury members or represent another person in court. In general, Texas law gave women fewer rights to litigate than it gave men. Women also continued facing some of the same social problems that they confronted in Mexico, but the legal means by which to resolve disputes changed. Women in Texas, like those in Mexico, filed the majority of lawsuits concerning sexual attacks, domestic disputes, and divorce. The outcome of such litigation, however, reveals important differences between women on opposite sides of the Rio Grande.

Scattered evidence on assault victims from border counties confirms previous patterns from Mexico. U.S. court records, however, often omitted the litigants' basic biographical information (age, marital status, occupation, etc.), the witnesses' testimony, and judges' commentaries. Although newspapers reported the male assailants' names, they often referred to their targets simply as "Mexican women." The exclusion of the victims' names is one measure of women's (especially tejanas') marginality within the U.S. legal system. As in Mexico, the aggrieved consisted of young women or girls. Most appeared to be nonelite; among those filing suits were washerwomen, ranch workers, servants, and homeowners. Several victims knew their assailants, who attacked women working alone in their homes or in isolated locations. Some of the women struck back or summoned help from passersby. Such was the case in July 1850, when a tejana whipped her husband after discovering that he had committed incest with their six-year-old daughter. The husband escaped further punishment by fleeing into Mexico. Another tejana made news in 1863 for stabbing a man over a disagreement while gambling at a local ranch.[33]

Women faced several obstacles to punish their assailants. Typically, tejanas appealed to the mayor's court first, probably because they were accustomed to taking disputes to *alcaldes* in Mexico. Victims sometimes faced delays if the mayor's court was not the appropriate venue and officials transferred the case to a higher tribunal. Any postponement made it more difficult for law-enforcement officials to apprehend attackers, who could flee. Judicial officials' subjective decisions presented additional impediments. Mayors often released assailants who were judged to pose a minimal risk. Yet, those released could escape into Mexico, while others might threaten their victims to drop their charges. Intimidation likely convinced a tejana victim to abandon her assault case against Macedonio Ramos, who was subsequently released.[34]

Even when women succeeded in punishing their attackers, some discovered the penalty did not fit the crime. After Eusabia Sánchez sued Louis Marchand for smashing her door and destroying household items, the mayor punished Marchand with thirty days in jail, imposed a five-dollar fine, and ordered him to pay for the broken items. Not all criminals were so expeditiously punished. When a man assaulted a victim using only his hands as weapons, officials had to decide whether the crime was a misdemeanor or a felony. The mayor's court could only adjudicate misdemeanors, meaning those assaults in which the attacker did not employ (or attempt to use) a deadly weapon. Telésforo Garza, who already had a history of physically attacking his family, benefited from a mayor's subjective decision after the military apprehended him for assaulting his sisters. One sister remained bedridden for a week from her injuries. Nevertheless, a judge decided to try Garza's aggravated assault and battery as a misdemeanor. Escaping a penitentiary sentence, Garza simply received a twenty-dollar fine after posting one-hundred-dollar bail.[35]

Sexual assault victims encountered additional obstacles. Some neglected to charge assailants because of shame, or fear of community pressure once their accusations became public. Others faced numerous delays from opposing lawyers' legal maneuvers, absent judicial officials, unavailable witnesses, and sundry technicalities. Wealthy men secured more advantages by hiring experienced lawyers, who convinced courts to offer bail, accept a change of venue, grant an appeal, or offer a new trial. The delays frustrated the victims, and provided ample time for prisoners to escape from notoriously insecure local prisons. In 1876, Fernando Glavecke paid a two-thousand-dollar bail to be released from custody pending his rape trial. After continuing his case for two years, the district attorney dropped it, possibly because the original litigants were no longer willing to testify. Incest victims and their families faced greater pressure still. The emotional and financial turmoil that a father's incarceration placed upon the family was often too much to bear. His family's economic necessity probably allowed León Estapa to avoid a penitentiary sentence in 1878. Following his arrest on an incest charge, Estapa paid a five-hundred-dollar bail to be released from the Hidalgo County Prison. He promptly fled, and later failed to appear in court. His trial was continued from term to term for eight years. Eventually officials rearrested Estapa and called four witnesses; however, the court ultimately dropped the charges against him.[36]

Despite numerous obstacles, sexual assault victims in Texas were more likely to see their assailants punished with prison sentences than were their counterparts in Mexico. Mexican officials could draw from a variety of punishments for convicted rapists, from exiling them to other communities or humiliating them with public whippings to sentencing them to public labor or lengthy presidio service. Rarely were sentences for rape or incest convictions longer than a few months. In contrast, several offenders received lengthy prison sentences for the same crimes in Texas border counties. State law defined rape as a felony and required a minimum one-year penitentiary sentence for convicted felons. Local magistrates typically issued sentences ranging from two years to life. Jacinto Torres received a fifteen-year sentence, while Víctor Flores incurred a twenty-five-year sentence for rape. Unlike Mexican courts, Texas tribunals did not offer religious pardons to men convicted of incest. Moreover, convicted felons usually served out the sentences in Texas because escapes from the penitentiary were less likely than from local Mexican prisons. Border county courts occasionally applied severe punishment, especially for nonwhite offenders. Post–Civil War racial antagonisms motivated a local tribunal to order the hanging of two African American Union soldiers convicted of raping a white woman.[37]

Texas considered both attempted rape and aiding and abetting the act of rape to be felonies. Magistrates imposed sentences ranging from two to four years for men guilty of attempted rape. At least two victims sued female accomplices of men accused of committing rape and incest. Kidnapping was also a felony punishable by a penitentiary sentence. A court sentenced the convicted kidnapper Manuel Vega to two years while Félix Martínez received a three-year sentence for "abduction of a female under the age of fourteen for the purposes of prostitution."[38]

Women's efforts to punish assailants revealed their limited power and subordinate position in society. The postwar jurisdictional change did not eliminate women's social problems, but it did give them more options to seek justice. Tejanas increasingly exercised these options to pursue successful convictions for physical or sexual attacks. While women in the villas del norte rarely witnessed assailants receive punishments, their counterparts in Texas saw attackers condemned to multiyear prison or penitentiary sentences. Yet, problems remained for Texas women because lawmakers and the judicial audience (both exclusively male) continued to devalue women's concerns. The judgments of border tribunals mirrored the state lawmakers who authored legislation that set minimal sentences for assaults against women. Local courts issued longer sentences for livestock theft than for sexual assaults. These uneven sentences suggest that men placed a higher value on protecting livestock than on ensuring women's safety.

"Seduction" and Domestic Abuse as Crimes

Despite more success in punishing assailants, tejanas no longer had options available in Mexico. The jurisdictional transfer meant that women lost the benefits of Mexico's protective legislation and the use of courts of conciliation. This loss is apparent in lawsuits over "seduction" and domestic abuse. While Mexico allowed this litigation to be resolved in civil tribunals, Texas adjudicated these cases in criminal courts. The legal difference reflected disparate approaches toward regulating sexuality and domestic relations. In Mexico, the state, church, and community continued to cooperate to enforce morality, while in the United States the regulation of morality by the state had been declining since the late eighteenth century. The market economy, the disestablishment of churches, and the population's increased geographical mobility combined to create less moral regulation by the mid-nineteenth century than in the preindustrial period. This distinction had important consequences, which made tejanas' lives different than the experience of women in Mexico.[39]

U.S. laws on seduction were different from those in Mexico, but the legislation in both nations shared patriarchal ideas about women's inequality and lack of control over their sexuality. The concept of seduction reveals the inherent inequality in each society's ideas about women, which were written into law. Derived from Spanish law, Mexico's protective legislation was based on the belief that women were inferior to men and required protection. The law permitted a woman's family (usually the father) to sue for civil damages if her suitor broke his marriage promise after consummating the relationship. The civil damage amount depended on the woman's class background and her sexual reputation. If premarital sexual relations resulted in pregnancy, the woman's family could also demand child support. In contrast, American seduction legislation had evolved from English common law that assumed a "master/servant" relationship within a patriarchal household, where a father could sue his daughter's lover for "loss of services" if she became pregnant. This legal framework addressed the father's rights (loss of his daughter's labor) while ignoring the daughter's rights and sexual consent. Female moral reformers in the 1830s spearheaded a campaign to convince state legislatures to enact statutes prosecuting male sexual assault, and to redefine seduction as a violation of the public trust. Beginning at midcentury, several states responded by passing legislation that criminalized seduction, and some replaced the original property basis ("loss of services") with a moral basis by recognizing seduction as a personal injury. By allowing women to sue in their own name (without their fathers' intervention), the new seduction statutes gave women more legal agency. This legislation reflected Victorian values maintaining that proper women were "passionless." Because women were expected to exercise sexual restraint, it was believed they would engage in premarital sexual relations only if deceived by men. Such prescribed and idealized sexual norms did not match the reality in the United States during the nineteenth century, when women engaged in a variety of extramarital behavior that confirmed their sexual agency and desire.[40]

Passed in 1858, the Texas law considered seduction a felony punishable by a fine not to exceed five thousand dollars or a penitentiary sentence of two to five years. States such as Texas that enacted criminal statutes for seduction did not allow women to sue for civil damages for their loss of virtue, their decline in status, or the burdens of maternity. Instead, these states punished perpetrators for violating public morals by deceiving women and undermining the marriage institution. The statute defined seduction as having carnal knowledge with an unmarried female under twenty-five years old with a promise to marry. This age requirement implied that the naïvité or immaturity of younger women led them to be deceived into sexual relations, which supported the Victorian idea of women as passive victims. Like Mexican law, a provision in the Texas law allowed the defendant to avoid prosecution if he offered to marry the complainant. A final stipulation exempted perpetrators from prosecution if they were married, and the woman knew of their marital status, which meant that they could not be deceived by a marriage promise. The law reinforced Victorian society's goal of limiting sexual activity within marriage, and protecting the "virtue and class status of unmarried women." The Texas statute, like similar legislation elsewhere, legally inscribed women as victims bereft of sexual agency.[41]

Despite the limitations of Texas's seduction statute, women along the border used it to pressure or punish men who broke marriage promises. By resorting to this law, some tejanas might have accepted Victorian ideals about proper sexual norms. Alternatively, they turned to this legal avenue because suing over a broken marriage promise was familiar from the Mexican period (despite the differences in punishments), and partly as a way of lessening the possible damage to their marriageability. Initiating sexual relations after a marriage pledge was socially accepted in Mexico; this promise, whether made verbally or in writing, had religious and legal obligations. Women who successfully sued their lovers over broken marriage promises could obtain community and church support for their eventual nuptials to others. Such a strategy might have motivated a young tejana who successfully sued a former lover, José María Vargas, in 1866 over a broken marriage pledge. The court found Vargas guilty of seduction and sentenced him to three years in the penitentiary. The claimant might have sought to pressure Vargas into honoring his marriage promise. When this failed, the court's punishment provided a public confirmation that she had been deceived into consenting to sexual relations, and thus her reputation was likely salvaged. In his 1895 trial for seduction, Carlos Guillén successfully avoided punishment by offering to marry Manuela Serrata in court, but she declined. Apparently, her intent was to punish Guillén for breaking his promise, rather than pressure him into honoring it. While the perpetrator escaped punishment, Serrata achieved another goal of preventing the irreparable damage to her marriageability. Eight years later, Serrata found a more suitable partner when she married Luis Gutiérrez in the Catholic Church. Had a claimant become pregnant, she could not obtain child support from her lover because Texas's seduction statute, unlike Mexican law, did not allow for civil damages. The Texas law introduced limitations and financial challenges for betrayed women who became pregnant. As unwed mothers, they were forced to rely on their families for financial assistance or to obtain employment while also caring for their children.[42]

Women also lost some legal avenues to combat domestic abuse because Mexico's courts of conciliation were not available in U.S. courts. Instead, women's first legal option to resolve marital problems was the mayor's court. Sista Villarreal successfully used the mayor's court in 1867 after her wayward husband abandoned their family, leaving them "short of rations." Mayor William Neale pressured Tomás Villarreal to return home by threatening to charge him with vagrancy, but Neale had no power to force him to fulfill marital obligations. Eschewing threats, mayors could impose lengthy prison sentences. While Mexico's courts of conciliation attempted to reconcile feuding couples, the goal of the Texas mayor's court was to punish violations of the law. This distinction had significant legal implications. Women could appeal to the mayor's court to charge their husbands with a crime, but not to salvage their marriages. Others relied on community pressure to reform their marriages, but this avenue lacked the legal backing of Mexico's courts of conciliation. Because tejanos' legal power and social status had diminished under American rule, tejanas adapted the "pluralization of patriarchs" strategy by appealing to Anglo American in-laws, employers, and neighbors.[43]

Although an avenue for conciliation was no longer available, domestic violence victims could more easily punish their husbands in the border counties than in Mexico. However, those who pursued criminal charges risked the possibility that their husbands' punishment might hurt their families' finances. In 1866, Mrs. Echarete protested her husband's arrest even after suffering his vicious assault, which provoked a miscarriage and threatened her life. She convinced the court to dismiss the domestic violence charges against her husband because her family needed his financial support. Two years later, however, he was convicted of theft and sentenced to two years in the penitentiary. A mayor could impose a fine, jail time, or hard labor on public works projects for domestic abuse crimes. Thus, Jesús Ramírez received ten days of public works labor for beating his wife. For domestic abuse involving a felony, officials transferred the cases to district courts, where the accused could receive up to ten years in the penitentiary.[44]

The loss of options to resolve seduction and domestic dispute cases had mixed results for Mexican Texan women. Undoubtedly, some preferred the use of Mexican tribunals to harness community, church, and state pressure on guilty men. Yet, others welcomed the ease with which they could file criminal charges and see assailants punished in Texas. Scattered evidence suggests that tejanas made extralegal appeals for community involvement in resolving these issues. However, for tejanas accustomed to resolving seduction and domestic abuse cases through courts of conciliation, life under U.S. rule had distinct disadvantages.

Marriage Transformed

The institution of marriage is important to nation-states; it plays an important part in molding gender roles for husbands and wives, in the raising of children, and in transferring property to successive generations. Because marriage is critically important to reproducing citizens, and ordering society, nations are invested in creating marriage policy and laws. By regulating marriage, nations sanction certain unions, while prohibiting others as "unnatural." Marriage regulations, therefore, shape societal practices by, for example, promoting monogamy, intraracial unions, and patriarchal households. In the United States, marriage required secular authorization and its rights and responsibilities varied by state. By permitting civil or religious wedding ceremonies, recognizing "common law" marriages, and legitimizing unions certified in other jurisdictions, states encouraged and facilitated marriages. Although they made legal unions easy for some, state laws also made it impossible for others. Texas, for example, enacted an antimiscegenation law (passed in 1837) that barred marriage between individuals of European and African descent, but did not explicitly name Mexicans. Since tejanos were considered legally white, they could marry Anglos or European immigrants but not Africans. By imposing racial prohibitions on marriages (which were absent in nineteenth-century Mexican law), American laws had the potential of altering Mexicans' practice of engaging in marriages that would be considered racially mixed in the United States. However, antimiscegenation laws were rarely applied to Mexicans who married individuals of African ancestry (including *afromestizos* [Mexicans with African ancestry]) because most Mexicans were viewed as nonwhite. In early nineteenth-century Mexico, the Catholic Church had sole authority to sanction marriage, and was the only recognized church. Therefore, when the Rio Grande settlements came under American control in 1848, marriage options and religious choices expanded. Each development would alter local society.[45]

As Texas residents, women in the Rio Grande region benefited from the state's adoption of aspects of Mexican law on family relationships, including marriage. Their legal rights depended on their age and marital status. Before reaching the age of maturity (twenty-one years), young people were under the control of their fathers or guardians. Unmarried adult women had the right to establish contracts, sue and be sued in court, control and own their property, and choose their home without male interference. Upon marriage, women obtained legal emancipation regardless of their age. As in other southwestern states ceded by Mexico, married women in Texas exercised greater rights than married women elsewhere in the United States. Even after the passage of "married women's property" laws from the 1830s to 1870s, which gave married women in other states similar rights to those enjoyed by Texas women, the latter enjoyed more property rights.[46]

Texas women lost rights with marriage and exercised significantly fewer legal rights than did married men. However, unlike in other parts of the United States (including territorial New Mexico), married women did not become *feme coverts* (women who were legally subsumed under their husbands concerning their rights of person and property). Instead, Texas, like California, continued the Spanish practice of giving married women specific, but limited, rights. After 1840, married women could own separate property and share equally with their husbands in the profits obtained during marriage. Husbands had the right to manage the couples' separate and community property, but could not sell their wives' property without permission. In turn, wives could not sell their real estate, stock, or bonds without their husbands' permission. However, women could legally challenge their husbands' control of property if the men mismanaged it. If widowed, women had sole custody of their children. Adult women could petition the state to become legal guardians or to adopt children. After 1856, single and married women obtained the right to compose their own wills and, therefore, choose their legal heirs. These rights gave them more independence than minors, but less than single adult men. Whereas married women could only establish contracts to which they were specifically entitled, married men could establish any contract unless expressly forbidden. As in Mexico, marital regulations in Texas structured gendered inequality by giving husbands more property and legal rights, and constructing wives as dependent on husbands as providers.[47]

For couples along the Rio Grande, a significant transformation in 1848 was the transfer of control over marriage from Mexican ecclesiastical authorities to U.S. civilian officials. Border residents witnessed the Catholic Church's loss of power over matrimonial matters in the United States, but its continued control over marriage in Mexico. Couples in the United States, unlike in Mexico, could marry through various churches (whose authorities officiated with state permission) or opt for a civil ceremony before a justice of the peace or a district judge. Some Protestant churches allowed individuals of different faiths to marry; Mexico's Catholic Church did not allow marriage to non-Catholics. Moreover, a civil ceremony provided more freedom than a religious one because some churches prohibited divorced members from remarrying as long as their ex-spouse lived.

A principal obstacle for tejanos wishing to marry in a religious ceremony was the clergy's unavailability. Couples often married outside of the Catholic Church because priests were absent for long periods from Mexican Texan communities. Jurisdictional changes contributed to the problem as priests based in the United States replaced Catholic officials based in Mexico. After the war, several religious orders from the United States faced the arduous task of providing clergy to a vast area. The Catholic Church faced a daunting challenge because many tejanos, who were predominantly Catholic, lived in the countryside—far removed from the towns' churches. Priests traveled long distances on horseback, while under constant risk of Indian attacks, to minister to tejanos. Small clergy numbers exacerbated these problems; twelve priests attended to approximately twenty thousand Catholics in the state in 1849. Many rural residents met with a priest only a few times a year. Moreover, churches were frequently without a permanent priest, and some clergy often expressed displeasure at working among tejanos—especially in isolated areas. Although the border counties were remote, they boasted more Catholics (some 10,500) than the city of San Antonio, which had about seven thousand worshipers.[48]

A jurisdictional change within the Catholic Church further complicated parishioners' choices. The U.S. Diocese, based in Galveston, gained jurisdiction over churches on the left bank of the Rio Grande from the Mexican Diocese, based in Monterrey, in 1848. Most newly established border towns, however, lacked priests and churches. This changed with the arrival of French priests, from the Oblates of Mary Immaculate, who built a modest chapel in Brownsville in 1849. Tejano parishioners adjusted slowly to the French clergy. Several couples, such as Néstor Treviño and María Rita Garza, crossed into Mexico to marry instead of having French priests officiate at their weddings. By contrast, Laredo already had an established church presided over by José Trinidad García, a Mexican priest, who remained in his position until 1851 (by permission of the Texas bishop John Odin). In 1853, two French priests, Louis Marie Planchet and Louis Claude Dumas, took over Laredo's parish. Young and energetic, Planchet and Dumas adapted well to the cultural conditions along the border. They learned Spanish, retained some Mexican Catholic traditions, and were well received by the town's parishioners.[49]

Unlike Laredo's young French priests, many non-Mexican clergy complained bitterly about their assignments to remote border counties and expressed anti-Mexican prejudices. Most clergy were foreign-born Europeans with limited knowledge of the Spanish language and of Mexican Catholic practices. A French Oblate missionary, Augustin Gaudet, Brownsville's father superior (1857–74), displayed extreme antipathy toward Mexican Texans. Gaudet never learned Spanish and barely spoke English during his seventeen-year tenure. The clerics who replaced Gaudet were no more enthusiastic. Several considered their appointments to south Texas to be "the worst sentence" they could receive. Dominic Manucy believed "the Catholics were almost exclusively *greaser* Mexicans—cattlemen and thieves."

Another priest expressed relief when tejanos fled across the Rio Grande to escape the anti-Mexican climate in the Texas Revolution's aftermath. Instead of having to minister to tejanos with "thin" Catholic practices, the priest reasoned, their departure would enable him to work among non-Mexican parishioners. Other French-born priests frequently complained about Mexican Texans' "inadequate" Catholic practices. Typical was the opinion of the former prefect apostolic John Timon, who believed "the poor Mexicans would die for their religion, yet they hardly knew what their religion was." Even an ally of tejanos, Emmanuel Domenech, complained about how "the religion of the great majority is very superficial . . . and the most essential duties of a Christian neglected."[50]

Tejanos' perceived lack of religious devotion was partly explained by their poverty. A few priests acknowledged that their parishioners neglected religious weddings and baptisms because of their inability to pay clergy. During a visit to Laredo in 1850, Bishop Odin excused a poor couple from paying wedding fees. Soon other clergy followed his example. Bishop Pedro Verdaguer observed that some priests did not charge for marriage ceremonies lest couples marry in civil courts. Other Oblate fathers, however, were disconnected and indifferent. Manucy acknowledged that his peers' inability to speak Spanish impeded their ministering efforts. Yet, he could not understand the parishioners' low level of tithing because he ignored the population's poverty.[51]

The Catholic Church's challenges presented an opening for Protestant outreach efforts. Border residents began attending Protestant services within a year of annexation by the United States. Construction of Protestant churches took time, as did the arrival of full-time ministers to lead them. In the meantime, itinerant preachers visited and at least one americano began a Sunday school. Early Protestant efforts focused on Cameron County, given its higher concentration of Anglos, and Brownsville's strategic location from which to launch outreach into Mexico. As elsewhere in the American West, the main advocates for construction of Protestant churches were americanas. By the early 1850s, ministers from Methodist, Episcopal, and Presbyterian denominations had arrived with plans for constructing churches.[52]

Protestants found few Mexican Texans willing to convert. In 1849, R. N. Stansbury began a Methodist Sunday school in Brownsville, and the following year had seventy-two students (half were tejanos) and sixteen teachers. Although Mexican Texans sent their children to the Sunday school for English-language instruction, they shunned its religious teachings. Their discerning use of language instruction was similar to Mexican Americans' selective adaptation of Americanization programs elsewhere in the American West. In 1859, Brownsville's Methodist Church struggled with eight members and one probationer. Methodists in Laredo, Rio Grande City, and Eagle Pass fared even worse; their projected missions were not fully staffed until the 1870s. The Episcopalians and Presbyterians established churches in Brownsville, but did not expand to other border towns until the twentieth century.[53]

Protestant ministers, like their Catholic counterparts, complained about being stationed in a remote region and among an "inferior" Mexican Texan population. Infused with the ideas of Manifest Destiny, Protestant clergy accepted the commonly held American views of Mexicans as indolent, corrupt, filthy, immoral, and racially degenerate. Moreover, Protestant ministers blamed Mexicans' perceived failings on their "superstitious" beliefs in Catholic saints. One missionary, Dr. Baker, argued that the region was ripe for Protestant conversion. However, his characterization of tejanos as "heathens" probably made his intended audience somewhat dubious. According to Baker, "Romanism [Catholicism], among the Mexicans, is only another form of paganism, and very many of these poor deluded creatures greatly desire to learn our language and religion too!" Other missionaries were no less sanguine about race. The Methodist minister Oscar M. Addison described Brownsville's Mexicans as "a class inferior to common niggers." These religious and racial views undoubtedly hampered Protestant outreach efforts.[54]

Protestants did make some gains through interethnic marriages in which Mexican Texan spouses converted. In Cameron County, nineteen of twenty-six interethnic marriages occurred in Protestant churches or in civil ceremonies during the first four years of rule by the United States. J. W. Hill and Hannah Zarate, one such interethnic couple, wed in a Methodist ceremony. The patterns of interethnic unions varied widely across the border counties. Only one interethnic couple married during the same period in Webb County, and they wed in the Catholic Church. A few Protestant marriages involved interfaith couples in Mexico who could not marry in the Catholic Church. Illustrative were Dr. Grayson Prevost and Doña Mariana Cosio, who had produced offspring but had to cross the Rio Grande to marry in Brownsville's Presbyterian Church in 1850. Prevost was unwilling to convert to Catholicism but wished to legitimize their children. Without a nearby Protestant church, interfaith couples in Webb County could marry in a civil or Catholic ceremony after obtaining a dispensation. Unlike Mexico's Catholic Church, Texas's Catholic Church routinely offered dispensations for couples of different religions. Adolpho Staacke and Alejandra Pérez obtained such a dispensation to marry in an 1867 Catholic ceremony.[55]

Individuals had various marriage choices depending on their county of residence. Until 1878, the only alternative to a Catholic wedding in Webb County was a civil ceremony. Not surprisingly, the vast majority (613) of weddings took place in the Catholic Church (where border priests based in the United States gave dispensations to non-Catholic spouses), while only sixty-four occurred in civil courts between 1848 and 1877. No Protestant weddings occurred in Laredo until 1878, when two Mexican couples wed in the Methodist Church. Residents in Hidalgo, Starr, and Zapata Counties were also limited to Catholic or civil ceremonies until the late nineteenth century. Couples in Cameron County, however, had more options. They could choose between a civil, Catholic, Presbyterian, or Methodist wedding. From 1848 to 1860, most couples (81 of 142) wed in religious ceremonies, while sixty-one married in civil ceremonies. Among religious weddings, most (53) occurred in the Catholic Church, followed by the Presbyterian (20) and Methodist (8) churches.[56]

Initially, interethnic marriages were mostly between newly arrived americanos and elite tejanas. This pattern is partly explained by local demographics. As elsewhere in the American Southwest, single americanos outnumbered unmarried americanas, and thus were more likely to intermarry. Male newcomers mostly wed elite tejanas because the wealthy were seen as white, while poor Mexican women were racialized as nonwhite. Intermarriage allowed Anglo men to obtain land, social connections, and political influence by becoming part of their wives' extended family. Such acculturation occurred in south Texas, when male newcomers became "Mexicanized" as a result of their marriage to local tejanas. This acculturation was critical for male newcomers, especially in regions with majority Mexican populations, such as south Texas. This trend mirrored the intermarriage patterns found in Arizona, California, and New Mexico. Such marriages, however, did not necessarily signal interethnic harmony. Along the Rio Grande, elite tejanas often married americanos—family ties with Anglos providing some protection from ethnic violence and land loss. Yet, it is worth nothing, as the historian Deena González reminds us for New Mexico, that the majority of Mexicans continued marrying other Mexicans.[57]

A different intermarriage pattern emerged in Hidalgo County, where Mexican Texans and African Americans intermarried. In the 1850s, Matilde Hicks, of French and Cherokee ancestry, and Silvia Hector, a former

11. Born in Alabama in 1848, Louisa Singleterry moved to Hidalgo County with her parents at age seven and lived in a community of ethnically mixed families. Classified as a mulato in the 1860 census, Louisa married L. H. Box in 1874. L. H. Box, classified as white in the 1880 census, worked as U.S. deputy collector of customs. Louisa Singleterry, circa 1870s. Courtesy of Museum of South Texas History, Edinburg, Texas.

slave, arrived in Hidalgo County accompanying their husbands, Nathaniel Jackson, a Cherokee Indian, and John F. Webber, a white man who settled in the area. Their ranches became refuge communities for escaped and freed slaves before the Civil War. As more African Americans arrived, the number of mixed-race and black offspring increased, augmenting the community's *mestizaje*. From 1852 to 1888, the community witnessed eleven unions between African Americans and Mexican Texans (five women and six men), and five marriages between African American women and Anglo American men (see, e.g., figure 11). In addition, there were ten marriages of mixed-raced individuals and five endogamous unions of African Americans. Unlike marriages between americanos and tejanas, the marriages between African Americans and tejanos did not involve the elite. Although some unions violated the state's antimiscegenation laws, the spouses' class background partly explains why local authorities did not prosecute them. Poor couples were likely not prone to inheritance disputes, which triggered appeals to antimiscegenation statutes. Additionally, poor tejanos were usually seen as nonwhite and therefore not subject to enforcement. Finally, local officials were unlikely to apply antimiscegenation prohibitions to

12. Martin Jackson, son of Nathaniel Jackson and Matilde Hicks, was born in 1837 in Alabama. Martin, whose ancestry was African American and Native American, married Esperidonia Carillo in 1882 in Reynosa. Subsequently they lived in Hidalgo County and raised eleven children. Martin Jackson, circa 1900 to 1910. Courtesy of Museum of South Texas History, Edinburg, Texas.

marriages that local residents readily accepted as part of Mexican cultural tradition.[58]

Residents intermarried throughout the nineteenth century, reflecting population growth and the persistent acculturation of newcomers. Tejanas continued intermarrying in greater numbers than tejanos. In Hidalgo County, between 1880 and 1900, thirty-four tejanas and twenty-three tejanos married Anglo American, mixed, or African American spouses. Cameron County witnessed a similar pattern as thirty-five interethnic unions (involving twenty-one tejanas and fourteen tejanos) occurred between 1883 and 1887. The most significant change was the increasing number of exogamous marriages between tejanos and americanas. The overall intermarriage patterns suggest that Anglos and African Americans (see figure 12) were becoming more acculturated to tejano society. The persistence of intermarriage in the border counties, as opposed to its decline in other parts of the American Southwest and elsewhere in Texas, suggests that such unions remained socially accepted, and continued to acculturate newcomers to local communities as well as Mexicans Texans to the larger American society.[59]

As intermarriage continued, religious weddings underwent a transformation. The changes again varied by county. Protestant weddings in Webb County increased after the Methodists established a church in 1878. The percentage of civil marriages also rose gradually in the 1880s. While residents of Webb County increasingly chose non-Catholic ceremonies, residents of Cameron County began favoring religious weddings. Although interethnic couples initially chose civil or Protestant ceremonies, most interethnic marriages were in Catholic ceremonies by the 1880s. This trend suggests parishioners' increasing comfort level with foreign priests, and the clerics' gradual acculturation to border society. From 1883 to 1887, Catholic clergy officiated over all but four of the religious ceremonies (434) in Cameron County out of 618 total weddings.[60]

The jurisdictional changes introduced by American annexation helped shape marriage patterns in the border counties. Mexican Texans increasingly chose partners of different ethnic backgrounds, leading to an upswing in intermarriage. The arrival of Anglo, African American, and European newcomers contributed to this growth, as did the civil control over marriage. The establishment of churches of various denominations and the availability of civil weddings allowed interfaith couples to wed, which likely motivated Catholic clergy to permit parishioners to marry partners of different faiths. Initially, tejanas participated in exogamous marriages more than tejanos. By the end of the nineteenth century, intermarriage across ethnic and faith divides had become common among Mexican Texan women and men in the border counties. This pattern illustrates their growing acculturation to American society, and their growing difference with their Mexican counterparts across the Rio Grande.

The Option of Real Divorce

While Texas women's marital rights resembled rights in Mexico, their ability to end their marriages was quite distinct. Under American rule, Mexican Texan women obtained the ability to permanently end their marriages. By taking advantage of this new right, tejanas abandoned patriarchal beliefs that had forced them to endure abusive, neglectful, or philandering husbands. Divorce, however, was a complicated benefit. Some women might have preferred to legally reconcile their marriages rather than ending them and, hence, assuming sole responsibility for supporting and raising their children. Under American rule, however, such women lost the use of courts

TABLE 9. Divorce Lawsuits by Gender, 1849–1900

Years	Number of lawsuits	Women as plaintiffs	Men as plaintiffs	Successful lawsuits (filed by women: filed by men)[a]
1849–1863	18	11	7	10 : 3
1864–1878	50	32	18	27 : 13
1879–1893	135	61	74	49 : 59
1894–1900	117	40	77	31 : 55

Sources: CCDCM; HCDCM; WCDCM; SCDCM; ZCDCM; CCMR; HCMR; WCMR; SCMR; ZCMR.
[a] Success rates are discussed in the chapter 5 text.

of conciliation to preserve their marriages. For others in unsalvageable marriages, filing for a permanent divorce in civil court was an absolute advantage over the difficult and lengthy process of obtaining a legal separation in Mexico through civil and ecclesiastical tribunals.

By 1848, when the lower Rio Grande region became part of Texas, the state's divorce laws had become more liberal and accessible. Texas initially allowed only a legislative divorce, which involved a petitioner asking the state legislature for a decree, and favored wealthy men with political connections. District courts obtained jurisdiction over civil divorce in 1837. Four years later, the state established precise grounds for granting a divorce, which included adultery, abandonment, and cruel treatment, all of which "made living together insupportable." Violence was not an acceptable cause unless "it was a 'serious' danger and might happen again." These stipulations made civil divorce increasingly popular along the border (see table 9). The rights that women exercised in marriage are often missing in historical records until marriages developed problems and lawsuits ensued. Although problematic because they are mainly adversarial, divorce lawsuits can serve as a window into marital relations.[61]

Mexican Texans who divorced in Texas shared some experiences with those attempting legal separations in Mexico. Husbands continued to hold an advantage during court proceedings because they controlled the couple's property until the divorce was finalized. The judicial audience—judges, jurors, lawyers, and interpreters—in Texas remained elite and male. Its ethnic composition, however, changed due to the more prominent representation of Anglos. Like their counterparts in Mexico, Texas women sought separations when their husbands committed adultery, inflicted physical abuse, or failed to provide financial support. The main motivation for husbands' filing separation lawsuits remained abandonment. As in Mexico, a spouse found guilty of adultery lost child custody. Moreover, plaintiffs continued to charge their spouses with multiple marital faults in their separation lawsuits.[62]

Women pursuing divorces in Texas enjoyed more freedom than did their counterparts in Mexico. Although they struggled to obtain a temporary or permanent legal separation in Mexico, women in Texas could divorce relatively easily. While their divorce lawsuits were pending in Texas, women arranged their own lodging unlike women in Mexico who were placed in *depósito* (a safe house). Many plaintiffs were living apart from their spouses, either with relatives or alone with minor children. The process was speedier in Texas because petitioners filed for divorce only in civil court, while those in Mexico were required to consult civil authorities before petitioning the ecclesiastical court. Moreover, the Catholic Church no longer held any legal influence on civil divorce proceedings in Texas. Several couples divorced within a year of marriage, an impossible outcome in Mexico, where courts of conciliation required disgruntled spouses to attempt reconciliation twice. Once the trial began in Texas, most verdicts followed quickly, with some decisions granted within a day. Unlike petitions in Mexico, where legal separations were rare, most divorce lawsuits in the border counties were successful. Among 320 divorce petitions filed between 1848 and 1900, 247 (77.2 percent) were successful, 10 were denied, 22 were dropped, and 22 were dismissed. Among the remaining 19 cases, 2 were probably successful because the defendants defaulted, but the resolution of the others is unclear, because the cases were changed to another county or the documentation ended.[63]

Few litigants successfully divorced by charging adultery, the most difficult charge to prove in court. If a couple had married elsewhere, Texas law required that they be state residents when the adultery occurred to accept infidelity as grounds for divorce. As in Mexico, neither an uncorroborated charge nor a spouse's admission of guilt was admissible. A third-party witness was required to verify adultery. This provision, similar to a stipulation in Mexican ecclesiastical law, sought to discourage spouses from lying about an extramarital affair in order to dissolve a marriage. Texas law also required that a noninvolved witness substantiate the charges to prevent a spouse from hiring a third party to seduce their partner into committing adultery. Among 320 petitions for divorce, only 15 successfully charged adultery. Nine defendants defaulted; some did not contest the charges, because they were living with their lovers. This pattern suggests that some

13. Louis and Bertha De Planque. Circa 1866. Louis De Planque, born in Prussia to French parents, worked as a photographer in Brownsville and Matamoros during the mid-1860s. In 1863, Louis married Bertha Cramer in Houston, and arrived in Matamoros in 1864. Louis secured a divorce from Bertha, charging adultery, on 21 August 1868 in Cameron County. Eight days later he married Eugenia Jenny Robert, born in France, before Justice of the Peace Israel B. Bigelow. Courtesy of the Brownsville Historical Association, Brownsville, Texas.

spouses were cohabitating with their preferred partner after leaving their legal spouse's residence. Several news items confirm this pattern. Plaintiffs occasionally accused their spouses of living in adultery or detailed their spouse's adulterous affairs in child custody lawsuits. Pascual Gonzales charged his wife, Trinidad Rivero, with adultery to successfully remove their daughter from her care.[64]

The difficulty of proving adultery led spouses to use other grounds to sue for divorce. Because unfaithful spouses had often left their homes, plaintiffs often alleged abandonment, cruel treatment, or multiple failings. Antonio Malleth charged adultery and abandonment to divorce Lorenza Malleth, who defaulted. Failing to prove adultery, Antonio successfully divorced on abandonment grounds. Women benefited from filing multiple charges because Texas courts enforced a double standard in divorce cases charging adultery. A man could obtain a divorce if "his wife shall have been taken in adultery" in a single instance (see figure 13). In contrast, a woman could obtain a divorce only if she proved her husband "*lived* in adultery with another woman."[65]

Multiple charges increased the likelihood of a successful divorce, but they were also symptomatic of a poor marriage. Mary Ghalson endured a terrible marriage until she successfully sued for divorce in 1862 on grounds of adultery and cruel treatment. James Ghalson had contracted a venereal disease, three witnesses argued, from prostitutes he met at "fandangos, bawdy houses, and other places where there were loose women." They characterized James, an army deserter, as an undependable person with no means of supporting his family. He had committed several burglaries and had been indicted for theft. After leaving him, Mary became solely responsible for the care and maintenance of the couple's four children by milking cows and laboring at other "industrious pursuits" at her home. The jury reached a quick verdict, dissolving the marriage because of the husband's excesses, which included "a series of infamous acts, outrageous conduct, and cruel treatment." Further, they granted Mary sole custody of the children and prohibited James from interfering in the children's upbringing.[66]

As the Ghalson case illustrates, women could secure divorces in Texas easier than in Mexico. Because Texas law was vague about the exact definition of "cruel treatment" as a reason for divorce, judges could interpret the provision liberally to include both physical and mental abuse. Moreover, a spouse could charge cruel treatment even if the couple were not state residents when the mistreatment occurred. Magistrates admitted a plaintiff's petition as valid if she/he had a reasonable fear about incurring bodily harm or mental anguish. A woman could charge mental cruelty if her husband wrongly accused her of infidelity in public but failed to prove his accusation. Men did not have a similar recourse. Spouses could also be held liable for mental anguish if they repeatedly insulted, outraged, or provoked their partner. Plaintiffs who accused their spouses of cruel treatment usually cited various failings, including drunkenness, criminal activities, adulterous relationships, and abandonment. Most secured divorces because Texas magistrates, unlike judges in Mexico, did not attempt to persuade spouses to reconcile. It was common for Mexican courts to reunite couples despite a pattern of abuse. Thus, the mid-nineteenth-century jurisdictional change gave tejanas more freedom to escape domestic violence. Court records verify that several tejana border residents took advantage of this increased freedom to divorce and leave abusive marriages, a choice not available to their counterparts in Mexico.[67]

Most successful divorce litigants charged their spouses with abandonment because it was the easiest charge to prove. Texas law defined abandonment as physical separation with an intention to leave the marriage. Plaintiffs were required to wait three years after the deserting spouse left their home before filing suit. The three-year period could be economically devastating: a family was often in financial hardship when a husband left, the wife lacked legal rights to the couple's property, and a husband could disappear with the profits from the sale of community property. The plaintiff could not be responsible for causing the separation, but a wife who left her husband to escape his cruelty could sue for divorce based on abandonment if she remained separated from him for three years. This provision and the fact that Texas officials, unlike Mexican authorities, could not force a wife to live with her husband, allowed women to successfully leave an abusive marriage. Wives had greater freedom in Texas than their counterparts in California, where as in Mexico courts could force women to reunite with their husbands. Texas law allowed a new resident to file for divorce based on abandonment even if the couple was not living in Texas when the abandonment began. Courts placed notices in local newspapers to allow a defendant an opportunity to contest the lawsuit. The deserting spouse usually defaulted, after which the court granted the divorce. Abandonment cases made up 54 percent of the divorce cases (seventy-six men and ninety-eight women were defendants). The high number of abandoned marriages in the border counties parallels the desertion trends in other parts of the nation.[68]

Abandoned spouses had more options to end their marriages in Texas than in Mexico. An abandoned wife in Mexico was required to prove that reconciliation was impossible in order to obtain a legal separation, thereby reclaiming physical independence and financial control. An abandoned husband retained control of the couple's property, but he too had to prove that his marriage was irreconcilable should he wish to obtain a legal separation. In either case, the couple remained married; absolute divorce was not allowed. In contrast, abandoned spouses in Texas could divorce and sever all links to their wayward partners. Divorce permitted an abandoned wife to reclaim her financial independence, receive child custody, and hold the option to remarry. These options were critical for wives whose husbands were philanderers, physically abusive, or financially unsupportive. In 1893, Virginia Fernández, a woman of mixed Mexican and Anglo American ancestry, successfully claimed abandonment to divorce José Leonardo Fernández. She reclaimed her maiden name of Campbell, and obtained custody of her four minor children. Within a year, she had married Manuel Cavazos in a civil ceremony.[69]

Several women had accompanied husbands to the border region but eventually returned to their former residences because they were unhappy with the region's rustic environment. Most spouses who abandoned their husbands migrated to another area within the state, moved elsewhere in the United States, or crossed the border into Mexico. A few took more drastic measures. Joseph Ximénez filed one of the most unusual abandonment cases in 1868. His wife, Aurelia Ximénez, had remained at their New Orleans home, refusing to join him after he moved to the border region in the early 1860s. Only after repeated requests did Aurelia join Joseph in Bagdad, Tamaulipas, where he, like many local merchants, had relocated during the American Civil War. According to Joseph, Aurelia became increasingly unfriendly, quarrelsome, and disgruntled. Life in the isolated outpost of Bagdad was unquestionably harder and less cosmopolitan than Aurelia's experience in New Orleans. Dissatisfied with her living arrangements, she eventually returned to Louisiana but remained unhappy. She attempted to convince Joseph to accompany her to France, but failed. Undeterred, Aurelia left without him to visit the World's Exposition in Paris. He subsequently filed for divorce in Cameron County. Although most women who abandoned their husbands did not have Aurelia's economic resources, they probably shared a similar desire to stop sacrificing their lives for a partner who could not provide a comfortable or happy home.[70]

Among those divorcing in Texas were couples who had recently become residents. Like other western states, Texas implemented liberal residency requirements to make it easier for newcomers to vote. Readily available residency, in turn, made divorce easier. By the mid-1880s, Texas consistently ranked among the top ten divorce-granting states, and occasionally it was in the top five states. The state's high divorce rate was part of a larger trend. Throughout the nineteenth century, the national divorce rate increased five times faster than the nation's population growth rate. The lax requirements increased the so-called interstate divorce trade, as when, for instance, residents of neighboring states moved to Texas to end their marriages. Others divorced after the state's boundaries expanded to include their settlements. Some couples married in the villas del norte while under Mexican jurisdiction and later divorced in a border town under American jurisdiction. María de las Nieves Salinas married Pablo José Mendiola in 1830 and lived with him in Laredo until 1857, when she sued for divorce in an American court. Despite the divorce, the parents remained observant Catholics and guided their children to marry in the same Catholic parish at which they had married.[71]

The "divorce trade" adopted international dimensions along the United States–Mexico border as a growing number of couples married in Mexico and later divorced in Texas. Several couples, including Francisco Abrego and Isabel Valdez Abrego, divorced within a few years of immigrating to the United States and some later remarried, demonstrating their acculturation to U.S. society. Others moved back and forth across the border to marry or divorce where convenient. This mobility also fits a national pattern of frequent moves by spouses who divorced or self-divorced and later remarried (often committing bigamy) in a complex "geography of remarriage" that the historian Hendrik Hartog identifies for the nineteenth century. In 1852, a sixteen-year-old, Antonia Díaz, and a twenty-nine-year-old, Felipe Cuellar, traveled from their homes in Carrizo, Texas, across the Rio Grande to Guerrero, Tamaulipas, to be married. They wed in Mexico because Guerrero was the site of the nearest Catholic Church and probably the home of some relatives. Four years removed from annexation by the United States, Carrizo did not have a church yet. The couple established a home in Texas, where they had two children who died shortly after birth. A third child, Josefina, was born in 1859. In that year, Felipe abandoned Antonia and returned to Mexico, whereupon Antonia filed for divorce in Zapata County. Their marriage had dissolved, according to Antonia, because Felipe "was guilty of excesses, cruel treatment, and outrages toward her of such a character as to render their living together insupportable." Antonia remained in Texas and gave birth to another daughter in 1863. As a single mother, she supported her surviving children as a seamstress, and witnessed Josefina marry in Mexico in 1874.[72]

The relatively mild consequences of divorce in Texas partially explain its frequency. A guilty spouse in Mexico was forced to pay court costs, relinquish child custody, and surrender ownership of community property. Mexican courts forced a guilty husband to support his family, while a guilty wife forfeited the right to her husband's financial support and ownership of her dowry. Although Texas courts charged the losing party with litigation expenses, they avoided harsh punishments unless a spouse was guilty of adultery or cruel treatment. In the border counties, only nineteen divorce litigants successfully charged adultery or cruelty, so most losing litigants escaped harsh legal punishments. A spouse found guilty of adultery forfeited his or her right to any community property and usually lost child custody. The court granted exclusive custody to a litigant only when a spouse was guilty of cruelty. If divorce resulted from abandonment, however, the losing party did not necessarily forfeit child custody.[73]

Child custody and alimony were contentious issues that highlighted male privilege. Judges usually granted women child custody, but occasionally they stipulated that former husbands retain visitation rights. The difficulty of supporting a family as a single mother is painfully clear from child custody lawsuits. Divorced mothers with little or no property often fell into poverty without a husband's support. Their former husbands could make their problems worse by suing them for custody, charging that the children were living in poverty. José Toribio Rodríguez pursued this tactic successfully by suing his ex-wife, Juana López, for custody. The court determined that López was living in poverty and was "unable and unfit" to care for her three minor children.[74]

Women's difficulty in securing alimony illustrates how state laws and local courts ensured their legal subordination. While divorce lawsuits were pending, Texas law allowed litigants to file for alimony. These support payments were minimal and difficult to procure, so litigants often relied on relatives for additional aid. Women were especially vulnerable because their husbands controlled the property and without their husbands' permission, they could not enter into any legally binding contracts. Men could use this power to pressure their wives to drop their suits. This was Frederick Schreck's strategy when he placed a newspaper announcement stating, "all persons are hereby notified and warned not to harbor or credit my aforesaid wife [Adela Chano de Schreck] on my account, as I will not be responsible for, or pay any debt of her contracting from and after this date." Despite Frederick's legal maneuvering, Adela persevered to obtain a divorce and child custody in 1869; she remarried (to John Mix, a Prussian immigrant) within seven months. Once a divorce was final, alimony payments were no longer required. Among the 320 divorce petitions, only eight women (and one man) secured alimony payments. Some women declined to file for alimony because litigants who did so were more likely to confront countercharges from their husbands, to be denied divorce, or to endure slower divorce litigation while the alimony was contested. Additionally, local tribunals (like courts throughout the nation) struggled to enforce alimony because husbands often moved away after deserting their marriages. Thus, women's success in securing divorces despite enduring a lack of alimony (and accompanying economic hardships) underscores their determination to abandon abusive marriages.[75]

In Texas, women gained greater advantages from divorce than did men. Divorcées usually regained legal control over their separate property and their share of community property. They could also litigate and establish contracts freely. After her divorce, María de las Nieves Salinas became a successful trader with her share of community property. Although she obtained financial independence, the divorce made her solely responsible for raising and supporting two minor children. Regaining control of property was critical for elite and middling women to prevent their spouses from mismanaging or selling it. For poor women, divorce gave them legal and economic independence to survive as single heads of households. In some border counties, female-headed households accounted for over 19 percent of all Mexican Texan households. As head of her household twelve years after her divorce, Juana Barbosa owned a house (where she took in boarders) and worked as a washerwoman to support three children.[76]

Divorce was mainly a woman's remedy until 1879, when men became the majority of litigants. This trend is partially explained by a change in Texas divorce law that led magistrates to give custody of younger children to mothers and custody of older boys to fathers. Subsequently, men were plaintiffs in thirty of sixty-two lawsuits involving child custody; twenty-five men received full custody, two split custody with their ex-spouses, and one obtained visitation rights. However, men also initiated divorces to leave unhappy marriages, abandon aging wives, or absolve themselves of family responsibilities. After 1879, men's divorce petitions (151) outnumbered women's suits (101). While several men obtained legal custody, some ex-wives ultimately raised the couple's children, undoubtedly after the men struggled with child care as single parents. Divorced fathers also turned to their own parents for help in raising children of whom they had custody.[77]

Anglos were overrepresented as divorce litigants, while Mexican Texans were underrepresented. Although americanos were a minority (from 2 percent to 16 percent) of the border counties' population, they were over one-third of all divorce litigants (see "Anglo and Europeans" in table 10)—a result explained by their familiarity with the legal system and divorce procedures. Americanos outnumbered americanas in both the border counties' general population and as litigants. Anglo American women were more likely to be plaintiffs than defendants, which indicates that they sought official divorces before leaving marriages. In most cases involving female plaintiffs (73 of 144), husbands defaulted, so these women divorced to legally extricate themselves from a marriage that had probably already ended. Mexican Texans accounted for less than two-thirds of all divorce

TABLE 10. Distribution of Divorce Litigants by Ethnicity and Gender, 1849–1900

	Total (by litigant category and total ethnicity)[a]	Percent by ethnicity (out of total plaintiffs, defendants, and litigants)	Women	Percent of women by ethnicity (out of total female litigants)	Men	Percent of men by ethnicity (out of total male litigants)
Mexican Texan plaintiffs	194	(60.6%)	83	(25.9%)	111	(34.7%)
Mexican Texan defendants	206	(64.4%)	134	(41.9%)	72	(22.5%)
Total Mexican Texans	400	(62.5%)	217	(67.8%)	183	(57.2%)
Anglo or European plaintiffs	123	(38.4%)	61	(19.1%)	62	(19.4%)
Anglo or European defendants	113	(35.3%)	41	(12.8%)	72	(22.5%)
Total Anglo and Europeans	236	(36.9%)	102	(31.8%)	134	(41.9%)
African American plaintiffs	3	(0.9%)	0	(0%)	3	(0.9%)
African American defendants	1	(0.3%)	1	(0.3%)	0	(0%)
Total African Americans	4	(1.3%)	1	(0.3%)	3	(0.9%)

Sources: CCDCM; HCDCM; WCDCM; SCDCM; ZCDCM; USCP 1850–1900.

Total lawsuits = 320 (see table 9).

litigants, which was lower than their proportion of the population (from 77 percent to 96 percent). Their underrepresentation might be the result of tejanos' lack of familiarity with the American legal system or their preference for self-divorce. Tejanas were mostly defendants while tejanos were mainly plaintiffs, which suggest men's greater familiarity with the courts. Over half of tejana defendants (78 of 134, or 58.2 percent) defaulted, which indicates that they had self-divorced.[78]

Divorce petitions from the border counties demonstrate changes in the legal expectations for marital relations. As in Mexico, divorce litigation in Texas reflected gendered marital expectations; that is, wives were responsible for child care and housework, while men were accountable for financial support. However, spouses rarely followed a domestic ideal that separated their roles into distinct spheres. In addition to completing domestic duties, many women worked to supplement their husbands' income. Marriages were far from the companionate ideal that scholars have described for some middle-class spouses. Nevertheless, a change occurred in the manner that spouses described their marital roles. Divorce petitions no longer mentioned wives' absolute subordination to their husbands—an essential element in marital dispute cases in Mexico. In legal records, at least, women no longer had to profess subservience in marriage in order to fulfill society's expectations. Moreover, women sought divorce for reasons other than cruel treatment, in contrast to the majority of wives in Mexico. The large number of abandonment cases suggests that deserted wives could gain legal redress under Texas law by divorcing, and thus regain financial and legal independence from absent husbands. Women's resolve to file for divorce or abandon a troubled marriage demonstrates what the historian Robert Griswold describes as a movement toward "self-assertion and a sense of personal efficacy."[79]

Women in the border counties gained the ability to remarry after a divorce, an option unavailable in Mexico. Of course, not all divorced individuals remarried; some chose to live alone, move in with relatives, or become boarders. However, the financial, domestic, and child-care struggles encountered by single heads of household persuaded many to remarry. Remarriage legitimated any future offspring, ensured inheritances, and eliminated the stigma of living together outside of marriage. Some were encouraged to remarry by overzealous officials. In the late 1860s, for example, Webb County officials charged several cohabiting unmarried couples with adultery or fornication, but dropped the charges when the couples legally married. Among the individuals who divorced, at least sixty-six remarried (twenty-four women and forty-two men) within the border counties. One of these was a Mexican revolutionary, Catarino Garza, who remarried in 1890 (to Concepción González), less than a year after Carolina Connor successfully sued him for divorce (see figure 14). It was easier to identify men than women who remarried because men kept their surname while women did not. Since many litigants moved away during or after their divorce, the total number of remarriages is undoubtedly higher. The number of divorced individuals who entered into pseudoremarriages (living as husband and wife without a legal marriage) is also impossible to

CATARINO Y CONCEPCION. 23 DE MAYO DE 1890. SAN DIEGO, TEXAS.

14. Catarino Garza and Concepción González on their
wedding day, 23 May 1890, in San Diego, Texas. Garza's first
wife, Carolina Conner, had successfully sued for divorce
from Garza on 13 November 1889 in Cameron County.
Courtesy of the Pérez and Tijerina families.

determine. Among the individuals who remarried were several plaintiffs
who married on the same day (or within weeks) of their divorce. On 23
November 1889, Tomasa Escamilla de Torres successfully divorced Baltazar
Torres, who defaulted. Later that day, Tomasa remarried Charles Fischer, a
forty-seven-year-old German immigrant and butcher with five children,
who himself had divorced thirteen months earlier. Among the divorced
individuals who later remarried, forty-four (67.7 percent) were plaintiffs in
their divorce suit, indicating that they divorced specifically to marry their

preferred partners. Most remarriages occurred in civil ceremonies within five years of the divorce.[80]

Alimony and child custody were at the center of a series of contentious lawsuits filed by María Brena de Llosas and Pedro Llosas. Married in a civil ceremony in 1851, the couple developed serious problems within five years. While pregnant with their fourth child in 1856, María sued Pedro for unspecified charges. Despite this outstanding lawsuit, they reunited to baptize two sons in February 1857 in Brownsville's Catholic Church. But the following month, Pedro sued María for divorce. Cameron County's court subsequently dismissed María's earlier lawsuit without explanation. Acting on María's petition for alimony and child custody, the judge split the provisional custody of the couple's four offspring; Pedro received custody of the two eldest, and María kept the two youngest children. María probably moved in with her sister, who lived next door. The court ordered Pedro to pay five hundred dollars a year in alimony and prohibited him from selling, transferring, or otherwise disposing of any community property. The judge asked three local men to obtain an inventory of the couple's property and appointed a merchant as receiver responsible for selling the couple's personal property at public auction to provide María with a monthly alimony allowance. In the ensuing year, the couple's legal battles would grow increasingly acrimonious.[81]

The couple's bickering demonstrated that husbands continued to have clear legal and financial advantages over wives during divorce proceedings. As a Spanish immigrant and a merchant, Pedro had extensive ties with local businessmen, lawyers, and magistrates. He had served as a juror for seventeen days during the spring term of 1857, while his divorce petition was pending. María's knowledge of judicial procedures was more limited, but she used her wealth to hire two lawyers. As she prepared for trial in the fall term, María's personal problems mounted. In May, her ten-month-old infant died of natural causes. María appeared to have trouble preparing her defense; she asked the judge for several delays when the court resumed. Finally in October 1857, Pedro and María appeared in court with their attorneys, but the jury could not reach a verdict, and the judge ordered the case continued. Pedro had refused to pay for María's lawyers, so she sued to recover attorney expenses. She won the suit, but Pedro immediately appealed. In April 1858, two fellow merchants sued Pedro for forty-five hundred dollars; he quickly admitted fault and waived his rights to appeal. The next day, Pedro agreed to pay his wife's litigation expenses and successfully asked the court to dismiss his divorce petition. Apparently, Pedro believed that this legal maneuver would end his alimony payments by exhausting his financial resources.[82]

The following month, María asked the court to investigate Pedro's legal machinations. The judge discovered that Pedro had retained complete control over the couple's community property by barring the receiver from selling it to pay for alimony, which María had not received for the past thirteen months. After asserting that Pedro and two merchants were colluding to defraud her of alimony payments, María asked the court to revoke the forty-five-hundred-dollar judgment against him. She had no right to interfere, a judge concluded, because she did not have a pending divorce suit. Undaunted by the ruling, she asked her attorneys to appeal the verdict.[83]

The outcome of the couple's litigation demonstrates the limits of Texas's liberal divorce laws. While awaiting her appeal in October 1858, María, then age thirty-six, was assassinated. After determining that Pedro was "unfit for the duties of guardian," the probate court appointed her sister, Crescencia Lewis, as administrator of María's estate and legal guardian of the couple's remaining three children. Although the magistrate did not explain why Pedro was unfit, events four months later provide some clues. In April 1859, the district attorney indicted Pedro Llosas for murder, and subsequently indicted his brother for perjury. As was typical in this period, court documents failed to indicate the name of Pedro's victim and the nature of his brother's perjury. No record of the Llosas brothers' arrest exists. They might have returned to Spain, escaped into Mexico, or moved to a distant American city. In 1867, when the court issued a final writ for their arrest, the case remained unresolved. Given the acrimony of their divorce proceedings, Pedro's subsequent murder indictment, and the probate's ruling declaring him unfit to be the children's guardian, it appears that Pedro killed María. This murder suggests that domestic violence might have plagued their marriage, and exemplifies women's fears of pressing charges against abusive husbands.[84]

The availability of divorce in the border counties provided new avenues for spouses to end troubled marriages, but the application of American laws did not create marital separations. Spouses in Mexico had been separating long before American annexation. In Texas, an increasing number of tejanas and tejanos left unsatisfactory marriages, obtained custody of their children, and remarried through civil channels. Their actions demonstrate an increasing independence for women and the Catholic Church's decreasing legal influence over marital relations. Yet, spouses who divorced did not necessarily abandon their religious beliefs; instead, they selectively chose to abide by some Catholic tenets and not by others. Their choices were not unusual, as their ancestors had made similar decisions. The difference was that after 1848, women and men in Texas could use secular law to sever marriages and begin new ones, instead of simply living apart but remaining legally married as they had done under Mexican rule. While a legal marital separation was exclusively a female option in the villas del norte, it became more complicated after 1848, as men increasingly filed for divorce. By successfully divorcing, Mexican Texans demonstrated their acculturation to American society, and their increasing difference with Mexicans across the river.

The introduction of the American legal system led to significant social change in the border counties. The Mexican Texan elite witnessed its power over workers diminish and their own property holdings decrease as Anglo American newcomers challenged their land titles. In order to counteract their displacement, the tejano upper class established political and social alliances (through intermarriage) with americanos. Adapting to the American legal system was difficult for the Mexican Texan elite, but it was much tougher for middling and poor workers, who had limited access to attorneys, fewer opportunities for alliances with the Anglos, and less legal knowledge. The postwar jurisdictional change did improve workers' mobility, because indebted labor was no longer legal in the annexed lands. This labor freedom attracted additional workers from Mexico who crossed the river to escape their debts. The flow of workers and artisans seeking higher wages in Texas represented an early immigration wave that reinforced Mexican culture but also created nascent tensions with Mexican Americans. Marital relations changed as women obtained more rights to sue over domestic abuse, file for divorce, and remarry in civil ceremonies. Overall, elite Mexican Texan men lost power, but the border counties' political and economic organization remained strongly patriarchal, with Anglo American men replacing the former Mexican elite.

The postwar period introduced patterns that would remain true for several generations. Mexican nationals began seeing the United States as a land of economic opportunity, while they acknowledged that life there had disadvantages. In addition to the class-based discrimination prevalent in Mexico, tejanos confronted new obstacles because of their ethnic background (which americanos perceived as their "race"). Moreover, Anglo newcomers launched Americanization programs designed to change Mexican Texans' choice of religion, language, and culture. Among the welcome changes were more permissive gender relations in the United States, which attracted female migrants. As they adapted to American control and racial discrimination, Mexican Texans began to understand that their American citizenship would increasingly be challenged.

6

Contested Citizenship
The Enduring Roles of Race and Class

On an early morning in September 1859, approximately seventy-five *mexicanos* (Mexicans) left a Mexican independence ball in Matamoros, rode across the Rio Grande, and gained control of Brownsville. Led by Juan Nepomuceno Cortina (see figure 15), they began searching for several *americanos* (American citizens) who had gone unpunished after killing Mexicans. The Cortinistas, as the men became known, skirmished with Brownsville's law-enforcement officials, shot some foes, and released prisoners from the county jail. Feeling overpowered, local authorities appealed to Mexico's National Guard, as well as to political and military leaders from Matamoros, who persuaded the Cortinistas to relinquish control of Brownsville that evening. The rebels, who suffered only one casualty, left four dead and a town in turmoil, but the conflict would continue for months.[1]

Two days later, the Cortinistas followed Mexican political tradition by issuing a *pronunciamento* (proclamation) to explain the purpose of their raid. Gathered at Rancho El Carmen, a portion of a Spanish land grant owned by Cortina's mother, the rebels addressed the inhabitants of Texas through a well-written tract defending their actions. Versions of the pronunciamento in both English and Spanish circulated on both sides of the border. The raid's purpose, they announced, had been to punish those persecuting and robbing them for "no other crime on our part than that of being of Mexican origin." Asserting their American citizenship, they protested the intervention of Matamoros officials and troops. "Not having renounced our rights as North American citizens," they stated, "we disapprove, and energetically protest, against the act of having caused a force of

15. Juan Nepomuceno Cortina, a descendant of a land-grant family in Cameron County, became famous for leading an 1859 rebellion, and later helping the Union Army recruit on both sides of the border. Juan N. Cortina in Mexican military uniform. Circa 1890s. Courtesy of the Brownsville Historical Association, Brownsville, Texas.

the national guards from Mexico to cross unto this side to ingraft [sic] themselves in a question so foreign to their country."[2]

Several local politicians and merchants portrayed the Cortinistas as outsiders. One group of Anglos and Europeans formed a safety committee to coordinate the city's defense, and requested military assistance from the Texas governor-elect and the U.S. president. They denounced the Cortinistas as nonresident criminals who had invaded Brownsville to kill every resident against whom they held a grudge. According to the committee members, the raiders had shouted pro-Mexico slogans and even threatened to raise the Mexican flag over the city. The local English-language newspaper characterized Cortina's followers as "all Mexicans by nativity" with "most of them [being] outlaws from Mexico" and accused them of "trampling on all law and upon the rights of our population."[3]

The contrasting views of americanos and Cortinistas illustrate that citizenship had become a contested issue in the border region within twelve years of American annexation. The competing discourses reflected a deep dispute over social and political belonging to local communities and to the larger imagined political community of the nation. The Cortinistas' actions also reveal transnational influences as *tejanos* (Mexican Texans) participated in a Mexican independence celebration in Matamoros, and afterward joined Mexican nationals in protesting injustice in the United States. While this cooperation might appear contradictory, the joint action illustrates social and cultural ties that transcended the international boundary. Such transnational influences emerged in the mid-nineteenth century precisely because the newly imposed boundary divided an ethnic community whose history on this land predated the reconfigured border. Ultimately, tejanos claimed the rights of American citizenship in order to secure equal treatment as landowners, litigants, voters, and officeholders. Tejano assertions of citizenship occurred in mostly male domains of armed struggles and electoral contests, so their actions can also be interpreted as masculine claims of belonging to local and national imaginaries. Their struggles reveal a determination to adapt to the imposed political structure by employing ethnicity and identity as tools to resist domination.[4]

"Flocks of Vampires" and Land Dispossession

The violation of property rights was a significant factor in the rebels' mobilization. As an heir of the vast Espíritu Santo Spanish land grant, Estéfena Goseascochea de Cortina, Cortina's mother, forfeited part of her estate to the city of Brownsville (see map 2). She lost additional property as a payment to lawyers for establishing legal claim to her land in American courts. Cortina believed attorneys and land speculators had conspired to dispossess his family and other tejanos. Squatters harassed and terrorized land-grant families, while land developers challenged tejanos' titles and forced them to defend their property in court. Simmering racial tensions were another factor in the widespread discontent. "Lawless and unprincipled Americans," wrote a visiting government official, "were much in the habit of grossly maltreating the Mexicans who visited Brownsville, even to the taking of life." Vigilantes had killed several mexicanos but had gone unpunished, which drew the rebels' ire. However, the spark that provoked the raid was an incident of police brutality. In July 1859, a Brownsville marshal had pistol-whipped a drunken former worker of Rancho El Carmen. Refusing Cortina's request to stop the beating, the marshal replied with an insult. Cortina then shot the marshal and rode out of town carrying the worker on his horse. Officials filed charges against Cortina, but failed to capture him. His unsuccessful efforts to have the charges dismissed, along with mexicanos' growing resentment, eventually led to the September raid.[5]

The raid led to a full-scale insurrection. Although the Cortinistas never recaptured Brownsville, they maintained control of the countryside for several months and stopped the town's mail. Cortina's forces, an estimated 350 to 600 men, gained popularity by defeating local and state militias. A combined force of Texas Rangers and federal army troops eventually suppressed the rebellion, but not before the conflict caused widespread devastation and the abandonment of many ranches from Brownsville to Rio Grande City. The towns and countryside became depopulated, when americanos and tejanos fled to Mexico for protection. American military inspectors, sent to the border to assess the violence in the raid's aftermath, accused both sides of damages; they charged the Cortinistas with destroying americanos' property, and criticized the Texas Rangers with raiding tejanos' ranches. The conflict's casualties, noted an army officer, were an estimated fifteen americanos, eighty "friendly Mexicans," and 151 rebels.[6]

The rebellion attracted considerable, but not uniform, support along the border. Victory over local militias coupled with the existing ethnic animosities attracted tejanos, Mexican nationals, and Tampacua Indians to the rebels. Although poor workers swelled their ranks, tejano elected officials and several large landowners also joined. Elite participants helped the raiders voice their complaints in written proclamations. Mexican nationals became involved through Cortina, who had previously served in the Mexican military. Aware of tejanos' disadvantaged position through various social and ethnic ties, some Mexican nationals joined to assist family and friends in Texas. Civilians on both sides of the border provided supplies and shielded the rebels from authorities. The Tampacuas' motivations are unclear, but their involvement recalls earlier *vecino-indio* (community members–Indians) alliances. They might have sought revenge for being forced to relocate to the Reynosa area by the U.S. Army after raiding Hidalgo County ranches and killing several Anglos in the early 1850s. Opposition to the rebels came from Anglos and several Mexican Texans, who cooperated with officials and organized armed patrols to suppress the rebellion. Mexico's authorities mobilized troops against the rebels to avert war with the United States. Ultimately, the rebellion challenged the stability of the "peace structure" and tested elite tejanos' loyalties. Nevertheless, Anglos and Europeans believed Cortina had unanimous support among mexicanos. Brownsville's postmaster, Gilbert Kingsbury, summarized this view: "The most striking feature in all these disturbances is the unanimity of Mexican sympathy with Cortina. . . . Whatever he writes is by high-born & low-born lauded as the perfection of logic & eloquence—Whatever he claims is approved as the purity of Justice."[7]

The Cortinistas' proclamations, along with word of mouth quickly carrying news of the conflict throughout the border region, helped popularize their grievances and garner support. Three weeks after the initial raid, the rebels issued their second pronunciamento, which was published in Spanish and English and distributed in both nations. Some of the grievances appealed to those elite who had lost land to newcomers. The proclamation writers avoided a blanket accusation against all newcomers by specifically accusing lawyers, judges, and law-enforcement officers of cooperating to deprive tejanos of property rights and equal protection under the law. Characterizing these arrivistes as "flocks of vampires in the guise of men who came and scattered themselves in these settlements," the rebels accused the newcomers of arriving "without any capital except the corrupt heart and the most perverse intentions." Lawyers secured tejanos' trust to obtain their land titles, but afterward, under "false and frivolous pretexts," they refused to return them. These arguments likely appealed to a cross section of mexicanos who had witnessed family and friends struggle to defend their land titles in American courts.[8]

By criticizing the justice system, the pronunciamentos attracted nonelite victims of targeted prosecution and criminalization. During the first raid, the rebels shot two americanos who were accused of killing Mexicans with impunity. Upon storming the jail, the rebels killed two more Anglos. The prisoners were freed, according to the insurgents, because local biases led to the frequent imprisonment of Mexican Texans. The pronunciamentos charged the county's sheriff, city marshal, and bailiffs with persecuting and killing Mexican Texans. "Inviolable laws, yet useless, serve, it is true, certain judges and hypocritical authorities," charged the rebels, "cemented in evil and injustice to do whatever suits them and to satisfy their avarice at the cost of your patience and suffering." Addressing tejanos' increasing statewide incarceration and mistreatment, the rebels argued, "through witnesses and false charges, although the grounds may be insufficient, you may be interred in the penitentiaries if you are not previously deprived of life by some keeper who covers himself from responsibility by the pretence [sic] of your flight." The rebels identified with other victims, arguing "many of you have been robbed of your property, incarcerated, chased, murdered, and hunted like wild beasts" because "justice has fled from this world, leaving you to the caprice of your oppressors." Tracing this unjust treatment to American annexation, they accused the United States of failing to uphold Mexican Texans' citizenship rights.[9]

The Cortinistas identified as U.S. citizens and argued for the same legal protection granted to other citizens. They characterized themselves as equal members of the region's towns, legal residents of Texas, and citizens of the United States. By asking the governor-elect and the American president to prosecute *americanos* accused of persecuting and robbing local *tejanos*, the rebels were claiming their rights to legal protection within the state and within the nation. Despite Mexican nationals' participation in the uprising, the proclamations emphasized the views of Mexican Texans. Tellingly, they did not appeal to the Mexican government for protection of Mexican Texans in the United States. On the contrary, the rebels protested against the intervention of the Mexican National Guard, and emphasized their alienation from Mexico.[10]

The rebellion gave the Cortinistas an opportunity to describe their dashed expectations of American citizenship. Both *tejanos* who were born in the region and naturalized Mexicans, the rebels argued, had viewed the United States as a land of liberty. Mexicans' choice of citizenship (Mexican or U.S.) figured prominently in both proclamations. They argued that Mexican nationals had chosen to live in the United States after witnessing Mexico's political turmoil and because "since the Treaty of Guadalupe Hidalgo, they have been attracted to its soil by the soft influence of wise laws and the advantages of a free government." These expectations, however, were not fulfilled. Summarizing their disappointment, the Cortinistas claimed that the promises offered by American citizenship were, in reality, "the baseless fabric of a dream."[11]

By appealing to the state and national governments, the rebels adopted the language of citizenship to advance their local interests. They asked specifically for the national government's intervention to protect *tejanos* from local police and from legal abuse. In this manner, the Cortinistas brought the "nation into the village" (or into the local community) just as they placed themselves within the nation by claiming American citizenship. Their articulation of a national identity illustrated the observation (in another context) of the historian Peter Sahlins that a people's "national identities were as much a legitimate expression and self-characterization as was the sense of identity tied to a particular place." Instead of the "imposition of politics, institutions, and cultural values from the top down and the center outward," Mexican Texans had taken part in state formation by claiming membership from below. Their national identities did not replace local ones, but rather as tejanos living along a contested border, they claimed multiple identities.[12]

Suspect Rebels

Several americanos also deployed the language of citizenship against the rebels. Identifying themselves as "fellow-citizens," they cast suspicion on the rebels' claim to U.S. citizenship by characterizing them as "immediately from Mexico," meaning Mexican nationals. Among officials who characterized the insurgents as "foreigners" were Stephen Powers, Brownsville's mayor and chief justice, and Frank W. Latham, Point Isabel's collector of customs, the latter claiming that neither Cortina nor his men had become naturalized American citizens. Local journalists asserted, "None of them [rebels] have any legal title to citizenship," and accused Cortina's men of "adhering to the common enemy" by aiding Mexico during the U.S.-Mexican War. The proximity of the border and the participation of some Mexican nationals in the uprising gave local americanos a convenient excuse to characterize all rebels as Mexican nationals.[13]

Opponents also labeled the rebels as criminals. In letters to Congress, they described the Cortinistas as "made up of the dangerous class of the Mexican population" who were "bandits," "outlaws," and "marauders." Moreover, some residents blamed the revolutions in Mexico for augmenting Cortina's forces with "peons and pelados" who escaped to Texas to avoid conscription into the Mexican Army. The *American Flag* called the rebels "graduates of the presidios of Mexico and the penitentiaries of Texas" who subsisted by stealing horses. What was the motivation for these spurious allegations? By portraying the rebels as noncitizens and criminals, americanos sought to dismiss the pronunciamentos' grievances, which accused local officials of denying tejanos their citizenship rights. Dismissing the proclamations' accusations, the *American Flag* argued, "All the complaints insinuated in this production are utterly without foundation." Denying the land dispossession claims, Charles Stillman, a prominent merchant, argued, "None of them are tax-payers or land-owners in Cameron County." Subsequently, the editors also argued that the rebels have "in this country neither properties nor homes, nor any thing but their own crimes to entitle them to any recognition under our laws." Such allegations ignored that the

[handwritten in left margin: word— "criminal"—]

rebels included local rancheros, land-grant owners, and political office-holders.[14]

A few rational voices expressed doubts about these wholesale depictions of the Cortinistas. Several U.S. Army officers believed the rebels to be American citizens. General Winfield Scott reported to the secretary of war, "The recent disturbances on our side of the lower Rio Grande were commenced by Texans, and carried on (vainly) by and between them. Cortinas [*sic*] himself and most of his brigands are natives of Texas." Some authorities reluctantly acknowledged that both tejanos and Mexican nationals became rebels. In asking the governor and the nation's president for help in quelling the rebellion, local officials described the rebels as "composed entirely of Mexicans, some of whom belong on this side of the river and some on the Mexican side, many of them *claiming* to be American citizens." Additional dissent came from John Haynes, Starr County's state representative, when he appeared before the state legislature as an expert witness, having lived in south Texas for more than thirty years. Haynes urged the national government to investigate the rebellion because it was "caused by a settled belief on the part of the citizens of Mexican origin [in] a deliberate attempt by certain persons to defraud them out of their lands." Federal court officials, Haynes asserted, were assisting this fraud.[15]

These conflicting characterizations illustrate the subjective nature of americanos' views concerning citizenship and the manner in which such outlooks could change. Before the rebellion, Anglos had accepted some Cortinistas as citizens. José María Cortina had served as tax assessor-collector, and Teodicio Zamora had been Hidalgo County's chief justice. Major S. P. Heintzelman wrote to Colonel Robert E. Lee: "Juan Nepomosina [*sic*] Cortinas, (or Cortina,) the leader of the banditti . . . is a ranchero, at one time claiming to be an American, and at another a Mexican citizen. . . . He had great influence with his class of the Mexican population, and thus, as he controlled so many votes, was courted at elections by politicians." Americanos had not questioned these tejanos' citizenship when they held elected office and rallied electoral support for local politicians. But when these same individuals accused the county's Anglos of obstructing the rights of Mexican Texans, americanos stripped the claimants of American citizenship. Nevertheless, a few "friendly" and "law-abiding" tejanos retained their good standing as Americans citizens by mobilizing other rancheros to fight the rebels, supporting the U.S. military's efforts to suppress the rebellion, or "overlooking whatever misfortunes fell on the lower class of Mexicans."[16]

The American government's earlier decision to withdraw troops from the border partly explains Anglos' stubborn insistence that the rebels were Mexican nationals. In January 1859, Major General D. E. Twiggs decided to relocate troops from the lower Rio Grande to the west Texas frontier to protect against Comanche attacks. Two months later, local politicians and merchants urged federal officials to keep the troops at Fort Brown (Brownsville), Ringgold Barracks (Rio Grande City), and Fort McIntosh (Laredo), to protect close to twenty million dollars in international trade. The petitioners warned that "bands of Mexican armed soldiers, highwaymen, and Indians, would cross into our Territory, plunder our commerce, murder our citizens, and make desert [of] our frontier." Dismissing the petitioners' fears, Twiggs wrote, "There is not, nor ever has been, any danger of the Mexicans crossing on our side of the river to plunder or disturb the inhabitants." He argued that residents were unhappy because "the citizens in the vicinity of those posts are very unwilling to lose the opportunity of handling a portion of the money necessarily expended by the government and troops." The Cortina rebellion gave local authorities a convenient excuse to pressure the national government to return federal troops to the border.[17]

By casting the rebels as criminals who threatened international trade, local politicians and merchants invoked the common stereotype of Mexican criminality, thereby converting a local dispute into a national issue. They attracted the federal government's attention by suggesting that Mexican soldiers and highwaymen were "invading" the nation's territory. These depictions also buttressed their earlier warning about attacks from bands of criminals if federal troops were removed. Within days of the Cortinistas' raid, americanos changed their initial depiction of the account from an incident involving a private grudge into a more threatening conflict. Gilbert Kingsbury, Brownsville's postmaster, described the rebellion as beginning as a riot, developing into an insurrection, turning into a war of races, and possibly heading into a war of nations. Such creative descriptions illustrate how americanos imagined the conflict's evolution. In letters to the state governor and the U.S. president, Anglos highlighted the Cortinistas' supposed allegiance to Mexico. To support their claim, they accused the rebels of attempting to hoist a Mexican flag on the unoccupied Fort Brown, and of pledging their allegiance to Mexico with shouts of "¡Viva México!"[18]

Americanos invoked national sovereignty by claiming that the rebels held an allegiance to Mexico. Having served as agents of the United States by establishing local governments after annexation, they now appealed for federal troops as privileged citizens. Local political leaders repeatedly reminded state and national officials of their humiliating reliance on the Mexican National Guard during Cortina's initial siege and the danger this posed because Mexico's military could not be trusted. One resident portrayed the Cortina raid as a conspiracy by the Mexican government to instigate an armed conflict between the United States and Mexico. The raid was "a national matter, and strictly a war of races," according to one correspondent. Ultimately, the Cameron County grand jury invoked national sovereignty when it described the Cortina raid as "an invasion of American territory by armed Mexicans under the Mexican flag." Governor Houston shared these views as he ordered state troops to the border to "repel invasions both from the Indians and Mexico." Ultimately, americanos highlighted national concerns to promote their local interests, namely, security from an insurrection and profits from locally stationed soldiers.[19]

Race and Nation

The Cortina uprising gave americanos an opportunity to voice their longstanding doubts about tejano sympathies. In addition to depicting the insurrection as an invasion, they characterized most tejanos as disloyal. One resident described Brownsville's population as consisting of only fifty "American citizens, native or naturalized, whose origin and sympathies are not Mexican." Israel Bigelow, the county judge, gave a similarly exaggerated view, complaining that only 150 males of the city's 2,500 residents spoke English and only 50 tejanos could be counted on to defend against rebel incursions. Such statements reflected americanos' belief that they had little support from most tejanos. They also reinforced Anglos' self-image as agents of the American government among a conquered, and possibly hostile, population. Finally, these statements implied a distrust of all monolingual Spanish-speaking Mexican Texans by linking language with national identity.[20]

Anglos viewed the rebellion as a manifestation of their worst fear—a race war. Because few tejanos defended Brownsville during the rebellion, a Cameron County grand jury's report charged that the state's entire Mexican Texan population was in sympathy with Cortina. Americanos believed that Mexicans on both sides of the border harbored deep hatred toward Anglos. One observer traced this animosity to the bitter feelings engendered by American soldiers during the U.S.-Mexican War. Recently arrived army officers concurred, arguing that mexicanos' "feeling against the Americans is very great." A *New Orleans Picayune* border correspondent believed that "under a polite exterior, the deepest, settled hatred exists in the Mexican mind towards us, running far back, but intensified since the late war with Mexico."[21]

Fueled by news reports of rebellions elsewhere in Mexico, americanos felt under siege by a mexicano majority. They feared that tejanos were obtaining aid from Mexican nationals and Mexico's government. Alarmist news reports even convinced some Texas Rangers, such as John Ford, who wrote, "The whole Mexican population on both sides of the river are in favor of him [Cortina]." Notwithstanding the aid provided by Mexico's National Guards and the safe haven for Cameron County's women and children offered by Matamoros's political authorities, Anglos believed that Mexican nationals were conspiring against them. Israel Bigelow voiced his fear by writing, "Mexican authorities are pretending to guard the right bank of the Rio Grande." However, this was only a pretense, Bigelow maintained, because the Cortinistas were frequently allowed to enter Matamoros, where they had been "publicly cheered and encouraged."[22]

Contemporary international and national events stoked these exaggerated fears. According to two presumed eyewitnesses who had fled shortly after the Cortinistas' raid, "the entire Mexican population on both sides of the Rio Grande, are up in arms, advancing upon us, to murder every white inhabitant, and to reconquer our country as far as the Colorado river." The Caste War in Yucatán and the Yaqui Indians' uprising in northwestern Mexico had alerted Americans about the possibilities of indigenous rebellions by oppressed majorities. Moreover, the Apaches had increased their attacks in Arizona and Sonora. Local fears about a race war were magnified further with news of John Brown's raid on Harper's Ferry in October 1859. Similarly, Cortina's rebellion posed a threat because of the setting and emotional circumstances in which Anglos found themselves along the border—outnumbered nine to one and without the protection of federal troops. One newspaper editor directly voiced this demographic fear by asserting, "On this whole frontier, the proportion of the Mexican to that of the American or Anglo Saxon race, on an average, is about as 10 to 1; but at some points . . . the population is about 25 to 1."[23]

Especially worrisome for white residents were the sympathies of poor tejanos, believed to hold grudges and posed to seek revenge. While previously silent or dismissive about ethnic tensions, journalists began asserting that they had "knowledge of the deep hatred . . . by the lower classes of Mexicans against us." Americanos' past treatment of Mexicans might have weighed on their conscience and spurred their creative imaginations. After traveling throughout south Texas, Abbé Domenech wondered about the simmering resentment caused by the prevalent ethnic tensions. He observed, "In these badly organized regions, the Mexican might have an easy vengeance on his persecutors, who are quite the minority on the Texan frontiers." Undoubtedly, similar thoughts and doubts were on the minds of local Anglos who had antagonized Mexican Texans.[24]

Americanos' views reflected their ideas about Mexicans as a "race." Mexicans' racial background had become a critical topic in debates about their citizenship during the Constitutional Convention of Texas (1845) and in the U.S. Congress amidst the U.S.-Mexican War. While the state and nation granted Mexicans the right to vote, both decisions were controversial because they centered on whether Mexicans would be considered "white" citizens. In the postwar period, questions about Mexicans' race and citizenship lingered. In newspapers, letters, and government reports, local americanos often pitted the interests of "American citizens" against those of "Mexicans." This dichotomy allowed Anglos to ignore distinctions between Mexican Texans with American citizenship and Mexican nationals with Mexican citizenship by portraying a homogenous group of "Mexicans" as the border community's racial "other." Throughout the Southwest, the presumed distinction between *white* and *Mexican* reflected regional and national trends in language use, according to the historian Lisbeth Haas, and confirmed that the "politics of race was anchored solidly in language." This discourse also illustrates how americanos used *Mexican* as a both a national and a racial category. Through such characterizations, they invested Mexicans' ethnic background with racial meaning, particularly for the poor. Thus, Anglo border residents continuously spoke disparagingly of "peons" and "pelados" when they mentioned the "Mexican race." By racializing most Mexicans through such discourse, Anglos gave meaning to the set of social relations that upheld white privilege.[25]

This racialization process informed Anglos' views of citizenship. Through the term *citizen* they identified residents with full rights. By using the terms *white inhabitants, American citizens,* and *Anglo Saxons* interchangeably, americanos tied citizenship to whiteness. References in newspaper advertisements and editorials described "meetings of citizens" for purposes of holding elections, organizing militias, and promoting commerce. The implied meaning of *citizen* was a white male resident. Echoing the ideology of racial Anglo Saxonism, local Anglos argued that American citizens stood for loyalty, order, and industriousness, while equating Mexicans with disloyalty, lawlessness, and laziness. The selective use of *citizen* to refer to Anglos racially "marked" most Mexican Texans as *noncitizens*, denying them full membership in the local community and the nation. Conversely, this discourse left americanos "unmarked" as citizens who represented "normative" behavior.[26]

Yet, Anglos nominally acknowledged tejanos as citizens when a particular action convinced them an individual provided a community service. When Mexican Texans captured and returned runaway slaves who had fled into Mexico, americanos depicted them as good citizens. In 1860 the *Ranchero* congratulated tejanos for capturing two runaway slaves. Offering qualified praise, the newspaper argued, "All must admit that *some* of our Mexican population *are of service* to the community at large, as well *as being law-abiding citizens*." Similarly, an americano in Laredo highlighted the exploits of Santos Benavides, who frequently crossed into Mexico to retrieve runaway slaves. His letter to the editor sought to correct the false impressions, the writer explained, "so generally entertained regarding the portion of our fellow-citizens of Mexican origin." Some tejanos were good citizens, he argued, since they were devoted to upholding "the interests of the country and the welfare of its citizens." Such interests, in this case, were tied to defending white supremacy. Ironically, Mexican Texans gained acceptance as legitimate American citizens when they denied freedom to African American slaves, who had no similar recourse to citizenship.[27]

An important class exemption was embedded within Anglos' generalizations about Mexicans. As the sociologist Tomás Almaguer argues, Anglo Americans considered poor Mexicans living in the annexed territories to be unassimilable and unambiguously nonwhite. They directed their opprobrium at the region's numerous poor Mexicans, considered "degenerate" and "mongrelized." By contrast, americanos viewed elite Mexicans as assimilable and white and thus eligible for intermarriage and citizenship. Americanos typically used terms such as *law abiding* or *good* to distinguish elite Mexicans from the poor. This class-based racialization corresponds with the argument of the historian Matthew Frye Jacobson that culture and politics rather than nature define race. The instability of race arises from cultural and political dynamics that alter which groups can claim the privileges of whiteness. While European immigrants might have been nominally white or nonwhite in eastern cities, they were unambiguously white along the border, where their low numbers and the presence of numerous Mexicans provided a different context. In contrast to the Mexican "race," various European immigrants along with Anglo Americans securely claimed whiteness. The flexibility of race allowed americanos to extend the privileges of whiteness to elite tejanos, and to withdraw these privileges from others who challenged their rule. In the border region, elite tejanos obtained political and social rights as citizens while nonelites obtained social rights but had limited political rights. Poor Mexican Texans, whom Anglos considered nonwhite, could not exercise their full citizenship rights. While Mexican nationals and Mexican Texans shared many attributes—culture, language, and ethnicity—they also had significant differences—namely, nationality, and civic experience.[28]

Development of Mexican Texan Identity

The pronunciamentos became manifestations of an emergent ethnic identity among Mexican Texans. In the first proclamation, the Cortinistas argued that certain americanos had persecuted and robbed their community "for no other crime on our part than that of being of Mexican origin." In this case, "Mexican origin" referred to an ethnic rather than a national identity. Noticeably absent was any mention of Mexican Texans' internal class divisions. Although some rebels belonged to the landed elite, they neglected to distinguish themselves from their poorer neighbors. Instead, they spoke as self-anointed representatives of a tejano community that shared "our identity of origin, our relationship, and the community of our sufferings." This constructed ethnic identity, however imagined, was similar to the vecino identity that existed among residents of the *villas del norte* (northern towns) who came together to repel Indian attacks. Border residents were once again constructing an identity in opposition to a "hostile" group, though now the heirs of the vecinos found themselves in a subordinate position, and they marshaled a counteridentity in response. American annexation had created a shared "community of sufferings" among Mexican Texans as the wealthy lost their land and the poor suffered unjust and excessive imprisonment under the American legal system.[29]

The Cortinistas recognized the ethnic ties between Mexican nationals and tejanos, while acknowledging differences between the groups. The second proclamation refers to Mexican citizens as "our relatives on the other side of the river" but identifies Mexican Texans as "the Mexican inhabitants of the State of Texas." This distinction in citizenship status clearly acknowledges the social and cultural links among Mexicans on both sides of the border. The unfilled promises of American citizenship are elaborated in their description of the flight of refugees into Mexico for safety. Some tejanos had escaped to Mexico after suffering land dispossession and physical persecution in the United States. By stating that "our families have returned as strangers to their old country to beg for asylum," the proclamation asserts that Mexican Texans had become alienated from Mexico's government after only eleven years as American citizens. Ultimately, the pronunciamentos position tejanos as distinct from Mexican nationals, and as a population without protection from either the American or Mexican governments.[30]

Although they shared a culture, language, and religion, tejanos' American citizenship separated them from their friends and families in Mexico. They had made gains unknown to Mexican nationals, such as higher-paying jobs, as well as the right to divorce and remarriage. But unlike Mexican nationals, Mexican Texans as a group lost large amounts of land, suffered disproportionate incarcerations, and were excluded from several political and judicial positions. They also experienced ethnic discrimination and second-class citizenship on a daily basis, unlike Mexican nationals, who did not live under American political and economic control. Their daily interactions with Mexican nationals and with americanos led some tejanos to develop a distinct counteridentity; they were not accepted as Americans and were no longer Mexican citizens.

Mexican Texans' quotidian encounters with Mexican nationals strengthened shared ties between the groups, but also highlighted differences. Social trips across the border were common among family and friends. Mexican nationals worked on Texas ranches and homes, while tejanos traveled to Mexico for cultural events, religious ceremonies, and shopping. Trade in livestock and manufactured goods increased commercial ties and strengthened social links. These daily encounters also accentuated differences in their social, legal, and political positions. Tejanos who crossed into Mexico witnessed Mexicans in control of local government while their own power had diminished in Texas. The constant flow of ethnically similar people across the international boundary provided Anglos with a convenient excuse to question Mexican Texan citizenship, especially when tejanos crossed the river to avoid prosecution or military service. These actions led americanos to accuse tejanos of being lawless and disloyal to the United States. The arguments over citizenship inevitably became more heated during local elections. Because the majority of eligible voters in the border region were tejanos, Anglo American politicians competed vigorously for their support. Yet, defeated candidates were the first to accuse ineligible voters from Mexico of corrupting elections.

American "Democracy"

Alliances between the americano and tejano elite helped broker political arrangements, but did not eliminate factions. Some divisions were reproduced from the Mexican period's alignments, and others formed from new issues, such as disputes over land. Ethnic or class differences, however, did not determine voting preferences, because americanos and tejanos of various socioeconomic classes participated in every political faction. Within each county, parties grew out of differing economic and political interests. While Anglo newcomers adapted to local political practices, they also altered them. Some became fluent in Spanish in order to campaign among the Mexican Texan electorate, while others depended on the tejano elite as intermediaries. They also used political insignias to bridge the gap resulting from language differences, and employed novel strategies for voter recruitment.

Voters divided themselves into political factions, the names of which varied by county. In Webb County, the *botas* (boots) and *guaraches* (sandals) parties developed after an Anglo American politician allied with his Mexican Texan brothers-in-law in the mid-1870s to challenge the Benavides family's political stranglehold. The Benavides faction adopted the guarache label to claim working-class support and called their opponents, the botas, a symbol of wealth. However, both parties included poor and rich as well as americano and tejano supporters. The Cameron County electorate split between the Red and the Blue Parties over land litigation and differences between large and small merchants. The Blue Party, led by small owners and professionals, supported Brownsville's claim to land within its city limits, which the state of Texas granted to the city by charter. Supported by large merchants and cattle barons, the Red Party backed the claims of the Brownsville Town Company, headed by Charles Stillman. "These colors were chosen in lieu of party names to designate the parties by, so that the Mexican voters might know to whom they belonged," noted an English immigrant, William Neale, "for it would have been a hopeless task to have made them understand either our political differences or our municipal affairs." Neale's condescension typified the political elite's attitudes toward the tejano electorate. Instead of promoting democratic practices, according to the claims of Manifest Destiny, americano politicians were concerned with controlling Mexican Texan voters so that they would remain in power.[31]

Anglo newcomers introduced other questionable political practices. Contemporary accounts describe political factions freely handing out liquor and food to influence voters. Each group set up tables on the street from which they dispensed whiskey to all passersby. They also distributed tickets with the names of candidates, hats, and colored ribbons. After plying the electorate with food and liquor, functionaries marched their new recruits, the so-called corral vote, to the polls. This type of democracy elected many judges, sheriffs, and mayors. "Viewing the manner in which the Texian judges are elected," a priest argued, "we cannot be surprised that impartiality is not considered by them a duty." Tejano and americano politicians became powerful political "bosses" who delivered numerous votes and enthusiastically participated in election-day festivities. They envisioned themselves as "fishers of men" who engineered elections, noted a candid politician. Abbé Domenech observed, "You might meet every evening in the streets numbers of electors drunk and battered; and not rarely might you recognise among their number the future magistrates for whom so much fuss was made, and so many bottles emptied."[32]

Americanos generally viewed elite Mexican Texans as fellow citizens, as long as they were subordinate or supported white supremacy. Tejanos obtained political positions under the supervision of americano politicians, and often in exchange for securing Mexican Texan support for Anglo American politicians. In 1858, Juan Cortina organized a tejano caucus to elect James G. Browne, an Irish immigrant, as sheriff. In exchange, a faction within the Blue Party helped elect Cortina's brother, José María Cortina, as tax assessor and collector. The defeated candidate for tax collector, Gilbert Kingsbury, would harbor resentment against Cortina and the tejano electorate for years. In penning a local history, Kingsbury described Mexicans as a people "who inherited by blood the vices of the Spanyard [sic] [and] Indian & negro & by tradition the a [sic] hatred to the very name of American." Juan Cortina would eventually drop out of favor, but his half-brother, Sabas Cavazos, continued to enjoy the privileges of alliances with the americano elite. Confirming this elite status, Governor Sam Houston provided a letter that allowed Cavazos to travel freely to pursue his business without fearing retribution from Anglo American law-enforcement officers. The political opportunities of nonelite tejanos were more limited and their status more fragile. Americanos routinely challenged their political participation, rarely treating them as fellow citizens. Typical confrontations involved questioning the legality of elections or threatening Mexican Texans with violence if they visited the polls.[33]

The proximity of the international border led to frequent accusations of voter fraud. Two years after the establishment of county governments, a journalist cited voting irregularities in precincts where the votes cast outnumbered the inhabitants. The correspondent blamed this irregularity on Mexican nationals who had crossed the Rio Grande to "avail themselves of the glorious privileges of the ballot box." The journalist surely knew, but failed to acknowledge, that the candidates had either accepted or taken part in the alleged voter fraud. When losing candidates challenged election re-sults, they blamed Mexican nationals but ignored the politicians responsi-ble for orchestrating the deception. According to William Neale, nineteenth-century elections "were combinations of force, fraud and farce, and the smartest 'fishers of men' like the apostles of old, gained the day." As a multiple officeholder, Neale failed to acknowledge the benefit he received from such practices. Instead, he highlighted the electorate's "ignorance" as the cause of corruption. While the number of Mexican nationals who voted in U.S. elections is unknown, critics routinely argued that illegal voters determined the outcome of local contests.[34]

Contemporary newspapers offered a different version that cast some of the blame on politicians. While losing candidates charged mexicanos with fraud, some journalists identified those Anglo American politicians who frequently used food and drink to "corral" voters. Similar reports from San Antonio and Beeville noted how brokers of political power would march Mexican nationals to the county clerk's office, pay a fee to have them declared citizens, and then lead them to the polls. Decades later, Catarino Garza, a Mexican revolutionary who organized in the border region, recog-nized that Mexican nationals' participation in this electoral fraud reflected poorly on them. However, Garza also identified tejano politicians and americano power brokers as the "political speculators" responsible for in-stigating this fraud to perpetuate their hold on electoral office.[35]

Voter fraud accusations conveniently masked americanos' opposition to Mexican Texans voters. Anglos believed that tejanos were ignorant, easily manipulated, and often duped by false rumors. Some cited the practice of "bloc voting" as evidence of tejanos' corruption. This vote was "controlled," the local newspaper argued, because it was common for an employer to "simply vote his hired Mexican." According to published accounts, the candidates who did not secure this vote charged "fraud, corruption," be-came "uproarious about the purity of the ballot box," and portrayed them-selves as "immaculate" in the electoral process. Americanos made these allegations despite having no accurate count of eligible voters in counties with seasonal labor migrations. "There are many Mexicans who are entitled to vote, and understand the principles and workings of our government, as well as any Americans," opined the *Ranchero*, "but the ignorant do not, and from the nature of circumstances, there must be many who have not the legal right to vote." Although the *American Flag* acknowledged not knowing the number of eligible voters in a Laredo election in which their candidate lost, they blamed Mexicans nevertheless for deciding the election. "We are opposed to allowing an ignorant crowd of Mexicans to determine political questions in this country, where a man is supposed to vote knowingly and thoughtfully," they editorialized.[36]

Intimidation often prevented tejanos from voting. Opponents stopped Mexican Texans from registering and prevented Mexican nationals from becoming naturalized American citizens. In response, groups mobilized to confront those organizations, such as the Ku Klux Klan, that attempted to intimidate Mexican Texan voters. In counties with smaller tejano populations, the intimidation was more direct and successful. Before the November 1860 presidential election, armed groups drove tejanos away from Nueces County. Some believed that Mexican nationals had previously voted illegally and feared that Mexican Texans, who held antislavery views, would vote for Abraham Lincoln. In a signed newspaper notice, several americanos warned employers and politicians to keep tejanos from voting. Characterizing Mexican Texan voters as easily manipulated and dependent, they argued, "It would be better for all parties concerned if Mexican voters were kept away from the polls; as the free and independent voters of the county do not think it right for them to vote." Authorities failed to take legal action against these vigilantes. Predictably, not a single tejano voted in the local election. Voting continued to be a contested issue for Mexican Texans throughout the rest of the nineteenth century.[37]

Americano newcomers claimed to bring democracy to the border. Yet, the political system that they, along with elite tejanos, controlled had undemocratic elements. Ironically, the political practices in the border counties were similar to those across the border, where *caudillos* (political strongmen) controlled politics. Although sharply critical of politics in Mexico, americanos benefited from machine politics that manipulated immigrant and poor voters. Several scholars have described the "Mexicanization" process by which americanos adopted cultural and social practices of the border's Mexican majority. On the one hand, the newcomers did adapt those local Mexican political conventions that suited their purposes. On the other, they added undemocratic practices reminiscent of political machines in large U.S. cities.[38]

Americanization Efforts

Newcomers believed Mexican Texans, perceived as "foreigners," needed to undergo Americanization. Distrusting monolingual Spanish speakers who continued following Mexican cultural practices, americanos sought to persuade tejanos to speak English, convert to Protestantism, and follow American customs. They carried out this policy zealously, if not always successfully, through American holidays, Protestant churches, and schools. Some believed the arrival of americanas would increase the morals of the border population and restrain excesses. Americanas took this charge seriously and began organizing Sunday schools, requesting missionaries for the area, and collecting funds to build churches. As in other parts of the American West, middle-class Anglo women in the lower Rio Grande region participated publicly in the Americanization of nonwhite "others." Assuming gendered roles as purveyors of "civilization" and "domesticity," they served as critical agents of imperial expansion by the United States.[39]

Americanos used national holidays and leisure activities to introduce American traditions to the border region. Towns celebrated the Fourth of July with speeches, military salutes, and parades. "The twenty-fifth day of December is no more sacred to Christians," noted a local newspaper, "than is the Fourth of July to 'Americans.'" By the nation's centennial celebration, some success was evident as a Mexican Texan brass band played while floats carrying young women (including three tejanas) passed along a Brownsville parade route. The newcomers also introduced the national pastime, baseball, to the region. Overall, americanos believed they were bringing morals and a better culture to tejanos. Yet, morality and culture were a matter of perspective. While they frowned upon Mexican Texans' habit of gambling at monte, Anglos wagered on horse races. Even tejanos' harshest critics, the editors of the *Ranchero*, enjoyed gambling on horses.[40]

Protestant missionary efforts began in Cameron County, which had the largest Anglo American population along the border, and slowly spread to other counties. Brownsville's first Sunday school, organized by the Methodist Church, had made inroads by July 1849, as nearly half of its students were Mexican Texans. The missionaries, however, did not always adapt their proselytizing efforts to the local population. Like the Catholic priests, some Protestant clergy disliked the border region's isolation and lack of urban comforts. Often their actions belied their pronouncements. While constantly clamoring for additional donations, the Presbyterian missionary Hiram Chamberlain appeared detached: he and his wife wore fine clothing

16. Schools were prominent instruments of Americanization and offered opportunities for school-children to enact patriotic war plays in the 1890s. Sons of several prominent Brownsville families a shown in this photograph. Standing from left to right: Manuel Orive, James B. Wells Jr., Ramon Re Sebastián Puente, Fred Harve, Gonzalo Fernández, Henry Harve, Robert Kingsbury, unidentified c and Edgar Hicks. Kneeling from left to right: Joseph K. Wells, Willie Turregano, Charles Turregano and James C. McAllen. Courtesy of Brownsville Historical Association, Brownsville, Texas.

and built a nicer home than those of their parishioners. By delivering monotonous sermons on the evils of the pope and the Catholic Church, he undermined his cause further. His successors were more diplomatic and, predictably, more successful. After establishing a base among tejanos, they cultivated native Spanish-speaking ministers. By the 1890s, the Presbyterian minister Leandro Garza y Mora offered Spanish-language services for Brownsville's substantial Mexican Texan congregation. The Presbyterians expanded to include a sister chapel in Matamoros; a mission in nearby Santa Rosalía, Texas; and a Brownsville Mission school for girls, which had about sixty tejana students. Its Sunday school had also grown, employing four teachers and serving nearly seventy-five students.[41]

Schools became an integral part of the "Americanizing" mission for the newcomers, especially for Protestant missionaries. Anglos believed the schools would increase literacy and permit border residents to read religious literature (see figure 16). Helen Chapman, a newcomer who was instrumental in petitioning several missionary boards, based her altruistic work on a belief in education to facilitate Protestant conversion. She argued, "The school master must precede or rather accompany the Bible. Without him, the distribution of this and all other good books is literally casting away pearls of wisdom." By 1850, twelve private schools (serving 296 students) and ten public schools (serving 119 students) existed in Cameron, Starr, and Webb Counties. Hidalgo County enrolled 215 students in its public schools by 1856. To address education needs in rural areas, some tejanos donated land and constructed school buildings. Urban centers offered both private and public schools, while rural communities were usually limited to public schools.[42]

Protestant missionaries established private schools with the goal of gaining Mexican Texan converts. Although they "lived hand to mouth," poor tejanos sacrificed to afford private schools, which their children attended consistently, earning admiration from Protestant newcomers. Among the most active educators was Melinda Rankin, a lay missionary, who opened a private school for girls in 1852. With Chamberlain's assistance, Rankin secured funding from the Presbyterian Board of Missions for a permanent building for the Rio Grande Female Institute. She credited her school's popularity among tejanos to its superior English lessons compared to the local Catholic school, where English was "imperfectly taught" by the school's French nuns. The Presbyterians sponsored the Spaniard Ramón Monsalvatge, a former Catholic monk, to organize a private school in the 1850s. After this school obtained mixed results because of local priests' opposition, Monsalvatge switched to teaching Spanish to Anglo children and offering private adult lessons. The Laredo Seminary, a private high school established in the late 1880s by the Southern Methodist Church, enrolled male and female students from a range of economic backgrounds by offering full scholarships, while Laredo's St. Ursuline Academy mainly drew elite students. Numerous students enrolled in Protestant schools, but few families attended Protestant churches, which illustrated Mexican Texans' continued selective cultural adaptation.[43]

Some tejanos avoided the "Americanization" programs altogether by enrolling their children in Catholic or Mexican schools. French nuns opened Brownsville's Convent of the Incarnate Word, the region's first Catholic school for girls, in 1853. Twelve years later, priests of the Oblates of Mary established St. Joseph's College to educate boys. Laredo's Catholic leaders also opened the Ursuline Academy in the 1860s, which filled a need resulting from sporadic funding for Laredo's public schools. Unfortunately, Catholic school tuition was out of reach for many tejanos. Yet, Catholic schools remained attractive because they offered English-language classes without the pressures of religious conversion. Facing limited school choices in rural areas, wealthy families often sent their children to Mexican schools in Saltillo or Monterrey.[44]

Public schools suffered from a lack of steady funding and untrained teachers. Throughout the nineteenth century, Texas struggled to establish a statewide public school system, so officials from border counties created semipublic schools, which operated sporadically because of minimal funding and the lack of permanent facilities. Laredo's government allocated partial funds for teachers' salaries, school furniture, and offered a meeting space rent-free. Due to limited school funding, children attended poorly ventilated, dimly lit, and underfurnished rooms. Lacking permanent school buildings, classes were held at various locations. This instability led to frequent teacher turnover. Rural children faced tougher obstacles because landowners discouraged laboring families from sending their children to rancho schools. These woefully inadequate schools held classes in thatched huts without desks or blackboards. Moreover, rural children received instruction from untrained teachers, who obtained their position through political connections rather than through merit.[45]

In the late nineteenth century, private Mexican schools emerged as an alternative to underfunded public schools. Attending poorly equipped public schools, tejano students grew more discouraged when they could not understand English-language lessons from teachers who prohibited them from speaking Spanish. Faced with these obstacles, Mexican Texan parents opted for private Mexican schools. Modeled after schools in Mexico, they offered Spanish-language classes in Mexican history, grammar, and civics. These schools' goals were to raise awareness of Mexican culture, and to instill ethnic pride. Despite some gains, close to 50 percent of urban students and over 60 percent of rural students remained illiterate at the close of the nineteenth century.[46]

Anglo newcomers supported U.S. nation building by seeking to "Americanize" tejanos, a population incorporated through conquest. Such efforts, typically directed at immigrants, sought to transform tejanos into English-speaking citizens who followed American customs. Yet, inadequate schools, overbearing religious conversion efforts, and Protestant missionaries' condescending views hampered the Americanization goals. While tejano enrollment at Protestant schools increased, religious conversions did not necessarily follow suit. Among the obstacles for religious conversions were the prejudicial views of Anglo missionaries and teachers. Americanization advocates failed to perceive the border population's needs and desires. Mexican Texans selectively chose English-language instruction at Protestant schools while rejecting their religious messages. Their strategic adaptation of American culture established patterns that future generations would follow. Mexican Texans' commitment to education, and to English-language instruction, indicated a desire to give their children the tools necessary to succeed in the United States. Ultimately, the lack of English-language skills among tejanos was a result of inadequate instruction rather than a lack of interest.

Language and Identity

Americanos had long been distrustful of tejano allegiances. Originating during the Texas Revolution, this suspicion grew during the U.S.-Mexican War, and continued in its aftermath, with some Mexican Texans assisting runaway slaves. The border region's americano minority had similar fears. A local merchant, W. G. Hale, articulated his suspicions of Mexican Texans by writing "Those of the higher classes only, have any attachment to the government under which they live." During the Cortina rebellion, Anglos doubted tejanos' commitment as scouts and militia members. Mexican Texans would leave for Mexico "when they" could "no longer bear the labor of watching and drilling," according to the army officer Loomis Langdon, because they were a "foreign population" who would look to "their own government" for protection. Like other americanos, Langdon accused tejanos of maintaining an allegiance to Mexico rather than to the United States.[47]

Visitors believed tejanos' inability or refusal to speak English was un-American, and found Spanish-language use by local officials unsettling. A *New York Times* correspondent expressed surprise at the particularities of Laredo's judicial system. Although the majority of Laredo's residents were tejanos, the journalist disapproved of the use of Spanish by jurors and of the need for an interpreter to translate court proceedings. Unbeknownst to the correspondent, Texas law required the appointment of interpreters when necessary. Other journalists were surprised and frustrated that American citizens along the border preferred communicating in Spanish. By continu-

ing to decry Spanish-language use, visiting journalists failed to acknowledge the long history of settlement and governance by Mexicans—conducted in Spanish since 1749—before americanos arrived in the region.
Nor did they consider that these residents had lived under American rule
for only a few years. The use of Spanish varied by county; counties with
higher numbers of Mexican Texan officials conducted more of their official
business in Spanish.[48]

Observations about tejanos' Spanish language often involved the serious
ramifications of Anglos mistaking language skills for patriotism. A local
resident, W. H. Chatfield, offered a unique explanation for poor tejanos'
Spanish use: "The lower classes adhere to it [the Spanish language] with an
obstinate persistence which may be laudable in the abstract, evincing a love
of their native land, but it is scarcely to be commended when it is considered that they are inhabitants of an American town, and are under the
protection of the laws of the United States. This trait is probably due to *the
Indian blood in their veins*; for an Indian will resort to every expedient before
he will admit that he understands or can speak Englssh [*sic*]." A federal
officer, sent to the Rio Grande border to investigate cattle raids, mistook
language for loyalty as well. Adjutant-General William Steele argued that
tejanos' inability to speak English proved they held stronger allegiances to
Mexico than to the United States. "This population has little knowledge of
the customs of the American people, and none of the laws which are
supposed to govern them . . . the result of which is," he added, "that county
officers, in some of the counties bordering on the Rio Grande, have little
qualifications, except that of being able to read the laws and talk Mexican."[49]

Rather than reflecting disloyalty, tejanos' continued use of Spanish confirmed that it was the border region's lingua franca. A few visitors acknowledged that people on both sides of the border shared a common culture and
language. "It is very difficult for any person not familiar with the boundary-
line to tell where Mexico leaves off and where the United States begin," the
infantry captain H. C. Corbin testified before a congressional committee.
"From any difference in the habits, customs, and appearance of the people.
From Brownsville to El Paso, even on our own bank of the Rio Grande, the
Spanish language is a common language."[50]

Knowledge of English did not correlate with patriotism, but rather with
an individual's political and economic ties beyond the local level. Merchants and itinerant workers were more likely to speak English than were
local rancheros and day laborers. Knowledge of English was also a sign of a

person's involvement in local politics. English was an administrative and economic language, while Spanish served as a social and cultural language among tejanos. To paraphrase the historian Peter Sahlins's analysis of a similar phenomenon along the French-Spanish border, fluid linguistic and identity boundaries persisted alongside the permeable territorial boundary between Mexico and the United States.[51]

Mexicans and the Civil War

During the Civil War, Anglo American doubts about Mexican Texans' citizenship receded into the background. This occurred because, as the border region's strategic and economic importance grew, the Confederacy and Union needed support from tejanos. The Confederacy began exporting cotton across the Rio Grande, one of the few areas to escape the Union blockade. Cotton initially flowed out of Brazos Santiago in Texas but Confederate officials, facing pressure from federal forces, shifted operations to the port of Bagdad, along the beach in Matamoros. This trade, which exported cotton from the southern states to Europe while importing manufactured goods and war supplies, fueled a period of prosperity and population boom along the border from 1861 to 1865.[52]

The Rio Grande region's strategic importance encouraged the Confederacy and the Union to enlist Mexicans regardless of citizenship. Recruited from both sides of the border, an estimated 2,550 Mexicans joined Confederate troops and 960 became Union soldiers (see figure 17). Texas's Confederate draft explains the skewed numbers. The forced conscription of Mexican Texans pulled so many cartmen out of work that it threatened to curtail trade between Texas and Mexico. Béxar, Refugio, and Webb Counties supplied many tejano Confederates, while Cameron, Hidalgo, and Nueces Counties contributed most tejano Unionists. Border Unionists launched their first armed action in April 1861 and fought one of the last battles of the war, in May 1865. Although most soldiers were concentrated along the border, Mexican troops fought battles throughout Texas, in neighboring Louisiana and New Mexico, and as far away as Virginia and Georgia.[53]

While the border economy was not dependent on slavery, the peculiar institution did influence the region and led Mexicans to participate in the war. Only fourteen slaves (all owned by Anglos) lived in the border counties in 1860 because slaves could easily escape into Mexico. Although tejanos owned slaves (sixty in 1860), most lived far from the border. Some Mexican

17. An unidentified Mexican Texan Union cavalry soldier. Circa 1864 to 1865. Mexicans and Mexican Texans volunteered for the Federal First and Second Texas Cavalry regiments. Courtesy of Museum of South Texas History, Edinburg, Texas.

Texans helped slaves flee across the international border, while others pursued runaway slaves into Mexico. The wealthy tended to side with the Confederacy due to alliances with Democrats and slave owners. In turn, a history of racial antagonisms along the border fueled the desire of poor mexicanos to seek revenge against the largely pro-Confederate americano minority by siding with the Union.[54]

A political disagreement in Zapata County demonstrates some of the region's ethnic and class divisions. The county's population (which boasted the largest percentage of tejanos along the border) consisted of numerous small landowners and agricultural workers along with a few elite tejanos allied with wealthy americano merchants and landowners. Among the elite were the county judge Isidro Vela, a large landowner, and Henry Redmond, an Englishman who had married the local resident Refugia Díaz. In January 1861, Zapata County joined Cameron, Hidalgo, Starr, and Webb Counties in voting overwhelmingly for secession. Zapata County recorded no ballots opposing secession, confirming the electoral influence of elite merchants and landowners. Judge Vela had threatened to fine secession opponents; he also arrested those who refused to vote. Yet, this plebiscite masked deep political divisions, evident three months later with a rebellion of tejano Unionists.[55]

In April 1861, Antonio Ochoa led fifty Mexican Texans in seizing control of a southern precinct in Zapata County. They claimed to owe no allegiance to the state or the Confederacy, and they threatened to sack the county's finances and hang the sheriff. Judge Vela persuaded Ochoa's troops to withdraw, but days later the insurrectionists presented Vela with a pronunciamento against the Confederacy. Alarmed, Vela and Redmond requested aid from nearby Webb County. Confederate soldiers surprised Ochoa's men, killing combatants and noncombatants alike. Tejano Unionists would later seek to avenge these deaths by attacking Redmond's fortified rancho complex. Reporting on this attack, an americano would claim "not a single citizen of the county came to our assistance." Subsequent news stories confirmed that most Zapata County residents sided with the Union or remained neutral.[56]

Dismissing the Unionists as ignorant criminal opportunists, local Confederates delegitimized the grievances of tejanos. Politicians and journalists were quick to characterize them as "bandits" and "assassins" from Mexico. According to Judge Vela, Ochoa had "collected all the thieves, murderers and assassins of Guerrero." Guerrero was located in Mexico opposite Zapata County. Ochoa's men asked Vela to forward their pronunciamento to federal officials, whom they believed were "a few miles on the other side of Bexar," according to Redmond. This led him to conclude that it was "hard to say how far their ignorance will lead them." Yet, Ochoa's supporters were far from ignorant; rather, they refused to continue accepting the patronizing control exercised by the county's political clique.[57]

Ochoa's men left few written records, so their motivations are difficult to discern. However, their actions offer some clues. Journalists reported that they had allegedly threatened to "kill the gringos" in the county. These reports might have been the exaggerated fears of Anglos, who were vastly outnumbered by Mexican Texans. On the other hand, the Unionists were likely venting their frustration at the powerful political control exercised by the americano and tejano elite. Ochoa's men also threatened to hang Sheriff Pedro Díaz and to seize the county's funds. Had they merely been displeased with the county's political machine, Ochoa's men had little reason to mention its support for the Confederacy. According to a local americano, "Fifty men of this county had armed themselves, and organized for the avowed purpose of keeping the county officers from taking the oath of office prescribed by the Convention. They had declared that they owed no allegiance to the State or Confederate States, and that they would not obey or respect the authorities holding office under either." The Unionists opposed the county's vote for secession and wanted to avoid fighting for a cause they did not support. Given the proclamation's various demands, the Unionists' motivations were more complicated than merely striking back at Zapata County's political elite.[58]

After Ochoa's uprising, local recruits swelled the Union ranks. While some joined as a result of Union recruitment, others enlisted for complex reasons. Among the Unionists were Teodicio Zamora, a former Hidalgo County judge, Octaviano Zapata, a small landowner in Zapata County, and several men allied with Juan Cortina. Unionists were soon harassing Confederate cotton shipments and engaging in cross-border raids. In December 1862, two hundred tejano Unionists demonstrated their resentment against the county's political elite by capturing Judge Vela at his ranch and hanging him from a tree. They left a note warning others not to remove the body unless they wished to suffer the same fate. The political divisions embodied in these conflicts reflected the tejano community's economic fissures, resentment over political subordination, and ideological differences over slavery.[59]

Various issues drew tejanos into the war. While many Union recruits were illiterate laborers, farmers, and herdsmen, their numbers also included

18. Laredo's men joined the Confederacy in large numbers under the influence of the Benavides family. Circa 1863 to 1864. Pictured from left to right: Captain Refugio Benavides, Lieutenant Atanacio Vidaurri, Captain Cristóbal Benavides, and Captain John Z. Leyendecker (a Benavides in-law). Courtesy of Webb County Heritage Foundation Collection, Laredo, Texas.

literate shoemakers, masons, and elected officials. Like Anglo American and African American soldiers throughout the nation, Mexican Texans had different degrees of literacy and understanding of the conflict. The Union's signing bonus of land and money undoubtedly attracted some recruits. Tejano Confederates included volunteers and draftees. Soldiers also chose sides based on the influence of their friends and family. Laredo's Benavideses, large landowners and perennial politicians, were fervent slavery supporters, who recruited others for the Confederacy (see figure 18). Cortina, Ochoa, and Zapata were equally crucial in recruiting for the Union. By joining the Union, tejanos struck back at their old enemies—the americano elite who had supported the Confederacy.[60]

Tejano Unionists were also motivated by antislavery feelings. Their sympathies were reinforced when slaves worked alongside Mexican Texan laborers on plantations elsewhere in Texas. Along the border, this interethnic bond was strongest in Hidalgo County, where several former slaves had married into local tejano families. Others took considerable risks to rescue slaves and transport them to Mexico for safety. Slaves, of course, also ran away on their own and escaped across the border in considerable numbers. Across Texas, Anglos adopted punitive measures against antislavery tejanos. Guadalupe County passed a resolution prohibiting "Mexican peons" from entering the county "because of their alleged sympathy with bondspeople."[61]

While living in Mexican border towns, fugitive slaves nurtured positive relations with Mexicans. Several former slaves married Mexican nationals and used their skills to obtain financial security. This positive relationship with tejanos' relatives and friends in Mexico undoubtedly fueled antislavery feelings. Although a few tejanos captured runaway slaves in Mexico, most border residents did not cooperate with slave owners despite bounties of two hundred to five hundred dollars on runaways. The friendship between fugitive slaves and Mexicans surprised supporters of slavery. "This admiration for negroes somewhat disgusted me with the Mexicans," wrote newcomer Teresa Vielé while visiting Rio Grande City. "For in spite of philanthropy, Christian charity, and liberal views, I do not believe that the colored and white races can ever by any possibility amalgamate to an equality!"[62]

The Civil War brought up several unresolved issues, such as slavery, citizenship, and political participation. While these issues had different salience along the border than in other regions of the United States, they nevertheless motivated residents to take sides. Like other communities throughout the nation, Mexican Texans displayed strong divisions during the Civil War and had complex, and often contradictory, reasons for participating. While few bondspeople lived along the border, slavery was still relevant because runaway slaves passed through the region and often settled across the river. Moreover, African Americans and mexicanos intermarried on both sides of the Rio Grande. Undoubtedly, many tejanos knew the conflict's causes and significance. By soldiering in the Civil War, they also staked a claim to American citizenship.

Unequal Soldiers

As in civilian life, mexicanos faced discrimination within the Confederate and Union Armies. While serving in segregated units under Anglo American commanding officers, they suffered from insufficient clothing, ammunition, and armaments. Language barriers magnified their problems. In

an effort to remedy their mistreatment, some Mexican Unionists unsuccessfully objected to the appointment of a monolingual English-speaking
officer to their regiment. The mistreatment included each army's failure to
compensate soldiers. Confederate officials failed to pay one local unit for
nine months. This problem exacerbated tejanos' existing poverty-stricken
conditions. Many families had crossed into Mexico to escape the violence
associated with the war. With their lands on the Texas side unattended,
these refugee families had little recourse but to sell their small herds of
livestock in order to obtain money for necessities.[63]

Mexicans in both armies experienced numerous discriminatory inci-
dents. One episode occurred in October 1861, when tejanos from Laredo
fulfilled their first six-month enlistment. Confederate officials attempted to
persuade them to reenlist for three years. The soldiers objected to such a
long commitment and their commander, Santos Benavides, asked the governor why his troops were asked to enlist for three years while other non-
Mexican troops could enlist for one year. Apparently, state officials distrusted Laredo's troops with newly issued firearms, believing the troops
might abscond with them when mustered out of service. The state legislature's distrust of Mexicans was apparent in another proposal to arm these
volunteers with lances. Charles Løvenskiold, a local Confederate recruiter,
acknowledged the problem. In letters to the governor, he argued that unequal treatment might hurt the Confederacy's recruiting efforts. "If the
Benavides company is not mustered into the service of the C.S. [Confeder-
ate States] now, they will of course disband, and it will be impracticable
hereafter to get any Mexican citizen to enlist or form another company,
while the state, as well as the Confederate Government, will be blamed and
rendered unpopular about it, as in their ignorance of matters they will
attribute their non-acceptance to prejudice against their nationality or origin." Eventually the governor agreed to allow Mexicans to enlist for only
one year, but these troops continued to receive substandard treatment.[64]

Not surprisingly, Mexican troops began deserting in large numbers from
both Confederate and Union units. Some left the service by escaping across
the border after receiving severe discipline. Others deserted to avoid trans-
fers out of state. The majority of desertions, however, occurred because
troops were unpaid and lacked clothing, supplies, or medicine. Upon leaving their units, impoverished troops improved their financial situation by
selling their arms and ammunition to soldiers in Mexico. Moreover, Mexicans became frustrated that their military service and lack of pay prevented
them from providing financial assistance to their families. One of these

soldiers was Adrián J. Vidal, who had initially joined the Confederate Army but later deserted, after which he recruited for the Union. Frustrated that his responsibilities as Union captain kept him from attending to his family, Vidal wrote to his superiors, "having a family in Brownsville who need my protection and help and the duties of the service will not allow me to devote the time necessary required to her interest." He asked for a leave while his resignation was processed, but grew tired of waiting and ultimately deserted. Unable to persuade officers of the need to financially support their families, many Mexican soldiers simply walked away.[65]

Union officials took advantage by recruiting Mexican Confederate deserters. Edmund Davis and John Haynes, former local officeholders, opposed secession and had crossed into Mexico after Texas joined the Confederacy. Haynes depended on long-time acquaintances, such as Antonio Abad Díaz and George Treviño, to recruit mexicanos. The U.S. consul in Matamoros, Leonard Pierce, assisted Davis and Haynes in establishing contact with Union leaders in New Orleans and in enlisting troops. Their success led the Confederate commander stationed at Fort Brown to complain bitterly to Mexican officials in an unsuccessful attempt to stop Union recruiting in Mexico.[66]

Anglo American military officers resorted to familiar characterizations of Mexicans when these soldiers switched sides or deserted. Confederate Colonel August Buchel characterized mexicanos as undependable, easily bribed, and vulnerable to corruption. Union Lieutenant Benjamin F. McIntyre believed Mexicans were deserting because they were "dishonest, cowardly, and treacherous and only bide their time to make good their escape." These characterizations recalled the charges of "unpatriotic" and "undependable" Mexicans during Texas's separatist revolt. Although Confederate officers characterized Anglo American deserters as "renegades" and "apostate Texans," they did not demean these men's racial or immigrant background. This noteworthy difference confirmed officials' heightened suspicions about tejano loyalties.[67]

Despite acknowledging problems with troop morale, some Anglo American officers reverted to racial arguments to explain the defections. In 1864 more than two hundred mexicano soldiers abandoned the Union Army. Colonel Edmund Davis acknowledged that the Union Army had not paid the enlistment bounty nor supplied sufficient clothing to these soldiers, and as a result "there is among them an impression that they have been badly treated." Nevertheless, he explained their defection by echoing prevalent racial Anglo Saxonism. Because of Mexicans' "Indian blood and nature, the discipline and restraint of this camp, and the value of their horses, arms and equipment proving too much of a temptation," argued Davis, "they take an opportunity to desert and carry them into Mexico." Yet, all officers did not share these views. Racial discrimination explained the neglect of mexicano Confederates, according to Charles Løvenskiold, a Confederate inspector who addressed Laredo's troops. Several military officers, Løvenskiold argued, believed, "that because [you are] citizens of Mexican origin[,] you neither could be trusted as far nor fight as well or as valiantly as those of your fellow citizens who have only Anglo-Saxon blood coursing through their veins." He also refuted the tendency of Anglos to claim "the exclusive right of calling themselves 'Americans'" by praising Laredo's Mexican Texans for their "valor and patriotism in the Southern cause."[68]

Tejano actions suggest another possibility—that they were adept at using multiple identities to better their lives. In 1863, after Texas instituted the Confederate draft for all "white men between the ages of eighteen and thirty-five," conscription agents scoured the countryside looking for able-bodied men. Casting aside their concerns about Mexican Texans' racial status and eligibility for citizenship, Confederate recruiters had no misgivings about considering them white citizens for draft purposes. Alerted to the recruiters' intentions, many fled to Mexico. Despite this large-scale departure, agents managed to conscript over three hundred men (including some Mexican nationals). Others avoided conscription by using an excuse that manipulated Anglo American prejudices. Frustrated about not finding any eligible recruits in areas that had previously polled many Mexican Texan voters, a conscription agent wrote, "nearly every other man I met claimed to be a citizen of Mexico, and therefore exempt from conscription." To avoid the draft, they strategically denied their membership in a nation that often did not uphold their citizenship rights. Not only did Mexican Texans cross the physical international border to escape conscription but they also intentionally blurred the figurative border of citizenship. Like people living in national borderlands elsewhere, tejanos embraced their ambiguous national identity to their advantage.[69]

Mexican Texans further exploited their unresolved citizenship to obtain temporary leaves or discharges from military service. While Americanos often cited tejanos' inability to speak English to show their loyalty as suspect, tejano soldiers manipulated this fear. Frustrated when they were denied leaves to visit their impoverished families, Mexican Texans claimed that their lack of English-language skills kept them from performing their jobs. Union Lieutenant Santos Cadena offered such an excuse to justify his

19. Quartermaster Sergeant José Lino Hinojosa and his brother-in-law Sergeant González served in the Union's Second Texas Cavalry. Circa 1863 to 1864. Courtesy of Museum of South Texas History, Edinburg, Texas.

resignation from the second Texas Cavalry in a Spanish-language letter. "I am entirely ignorant of the English language," he wrote, "and feel that I cannot acquire a knowledge of it sufficiently to enable me to become familiar with the United States Cav. [Cavalry] Tactics." His second reason for resigning, however, revealed a more pressing concern. "I have a large family from whom I have been long separated," stated Cadena, "and who now require my immediate presence and support." After commanding his unit for over six months, Union Captain Adrián Vidal made a similar claim in his resignation letter. "I find myself incompetent to carry on the company books," he argued in a letter dictated to his superiors, "as I do not understand nor have anybody in my company to understand the English language for this purpose." When the Second Cavalry (see figure 19) was transferred to Louisiana, several soldiers, including Captain Cesario Falcón, submitted their resignations, citing an inability to speak English. Falcón had fallen ill, longed to join his family in Mexico (where they had fled), and was upset upon learning of the deaths of his father and brother. While the inability to speak English could obviously impair communications with English-speaking troops and officials, tejano soldiers had previously not allowed this obstacle to hinder their military service. Officers such as Cadena, Vidal, and Falcón had performed their duties for several months without any problems. However, when soldiers realized that they could not resign or obtain a leave, they employed a common excuse to obtain a discharge.[70]

Several military officials acknowledged that mistreatment fueled desertions. According to Colonel John Haynes, the inactivity of camp life and the inability of soldiers to obtain furloughs to visit their families led to defections. He also blamed military authorities in Mexico, who enticed Union deserters with money for their firearms. The allure of money was great because soldiers were often not paid, Haynes maintained. Desertion and sale of military equipment became as common among Civil War soldiers as the capture and sale of Indian slaves had been among Spanish colonial soldiers, whose government also failed to pay them. In both cases, governmental neglect forced borderland residents to devise their own solutions.[71]

Despite risking their lives for the Confederacy, tejanos did not obtain acceptance from local journalists. Postelection comments reveal deep-seated racist views that excluded many tejanos from political participation. In 1863, after Laredo provided the swing votes to defeat the state representative candidate favored by americanos, local editors expressed hostility. The predominantly Mexican Texan electorate voted for Charles Callaghan instead of Sommers Kinney, who was supported by americanos in Corpus Christi. After serving as a Confederate lieutenant among troops commanded by Laredo's Santos Benavides, Callaghan was well known to tejanos. When Callaghan defeated Kinney, newspaper editors unleashed a vitriolic attack against the Laredo electorate. The *American Flag* portrayed Laredo's "lower order" of Mexican Texans as "not only abolitionists but amalgamationists" who married blacks and "always assist a runaway slave to escape from his master." Unacknowledged by the editors was a widely known fact—Laredo supplied a disproportionately high number of tejano Confederates compared to other regions of the state. The *Ranchero* disregarded this strong Confederate support, choosing instead to argue against the electoral rights of Mexican Texans: "The returns of the election show that Mr. S. Kinney is the choice for representative over Mr. Callaghan by fifteen voters out of every sixteen in every place where the English language is spoken; but, over yonder, where the Mexican language is spoken, the tables were turned, and Mr. Callaghan is the choice almost unanimously. We have no objection to Mr. Callaghan; nevertheless, we think American men in an American country should have a fair showing in shaping the destinies of the country, by their votes." The term *American men* implied Anglo American males. To explain the election results, the *Ranchero* trotted out the age-old allegation of imported voters from Mexico. The *American Flag*, in strong objection to Mexican Texans' political participation, wrote, "We affirm that it is inconsistent with our laws or our institutions that Mexicans should have the same political rights in this state as Americans."[72]

Faced with this type of fervent opposition, tejanos pursued avenues that would guarantee their rights. In April 1863 Hamilton Bee, the Confederate brigadier general stationed at Fort Brown, decided against enforcing the conscription law. The enforcement of the draft, Bee argued, would drive Mexican Texans across the border and convert them into enemies of the Confederacy. Instead, he implemented a "course of policy toward the Mexicans on this frontier by which I seek to protect them in their rights and immunities as *citizens* and thereby attach them to our cause." Bee concluded, "This plan is meeting with success." His alternative recruitment plan contained a veiled acknowledgment of a common problem facing tejanos—the denial of their rights. The plan's success suggests that Mexican Texans joined the military to obtain protection for their citizenship rights. Like African Americans, who expected to be rewarded for their patriotic Civil War participation with full citizenship rights, tejanos considered their military service as proof of their loyalty. In a petition to their superiors, George Treviño and other Mexican Texan Union officers alluded to this loyalty. They asked that "the Government may take into consideration our patriotic desires, and that we may, in future as in the past, have the pride of increasing the ranks of the Army of the United States, although we are the last soldiers." Among the reasons that tejanos joined the Confederate or Union Army was their belief that military service would act as a future guarantee of their citizenship rights.[73]

In the postwar period, Mexican Unionists derived fewer benefits from their military service than did Anglos. Reconstruction governments rewarded Union officers and soldiers with political posts, land, and other benefits. Edmund Davis became governor in 1870 under the Radical Reconstruction government, while John Haynes became collector of customs for Galveston and later for Brownsville and Brazos Santiago. Mexican Texans did not fare as well. One subsequently became justice of the peace in Zapata County, and several served as Cameron County constables. Most tejano Unionists, however, did not reap political or economic benefits. Mexican nationals who obtained an honorable discharge from the Union Army became eligible for naturalization after a year of residence. Despite their military service, however, these newly naturalized Americans were accused of voter fraud by americanos intent on limiting their electoral rights. Additionally, several Union veterans fell victim to a rash of racially motivated violence between 1865 and 1870 that resulted in over one hundred murders in the border region.[74]

After the Civil War, the ex-Confederates' view of Mexican Texans underwent a metamorphosis. The Reconstruction Congress passed laws disenfranchising ex-Confederates. Most tejanos were not affected by this legislation, because few had been officeholders who supported secession. Subsequently, Radical Republicans and ex-Confederates courted Mexican Texans. A *Daily Ranchero* editorial illustrates americanos' changing notion of citizenship based on new political circumstances. In sharp contrast to their prewar position, ex-Confederate editors acknowledged tejanos' American citizenship in a front-page appeal to "the Citizens of the United States, of Mexican origin, in Cameron County." Mexican Texans had a choice "between confiscation, negro equality and your ultimate extinction," the editors declared, "and on the other hand, liberty, rights of interest, and social distinction." In their most dramatic statement, the editors portrayed tejanos (irrespective of class) as "freeborn white citizens" and urged their "fellow-citizens" to register and vote against the Republican program. This dramatic reversal demonstrates how Anglos socially constructed citizenship to suit their needs. Tejanos had also socially constructed their citizenship, or sense of belonging to the nation, but with less freedom and political power.[75]

Transnational Ties

Border residents also became drawn into Mexico's struggle against French intervention during the U.S. Civil War. The Mexican conflict began after President Benito Juárez decided to suspend payments on Mexico's foreign debt—the nation was bankrupt after emerging from a devastating civil conflict (War of Reform, 1858–61) between liberal and conservative factions. His decision prompted England, Spain, and France (the nation's major creditors) to occupy Mexico's ports in 1862 in order to collect their claims. After realizing that Napoleon III intended to use the occupation to conquer Mexico, England and Spain withdrew their forces. French forces defeated Mexican troops to establish a monarchy that ruled Mexico until 1867, when *juaristas* (Juárez's forces) drove out the French Army. Preoccupied with its own civil war, the U.S. government eventually helped Juárez by allowing his agents to purchase weapons and ammunition, as well as to recruit volunteers in the United States. Juárez's victory boosted nationalism and confidence through Mexico. Along the border, mexicanos and tejanos fought for and against the French intervention, but most favored troops allied with President Juárez. While alliances shifted throughout the wars, the Unionists established stronger links to the juaristas, while the Confederates allied with the French. Various troops repeatedly crossed the border to pursue their opponents and to seek refuge. Deserters traversed the river in both directions, and sometimes joined the corresponding nation's armed conflict, especially if their unit leader switched alliances. Cross-border social ties shaped some decisions. Union deserters, for example, might join their families or friends in juarista units. As troops appropriated livestock and firewood, or imprisoned suspects for aiding their enemies, ranch owners and workers felt pressured from multiple sides. The border between the United States and Mexico failed to contain each nation's internal conflict. In addition to troops and supplies, ideas about nations, sovereignty, and freedom traversed the boundary to shape the views of local residents.[76]

The multiple national and local influences on Mexican Texan identities were richly illustrated at a Cinco de Mayo (Fifth of May) celebration in Zapata County in 1867. A local guitarist and songwriter, Onofre Cárdenas, composed two *corridos* (Mexican folksongs) for the festivities in San Ignacio, Texas. The first song honored the memory of Ignacio Zaragoza, a hero of the battle of Puebla on 5 May 1862, in which Mexican troops defeated the occupying French Army. Born in Goliad, Texas, Zaragoza attended school in Matamoros, where his family had fled to escape the racial violence in the

Texas Revolution's aftermath. Drawing on the national anthems of Mexico and France for the music, Cárdenas turned to local folklore tradition for his lyrics. "To Zaragoza" aptly illustrates Cardenas's knowledge of various international genres, as he borrowed from romantic Mexican ballads, Spanish musical comedies, and military rhythms.

> Dios te salve, valiente Zaragoza,
> invicto general de la frontera
> yo con los libres saludo tu bandera
> que en Puebla tremoló sin descansar.
> Los hijos de la patria te saludan
> Solemnizando tu triunfo de en esta día, . . .
> No olviden mexicanos que en el Cinco de Mayo
> los zuavos como un rayo corrieron . . . ¡para atrás! . . .

> God save thee, brave Zaragoza,
> unconquerable general of the border;
> I and all free men salute your flag
> That waved unceasingly in Puebla.
> The sons of the Fatherland salute you,
> Celebrating your triumph on this day, . . .
> Mexicans, don't forget that on the fifth of May
> The Zouaves, with lightning speed, ran . . . toward the rear! . . .

According to the folklorist Américo Paredes, "To Zaragoza" is emblematic of border tejanos' dynamic and contingent position within competing national imaginaries: the narrator is alternately a U.S. citizen, a Mexican citizen, and a proud *fronterizo* (borderland resident, or son of the *patria chica* [locality] of the border region). The corrido's narrative voice begins from the perspective of a fronterizo, who depicts Zaragoza as an "unconquerable general of the border" and not as a Mexican officer. This characterization suggests regional pride for a fronterizo who became a Mexican national hero. The narrator's perspective then shifts to that of U.S. citizens (namely Union supporters or "I and free men"), who salute Zaragoza's (meaning Mexico's) flag. The narrative voice ends with the views of Mexican citizens, "sons of the Fatherland," who revel with pride and nationalism at the French defeat. Municipal celebrations in border towns during subsequent years undoubtedly affirmed this binational and regional pride.[77]

The second song was musically similar to the first corrido, but it honored Ulysses S. Grant for leading the Union forces to victory. Alluding to the Union, liberty, and freedom, the narrator is initially an American citizen

("Long live Grant! citizens") but shifts to a Mexican citizen ("Mexico too exalts your name"). The final verses allude to Grant's support for Benito Juárez, and thus his support for the Mexican Constitution.

> ¡Viva Grant! ¡Viva Grant! ciudadanos,
> que cinco años la guerra sostuvo . . .
> Y después de sangrientos combates,
> do murieron valientes soldados,
> fueron libres aquellos estados
> que jamás pretendían la igualdad. . . .
> También México ensalza tu nombre,
> porque fuiste con él indulgente,
> fuiste siempre y serás el valiente
> que defiende la Constitución.

> Long live Grant! Long live Grant! citizens,
> who sustained the war for five years . . .
> And after bloody battles
> in which brave soldiers died,
> those states were free
> that had never aspired to equality. . . .
> Mexico too exalts your name
> because you were kind toward it;
> you have always been and shall be the brave one,
> who defended the Constitution.

As vehicles of popular sentiment, these corridos confirm that border Mexicans understood the ideological issues that provoked the American Civil War and Mexico's war against French intervention. Passed across multiple generations of fronterizos before being recorded, the corridos are local expressions of Mexican nationalism, American patriotism, and regional pride. Moreover, these folksongs tellingly reveal border residents' comfort with multiple identities, which appeared to be ambiguous to newcomers or visitors. Yet, locals' self-perception as Mexican nationals, Americans, and tejanos all at the same time appeared unambiguous to them. Mexican Texans expressed a political affinity with the United States, but also felt connected to Mexico, just as Mexican nationals had links to the United States. In addition to the corridos' international and local influences, the setting expressed transnational bonds, as the songs were performed at Cinco de Mayo festivities in which American citizens (Mexican Texans) celebrated Mexican nationalism in an American border town. Ultimately, the songs served as reminders that the processes of state formation of both nations influenced, but did not completely shape, the identities of Mexicans in the political and cultural borderland of south Texas.[78]

The Floating Population's Transnational Ties

In the aftermath of the U.S. Civil War, the "Cattle War" of the 1870s further soured relations among Anglos, Mexican nationals, and Mexican Texans. The conflict involved cattle rustling in the Nueces Strip, whose origins American investigators traced to the aftermath of Texas's secession. The separatist struggle, Mexico's attempts to reconquer the breakaway republic, and Anglo Texan attacks on the villas del norte generated widespread turmoil that worsened ethnic relations. Thieves capitalized on the disorder to raid the region's ranches for livestock, which numbered some three million. Many residents abandoned their homes and relocated closer to the Rio Grande for safety while most of their cattle were "abandoned or destroyed." The U.S.-Mexican War aggravated the turmoil and economic losses of the region's ranches. Subsequently, the creation of a new international boundary at the Rio Grande provided additional opportunities for cattle theft. By the 1860s, Mexican nationals had begun crossing into Texas to steal cattle from americanos and tejanos, triggering counterraids into Mexico. Indians robbed from both sides of the border and fled across the river to escape prosecution. Although various ethnic groups stole cattle, politicians and the press mostly blamed Indians and Mexicans. American military officers attributed the raids to Mexicans who harbored a "violent antipathy towards gringos." Mexican Texans and Mexican nationals conspired to steal from americanos, according to a congressional committee witness, because they were part of the same community—they were "Mexicans in feeling, thought, language, religion, and everything." The overwhelming Mexican majority along the border fueled Anglo fears of a cattle-rustling conspiracy. In 1870, the number of residents between the Rio Grande and Nueces rivers was about twenty-seven thousand, of whom approximately nine out of ten were Mexicans. Several observers estimated Mexico's border population at between fifty-four and eighty-one thousand. Greatly outnumbered, americanos felt overwhelmed.[79]

Although lumped together, tejanos and Mexican nationals experienced the turmoil of the Cattle War quite differently. Among the military officers who arrived on the border to capture cattle rustlers, a few noticed the distinct problems facing each group. "The interest of the common people on this side of the river are scarcely the interests of the people on the other side," replied H. C. Corbin to a congressional committee question. He proceeded to explain the vastly different economic realities confronting each group. "For instance, $5 is quite a fortune to a Mexican [national]. He can gamble and live a long time on $5. He crosses the river to the American side, kills a beef, gets the hide off and carries it to Matamoras [sic], where he can sell it for $5, and with that money he is well off for some time. That is done often, and it makes the people on this side mad with the people on the other." When asked whether tejanos were "naturalized," he replied, "Yes; they are voters and in many instances they are very excellent citizens." Explaining Mexican Texan rancheros' problems, Corbin argued that many had abandoned their ranches after growing alarmed by the livestock theft and the murders of their friends. Such testimony confirmed that Mexico's faltering economy led some Mexican nationals to cross the border and engage in cattle theft, which, in turn, hurt tejanos' livelihood. Despite sharing an ethnic background, tejanos and Mexican nationals were clearly separated by citizenship and stark economic realities.[80]

Although cattle thieves from Mexico were thought to be somewhat lenient on them, tejanos nevertheless incurred severe reprisals. "The raiders do not like to kill their Mexican friends as well as they like to kill what they call *gringos*," testified the lawyer John McCampbell. He continued, "They have an enmity toward the Americans stronger than toward the Mexicans; but still they rob Mexican ranches, and steal their cattle." Most Anglo American ranchers lived in the security of nearby towns, preferring to visit their ranches occasionally. According to McCampbell, Mexican Texans remained in their ranch homes because they were native to the region and had long-standing ties to their ancestral lands. These rancheros undoubtedly also remembered that when tejanos abandoned their ranchos during the Texas revolt, their land was seized by squatters and vigilantes. A Texas Ranger explained the predicament of the rancheros: "The Mexican owners of ranches on this side of the river, those who are citizens of Texas, are, almost to a man, as much opposed to this system of raiding as the American citizens of Texas are."[81]

Caught between Texas Rangers and Mexican cattle thieves, tejanos were hesitant to cooperate with law-enforcement officials. After years of enduring the rangers' harassment and intimidation, Mexican Texans were clearly distrustful of officials, but they also feared the possibility of reprisals from thieves. Nevertheless, tejanos provided information that helped capture rustlers, but some were subsequently killed for cooperating. The fear of reprisals was widespread. "The Mexican jurors are afraid [for] their lives," stated a lawyer. "If they would bring a bill of indictment against a cow-thief, or a raider from the other side of the river, those raiders would kill them." When law-enforcement officials confronted suspected cattle thieves in the countryside, the suspects often claimed to work on a nearby ranch. Workers from these ranches would confirm that the suspects were coworkers because they feared harassment and intimidation from these roving gangs. The rangers acknowledged that thieves pressured Mexican Texans, who were "powerless to resist [the thieves'] demands."[82]

Officials further complicated the precarious situation of Mexican Texans by blaming them for thefts carried out by Mexican nationals. In some cases, Anglo American ranchers killed tejano suspects, despite scant evidence linking the victims to the raiders. Instead of investigating the crimes to find the guilty parties, they lashed out at defenseless Mexican Texans. In 1873, an infamous thief from Mexico, Alberto Garza, crossed into Texas and stole a large quantity of livestock. In response, americanos in Corpus Christi hanged seven tejano shepherds who were suspected of assisting Garza, although a congressional committee found "no direct evidence" that the victims were Garza's accomplices. Unfortunately, officials failed to identify and punish the Anglo American vigilantes.[83]

The task of capturing cattle thieves was complicated by soldiers' inability to distinguish between Mexican nationals and Mexican Texans. Several newly arrived soldiers saw Mexicans as an undifferentiated whole, regardless of their citizenship status. "The personal appearance of the Mexican raiders on the American side does not differ any from the appearance of the Mexican inhabitants generally on the American side," Captain Clous noted. "Hence the pursuit of raiders in the interior of Texas is a matter of great difficulty. They look like all the other Mexicans," Clous complained, "and are armed nearly the same way; there is hardly any difference." Confounding matters further, military officers confirmed the presence of mexicanos, whose social and economic lives straddled the international border. According to Brigadier-General Ord, "The Mexican ranches under old Mexican titles embrace all that country between the Nueces and the Rio Grande and south of Fort Duncan. . . . A great many people who live in Mexico own ranches in Texas." The cattle raids forced American troops to confront the messy consequences of territorial conquest and the imposition of an international boundary in a region with a shared culture. These soldiers shared a similar problem with government officials along the border between the

United States and Canada, who struggled to identify Métis as American or Canadian because of this population's ambiguous citizenship as well as cross-border kin and trade networks. In both cases, a native population's transboundary social and economic practices (whose origins predated the international boundaries) undermined the efforts of nation-states to enforce their territorial boundaries.[84]

The Cattle War offered state and national leaders another opportunity to link class with citizenship by praising elite tejanos' respect for the law. Congressional investigators described them as "good, honorable, law-abiding men, citizens of this state and fully entitled to the protection of the law." According to congressional reports on the cattle raids, Mexican Texan landowners were good citizens who suffered greatly from cattle thieves preying on their stock. Texas's governor, in congressional testimony, confirmed the loyalty and responsibility of Mexican Texans. After consulting local ranchers familiar with border residents, the congressional investigators gave individual tejano rancheros special accolades. "Far from sympathizing with the robbers and raiders, they have often been foremost in the defense of our border, and in the punishment of invaders," the committee reported.[85]

In response to the widespread raids, the Mexican and American governments sent investigative committees to the border. Predictably, each committee's report alleged that the cattle rustlers lived in the opposing nation, where they operated with impunity. The Mexican commissioners believed Mexican Texans and Anglo Americans stole livestock from Mexico with the assistance of Texas county officials. In particular, they accused Thadeus Rhodes, Adolphus Glavecke, and León and José Estapa of cattle theft. Rhodes had been an Hidalgo County justice of the peace in 1873; León Estapa had served as sheriff while José Estapa had been tax collector of the same county. Glavecke had been a juror in Cameron County and a Brownsville alderman. The Mexican commissioners cited Texas newspaper accounts to emphasize that cattle rustling was widespread throughout Texas and not limited to the Nueces Strip. Most stolen livestock, they argued, was skinned immediately to sell as hides. Several Anglo American ranchers, such as Richard King and Mifflin Kenedy, had increased their livestock greatly while Mexican Texan stock raisers suffered devastating losses. Noting this pattern, the commissioners accused these wealthy americanos of profiting from the contraband livestock trade. Regardless of the smugglers' origins or the direction of the contraband, the prevalence of the illegal trade demonstrated the impossibility of restricting the movement of cattle across a sparsely monitored border. This boundary, as the historian Rachel St. John argues for the western United States–Mexico borderlands, "is not a space of absolutes," where territorial sovereignty can be rigidly enforced. Instead, it is a region where native populations (of humans and animals) engage in daily practices that blur the neat national boundaries found on maps.[86]

American military officers believed that livestock theft and land disputes created simmering ethnic tensions along the border. Mexican nationals, especially the poor, expressed considerable animosity toward americanos, argued H. C. Corbin. Mexican government officials "seem to cultivate and foment all the hostility that they can against 'los Yankees,' with a view to maintaining themselves in the good will of the people," testified another army officer. American officials believed these views led Mexican nationals to justify cattle theft. Ultimately, the American congressional committee blamed Indians and Mexican nationals for stealing livestock in Texas to sell in Mexico. State officials of Tamaulipas failed to prosecute the criminals, the investigators charged, and in some cases, colluded with them to dispose of stolen livestock. Such accusations supported the charges of many Anglo American ranchers, who deeply distrusted Mexican border town officials.[87]

Variously described as a "robber population" and a "floating population," Mexican nationals crossed the border repeatedly for temporary employment. As seasonal workers, they sheared sheep, branded cattle, and built fences. According to a U.S. congressional investigative committee, border residents in Mexico owned little livestock and, the report stated, "their agriculture is not enough to support but a small portion of their number, notwithstanding which they live better, dress better, and are mounted and armed better than the same class elsewhere in Mexico." The floating population increased constantly, augmented by soldiers deserting revolutionary activity and political disturbances in Mexico. These deserters fled into Texas to search for political refuge and jobs and, occasionally, for merchandise to steal. Moreover, mechanization and land concentration during the Porfiriato pushed the unemployed and landless out of Mexico, while higher wages in agriculture and ranching pulled workers into Texas.[88]

The ambiguous citizenship status of the floating population prevented American military officials from stopping the raiders. Some had become naturalized U.S. citizens, but others remained temporary residents. William Steele, Texas's adjunct general, admitted that "it is very hard to define who is a citizen" along the border. Similarly, S. H. McNally acknowledged the intricate kinship, labor, and cultural ties that straddled the border, arguing

The large proportion of the Mexican settlers on this side of the river is a floating population, who vote on this side as well as on the other. Many of them have been born and claim citizenship in Mexico. A large proportion of the Mexican population on this side of the river have [sic] their homes on the other side. They live over here, and are employed on this side; but they claim no citizenship here, and they are in active, direct sympathy with the raiders. They are their kinsfolk, their cousins, uncles, and brothers—for it seems to me as if all the Mexicans on both sides of the river are relatives.

Local residents and visiting military officers blamed the floating population for aiding the raiders by acting as their scouts. "They are Mexicans, decidedly, in all their habits and feelings," argued McNally, referring to the floating population of workers, "having a violent antipathy to the *gringos*, or Americans." Pursued by American military authorities, the raiders fled into Mexico and claimed Mexican citizenship to avoid extradition to the United States, American officials contended. "And then they have, on the opposite side, a large population of roving Mexicans, who can be citizens on either side, and who are thus exempt from arrest on the other," argued Brigadier General E. O. C. Ord.[89]

This floating population became adept at blurring their citizenship in order to escape reprisals. "The population is changing all the time," stated Ord, "and Mexicans from the west bank claim a residence on either, to suit their convenience, and claim immunity as American citizens from any interference by the military without due process of law." Mexicans were not wholly responsible for this subversion of citizenship along the international border. Also benefiting were local Anglo American politicians. Voter fraud complaints in a congressional committee's report described a mutual interdependence:

> By the provisions of our State constitution every male person who shall have declared his intention to become a citizen of the United States and who shall have resided in the State one year is entitled to register as a voter. Many of the squatters, heretofore described, make this declaration of intention in order to make entry of land as a settler and to register as voters, whereby they manage to secure a certain degree of impunity by placing themselves under the protection of politicians, who are called upon to defend them in the courts, by which service the aid of these characters is secured in our elections.[90]

Neither the Mexican nor the American governments could control the flow of people or goods across a permeable border. Just as workers and soldiers crossed the Rio Grande for economic opportunity or political refuge, cattle rustlers used the river for illicit commerce. Both nations failed to stop the raiding, because border residents frequently outsmarted government officials. Visiting American troops acknowledged that kinship, labor, and trade networks united residents on either side, while a common culture made it difficult to distinguish Mexican Texans from Mexican nationals. Thus, the "unruly realities of the borderlands," in Michel Hogue's apt phrase, prevented federal officials not only from enforcing strict national boundaries, but also from easily mapping the nationality of border residents. Yet distinct citizenship separated border residents, with tejanos experiencing a different economic reality than their counterparts in Mexico. Mexican Texans not only lost property to cattle thieves; they also endured suspicion for colluding with the raiders. In turn, landowners benefited from the continuous supply of workers, and border politicians used the floating population to manipulate the vote. Suspicions about Mexican nationals voting in local elections created a volatile environment for Mexican Texans. Some politicians took advantage of voting irregularities to question the citizenship of all residents of Mexican descent. Critics charged that Mexicans were abusing liberal naturalization laws to obtain "quasi-citizenship." Ultimately, the presence of Mexican nationals in Texas hindered the tejano struggle for voting rights, illustrating the complex and contradictory nature of the relationship between Mexican nationals and Mexican Texans.[91]

Naturalization Debate

Debates over citizenship and voter registration continued throughout the last quarter of the nineteenth century. Complicating this debate was Mexican nationals' increasing practice of becoming naturalized American citizens. Among those choosing naturalization were Union Army veterans who had remained in Texas after the Civil War. Joining them were Mexican Army deserters, laborers, and political exiles. The naturalization debate, initially between U.S. politicians and English-language journalists, eventually drew new participants: Mexican consuls, Mexican official newspapers, and naturalized American citizens.[92]

The views expressed by the Mexican government and its former citizens revealed stark differences regarding naturalization. In 1869, Manuel Treviño, the Mexican consul in Brownsville, warned Mexican nationals against registering to vote in Texas elections lest they lose their Mexican citizenship. It is unclear whether he meant to discourage voter fraud, dissuade naturalization, or both. In response, the *Daily Ranchero* noted that only American citizens could legally vote in Texas, and they defended the right of Mexican nationals to become naturalized U.S. citizens. Expressing a more cynical view was the Matamoros-based *Observador*, which described Mexican nationals who became U.S. citizens as unpatriotic "peons" managed by American politicians. A sharp critique of the *Observador* and the Mexican government appeared in a letter to the *Daily Ranchero* signed by "various naturalized Mexicans." Addressing patriotism, they argued that Mexican soldiers had served their country dutifully, but Mexico had failed to provide for disabled veterans. Moreover, soldiers deserted to the United States for safety from forced military service that only fell on the "poor and ignorant classes" in Mexico. Immigrants would continue seeking "naturalization," the writers asserted, until they could safely live in Mexico without "molestation." Acknowledging that some naturalized Mexicans might be manipulated for their vote and alleging that Mexico had failed to educate its citizens, they blamed Mexico for this problem. Other disaffected socioeconomic classes besides the poor sought naturalization, according to the writers. Addressing the *Observador*'s charge about manipulation, they argued that twenty-one-year-old adults who had lived in the United States for five years (which were the naturalization requirements) were well aware of their voluntary choice to become naturalized citizens. They did not need any protection from the Mexican government, the writers concluded, which had never given them any help.[93]

The new voices in the naturalization debate transformed a local issue into an international concern. The Mexican government appears to have wanted to protect Mexican nationals in the United States from running afoul of voter registration laws, and to prevent large numbers of naturalizations. By suggesting that Mexican nationals were voting in Texas elections, Mexico acknowledged the possibility of voter fraud, ironically reproducing Anglo American politicians' charges against Mexican voters. The Mexican nationals who became American citizens were indirectly pointing to Mexico's inability to provide for its citizens. The Mexican government's views mirrored Canadian officials' fear and dismay at their nation's loss of people along the U.S.-Canadian border during a similar period. Mexican nationals' choice to live in Texas was noteworthy because they were willing to endure the state's heightened ethnic tensions in order to make a living. The immigrants' written response accused Mexican government representatives of paternalism and revealed their continued alienation from Mexico's government. It also demonstrated a thorough knowledge of American naturalization requirements and citizenship rights. Perhaps most importantly, their written response was an indictment of the Mexican government's failures, and an assertion of their choice to reject Mexican citizenship in favor of American citizenship. Such choices and recriminations would continue to resonate for multiple generations along the border.[94]

Enduring Ethnic Tensions and Citizenship Challenges

In the waning years of the nineteenth century, local constables and Texas Rangers continued to harass tejanos and to incur minimal punishment after unprovoked civilian killings. Mob lynchings of mexicanos on both sides of the border also remained common. Contributing to the tense situation were those Mexican nationals who sought refuge in Texas from the dictatorship of Porfirio Díaz. Among the political exiles were Ignacio Martínez and Catarino Garza, who organized against Díaz from the border region. Through political organizations and anti-Díaz newspapers, these refugees led opposition movements among mexicanos on both sides of the border. The Mexican government responded by repressing dissidents and assassinating exiles. As opponents launched a series of armed assaults on the Díaz regime from the mid-1880s through the 1890s, the Mexican government's repression intensified and drew the American military into the conflict. The ensuing political strife inflamed ethnic tensions and increased the number of extralegal killings of innocent victims by Mexican and American government forces. As was their custom, American officials failed to prosecute the assailants, adding to tejano resentment about injustice. Once again, border mexicanos became involved in international conflicts across a permeable border, and their actions highlighted their alienation from both the Mexican and American governments.[95]

The border region's political and social landscape had changed significantly since the mid-nineteenth century, but some patterns remained consistent. Mexican Texans continued to face an entrenched political machine that manipulated their votes and challenged their citizenship. While tejano politicians had made inroads, americanos endured as political brokers who were instrumental in sustaining boss politics yet blamed mexicanos for corruption. As ethnic riots and politically motivated violence erupted during Garza's revolution, English-language newspapers rehashed "bandits" and "aliens" as epithets to racially mark mexicanos as noncitizens. Yet, some newspapers made a careful class distinction by noting that the "rioters" were mostly poor, whereas the "better class" of Mexicans cooperated with American officials. Class continued to shape, but not determine, mexicanos' response as it had at midcentury. Sensationalizing the violence, the press called it a "race war" that would provoke an international conflict between the United States and Mexico. This recycled logic recalled the faulty excuses offered during Cortina's rebellion. While Garza, like Cortina, obtained widespread support across the border, some tejanos and Mexican nationals, especially among the elite, worked to suppress his forces. As earlier rebels had done, Garza's supporters engaged in dissimulation to resist official investigations and eluded authorities by repeatedly crossing the Rio Grande.[96]

Once again, local journalists and officials conveniently ignored differences between Mexican Texans and Mexican nationals in order to serve their political purpose of casting the troubles solely as a result of "foreign" involvement. They accused tejano officials of English-language illiteracy to cast doubt on their legitimacy and patriotism. Recycling claims of an "invasion" by armed Mexican nationals to explain the political disturbances, the press denied tejano grievances about local injustices. As they had done during earlier conflicts, local americanos emphasized their isolation and precarious situation amidst an overwhelming mexicano population when they asked for state and federal military protection. Unlike the midcentury conflicts, however, the last decades of the nineteenth century witnessed higher numbers of Mexican Texan judicial officials and law-enforcement officers. Some of these officials might have tempered Anglo American abuse. Other tejano officeholders, however, cooperated with americanos in suppressing dissent. Charging Mexican Texan politicians with collusion were various Spanish-language newspapers, a new development that provided an alternate view of local and national politics. Directed by Mexican exiles and local tejanos, the Spanish-language press offered sharp critiques of corrupt local politics and the persistent injustice of the legal system.[97]

Mexican Texans and Mexican nationals assumed several identities as men struggling to adapt to the structures of domination imposed by Mexico and the United States. They claimed to be American citizens when they believed this identity would improve their lives, and they claimed themselves citizens of Mexico when American citizenship proved detrimental. Their situational self-identification was consistent with the experience of others struggling to survive along contested borders. The ability of border residents to assume various concurrent national, regional, and ethnic identities reveals the dynamic nature of identity formation. Yet cleavages between Mexican nationals and Mexican Texans did emerge in the nineteenth century as a result of Mexican immigration to the United States, which complicated voting, citizenship, and economic opportunities for tejanos. These divisions and Mexican Texans' daily experience as subordinate members of U.S. society led to the development of an emergent ethnic identity that separated Mexican Texans from Mexican nationals.[98]

The promises of American democracy were unfulfilled for many tejano men even as they came under increasing pressure to "Americanize" to prove their loyalty. Exercising full citizenship rights proved elusive for many. Yet, a few became accepted as "white" citizens based on their elite class and on their ideological positions. Americanos accepted tejanos as U.S. citizens if the latter were subordinate participants, but they denied this recognition when Mexican Texans asserted their electoral independence. Mexican Texans also obtained recognition as American citizens by upholding white supremacy. Elite tejanos were comfortable with enforcing a racial hierarchy that privileged whiteness, as their ancestors had participated in, and benefited from, the Spanish casta system, which afforded more prestige and legal rights to "white" Spaniards. By the early nineteenth century, casta classifications had broken down and softened the racial hierarchy along New Spain's northern frontier. Yet, border residents' preferential attitudes toward those perceived as "white" remained.[99]

Political conflicts and civil wars in both nations attracted male border residents simultaneously, and encouraged border mexicanos to assume transnational identities. Mexican nationals supported the Cortinistas, while tejanos lent support to various political factions in Mexico. Several Cortinistas subsequently fought with the Mexican Liberal Army, but also became important military allies to Union forces in Texas. Other border mexicanos joined the Confederacy and supported the French intervention in Mexico. The concurrent civil wars created a chaotic situation along the Rio Grande because of the frequent incursions of military forces into the neighboring country and the constant back-and-forth flow of deserters. In the United States, Mexicans participated in a civil war concerned with citizenship, freedom, and the abolition of slavery; in Mexico, they participated in a struggle over Mexico's sovereignty against an invading European power. In both wars, they involved themselves in the processes of nation building and asserted their respective identities as border residents, American citizens, Mexican nationals, and transnational actors. Mexican nationals fled from political instability and dire economic circumstances, while Mexican Texans escaped into Mexico to avoid discrimination and legal injustice. Both groups manipulated citizenship laws to their advantage and demonstrated their strategic adaptation to respective national cultures. These aggregate actions revealed that the border remained permeable, with each nation failing to control population movements.[100]

Tejano men assumed ambiguous and contradictory identities as a way of carving out a social space from which to improve their lives. Their "economic and political survival" may have depended on what the historian Peter Sahlins in a different context refers to as the "adroit manipulation and maintenance of these ambiguities, [and] on keeping options and connections open." It is not surprising to discover people preferring multiple, situational, and dynamic identities as opposed to static, singular self-characterizations. Members of a nation do not necessarily "aspire to a clear and unambiguous status as national citizens at the expense of other ties of loyalty and identity." Ultimately, Mexican Texans living along the Rio Grande embraced ambiguous identities in order to pursue local concerns and subvert government restrictions at odds with the realities of the borderlands.[101]

Conclusion

Following his 1859 raid, Juan Cortina moved to Mexico, and plunged head-long into politics. He joined the Mexican Army, led the Matamoros *ayunta-miento* (town council), and ultimately became the governor of Tamaulipas. As a Mexican Army commander, Cortina assisted Union forces, and inter-ceded on behalf of *tejanos* (Mexican Texans) mistreated during the U.S. Civil War. Subsequently, he allied himself with the liberal forces of Benito Juárez against French occupation, and fought incessant power struggles with northern Mexico's political strongmen. By 1875, Cortina had left the governor's office and regained leadership of the Matamoros ayuntamiento. When the "Cattle War" erupted, U.S. authorities accused Cortina of master-minding livestock theft throughout the border region.[1]

Pressured by ranchers in south Texas, local U.S. and Mexican officials asked the Mexican government to remove Cortina from the border region. After initially refusing to take action, Mexican authorities relented by jail-ing Cortina in Mexico City's Santiago Tlatelolco Prison. Upon his release a year later, Cortina issued a *pronunciamento* (proclamation) supporting Gen-eral Porfirio Díaz, then returned to the border. Díaz had captured control of the national government but could not obtain recognition by the United States for his administration until he stopped the raids across the Tamaulipas-Texas border. To obtain such support, Díaz ordered Cortina rearrested and brought to Mexico City, where the *caudillo* spent the next sixteen years in prison and under house arrest until his death in 1894.[2]

By pressuring the Mexican government to remove Cortina from the border, his enemies successfully turned a local issue into an international one. They brought the nation into the village, when they converted a local concern, cattle theft, into a national security issue—the control of the international border. Cortina's long career in Mexico testifies to the caudillo's charisma, political resolve, and transnational influence. Like Juan Seguín, San Antonio's former mayor who escaped death threats by fleeing to Mexico, Cortina spent the rest of his life serving a government from which he and other tejanos had grown distant after annexation by the United States in 1848. Both died broken men and political outcasts far from their native lands. Cortina's denouement demonstrates the border's growing importance to both nations, and its communities' increasingly transnational connections.

Although the Mexican and American governments considered Cortina a pariah, he became a folk hero among *mexicanos* (Mexicans) on both sides of the Rio Grande. They recounted his exploits in several *corridos*, of which three fragments from different songs have survived. The first corrido refers to his 1859 shooting of Marshal Shears to end the officer's pistol-whipping of a mexicano worker:

> Ese general Cortinas
> es libre y muy soberano,
> han subido sus honores
> porque salvó a un mexicano.

> The famed General Cortinas
> is quite sovereign and free,
> the honor due him is greater,
> for he saved a Mexican's life.

The song acknowledges Cortina's rank in the Mexican military, and characterizes him as autonomous—perhaps alluding to the caudillo's political independence. His esteem derives not from his military exploits, but rather from his role in saving a mexicano from police brutality. "Mexicano" refers to ethnic identity and not nationality, which confirms the importance of shared ethnic ties among Mexican communities divided by an international border. Dating to the 1860s, this corrido is one of the earliest extant examples alluding to the region's intercultural conflict. Fittingly, this corrido celebrates the first man, according to the folklorist Américo Paredes, to organize Mexican Texan protest against abuses from the Anglo-controlled power structure.[3]

The second corrido refers to Cortina's visit to the border in the 1890s, following his initial imprisonment in Mexico City:

> Viva el general Cortinas
> de su prisión salió,

vino a ver a sus amigos
que en Tamaulipas dejó.

Long live General Cortinas,
who has come out of prison;
he came to visit his friends
that he had left in Tamaulipas

In its recounting of Cortina's trip to Tamaulipas, the song can be read as a reminder of the caudillo's persistent political and social ties to border residents. Such relationships account for his enduring influence among mexicanos on both sides of the Rio Grande. The song is also an expression of pride in a northern Mexican regional identity (in a *patria chica* [locality]), and demonstrates the persistent difficulties faced by the Mexican federal government in forging a nation in the nineteenth century.

The third corrido describes the joy *americanos* (American citizens) expressed over Cortina's death in 1894, and was likely written in the late 1890s:

Los americanos hacían huelga,
borracheras en las cantinas,
de gusto que había muerto
ese general Cortinas

The Americans made merry,
they got drunk in the saloons,
out of joy over the death
of the famed General Cortinas.

By identifying Americans as joyful over the death while neglecting to note that Cortina's enemies in Mexico were probably similarly pleased, the song emphasizes the role of the caudillo in influencing developments north of the border. The absence of Cortina's tejano foes in these lyrics constructs the border troubles as primarily rooted in ethnic conflict. The songs' omission of class divisions among mexicanos suggests Cortina's ability to attract support among the poor, through patronage and his ability to give voice to their concerns. Composed and sung primarily by men, these corridos can also be interpreted as male expressions of approval; they celebrate Cortina's performance of masculinity as a patriarch who defended his community from outsiders.

Since folksongs are expressions of community sentiment, these surviving fragments are exemplary of the popular memories of *fronterizos* (borderland residents). While newspapers minimally acknowledged Cortina's death, mexicanos honored him with corridos immortalizing his influence. Notably, none of the surviving corrido fragments refer to class or citizenship divisions among mexicanos. While poor residents were obviously aware of these divisions, since they had a daily impact on their lives, their choice to deemphasize them in these corridos speaks to another aspect of border life. By the late nineteenth century, its residents had grown accustomed to the transnational influences that shaped their lives and connected communities across an international border. Far from passive, fronterizos were active agents in asserting an early type of transnational citizenship in which they expressed allegiances to Mexico and the United States. Yet, at other times, they remained ambivalent to each nation, especially when central governments ignored their needs. As the scholars Michael Peter Smith and Matt Bakker remind us, loyalty is "never unalloyed and always contingent."[4]

Few had the opportunities available to elite men such as Cortina and Seguín. Unlike these powerbrokers, most tejanos lacked critical contacts for political and economic advancement in Mexico. Instead of relocating across the Rio Grande after 1848, they remained on their lands and became American citizens. While losing economic, social, and political power, Mexican Texans took advantage of new opportunities created by the jurisdictional change. Internal class divisions, however, shaped their accommodation: wealthy tejanos created alliances with Anglo Americans, who usually racialized elites as white and poor Mexican Texans as nonwhite. The imposition of the international boundary at the Rio Grande increased the economic importance of the region. As twin cities emerged along the river, binational trade (legal and illegal) became embedded in the region's economy. A floating population of laborers from Mexico crossed the river to escape their debts and to secure higher wages in Texas. Gender relations became more permissive on the river's left bank because American jurisdiction permitted civil marriage and made permanent divorce relatively easy. Although the border served as a political divider of previously intact communities, Mexican nationals and tejanos continued to travel across the river for social occasions—to marry, visit friends and relatives, and divorce (if you can call divorce a social occasion).

A new cultural identity emerged among tejanos as a result of their political and economic marginalization within the United States, their racialization, and their struggle to claim citizenship rights. Religious differences with Anglos, intermarriage with immigrants, and familial ties with relatives across the border also altered their identities. This process of identity destabilization, fragmentation, and reformation continued with the U.S. Civil War. Both the Union and Confederacy attempted to obtain the allegiance of tejanos, complicating their national and ethnic identifications. The constant arrival of Mexican immigrants reinforced Mexican culture among tejanos, but this floating population's itinerancy complicated tejanos' daily lives by inviting voter fraud allegations. Mexican Texans inhabited complex in-between social positions, as illustrated by their animosity toward Mexican nationals who stole their cattle and their distrust of Anglos who accused them of perpetuating the same thefts. Ultimately, tejanos continued to hold weak national identities owing to their ambiguous position as American citizens and their fluid subjectivities as mexicanos living along the international border. Such ambiguity and fluidity would remain cornerstones in the region's ethnic mortar into the twenty-first century.

Residents of the lower Rio Grande region used the border to resist national control and subvert local authorities. Everyday resistance is contingent on the institutional apparatus used to enforce rule and on the existing environment. Writing about this relationship in another context, the scholar Paul Gilroy argues, "The form of the state structures the form of the political struggles." To undermine national rule, Mexican Texans and Mexican nationals repeatedly crossed the border, ignored trade restrictions, and adopted strategic civic identities. Like their Spanish colonial ancestors who used their isolation to evade royal directives, border residents became adept at using the international boundary to subvert government restrictions. Some helped runaway African American slaves escape into Mexico, while others fled across the border to avoid conscription or criminal prosecution. Ultimately, Mexican Texans underwent a cultural transformation that distinguished them, as American citizens, from their friends and families across the border, who remained Mexican citizens. As they strategically adapted to the disciplining effects of the American legal and political systems, they created precedents for social and cultural processes that continue today.[5]

The jurisdictional change along the lower Rio Grande in the mid-nineteenth century initiated long-standing social interactions. Before the takeover by the United States, the *villas del norte* (northern towns) had begun absorbing foreign influences due to the region's position as a trading zone for Anglo American and European merchants. The process of change accelerated after 1848, with border communities becoming increasingly bilingual and bicultural. On the river's left bank, residents intermixed the Spanish and English languages when they appeared in American courts, appealed to government officials, and interacted daily with Anglos and African Americans as friends, employees, or spouses. The geography of border communities fostered binational cultural influences, for example, when municipal governments began observing Mexican and American celebrations and holidays (often in conjunction with their Mexican twin-city counterparts). Protestant churches made inroads into border society as part of Americanization attempts aimed at Mexican border residents. Although tejano children learned English in Protestant Sunday schools and secular public schools, their families resisted religious conversion efforts. Future generations of Mexican Americans and Mexican immigrants would repeat this selective adaptation and cultural hybridization (labeled "cultural coalescence" by the historian Vicki Ruiz) by learning English and incorporating some American customs, but rejecting Americanization efforts to eliminate Mexican cultural practices. Today, the region's transnational influences and cultural hybridity are manifested in residents' continued Spanish-language use, binational celebrations, and fusion of Mexican and American popular cultures.[6]

The jurisdictional transformation in 1848 had long-term consequences for border society. On the river's left bank, demographic diversity increased as civil marriage permitted spouses of various religious, ethnic, and racial backgrounds to intermarry. Divorce through civil courts allowed spouses to end irreconcilable unions, and offered the option to remarry. American legislation provided greater flexibility in marriage and divorce for U.S. residents than did Mexico's laws for Mexican residents throughout the nineteenth century. Differences in each nation-state's marital legislation influenced local society; for instance, women and men on the U.S. side had greater freedom than their counterparts in Mexico in constructing their domestic households. This greater social freedom along with wider economic opportunities in the United States initiated a migratory stream that continues today, in which Mexican immigrants help enrich and expand Mexican American communities. The racialization and criminalization of Mexicans' cultural practices (e.g., fandangos, monte games) begun in the nineteenth century also has contemporary counterparts throughout the American Southwest, where communities have passed ordinances against home-based shops offering car repairs, day laborers seeking employment, and street vendors plying their goods. The legacy of the mid-nineteenth century practice of questioning tejanos' citizenship lingers in immigration debates that contest the legitimacy of Latinos in U.S. society. Mexico's political elite expressed similar distrust of the floating population of poor

Mexicans who have left for seasonal jobs in the United States. The migrants' steady and considerable remittances, however, have increased their political clout in Mexico and gradually changed elite perceptions. Improvements in transportation have also broadened migrants' circular migration beyond the immediate geographic border region. The back-and-forth migration pattern links south Texas to borderlands elsewhere in the world, where political and economic disparities have created populations of workers (similarly scorned and suspected of disloyalty) that easily migrate across international boundaries.[7]

The nineteenth-century political experiences of tejanos serve as reminders that their civil rights struggles precede the twentieth century. The first generation to live under American rule was also the first group of Mexican Americans to ask the United States to live up to its ideals and promises. They elected municipal and state representatives, filed lawsuits in pursuit of justice, and issued civil rights appeals to state and federal officials. In the late 1920s, when members of the League of United Latin American Citizens (LULAC) staked claims to American citizenship, asked for legal equality, and fought against racial segregation, they were continuing a struggle begun by their nineteenth-century forebears. Unlike its predecessors, however, LULAC exploited citizenship divisions that had fractured the nineteenth-century mexicano community to become the first Mexican American organization to exclude Mexican nationals from membership. Within years of the American conquest, Mexican Texans identified the lack of equal legal protection and inequitable jury representation as reasons for their increasing numbers of incarcerations. In 1954, this lingering inequality motivated the lawyers Gus García and Carlos Cadena to convince the U.S. Supreme Court, in *Hernandez v. Texas*, to reverse the long-standing practice of excluding Mexican Americans from juries. Since the nineteenth century, U.S. society has questioned the citizenship of Mexican Americans and challenged their voting rights. Some, such as low-wage workers and landless agricultural laborers, have been more easily manipulated as "coral" or machine voters. In early twentieth-century Texas, politicians persisted in managing the vote with a practice known as "herding Mexicans." The Great Depression offered Texas state administrators the opportunity to deny Mexican laborers relief by resurrecting the belief that Mexican Texans were neither American citizens nor taxpayers. Poll taxes and whites-only primaries emerged in the twentieth century to further disenfranchise tejanos, while the Texas Rangers persisted in intimidating voters during elections. Unfortunately, contemporary tejanos (and Mexican Americans across the nation) continue to confront lingering doubts about their status as American citizens.[8]

Undaunted by intimidation of voters and by doubts about their American citizenship, Mexican Texans engaged in political and social strategies that established patterns for future generations. The Cortina rebellion's armed struggle and transnational influence established precedents for the Plan de San Diego uprising in 1915, in which ethnic Mexicans led an irredentist rebellion with support from Mexican revolutionaries. The twentieth-century rebellion also unleashed state repression against tejanos, but most significantly, it drew attention to their civil rights claims. Although both rebellions gained widespread support among poor Mexican Texans and Mexican nationals, they also fueled opposition from elite tejanos interested in maintaining the political status quo. Like their nineteenth-century counterparts, elite Mexican Texans distanced themselves from the poor in the early twentieth century and often hindered the latter's struggles for justice. Protests against abuse from law officers also had earlier roots. Sixty years after Cortina's proclamations called on the state's governor for protection from abusive law-enforcement officers, the state representative José T. Canales, Cortina's distant relative, held a series of historic legislative hearings that brought this abuse to light. In the wake of numerous killings and intimidation of tejanos by the Texas Rangers, Canales introduced a bill to restructure this armed force in 1919. During the nineteenth century, tejanos served in the military to underscore their claims to American citizenship despite suffering from inadequate equipment, lack of pay, and racial discrimination. Few veterans were fully rewarded for their participation, but they established a pattern linking military service with citizenship claims that the American GI Forum, which fought for the rights of Mexican American veterans, reproduced in the late 1940s.[9]

Nineteenth-century border residents also established enduring economic practices. Residents had begun smuggling before the international border divided their communities. The imposition of an international boundary at the Rio Grande fueled contraband, making it an everyday practice and leading to the idealization of smugglers. The border's illicit trade created several nineteenth-century fortunes, which later funded multinational corporations, including the Stillman-backed National City Bank and the King Ranch. Twenty-first-century *narcocorridos* (folksongs about drug trafficking) have clear antecedents in nineteenth-century versions commemorating *contrabandistas* (smugglers). While smugglers' popularity has endured, the types of contraband goods have shifted from manufactured items, cattle, and cotton to liquor, pharmaceuticals, guns, and drugs. More importantly, the direction of most clandestine trade has reversed; while contraband flowed south into Mexico in the nineteenth century, most now travels north into the United States. One constant over the years has been the economic pull of the United States as undocumented workers have replaced the indentured servants of the nineteenth century. Even the North American Free Trade Agreement (NAFTA) had its nineteenth-century counterpart (although not equal in scope or intent) in Tamaulipas's Free Trade Zone. While both nations have encouraged the free flow of legal goods, they have been less tolerant of human migrations. Immigration checkpoints and Border Patrol stations have replaced nineteenth-century forts. The border's militarization has increased dramatically; helicopters, night-vision goggles, and high-speed boats have superseded the horses and rifles of frontier soldiers. The most extravagant and controversial change in policing has been the construction of a border wall. Aimed at interdicting drugs and undocumented workers, the wall has generated controversy for its role in destroying ecosystems, dividing private land, and aggravating binational relations. While this wall is politically expedient for politicians interested in the illusion of control, it has been repeatedly subverted by various populations, whose efforts remind us that the United States–Mexico boundary will remain porous.[10]

The international boundary continued to pose challenges for both nations in the early twenty-first century. The significance of the border was apparent in its attention from the press, politicians, and the public. For many immigrants, it had replaced Ellis Island as the unofficial port of entry. These new arrivals have contributed to reinforcing cultural traditions in Mexican American communities, and expanding them to regions without a previously significant Latino population. Mexican music, food, and traditions had spread beyond the southwest borderlands to unlikely outposts in Alaska and Iowa. Since NAFTA's passage, the United States had remained Mexico's first trading partner, and its most significant foreign cultural influence (to the consternation of some Mexicans). Both governments have exerted more control over their shared boundary, but residents have also persisted in undermining restrictions. The United States continued to pressure the Mexican government to control its northern border in exchange for future American government aid and assistance. The fortified "border wall" appeared like a relic of bygone eras, when nondemocratic regimes attempted to keep people from crossing international boundaries. Yet, it did not stop drug smugglers and undocumented immigrants, who have dug tunnels and used ramps to bypass the structure or have taken to transporting contraband by air and sea. The border wall did succeed in poisoning binational relations, and confirming the view of borderland residents that distant central governments continue to misunderstand the needs of the region. By 2010, fewer immigrants were making the journey north because of an economic recession in the United States, but the increased security also kept undocumented workers in the United States longer, as circular migration became more difficult. The demand for contraband goods and inexpensive labor, as in the nineteenth century, endured in the United States. American politicians and a segment of the public, however, remained wary of immigrants who might become permanent residents of the United States and eventually press for full citizenship rights. The presence of undocumented immigrants also raised suspicions about the legal status of many Latinos, even those with U.S. citizenship. Therefore, Latinos continued to struggle to enjoy the symbolic and real benefits of full citizenship rights in U.S. society.[11]

The United States–Mexico border has become a trope and a cultural symbol in literature, music, and art. Yet, its history is relatively unknown to the general public. Most Americans do not know that civil right struggles in the early twenty-first century have nineteenth-century origins. Nevertheless, history can provide important lessons and serve as inspiration. Economic opportunities in the United States continue to attract Latinos (mainly Mexicans). Immigration raids and the threat of additional punitive legislation motivated large-scale protests in 2006 urging legislative reform. These immigrant-rights demonstrations have emphasized Latinos' long history of laboring in the United States. Brought into sharp relief by the raids and subsequent deportations are so-called mixed families, which consist of members with a variety of immigration statuses (citizens, permanent residents, undocumented workers, etc.). These family and labor arrangements are not new; mixed families and Mexican itinerant workers were common along the lower Rio Grande region in the mid-nineteenth century. In that period, border residents became transnational actors, establishing precedents for contemporary expressions of transnational citizenship. Immigrant rights marches have led scholars to point to Latino workers as the future of organized labor, and as significant contributors to the Latinoization of the United States. Similarly, observers have argued that Latinos are the key to turning politically conservative states (such as Texas) into more moderate or progressive ones. Whether or not this political shift is realized, the expected increase in the population of Latinos—as well as their civil rights struggles within, economic contributions to, and cultural influence on U.S. society—will remain a legacy of the efforts begun by nineteenth-century residents of the Rio Grande borderlands. They initiated enduring transnational patterns of migration, trade, politics, and social relations that challenge the power of nation-states to control populations along their borders.[12]

Notes

Introduction

1. Mexicans referred to the river as the Río Grande, Río Grande del Norte, and Río Bravo. Horgan, *Great River*, 257; Zorrilla, Miró Flaquer, and Herrera Pérez, *Tamaulipas: Una historia compartida I*, 25, 28, 162–68; Osante, *Orígenes del Nuevo Santander*, 18, 85; AHM-COL 1:8, 15 enero 1815. For incisive critiques of borderlands history, see Hämäläinen and Truett, "On Borderlands," 338–61; Gutiérrez and Young, "Transnationalizing Borderlands History," 27–53; Johnson and Graybill, "Introduction: Borders and Their Historians in North America," 1–29; Adelman and Aron, "From Borderlands to Borders," 814–41; and Truett and Young, "Introduction: Making Transnational History," 1–32.

2. Salinas, *Indians of the Rio Grande Delta*, 69.

3. Corrigan and Sayer, *The Great Arch*, 1–13.

4. Marshall and Bottomore, *Citizenship and Social Class*, 8; Bosniak, "Citizenship Denationalized," 456–89; Horsman, *Race and Manifest Destiny*, 241 (quote).

5. Sánchez, *Becoming Mexican American*, 11–13; Stets and Burke, "Identity Theory and Social Identity Theory," 224–29; Hall, "Cultural Identity and Diaspora," 225–27; Hall and Du Gay, *Questions of Cultural Identity*, 3–6; Sahlins, *Boundaries*, 110–13, 267–76; Haas, *Conquests and Historical Identities in California*, 9–44.

6. Wilson and Donnan, *Border Identities*, 13, 26 (quote).

7. Lockhart and Schwartz, *Early Latin America*, 290–95.

8. Bolton, *Wider Horizons in American History*, 55–106; Limerick, *The Legacy of Conquest*, 227; Weber, *The Spanish Frontier in North America*, 12.

9. Gutiérrez, "Claims and Prospects," 35; Engstrand, Griswold del Castillo, and Poniatowska, *Culture y Cultura*; Roa Bárcena, *Recuerdos de la invasión norteamericana*.

10. Delay, *War of a Thousand Deserts*, 61–138.

11. Montejano, *Anglos and Mexicans in the Making of Texas*, 34–37; Omi and Winant, *Racial Formation in the United States*, 64; Almaguer, *Racial Fault Lines*, 45–74.

12. R. Smith, *Civic Ideals*, 165–66, 200 (quote), 206 (quote); Guardino, *Peasants,*

ation of Mexico's National State, 174–75; Mora, _Border Dilemmas_,

Captives and Cousins, 31; Hämäläinen, _The Comanche Empire_, 2–9; _Came in the Form of a Woman_, 15, 118; Hämäläinen and Truett, "On _ands_," 347.

. Wunder and Hämäläinen, "Of Lethal Places and Lethal Essays," 1229; Hämä-inen and Truett, "On Borderlands," 352.

15. Truett and Young, "Introduction: Making Transnational History," 14–17; Johnson and Graybill, "Introduction: Borders and Their Historians in North America," 6–9, 24; Reséndez, _Changing National Identities at the Frontier_, 3–6, 56–123; Ramos, _Beyond the Alamo_, 93, 105, 128–30; Adelman and Aron, "From Borderlands to Borders," 816; Sahlins, _Boundaries_, 127–32; Baud and Van Schendel, "Toward a Comparative History of Borderlands," 235.

16. Nugent, "Are We Not Civilized Men?"; Alonso, _Thread of Blood_; Osante, _Orígenes del Nuevo Santander_; Reséndez, _Changing National Identities at the Frontier_, 56–123; Guardino, _Peasants, Politics, and the Formation of Mexico's National State_, 86; Truett, _Fugitive Landscapes_, 6; Almaguer, _Racial Fault Lines_; Meeks, _Border Citizens_; Benton-Cohen, _Borderline Americans_; Mitchell, _Coyote Nation_.

17. Gutiérrez, _When Jesus Came, the Corn Mothers Went Away_; A. Castañeda, "Presidarias y Pobladoras"; Monroy, _Thrown among Strangers_; D. González, _Refusing the Favor_, Chávez-García, _Negotiating Conquest_; Casas, _Married to a Daughter of the Land_; Heidenreich, _"This Land Was Mexican Once"_; Reyes, _Private Women, Public Lives_; Haas, _Conquests and Historical Identities in California_; Ramos, _Beyond the Alamo_; Montejano, _Anglos and Mexicans in the Making of Texas_.

18. Gutiérrez, _Walls and Mirrors_, 7; Paredes, _Folklore and Culture on the Texas-Mexican Border_, 29; Sánchez, _Becoming Mexican American_; Gutiérrez and Young, "Transnationalizing Borderlands History," 50; Meeks, _Border Citizens_; Benton-Cohen, _Borderline Americans_; Gómez, _Manifest Destinies_; Mora, _Border Dilemmas_.

19. On the absence of borderland stories from national narratives, see Truett and Young, _Continental Crossroads_, 2; Johnson and Graybill, _Bridging National Borders in North America_, 1–2; Saldívar, _Borderlands of Culture_, 8; and Cotera, _Native Speakers_, 118–20.

20. The villas del norte's vecinos used the following terms interchangeably: _americanos_, _norteamericanos_, _anglo americanos_, and _americanos del norte_. For examples, see AHM-JUD 2:4, 27 mayo 1822; AHM-JUD 2:9, 24 marzo 1824; AHM-JUS 1:27, 24 septiembre 1827; AHM-PRE 1:2, 20 febrero 1825; AHR-PRE 1:6, 15 abril 1847; and AHR-PRE 3:17, 30 marzo 1853.

1. Constructing _Vecinos_, _Indios_

1. AHM-JUD 1:1, 4 julio 1804.

2. Gutiérrez, _When Jesus Came, the Corn Mothers Went Away_, 149; Brooks, _Captives and Cousins_, 121–42.

3. Alonso, _Thread of Blood_, 90–98.

4. Osante, *Orígenes del Nuevo Santander*, 116.

5. Ibid., 57, 62–65, 72, 84–91, 96.

6. Jones, *Los paisanos*, 65–66; Hill, *José de Escandón and the Founding of Nuevo Santander*, 4; Osante, *Orígenes del Nuevo Santander*, 95–98, 106; Bolton, "Defensive Spanish Expansion and the Significance of the Borderlands," 71–95, in Herbert E. Bolton, *Wider Horizons of American History*; Cruz, *Let There Be Towns*, 81–82; Weber, *The Spanish Frontier in North America*, 181–82, 194.

7. Hill, *José de Escandón and the Founding of Nuevo Santander*, 16–31.

8. Scholar's estimates on the number of precontact indigenous groups range from 72 to 195. Osante, *Orígenes del Nuevo Santander*, 22, 30; Campbell, "Coahuiltecans and Their Neighbors," 343–58; Hill, *José de Escandón and the Founding of Nuevo Santander*, 49; Salinas, *Indians of the Rio Grande Delta*, 81, 142–47.

9. Osante, *Orígenes del Nuevo Santander*, 55–69, 146–48.

10. Salinas, *Indians of the Rio Grande Delta*, 14–20; Hill, *José de Escandón and the Founding of Nuevo Santander*, 52–55; Valdés, *La Gente del Mezquite*, 189; Osante, *Orígenes del Nuevo Santander*, 36n70, 57–58.

11. Lockhart and Schwartz, *Early Latin America*, 44–46; Salinas, *Indians of the Rio Grande Delta*, 14–20; Osante, *Orígenes del Nuevo Santander*, 34–39, 96.

12. Osante, *Orígenes del Nuevo Santander*, 18n5, 102–19; Thompson, "Historical Survey," 18–19, 85; Hill, *José de Escandón and the Founding of Nuevo Santander*, 56–88.

13. Subsequently, Dolores and Refugio became part of the villas del norte, also known as the *cordillera del norte* (belt of the north). Osante, *Orígenes del Nuevo Santander*, 93–125; Wright, "Popular and Official Religiosity," 383–84.

14. Hill, *José de Escandón and the Founding of Nuevo Santander*, 104, 105n40; IR (quote).

15. Zorrilla, *El poder colonial en Nuevo Santander*, 35–39, 52, 84–91, 118, 176–78, 202–3; Hill, *José de Escandón and the Founding of Nuevo Santander*, 104; Zorrilla, Miró Flaquer, and Herrera Pérez, *Tamaulipas: Una historia compartida I*, 35, 40; Salinas, *Indians of the Rio Grande Delta*, 153–58, 162; Osante, *Orígenes del Nuevo Santander*, 225–26.

16. Salinas, *Indians of the Rio Grande Delta*, 138–39; Campbell, "Coahuiltecans and Their Neighbors," 350; Osante, *Orígenes del Nuevo Santander*, 234; Hinojosa, *A Borderlands Town in Transition*, 28–36, 124; Herrera Pérez, *Monografía de Reynosa*, 126; MAA 2:132–35, 15 agosto 1814; AHM-COL 1:17, 31 diciembre 1820.

17. The vecinos identified several Indian nations as Carrizos (literally, "canes" or "reeds"), so scholars distinguish between Western and Eastern Carrizos. Salinas, *Indians of the Rio Grande Delta*, 91–94; Wright, "Popular and Official Religiosity," 381–83.

18. Weber, *The Mexican Frontier*, 212; LA 59:23, 18 julio 1815; LA 59:1, 5 enero 1815; LA 63:26, 19 octubre 1818; LA 63:28, 6 noviembre 1818; AHM-JUD 1:1, 4 julio 1804; AHM-COL 1:16, 21 enero 1819; AHM-JUD 2:5, 23 febrero 1822; Hinojosa, *A Borderlands Town in Transition*, 19; Salinas, *Indians of the Rio Grande Delta*, 40–41; MAA 16:32, 13 agosto 1814; Weber, *Bárbaros*, 238.

19. AMR-PRE Juan Antonio Ballí, Joseph de Trejo, and Antonio Margil Cano, "De

José Abito Cantú, Apolinario Moya, y Lúcas Sosa vecinos de esta Jurisdición por la acusación de haver extrahido un indito de poder de sus padres indios de la Nacion de los Mulatos: hayase incurso tambien un indio Christiano reducido a esta misión llamado José Miguél," 1777. Vecinos identified two unrelated groups of Indians from Tamaulipas as Mulato Indians. Salinas, *Indians of the Rio Grande Delta*, 51–52.

20. AHM-PRE 1:6, 10 junio 1826. The Laws of the Indies (1680) reinforced the ban on Indian slavery, but war captives could be enslaved under the "just war" doctrine. Gutiérrez, *When Jesus Came, the Corn Mothers Went Away*, 150–51; Brooks, *Captives and Cousins*, 50–51, 124–25; 234; Barr, *Peace Came in the Form of a Woman*, 165, 170; Weber, *Bárbaros*, 234–36; Zavala, *Los esclavos indios en Nueva España*, 265–74; Simmons, *Little Lion of the Southwest*, 34–35; Weber, *The Mexican Frontier*, 212.

21. Weber, *The Mexican Frontier*, 212; AHM-JUS 1:13, 15 Mayo 1822, will of Doña María Nicolasa Longoria de Ramírez; Hinojosa, *A Borderlands Town in Transition*, 19. New Mexican colonists also euphemistically referred to "adopted" Indian children as *criados* to obscure their use as domestic slaves. Gutiérrez, *When Jesus Came, the Corn Mothers Went Away*, 154–55, 181; Brooks, *Captives and Cousins*, 125, 144.

22. RBR, 30 junio 1791.

23. Don Vicente González de Santianes, quoted in Zavala, *Los esclavos indios en Nueva España*, 270; AEM-BAU 1 and 2; CCBR 1–9.

24. Mörner, *Race Mixture in the History of Latin America*, 41–45, 53–59; León, *Las castas del México colonial o Nueva España*; Haas, *Conquests and Historical Identities in California*, 30–31; Vidaurreta Tjarks, "Comparative Demographic Analysis of Texas," 135–69; Lockhart and Schwartz, *Early Latin America*, 129–31, 315–17; Gerhard, *The Northern Frontier of New Spain*, 27; McAlister, "Social Structure and Social Change in New Spain," 356; Gutiérrez, *When Jesus Came, the Corn Mothers Went Away*, 193–94; De la Teja, *San Antonio de Béxar*, 24–26; Jones, *Los paisanos*, 246–47.

25. CCBR 1–9; DG 1, 19, Laredo Census (1788 and 1789). On Indian naming patterns, see Lockhart, *The Nahuas after the Conquest*, 117–30.

26. Gudeman and Schwartz, "Cleansing Original Sin," 40–48; Gutiérrez, *When Jesus Came, the Corn Mothers Went Away*, 182; Brooks, *Captives and Cousins*, 236–37; RBR 27 octubre 1791 (quote).

27. Berlandier, *Journey to Mexico during the Years 1826 to 1834*, 245–46, 430; Brooks, *Captives and Cousins*, 237; Gutiérrez, *When Jesus Came, the Corn Mothers Went Away*, 295–97. AEM Libro de Matrimonios no. 1. The number (840, or 38 percent) of mestizo baptisms (see table 5 in chapter 2) suggests substantial miscegenation; it should be viewed cautiously, though, as casta classifications were very subjective (as explained in chapter 2).

28. AEM Libros de Bautismos nos. 1 and 2. Amos in New Mexico also fathered a significant portion of out-of-wedlock children born to Indian criadas. Gutiérrez, *When Jesus Came, the Corn Mothers Went Away*, 155–56, 184; Brooks, *Captives and Cousins*, 147, 237, 335.

29. Gutiérrez, *When Jesus Came, the Corn Mothers Went Away*, 149–51; Brooks, *Captives and Cousins*, 45–79; Blackhawk, *Violence over the Land*, 16–54.

30. AHM-JUD 1:1, 4 julio 1804. Indigenous nations along the Rio Grande likely

shunned detribalized Indian criados as occurred in colonial New Mexico. Brooks, *Captives and Cousins*, 123–25, 234–35; Gutiérrez, *When Jesus Came, the Corn Mothers Went Away*, 155–56, 295; Weber, *The Mexican Frontier*, 212–13.

31. LA 59:25, Ramón Perea to Don José Maria Tovar, 1 agosto 1815; Hinojosa, *A Borderlands Town in Transition*, 34n18; LA 63:28, 6 noviembre 1818; LA 63:26, 19 octubre 1818; Katz, "Labor Conditions on Haciendas in Porfirian Mexico," 7–8; Gutiérrez, *When Jesus Came, the Corn Mothers Went Away*, 321–26.

32. MAA 16:32, 14 noviembre 1814; LA 59:25, 1 agosto 1815; LA 59:23, 18 julio 1815; LA 59:1, 5 enero 1815; AHM-JUD 1:1, 4 julio 1804.

33. Hinojosa, *A Borderlands Town in Transition*, 33–34; MAA 2:32, 15 agosto 1814; Wilkinson, *Laredo and the Rio Grande Frontier*, 67.

34. AHM-COL 1:2, 17 mayo 1810, will of Doña Juana Girón, [1806 or 1807], will of Don Antonio Gutiérrez; AHM-JUD 1:1, 4 julio 1804; LA 63:28, 6 noviembre 1818; Haas, *Conquests and Historical Identities in California*, 43; Gutiérrez, *When Jesus Came, the Corn Mothers Went Away*, 181.

35. The meaning of the term *ladino* (Indians who spoke Spanish and were acculturated into vecino society) in the villas differs from its meaning in other regions of Latin America. AHM-JUD 1:1, 4 julio 1804. New Mexican colonists also believed that they were "civilizing" the Indians. Gutiérrez, *When Jesus Came, the Corn Mothers Went Away*, 185.

36. AMR-PRE, Documentos Diversos, "Libro donde constan los indígenas que por no tener oficio . . ." 19 abril 1831.

37. Haas, *Conquests and Historical Identities in California*, 31.

38. AHM-JUD 1:1, 4 julio 1804; AHM-JUD 1:2, 3 noviembre 1807.

39. John, "Independent Indians and the San Antonio Community," 123; Hinojosa, *A Borderlands Town in Transition*, 12–13; Weber, *Bárbaros*, 68–76; MAA 14:34–7, 29 septiembre 1825; MAA 16:32, 13 agosto 1814; DeLay, *War of a Thousand Deserts*, 141–296, 303–10.

40. DRI 1, Don Vicente González de Santianes to Thomas Sánchez, 2 diciembre 1773; AHM-PRE 6:12, *Gaceta del Gobierno de Tamaulipas*, 16 diciembre 1841, 4; MAA 16:144, 10 junio 1823; Hämäläinen, *The Comanche Empire*, 220. On vecinos' views of Lipán Apaches and Comanches, see MAA 5:65–66, 9 septiembre 1821; MAA 14:34–7, 29 septiembre 1825; AHM-PRE 4:20, 4 marzo 1834; and AHM-PRE 6:12, *Gaceta del Gobierno de Tamaulipas*, 16 diciembre 1841, 4, 7 agosto 1841, 2. For reprisals against enemy Indians, see AHM-PRE 1:1, 10 septiembre 1825; and DRI 23–25, 8 agosto 1825. On colonists' community identity and warrior ethic, see Nugent, "Are We Not [Civilized] Men?," 206–39; Gallegos, "'Last Drop of My Blood' Col. Antonio Zapata," 43–60; Alonso, *Thread of Blood*, 51–71, 93–94; and Mora-Torres, *The Making of the Mexican Border*, 11–20. On the vecino practice of scalping, see DRI 15–16, Nemesio Salcedo to Don José Yturrigaray, 30 julio 1804.

41. On peace treaties with Lipán Apaches, see DRI 14–15, El Conde de Sierragorda to Sr. teniente Don José Gonzales, 15 marzo 1791; and DRI 17–18, Herrera to Sres. Alcaldes de la Provincia, 17 agosto 1822. For peace treaties with Comanches, see DRI 23–25, Ayuntamiento de Laredo to Sr. Governador del Estado de Tamaulipas, Fernando Garcia Davila, 8 agosto 1825; and DRI 28–29, Antonio Elosua to

Comandante de Coahuila, Tamaulipas, y N. León, 23 junio 1827. On failed peace treaties, see Wood, *Life in Laredo*, 84–86; and MAA 5:65–66, 9 septiembre 1821.

42. The colonization plan gave land to those Anglo American colonists who pledged to obey Mexican laws and practice Christianity and who "prove their morality and good habits." Calvert and De León, *The History of Texas*, 48–51. On Indian attacks, see Newcomb, *The Indians of Texas*, 348–50; MAA 25:188–89, 17 marzo 1837; Vigness, "Indian Raids on the Lower Rio Grande," 14–23; and Hämäläinen, *The Comanche Empire*, 151, 194, 221–26. For joint Anglo Texan and Comanche incursions, see Hinojosa, *A Borderlands Town in Transition*, 27, 44; and AHM-PRE 8:15, *Gaceta del Gobierno de Tamaulipas*, 15 febrero 1845, 4. On trade between enemy Indians and Anglo Texans, see AHM-PRE 4:14, *Mercurio del Puerto de Matamoros*, 15 septiembre 1837, 360. For unfulfilled military assistance requests, see AHM-PRE 6:12, *Gaceta del Gobierno de Tamaulipas*, 7 agosto 1841. For national government appeals, see AHM-PRE 4:14, *Mercurio del Puerto de Matamoros*, 15 septiembre 1837, 360.

43. DRI 6–8, Alcaldes of Camargo, Reynosa, Mier, Revilla, and Laredo to Exmo. Sr. Virrey, 30 marzo 1783; DRI 42–43, Rafael Ramires Eizaguirre to Ilustre Ayuntamiento de C. Guerrero, 15 marzo 1834; MAA 9:22, 1 noviembre 1824; MAA 21:138–40, 29 enero 1830; AHM-PRE 4:20, 9 marzo 1837 (quote).

44. Hinojosa, *A Borderlands Town in Transition*, 44; MAA 25:188–9, 17 marzo 1837; AHM-PRE 4:6, 22 junio 1836. Zorrilla, *Historia de Tamaulipas*, 26; MAA 26:176–9, 7 junio 1836; DHL 71:120:1, Basilio Benavides to Governador, 10 abril 1836; MAA 25:146–7, 12 mayo 1837; MAA 25:68–71, 25 mayo 1837.

45. Letter from Basilio Benavides in *Mercurio del Puerto de Matamoros*, 22 abril 1836, quoted in Wright, "Popular and Official Religiosity," 509; AHM-PRE 6:12, *Gaceta del Gobierno de Tamaulipas*, 16 diciembre 1841, 4, 7 agosto 1841, 2 (quote).

46. Hämäläinen, *The Comanche Empire*, 233. On the borderland colonists' isolation and neglect, see Weber, *The Mexican Frontier*, chap. 6.

47. Hinojosa, *A Borderlands Town in Transition*, 19; DG 1–2, Census of 1788; DRI 9–14, Testimony taken by Joseph Gonzales, 14–17 junio 1790; Salinas, *Indians of the Rio Grande Delta*, 17, 40–41, 93–94, 132; MAA 16:32, 13 agosto 1814; AHM-PRE 4:20, 19 abril 1837; Berlandier, *Journey to Mexico during the Years 1826 to 1834*, 244–45.

48. Salinas, *Indians of the Rio Grande Delta*, 62–63, 96–97; Berlandier, *Journey to Mexico during the Years 1826 to 1834*, 428–29.

49. On the alliance between Tancahues and vecinos, see AHM-PRE 4:20; and AMR-PRE:1 "Año de 1837, Cuaderno borrador de oficios del Ayuntamiento y Juzgado," Julian Guerra to E. S. en Gefe del Ejército, 4 junio 1837. On conflicts between Lipán Apaches and Comanches, see DRI 20–21, letter from José Francisco de la Garza, 11 marzo 1824; DRI 21–22, letter from José Francisco de la Garza, et al., 25 marzo 1824; and MAA 26:176–79, letter from J. N. Molano, 7 junio 1836. For alliance with Lipanes, see DRI 23–25, Laredo Ayuntamiento to Tamaulipas governor Fernando García Dávila, 8 agosto 1825.

50. AHM-PRE 4:20, 24 julio 1837.

51. Despite the label "mission Indians," Carrizos no longer lived in the mission, which had ceased operating in the late eighteenth century. AHM-PRE 4:20, 19 abril 1837.

52. Barr, *Peace Came in the Form of a Woman*, 119, 135–36.

53. For interdependence of colonists with Indians elsewhere in the borderlands, see Brooks, *Captives and Cousins*, 30–33; and Barr, *Peace Came in the Form of a Woman*, 119–58.

2. Fragmented Communities

1. Corrigan and Sayer, *The Great Arch*, 3–4.

2. Vigness, "Nuevo Santander in 1795," 477 (second quote); Osante, *Orígenes del Nuevo Santander*, 136–37, 146, 155 (first quote), 156–57; Jones, *Los paisanos*, 66, 72; Miller, *José de Escandón*, 14, 22; Alonzo, *Tejano Legacy*, 28–29; EGF 1:105; Weber, *The Mexican Frontier*, 188–90.

3. Alonso, *Thread of Blood*, 23; Myres, "The Ranching Frontier," 88; Alonzo, *Tejano Legacy*, 15–20, 28; Osante, *Orígenes del Nuevo Santander*, 143, 179.

4. Alonzo, *Tejano Legacy*, 35–39; EGF 1:39; Vigness, "Nuevo Santander in 1795," 476n30; Zorrilla, Miró Flaquer, and Herrera Pérez, *Tamaulipas: Una historia compartida*, 1:24; Miller, *José de Escandón*, 33–34; Osante, *Orígenes del Nuevo Santander*, 158–76; Castillo Crimm, *De León*, 17, 252n33; Jones, *Los paisanos*, 72–73; Scott, *Historical Heritage of the Lower Rio Grande*, 64, 74–97.

5. Scott, *Historical Heritage of the Lower Rio Grande*, 65–68, 84–85; Alonzo, *Tejano Legacy*, 38–39; Miller, *José de Escandón*, 34.

6. Scott, *Historical Heritage of the Lower Rio Grande*, 103, 107; Goldfinch and Canales, *Juan N. Cortina*, 11. A hacienda measured at least five sitios. Myres, *The Ranch in Spanish Texas*, 22; Herrera Pérez, "Del señorío a la posrevolución," 7; Alonzo, *Tejano Legacy*, 44; Jones, *Los paisanos*, 69; Vigness, "Nuevo Santander in 1795," 474.

7. Vigness, "Nuevo Santander in 1795," 472–78; Zorrilla, *El poder colonial en Nuevo Santander*, 183; EGF 1:16; Graf, "The Economic History of the Lower Rio Grande Valley," 15; Alonzo, *Tejano Legacy*, 68–70; John, *Storms Brewed in Other Men's Worlds*, 482.

8. Alonzo, *Tejano Legacy*, 36–40; Paredes Manzano, *Homenaje a los fundadores de la heroica, leal e invicta Matamoros en el sesquicentenario de su nuevo nombre*, 52; Rivera Saldaña, *Frontera heroica*, 47–65, 69; Jones, *Los paisanos*, 69, 281n13; Vigness, "Nuevo Santander in 1795," 474–75.

9. Jones, *Los paisanos*, 71; Graf, "The Economic History of the Lower Rio Grande Valley," 427–28, 435–36; Berlandier, *Journey to Mexico during the Years 1826 to 1834*, 1:266; Alonzo, *Tejano Legacy*, 34; EGF 1:16, 105–9, 113–19.

10. Weber, *The Spanish Frontier in North America*, 175.

11. Gerhard, *The Northern Frontier of New Spain*, 27. Osante, *Orígenes del Nuevo Santander*, 121, 154–55; Zorrilla, *El poder colonial en Nuevo Santander*, 32–33; Alonzo, *Tejano Legacy*, 48–49; Gallegos, "Last Drop of My Blood," 6–7.

12. Haas, *Conquests and Historical Identities in California*, 30; Hinojosa, *A Borderlands Town in Transition*, 33, 43; Wright, "Popular and Official Religiosity," 426; DG 21.

13. While priests José Darío Zambrano (1800) and José Felipe de la Garza y Guerra (1804–6) used the mulato label, clerics Nicolás Ballí (1800–22) and José Fernández (1807) did not: AEM-BAU 1 and 2; Rendón de la Garza, *Bicentenario de Nuestra Señora del Refugio de los Esteros*, 114; De la Teja, *San Antonio de Béxar*, 27; Gutiérrez, *When Jesus Came, the Corn Mothers Went Away*, 196–97; EGF 2:443–44, Santa María; Salinas, *Indians of the Rio Grande Delta*, 54–55. Baptisms of Medrano Gutiérrez children: AEM-BAU 1, María Gertrudis Ysidora (18 mayo 1800), Ygnasia (4 marzo 1802), María del Carmen (28 enero 1804), and José Serbeliano (27 septiembre 1805).

14. De la Teja, *San Antonio de Béxar*, 24–28; Haas, *Conquests and Historical Identities in California*, 30; Hinojosa, *A Borderlands Town in Transition*, 101; Gerhard, *The Northern Frontier of New Spain*, 27, 366; Weber, *The Spanish Frontier in North America*, 326–28; Alonso, *Thread of Blood*, 64–68; Poyo and Hinojosa, *Tejano Origins in Eighteenth-Century San Antonio*, 139; Poyo, "Immigrants and Integration in Late Eighteenth-Century Béxar," 86–87; Jackson, *Race, Caste, and Status*, 4–5; Gutiérrez, *When Jesus Came, the Corn Mothers Went Away*, 190–94; Wright, "Popular and Official Religiosity," 453–44.

15. Alonzo, *Tejano Legacy*, 83. On the Ballís's properties, see Vigness, "Nuevo Santander in 1795," 477–78. On Capistrán's properties, see AHM-COL 1:1, 3 septiembre 1806. For merchants and foreign smugglers, see Herrera Pérez, *Monografía de Reynosa*, 126; Jones, *Los paisanos*, 71; AHM-JUD 1:1, 3 julio 1804, 28 junio 1804; AHM-JUS 1:3, 14 diciembre 1810; AHM-JUS 1:18, 14 septiembre 1823; and AHM-JUS 1:38, 13 julio 1830.

16. AHM-COL 1:1, 4 mayo 1802, will of Blas de la Garza, 3 septiembre 1806, will of Antonio Capistrán. José Nicolás Ballí, Refugio's priest, was the son of José María Ballí and Rosa María de Hinojosa. AHM-COL 1:1, 2 enero 1804.

17. AHM-COL 1:1, 29 octubre 1803, will of María Fijenia Ramirez; AHM-COL 1:1, 4 mayo 1802, will of Blas de la Garza; MAA 16:77, 19 julio 1816; Hinojosa, *A Borderlands Town in Transition*, 17, 21; Jones, *Los paisanos*, 75–76, 263; Wright, "Popular and Official Religiosity," 426.

18. AHM-JUD 1:1, 3 julio 1804; AHM-JUD 1:2, 3 noviembre 1807. Approximate wages based on salaries paid on Sánchez Navarros's Coahuila hacienda. Harris, *A Mexican Family Empire*, 213–16. Domestic servants earned approximately six pesos per month and a *cuartilla* (one and one-half pecks) of corn per week by the mid-nineteenth century. Paredes Manzano, *Homenaje a los fundadores de la heroica, leal e invicta Matamoros en el sesquicentenario de su nuevo nombre*, 32.

19. For *avíos* in colonial Mexico, see Van Young, *Hacienda and Market in Eighteenth-Century Mexico*, 255; and Martin, *Governance and Society in Colonial Mexico*, 59. For avíos and work contracts in the villas del norte, see AHM-JUD 2:28, 6 diciembre 1826; AHM-JUS 3:8, 18 marzo 1835; and AHM-JUS 3:16, 13 enero 1836. On papel de cuentas and indebted workers' switching jobs, see IMC 52:132:22, 11 octubre 1837; IMC 55:135:4, 20 marzo 1838; AHM-PRE 8:9, 5 abril 1844, 17 junio 1844; Wood, *Life in Laredo*, 123–25, 172; AHM-JUS 3:7, 28 abril 1835; Hinojosa, *A Borderlands Town in Transition*, 34n18; and AHM-COL 1:2, 16 enero 1808, will of Lorenzo Serna.

20. On artisans and professionals, see Herrera Pérez, *Monografía de Reynosa*, 126; MAA 2:129, 15 febrero 1814, MAA 16:53, 3 noviembre 1814; MAA 16:29, 15 febrero 1814; MAA 16:32, 13 agosto 1814; and Paredes Manzano, *Homenaje a los fundadores de la heroica, leal e invicta Matamoros en el sesquicentenario de su nuevo nombre*, 49–50. On homeownership, see AHM-JUD 2:17, 22 julio 1826; and AHM-JUD 3:58, 15 abril 1833. For grants of vacant lots, see AHM-PRE 4:26, 27 enero 1838; AHM-JUS 1:28, 3 septiembre 1827; and Wood, *Life in Laredo*, 151–55.

21. Poyo, "Immigrants and Integration in Late Eighteenth-Century Béxar," 86; AHM-COL 1:17, 31 diciembre 1820; Paredes Manzano, *Homenaje a los fundadores de la heroica, leal e invicta Matamoros en el sesquicentenario de su nuevo nombre*, 58, 66, 86; Graf, "The Economic History of the Lower Rio Grande Valley," 24–25, 45–46; Kearney and Knopp, *Boom and Bust*, 29, 31; AHM-PRE 1:6, 10 junio 1826; Zorrilla, Miró Flaquer, and Herrera Pérez, *Tamaulipas: Una historia compartida*, 1:90; Canseco Botello, *Historia de Matamoros*, 24; Cuéllar, *De Matamoros a México con sus gobernantes*, 9.

22. Hinojosa, *A Borderlands Town in Transition*, 39; Mora-Torres, *The Making of the Mexican Border*, 30–31; Herrera Pérez, *Monografía de Reynosa*, 57; Graf, "The Economic History of the Lower Rio Grande Valley," 4–5, 56–57; Berlandier, *Journey to Mexico during the Years 1826 to 1834*, 2:438.

23. MAA 26:133–35, 31 enero 1823; AHM-PRE 1:6, 10 junio 1826; MAA 26:161, 27 febrero 1836; MAA 26:165–66, 2 marzo 1836; Kearney and Knopp, *Boom and Bust*, 32; Graf, "The Economic History of the Lower Rio Grande Valley," 733; AHM-PRE 1:2, 18 agosto 1825, 18 enero 1825; Berlandier, *Journey to Mexico during the Years 1826 to 1834*, 2:435, 437–38.

24. On merchants, see AHM-PRE 1:6, 10 junio 1826; AHM-JUD 2:6, 30 noviembre 1823; Graf, "The Economic History of the Lower Rio Grande Valley," 48–49; DG Censuses of 1824 and 1829, 33, 72; and Wood, *Life in Laredo*, 169–71. On soldiers and immigrants, see AHM-JUD 5:5, 25 abril 1835; AHM-JUD 4:11, 25 noviembre 1833; AHM-JUD 7:19, 5 marzo 1835; AHM-JUD 3:58, 15 abril 1833; Hinojosa, *A Borderlands Town in Transition*, 64; and Berlandier, *Journey to Mexico during the Years 1826 to 1834*, 2:433.

25. Graf, "The Economic History of the Lower Rio Grande Valley," 48, 79–81; AHM-PRE 1:1, 17 diciembre 1826, 10 mayo 1826, 24 agosto 1825, 18 mayo 1826; Kearney and Knopp, *Boom and Bust*, 35–36.

26. Graf, "The Economic History of the Lower Rio Grande Valley," 63, 68.

27. On service jobs, see AHM-JUD 3:44, 5 marzo 1832; AHM-JUD 3:58, 15 abril 1833; AHM-JUD 3:63, 29 agosto 1833; and AHM-JUD 3:65, 16 octubre 1833. For transportation workers, see AHM-JUD 2:5, 23 febrero 1822; AHM-JUD 22:1, 8 marzo 1841; AHM-JUD 3:44, 5 marzo 1832; and AHM-JUD 3:45, 24 febrero 1831. For seamstresses and planchadoras, see AHM-JUD 3:42, 31 diciembre 1831; and AHM-JUD 16:3, 19 julio 1838. On boardinghouses, see AHM-JUD 2:35, 13 marzo 1831. On female-owned boardinghouses elsewhere, see D. González, *Refusing the Favor*, 20–21, 29; Ruiz, *From out of the Shadows*, 23; and Martin, *Songs My Mother Sang to Me*, 97, 102–3, 110–12, 201.

28. Mora-Torres, *The Making of the Mexican Border*, 9, 30–31.

29. Vigness, "Nuevo Santander in 1795," 475; Jones, *Los paisanos*, 75–77; DG Census of 1789, 6; Hinojosa, *A Borderlands Town in Transition*, 40; MAA 16:77, 19 julio 1816; AHM-PRE 1:6, 10 June 1826; DG Census of 1833, 92; Canseco Botello, *Historia de Matamoros*, 70–71. On foreign architectural influences and workers' housing, see Zorrilla, Miró Flaquer, and Herrera Pérez, *Tamaulipas: Textos de su historia*, 1:242–46; Berlandier, *Journey to Mexico during the Years 1826 to 1834*, 2:434; and AHM-PRE 4:1, 6 enero 1836, 27 diciembre 1835. For a house sold for twenty thousand pesos, see AHM-JUS 2:7, 27 abril 1832.

30. On cultural practices, see AHM-PRE 4:7, 17 octubre 1836; AHM-JUS 3:8, 7 marzo 1835; MAA 10:24, 17 abril 1823; Paredes Manzano, *Homenaje a los fundadores de la heroica, leal e invicta Matamoros en el sesquicentenario de su nuevo nombre*, 39–44; Zorrilla, Miró Flaquer, and Herrera Pérez, *Tamaulipas: Textos de su historia*, 1:243–44; *Mercurio del Puerto de Matamoros*, 22 diciembre 1837; and *El Látigo de Tejas*, 22 febrero 1844, 8 abril 1844, 7 octubre 1844. On Laredo's regulations, see DHL 40:32:13, 6 septiembre 1788; DHL 40–41:34:9, 22 agosto 1790; Jones, *Los paisanos*, 74–75; Wood, *Life in Laredo*, 127–29; and Hinojosa, *A Borderlands Town in Transition*, 23. On Matamoros's regulations, see *El Látigo de Tejas*, 25 enero 1844; AHM-PRE 2:1, 21 enero 1832; AHM-PRE 2:25, 22 mayo 1834; MAA 2:121, 22 junio 1811; AHM-PRE 6:15, 1 septiembre 1842, 24 octubre 1842; AHM-PRE 1:2, 29 abril 1825, 31 mayo 1825; and AHM-PRE 6:4, 20 marzo 1841.

31. On honorifics, see AHM-COL 1:7, 30 noviembre 1814; Hinojosa, *A Borderlands Town in Transition*, 18–19; and Wood, *Life in Laredo*, 112. In his second will, Lorenzo Serna identifies his workers by occupation. AHM-COL 1:1, 16 enero 1808. On uses of *ciudadano* and *paisano*, see MAA 21:132–35, 16 julio 1830; MAA 26:22–23, 18 julio 1836; Wood, *Life in Laredo*, 113; and AHM-JUS 1:25, 27 septiembre 1827 (first quote). On elite self-views, see AHM-PRE 8:24, 2 julio 1845 (second quote).

32. Osante, *Orígenes del Nuevo Santander*, 123, 169, 257; Jones, *Los paisanos*, 72–73; Wood, *Life in Laredo*, 34, 112; De la Teja, *San Antonio de Béxar*, 44; Lomnitz, "Modes of Citizenship in Mexico," 304–7; Guardino, *Peasants, Politics, and the Formation of Mexico's National State*, 174.

33. Cruz, *Let There Be Towns*, 148; Tijerina, *Tejanos and Texas under the Mexican Flag*, 39–42; Wood, *Life in Laredo*, 111, 117–18; Weber, *The Mexican Frontier*, 39; AHM-JUS 2:3, 11 agosto 1832.

34. AHM-PRE 4:20, 7 agosto 1837.

35. On the courts' sexual double standard in California and New Mexico, see Chávez-García, *Negotiating Conquest*, 25–85; and D. González, *Refusing the Favor*, 17–37.

36. On land and livestock disputes, see DHL 98–99:68:6, 6 junio 1822; DHL 99:71:15, 31 enero 1824; AHM-JUS 1:7, 6 octubre 1815; AHM-JUS 1:5, 7 diciembre 1824; AHM-COL 1:2, 14 junio 1810; AHM-JUS 1:38, 13 julio 1830; and AHM-JUS 2:3, 5 octubre 1832. Breach-of-contract suits are found in IMC 37–38:105:71, 18 octubre 1834; AHM-COL 1:7, 14 junio 1814; AHM-JUS 2:14, 7 mayo 1833; and AHM-JUS 3:13, 29 marzo 1836. On rental disputes, see AHM-JUS 1:3, 14 diciembre 1810; and AHM-JUS 2:14, 14 junio 1833, 24 octubre 1833. For disputes over manufactured items, see AHM-JUS 3:13, 28 marzo 1836; AHM-JUS 2:26, 10 noviembre 1834; and AHM-COL 1:7, 9 julio 1814.

37. On servants as property, see IMC 27:105:16, 22 febrero 1834; and AHM-COL 1:3, 23 abril 1810. For vagrants and vagrancy laws, see MAA 16:52–53, 13 noviembre 1814, 2 diciembre 1814; MAA 16:2, 16 agosto 1814; MAA 10:11–12, 23 diciembre 1823; *El Látigo de Tejas*, 25 enero 1844; AHM-JUD 3:66, 17 octubre 1833; DHL 40:34:9, 22 agosto 1790; MAA 10:86, 13 febrero 1823; AHM-JUD 3:42, 31 diciembre 1831; and AHM-PRE 2:19, 15 marzo 1834. On Indians' impressment into domestic service, see AHR-PRE 1, Documentos Diversos, "Libro donde constan los indígenas que por no tener oficio," 19 abril 1831; and Monroy, *Thrown among Strangers*, 150–54.

38. AHM-JUS 3:16, 13 enero 1836 (quote). On laws prohibiting indiscriminate punishments, see MAA 16:2, 2 agosto 1814; MAA 16:133–39, 23 febrero 1823; and Hinojosa, *A Borderlands Town in Transition*, 33. For lawsuits against servants, see IMC 46:126:31, 31 octubre 1836; IMC 53:132:25, 12 octubre 1837; IMC 43:126:11, 11 abril 1836; AHM-JUS 2:11, 22 julio 1833, 10 agosto 1833; AHM-JUS 2:3, 25 octubre 1832; and AHM-JUS 5:4, 10 febrero 1841.

39. AHM-JUS 2:11, 11 septiembre 1833; AHM-JUS 2:3, 29 octubre 1832; AHM-PRE 2:4, 7 junio 1832.

40. Graf, "The Economic History of the Lower Rio Grande Valley," 75–76, 123; AHM-JUS 1:29, 14 noviembre 1828; AHM-JUS 5:12, 22 junio 1841; AHM-JUS 3:16, 17 marzo 1836, 28 marzo 1836; AHM-JUS 5:4, 23 abril 1841; AHM-JUS 5:7, 27 marzo 1841, 14 abril 1841, 15 mayo 1841; AHM-PRE 1:2, 25 junio 1825; AHM-PRE 6:14, 21 febrero 1842; AHM-JUS 2:3, 27 agosto 1832, 4 septiembre 1832, 6 septiembre 1832; AHM-JUS 2:7, 8 mayo 1833; AHM-JUS 1:25, 12 marzo 1827.

41. On Smith, see Graf, "The Economic History of the Lower Rio Grande Valley," 76–82; AHM-JUS 3:16, 21 abril 1836; MAA 12:72, 22 junio 1825; AHM-JUS 1:35, 29 abril 1830; AHM-JUS 1:41, 27 enero 1831; AHM-JUS 2:10, 7 octubre 1833; AHM-PRE 2:26, 17 diciembre 1834; AHM-JUS 3:9, 28 abril 1835; AHM-JUS 1:18, 14 septiembre 1820; AHM-JUS 1:29, 14 noviembre 1828; AHM-PRE 1:7, 13 julio 1826; and AHM-PRE 1:1, 5 julio 1824. For the legal disputes of Prussia's vice-consul J. P. Schatzell, see AHM-JUS 5:7, 22 abril 1841, 23 abril 1841, 15 septiembre 1841; and AHM-JUD 6:5, 30 octubre 1835.

42. On foreign workers and former slaves, see AHM-JUD 2:6, 30 noviembre 1823; AHM-JUS 2:3, 4 septiembre 1832, 12 octubre 1832; AHM-JUS 3:13, 10 octubre 1836, 13 junio 1836; AHM-JUD 4:30, 7 mayo 1834; AHM-JUD 2:18, 9 agosto 1826; AHM-JUD 2:6, 30 noviembre 1823; Green, *Journal of the Texian Expedition against Mier*, 122–24; Schwartz, *Across the Rio to Freedom*, 26–27, 32–38, 43–46; Vielé, "*Following the Drum*," 157–58; and AHM-JUD 3:44, 5 marzo 1832 (quotes).

43. IMC 56:135:9, 23 mayo 1838; AHM-JUS 2:3, 20 agosto 1832, 25 agosto 1832, 31 agosto 1832; AHM-JUD 3:45, 24 febrero 1831.

44. AHM-JUS 3:16, 29 abril 1836; AHM-JUD 2:11, 18 noviembre 1824; AHM-JUS 2:3, 23 agosto 1832, 4 septiembre 1832, 25 octubre 1832; AHM-JUS 2:11, 22 noviembre 1833; IMC 46:126:31, 31 octubre 1836; IMC 23:97:5, 17 septiembre 1832.

45. On laws curbing children's indenture, see AHM-PRE 8:5, *El Látigo de Tejas*, 25 enero 1844. For orphans as indentured servants, see AHM-JUD 7:19, 5 marzo 1835. On children as domestic servants and apprentices, see AHM-JUS 2:3, 24 octubre

1832; AHM-JUS 3:8, 18 marzo 1835; AMR-JUZ 1, "Juicios Verbales, 1841," 16 febrero 1841, 26 octubre 1841; AHM-PRE 8:9, 8 junio 1844; AHM-JUS 3:16, 9 abril 1836; and AHM-JUS 5:7, 22 marzo 1841, 2 agosto 1841.

46. MAA 16:132, 31 enero 1823; Wood, *Life in Laredo,* 172. For workers' lawsuits, see AHM-JUS 3:16, 13 marzo 1836, 17 marzo 1836; AHM-PRE 4:6, 24 abril 1836; LA 59:1, 5 enero 1815; LA 59:2, 8 enero 1815; LA 59:23, 18 julio 1815; AHM-JUS 2:3, 31 agosto 1832, 5 septiembre 1832; AHM-JUS 5:3, 25 febrero 1841; AHM-JUS 5:7, 21 junio 1841; and MAA 16:133, 31 enero 1823. For petition and governor's denial, see MAA 10:109, 13 febrero 1823.

47. AHM-JUD 7:19, 28 febrero 1835.

48. AHM-JUS 5:7, 12 julio 1841, 7 septiembre 1841; AHM-JUS 2:3, 25 agosto 1832; AHM-JUS 3:7, 28 abril 1835; IMC 29:105:32, 1 mayo 1834; IMC 29:105:33, 9 mayo 1834; MAA 27:159, 26 abril 1838.

49. LA 135:1–4, 20 marzo 1838, in Wood, *Life in Laredo,* 123–24; Hinojosa, *A Borderlands Town in Transition,* 41; AHM-JUS 5:7, 7 septiembre 1841; AHM-JUS 5:4, 10 febrero 1841. On runaway notices, see AHM-PRE 1:29, 7 octubre 1832; AHM-PRE 8:9, 5 abril 1844, 15 abril 1844, 17 julio 1844; and MAA 9:17–18, 9 septiembre 1824. On law permitting whippings, see MAA 2:121, 19 febrero 1814. For workers' punishments, see AHR-JUZ 1, "Juicios Verbales, 1830–1895," 31 diciembre 1845; AHM-JUS 2:16, 21 marzo 1833; AHM-JUS 2:3, 18 octubre 1832; and IMC 46:126:31, 31 octubre 1836. On runaways, see AHM-JUS 2:16, 11 abril 1833; AHM-JUS 2:11, 19 julio 1833, 22 julio 1833; AHM-JUS 2:3, 29 octubre 1832; MAA 29:23, 19 abril 1838; MAA 27:159, 26 abril 1838; AHM-PRE 4:3, 23 agosto 1836; AHR-JUZ 1, "Juicios Verbales, 1830–1895," 31 diciembre 1845; MAA 21:189–90, 2 agosto 1830; MAA 21:186–87, 3 agosto 1830; and MAA 29:195–96, 1 mayo 1839.

50. Arrom, *The Women of Mexico City,* 56–64; Lavrin, "Sexuality in Colonial Mexico," 65.

51. Arrom, *The Women of Mexico City,* 57–61; IMC 51:132:14, 21 agosto 1837; IMC 50:132:9, 4 abril 1837; IMC 46:126:34, 24 noviembre 1836; AHM-COL 1:7, 14 julio 1814; AHM-JUS 2:3, 24 octubre 1832; AHM-JUD 32:5, 5 enero 1846; González, *Refusing the Favor,* 17–37.

52. AHM-JUD 2:28, 6 diciembre 1826; AHM-JUD 16:3, 19 julio 1838; AHM-JUD 32:1, 8 marzo 1841; AHM-JUD 22:1, 8 marzo 1841; DHL 38:28:1, 3 mayo 1784; MAA 27:164, 15 enero 1838. On underreported sexual assaults, see Castañeda, *Violación, estupro y sexualidad,* 69, 78, 115, 166–69; and Lavrin, "Sexuality in Colonial Mexico," 71. On sexual assault lawsuits in the villas, see AHM-JUS 3:9, 28 abril 1835; AHM-JUS 3:13, 19 may 1836; AHM-JUD 26:15, 4 abril 1844; AHM-JUD 32:5, 5 enero 1846; AHM-JUS 2:11, 11 octubre 1833; AHM-JUD 2:22, 28 febrero 1827; AHM-JUD 5:22, julio 1834; AHM-JUD 16:12, 10 octubre 1838; AHM-PRE 1:29, 11 mayo 1832; AHM-PRE 8:14, 26 junio 1845; AHM-JUD 16:11, 3 octubre 1838; and MAA 27:164, 15 enero 1838.

53. Castañeda, *Violación, estupro y sexualidad,* 120. For Gudiño's case, see AHM-JUD 2:22, 28 febrero 1827, 8 marzo 1827. On medical examinations, see Lavrin, "Sexuality in Colonial Mexico," 71; and AHM-JUD 26:15, 4 abril 1844. For an incest case and García's lawsuit, see AHM-JUD 5:22, 5 agosto 1834; and AHM-JUD 32:5, 5 enero 1846.

54. Castañeda, *Violación, estupro y sexualidad*, 124, 130–31; Lavrin, "Sexuality in Colonial Mexico," 70–72. AHM-JUD 16:12, 10 octubre 1838.

55. Arrom, *The Women of Mexico City*, 63; Castañeda, *Violación, estupro y sexualidad*, 125, 168; Lavrin, "Sexuality in Colonial Mexico," 71; AHM-JUS 2:11, 11 octubre 1833; AHM-JUD 5:22, 5 agosto 1834. For successful prosecutions and family honor discussions, see Chávez-García, *Negotiating Conquests*, 36–38; and Gutiérrez, *When Jesus Came, the Corn Mothers Went Away*, 207–26.

56. AHM-JUD 2:22, 28 febrero 1827; Arrom, *The Women of Mexico City*, 58; Lavrin, "Sexuality in Colonial Mexico," 71.

57. Arrom, *The Women of Mexico City*, 57–63; Twinam, "Honor, Sexuality, and Illegitimacy in Colonial Spanish America," 123–24; IMC 51:132:14, 21 agosto 1837; Wood, *Life in Laredo*, 122–23.

58. AHM-COL 1:1, 25 mayo 1804; Lavrin, "Sexuality in Colonial Mexico," 55–56.

59. Gutiérrez, *When Jesus Came, the Corn Mothers Went Away*, 208–9; IMC 33:105:48, 25 junio 1834; AHM-JUS 2:3, 2 octubre 1832; AHM-JUS 2:11, 24 enero 1833, 17 junio 1833, 11 octubre 1833; IMC 50:132:9, 4 abril 1837; AHM-JUS 1:10, 21 agosto 1820.

60. AHM-JUS 5:7, 4 febrero 1841; Arrom, *The Women of Mexico City*, 57, 72, 307n71; AHM-PRE 1:29, 10 febrero 1832; AHM-JUS 2:3, 2 octubre 1832; AHM-PRE 1:31, 11 septiembre 1832; AHM-JUS 2:11, 15 julio 1833.

61. Lavrin, "Sexuality in Colonial Mexico," 61; Arrom, *The Women of Mexico City*, 63. For fathers' lawsuits, see AHM-JUS 2:11, 24 mayo 1833, 22 noviembre 1833; AHM-JUS 5:7, 2 agosto 1841; AHM-JUD 24:25, 8 junio 1842; and AHM-COL 1:7, 14 junio 1814. For a mother's lawsuit, see AHM-COL 1:7, 30 noviembre 1814.

62. Seed, *To Love, Honor, and Obey in Colonial Mexico*, 101; Lavrin, "Sexuality in Colonial Mexico," 61–63; Gutiérrez, *When Jesus Came, the Corn Mothers Went Away*, 215–26; AHM-JUS 5:7, 2 agosto 1841.

63. AHM-COL 1:7, 30 noviembre 1814; Arrom, *The Women of Mexico City*, 63–65.

64. Arrom, *The Women of Mexico City*, 63, 305n54; Lavrin, "Sexuality in Colonial Mexico," 55–56; AHM-JUS 2:11, 22 noviembre 1833; AHM-JUD 24:25, 8 junio 1842 (quote).

65. Arrom, *The Women of Mexico City*, 64, 79; AHM-JUS 2:14, 6 junio 1833; AHM-JUS 2:11, 22 mayo 1833, 1 junio 1833; AHM-JUS 1:25, 15 mayo 1827.

66. AHM-JUS 2:11, 9 octubre 1833, 20 septiembre 1833; AHM-JUS 2:14, 6 junio 1833; Arrom, *The Women of Mexico City*, 58–61.

67. MAA 10:63, 12 septiembre 1823; AHM-JUS 1:25, 23 octubre 1827; AHM-JUS 1:26, 15 diciembre 1827 (quote).

68. Alonso, *Thread of Blood*, 75–79, 88–91; Gutiérrez, *When Jesus Came, the Corn Mothers Went Away*, 208–26.

69. Arrom, *The Women of Mexico City*, 65–70; González, *Refusing the Favor*, 17–37; Chávez-García, *Negotiating Conquest*, 52–85; LeCompte, "The Independent Women of Hispanic New Mexico."

70. Arrom, *The Women of Mexico City*, 218; Stern, *The Secret History of Gender*, 99–107; AHM-JUS 3:16, 16 abril 1836; IMC 39:105–1:76, 4 noviembre 1834, *Antonio Castillo v. Andrés García*.

71. Chávez-García, *Negotiating Conquest*, 29–30; Arrom, *The Women of Mexico City*, 65. On women who refused to accompany husbands, see AHM-JUS 5:6, 14 enero 1841; AHM-JUS 5:4, 5 febrero 1841; AHM-PRE 1:29, 28 julio 1832; AHM-JUS 3:16, 20 abril 1836, *Ylario Villarreal v. María Reducinda Gutiérrez*; and AHM-JUS 5:4, 5 febrero 1841, *Filomeno Lopes v. esposa* (wife's name not given). For women compelled to work as domestic servants, see AHM-PRE 1:29, 23 julio 1832; and AHM-JUS 3:16, 27 abril 1836.

72. IMC 34:105–1:54, 28 julio 1834, *Josefa de Luna v. Domingo Siprián*; AHM-JUS 2:3, 21 agosto 1832; AHM-JUS 2:11, 17 junio 1833; AHM-JUS 5:7, 4 mayo 1841. After 1845, Mexico allowed criminal charges for frequent and extreme domestic abuse. Arrom, *The Women of Mexico City*, 211, 237; Chávez-García, *Negotiating Conquest*, 29–30.

73. Arrom, *The Women of Mexico City*, 208 (quote); Cummins, "Church Courts, Marriage Breakdown, and Separation in Spanish Louisiana, West Florida, and Texas," 97–114; AHM-JUS 2:11, 10 enero 1833. I identified twenty-nine domestic reconciliation cases in IMC and AHM.

74. AHM-JUS 3:7, 1 mayo 1835, *Eulogio Peres v. esposa* (wife's name not given); AHM-JUS 5:5, 6 agosto 1841; AHM-JUS 2:11, 10 enero 1833; AHM-JUS 2:4, 30 abril 1832.

75. Arrom, *The Women of Mexico City*, 211; AHM-PRE 4:3, 14 septiembre 1836; AHM-JUD 23:9, 23 julio 1841; AHM-JUS 5:5, 3 diciembre 1841, *Benito Bon v. Manuela Núñez*; AHM-JUS 2:11, 10 enero 1833, *Pedro Torres v. María Gertrudis*; AHM-JUS 2:24, 9 mayo 1834, *María Concepción Flores v. Francisco Quintanilla*.

76. I found no annulment records in the villas del norte. Cummins found two annulment cases over a seventy-four-year period for Spanish Louisiana, west Florida, and Texas. Cummins, "Church Courts, Marriage Breakdown, and Separation in Spanish Louisiana, West Florida, and Texas," 100. Arrom identified seven annulment requests in Mexico City for a sixty-eight-year period. Arrom, *The Women of Mexico City*, 208–12, 336n6; Arrom, "Changes in the Mexican Family Law in the Nineteenth Century," 305, 310–12. See also Nizza da Silva, "Divorce in Colonial Brazil," 313.

77. AHM-JUS 5:19, 3 mayo 1842, *Cecilia Figueroa v. Francisco Leal*. On women's use of the term *mala vida*, see Boyer, "Women, *La Mala Vida*, and the Politics of Marriage," 252–86; Arrom, *The Women of Mexico City*, 209, 218; and AHM-JUS 5:7, 2 septiembre 1841, *Brigida Ramires v. Pedro González*, 6 diciembre 1841, *Jesús Guadalupe Olvera v. Marta de Ávila*.

78. Arrom, *The Women of Mexico City*, 210; AHM-JUD 7:23, 13 mayo 1835, *Manuela Delgadillo v. Manuel Quintanilla*; AHM-JUS 2:24, 9 mayo 1834, *María Concepción Flores v. Francisco Quintanilla*.

79. Lavrin, "Sexuality in Colonial Mexico," 58–67; Seed, *To Love, Honor, and Obey in Colonial Mexico*, 62–64; Gutiérrez, *When Jesus Came, the Corn Mothers Went Away*, 207–40; Hunefeldt, *Liberalism in the Bedroom*, 219, 352–53; Arrom, *The Women of Mexico City*, 212–16; AHM-JUD 22:5, 12 marzo 1841, *María Concepción Solís v. Sabas Olivares*; AHM-JUS 5:12, 22 junio 1841, *María de la Luz Barrera v. Juan Nicolás Boden*; AHM-JUS 2:14, 9 mayo 1833, *Mónica Carriaga v. Francisco Gamilla*; AHM-JUS 2:24, 9 mayo 1834, *María Concepción Flores v. Francisco Quintanilla*.

80. AHM-JUD 22:5, 12 marzo 1841, 11 mayo 1841 (quote); AHM-JUS 5:4, 27 marzo 1841; AHM-JUS 5:7, 24 mayo 1841, 28 julio 1841; AHM-JUD 23:9, 23 julio 1841.

81. AHM-JUD 16:6, 15 agosto 1838, *Juicio criminal v. Francisco Alvian por muerte de su esposa Rafaela Sánchez*; AHM-PRE 1:29, 22 julio 1832; AHM-JUS 2:14, 9 mayo 1833, *Mónica Carriaga v. Francisco Gamilla*; AHM-JUS 2:24, 9 mayo 1834, *María Concepción Flores v. Francisco Quintanilla*.

82. Arrom, *The Women of Mexico City*, 210, 226–28; Nizza da Silva, "Divorce in Colonial Brazil," 319; AHM-JUS 2:11, 10 enero 1833, *Pedro Torres v. María Gertrudis* (no surname given). Without access to ecclesiastical court records, I could not determine the number of successful divorces and annulments.

83. AHM-JUD 7:23, 13 mayo 1835; AHM-JUS 2:24, 9 mayo 1834; AHM-JUS 5:7, 6 diciembre 1841, *Jesús Guadalupe Olvera v. Marta de Ávila*. Ávila's statement alluded to the Catholic Church's exhortation about martial power relations during the marriage ceremony, in which the husband is cautioned, "We do not give you a slave but rather a wife." Arrom, *The Women of Mexico City*, 230.

84. Arrom, *The Women of Mexico City*, 219–22.

85. Ibid., 230–32; Rodríguez S., "Civilizing Domestic Life in the Central Valley of Costa Rica," 85–107; AHM-JUS 3:7, 1 mayo 1835, *C. Eulogio Peres v. su muger* (wife's name not given); AHM-JUS 5:19, 3 mayo 1842, 26 agosto 1842 (first quote) *Cecilia Figueroa v. Francisco Leal*; AHM-JUS 2:24, 9 mayo 1834, *María Concepción Flores v. Francisco Quintanilla*.

86. Corrigan and Sayer, *The Great Arch*, 12.

3. Opposing Forces

1. Nugent, "Are We Not [Civilized] Men?," 206–39; Nugent, *Spent Cartridges of Revolution*, 50.

2. Alonso, *Thread of Blood*, 25.

3. Zorrilla, *El poder colonial en Nuevo Santander*, 242; Osante, *Orígenes del Nuevo Santander*, 257–60; Zorrilla, Miró Flaquer, and Herrera Pérez, *Tamaulipas: Una historia compartida I*, 18; Scott, "Spanish Colonization of the Lower Rio Grande," 17–18; Wright, "Popular and Official Religiosity," 416–17.

4. Zorrilla, Miró Flaquer, and Herrera Pérez, *Tamaulipas: Una historia compartida I*, 20; Gerhard, *The Northern Frontier of New Spain*, 10–19, 363.

5. Osante, *Orígenes del Nuevo Santander*, 257; Zorrilla, Miró Flaquer, and Herrera Pérez, *Tamaulipas: Una historia compartida I*, 16; Miller, *José de Escandón*, 14; Zorrilla, *Estudio de la legislación en Tamaulipas*, 12; Cruz, *Let There Be Towns*, 74–75, 150, 164; Hinojosa, *A Borderlands Town in Transition*, 13.

6. Zorrilla, *Estudio de la legislación en Tamaulipas*, 11–12; Zorrilla, Miró Flaquer, and Herrera Pérez, *Tamaulipas: Una historia compartida I*, 21; Gerhard, *The Northern Frontier of New Spain*, 363; Zorrilla, Miró Flaquer, and Herrera Pérez, *Tamaulipas: Textos de su historia*, 1:17–22; MAA 16:28, 1814 (no month, day); MAA 16:38, 12 diciembre 1814; AHM-COL 1:15, 3 septiembre 1819, 13 diciembre 1819.

7. MAA 16:35, 23 octubre 1815; AHM-COL 1:15, 27 marzo 1819; Gutiérrez, "Un-

raveling America's Hispanic Past," 80–82; Gutiérrez, "Migration, Emergent Ethnicity, and the 'Third Space,'" 484; Weber, *The Mexican Frontier*, 240; Sahlins, *Boundaries*, 110–11, 146; Poyo and Hinojosa, *Tejano Origins in Eighteenth-Century San Antonio*, 140–41; Matovina, *Tejano Religion and Ethnicity*, 5–6, 9–10; Haas, *Conquests and Historical Identities in California*, 32–38.

8. Sahlins, *Boundaries*, 111–13, 146; Marzahl, *Town in the Empire*, 37, 63; Jones, *Los paisanos*, 13, 266; Gutiérrez, *When Jesus Came, the Corn Mothers Went Away*, 190–94; De la Teja, *San Antonio de Béxar*, 44; Lockhart and Schwartz, *Early Latin America*, 96; Cruz, *Let There Be Towns*, 116, 117, 126, 133; Frank, *From Settler to Citizen*, 176–81; Mora-Torres, *The Making of the Mexican Border*, 15–16.

9. Weber, *The Mexican Frontier*, 238–41; Gutiérrez, "Unraveling America's Hispanic Past," 81–82; Ramos, *Beyond the Alamo*, 85, 128; Reséndez, *Changing National Identities at the Frontier*, 148–49; Reséndez, "National Identity on a Shifting Border," 690; Wilkinson, *Laredo and the Rio Grande Frontier*, 55–56, 63–64; Alonzo, *Tejano Legacy*, 68–70.

10. Jones, *Los paisanos*, 250; Osante, *Orígenes del Nuevo Santander*, 267; Wilkinson, *Laredo and the Rio Grande Frontier*, 63–64; Vigness, "Nuevo Santander in 1795," 476, 478, 479; Zorrilla, Miró Flaquer, and Herrera Pérez, *Tamaulipas: Una historia compartida I*, 27–29; Zavala, "The Frontiers of Hispanic America," 190–91; Weber, *The Mexican Frontier*, 284; Poyo and Hinojosa, *Tejano Origins in Eighteenth-Century San Antonio*, 140–41.

11. Weber, *The Mexican Frontier*, 124 (quote); Osante, *Orígenes del Nuevo Santander*, 267.

12. Weber, *The Mexican Frontier*, 123–24; Meyer, Sherman, and Deeds, *The Course of Mexican History*, 145; Vigness, "Nuevo Santander in 1795," 467, 477–79, 467, 491–506.

13. Meyer, Sherman, and Deeds, *The Course of Mexican History*, 224; Weber, *The Mexican Frontier*, 123; MAA 16:33, 30 agosto 1814; MAA 2:132, 15 agosto 1814; Wright, "Popular and Official Religiosity," 449–50.

14. Alonzo, *Tejano Legacy*, 68; Wilkinson, *Laredo and the Rio Grande Frontier*, 72; Graf, "The Economic History of the Lower Rio Grande Valley," 15, 52–56; Weber, *The Mexican Frontier*, 123, 125 (quote); Kearney and Knopp, *Boom and Bust*, 19, 36–37; Sahlins, *Boundaries*, 129, 140–41; Lattimore, "The Frontier in History," 470; Canseco Botello, *Historia de Matamoros*, 71.

15. Herrera Pérez, *Monografía de Reynosa*, 50–51; MAA 16:70, 14 agosto 1816.

16. Miller, *José de Escandón*, 14; Osante, *Orígenes del Nuevo Santander*, 259; Weber, *The Mexican Frontier*, 123–25, 149; MAA 16:70, 14 agosto 1816.

17. Zorrilla, Miró Flaquer, and Herrera Pérez, *Tamaulipas: Una historia compartida I*, 51–52.

18. Ibid., 47–69; Alessio Robles, *Coahuila y Texas en la época colonial*, 635–36, 655–61; Jarratt, *Gutiérrez de Lara, Mexican Texan*, 13–67; Milligan, "José Bernardo Gutiérrez de Lara," 76–105.

19. Zorrilla, Miró Flaquer, and Herrera Pérez, *Tamaulipas: Una historia compartida I*, 65–66; Hinojosa, *A Borderlands Town in Transition*, 26–27; Herrera Pérez, *Monografía de Reynosa*, 52–53; Zorrilla, Miró Flaquer, and Herrera Pérez, *Tamaulipas: Textos de su historia*, 1:60–68.

20. Zorrilla, Miró Flaquer, and Herrera Pérez, *Tamaulipas: Una historia compartida I*, 68; Herrera Pérez, *Monografía de Reynosa*, 55; Zorrilla, Miró Flaquer, and Herrera Pérez, *Tamaulipas: Textos de su historia*, 1:78–81; Van Young, *The Other Rebellion*, 127–38.

21. Hinojosa, *A Borderlands Town in Transition*, 23, 28, 36–37; Martin, *Governance and Society in Colonial Mexico*, 103–5; MAA 15:195, 8 junio 1814; MAA 16:5, 24 septiembre 1814; MAA 15:177, 20 julio 1814; MAA 15:176, 21 julio 1814; LA 29:1, decree signed by Santiago de Jesús Sánchez, 6 January 1785, in DHL 48; MAA 16:29, 15 febrero 1814.

22. TePaske, "The Financial Disintegration of the Royal Government of Mexico during the Epoch of Independence," 71; Zorrilla, Miró Flaquer, and Herrera Pérez, *Tamaulipas: Una historia compartida I*, 65; MAA 2:121–23, 23 febrero 1811; MAA 16:18, 8 julio 1814; MAA 15:195, 8 junio 1814; MAA 16:65, 13 noviembre 1816; AHM-COL 1:15, 28 marzo 1819; HM 9, letter by José González, 9 March 1813.

23. TePaske, "The Financial Disintegration of the Royal Government of Mexico during the Epoch of Independence," 63–83; Archer, "'La Causa Buena,'" 106–7.

24. AHM-COL 1:13, n.d.; AHM-COL 1:15, 26 marzo 1819, 27 marzo 1819; AHM-COL 1:18, 10 agosto 1820, 21 noviembre 1820, 28 diciembre 1820; MAA 15:80, 22 abril 1814; MAA 16:47, 7 diciembre 1814; MAA 15:127–28, 12 junio 1814; MAA 16:30, 17 mayo 1814; MAA 16:65, 13 noviembre 1816; MAA 16:84, 23 noviembre 1816; Hinojosa, *A Borderlands Town in Transition*, 28–29.

25. MAA 2:136, 18 agosto 1814; Zorrilla, Miró Flaquer, and Herrera Pérez, *Tamaulipas: Textos de su historia I*, 84–88; Hinojosa, *A Borderlands Town in Transition*, 29; Herrera Pérez, *Monografía de Reynosa*, 55–56; Wright, "Popular and Official Religiosity," 475; AHM-COL 1:15, 27 marzo 1819; MAA 5:67, 6 noviembre 1821.

26. Wright, "Popular and Official Religiosity," 475; MAA 16:30, 20 marzo 1814; MAA 15:127–29, 12 junio 1814; Hinojosa, *A Borderlands Town in Transition*, 30–32; Herrera Pérez, *El norte de Tamaulipas y la conformación de la frontera México–Estados Unidos*, 28–29.

27. Hinojosa, *A Borderlands Town in Transition*, 31; MAA 16:31, 13 junio 1814, MAA 16:33, 18 agosto 1814; AHM-COL 1:15, 28 marzo 1819.

28. Wright, "Popular and Official Religiosity," 476–77; MAA 16:33–34, 21 agosto 1814; DRI 17, letter from José María de Echeagaray, 8 October 1819; Hinojosa, *A Borderlands Town in Transition*, 30–31; Wood, *Life in Laredo*, 85.

29. AHM-COL 1:15, 27 marzo 1819; MAA 5:67, 6 noviembre 1821; MAA 16:65, 13 noviembre 1816, MAA 16:84, 23 noviembre 1816; Scott, *Weapons of the Weak*, 33–38; Sahlins, *Boundaries*, 22, 127–32.

30. AHM-COL 1:18, 10 octubre 1820; AHM-COL 1:8, 21 febrero 1815; Hinojosa, *A Borderlands Town in Transition*, 31–32.

31. MAA 16:1, 3 septiembre 1814; MAA 15:77, 19 julio 1816; MAA 16:71, 2 septiembre 1816; MAA 16:84, 23 noviembre 1816.

32. Krauze, *Mexico*, 132; Anderson, *Imagined Communities*, 44–46, 61–65; Zorrilla, Miró Flaquer, and Herrera Pérez, *Tamaulipas: Una historia compartida I*, 138–39.

33. Zorrilla, Miró Flaquer, and Herrera Pérez, *Tamaulipas: Una historia compar-*

tida I, 139; Reséndez, "National Identity on a Shifting Border," 691; Green, *The Mexican Republic*, 99–111; DHL 49–56, letter from José Francisco de la Garza, 19 January 1818, letter from Francisco Fernández, 5 November 1821, monthly reports of Laredo schools from the 1822, 1823, 1826, and 1827; Hinojosa, *A Borderlands Town in Transition*, 36–37, 40.

34. Reséndez, "National Identity on a Shifting Border," 675. "Tamaulipas" is from the Huasteca-language word "Tamaholipan" with several meanings, including "place with high mountains" and "place where much prayer occurs." Zorrilla, Miró Flaquer, and Herrera Pérez, *Tamaulipas: Una historia compartida I*, 90; Zorrilla, Miró Flaquer, and Herrera Pérez, *Tamaulipas: Textos de su historia*, 1:162; Cuellar, *De Matamoros a México con sus gobernantes*, 9, 29; Meade, *Etimologías toponímicas indígenas del Estado de Tamaulipas*, 29; Zorrilla, *Tamaulipas—Tamaholipa*, 7–8, 49n1; MAA 9:158, 23 marzo 1824; Zorrilla, *Estudio de la legislación en Tamaulipas*, 15. Priest Mariano Matamoros was José María Morelos y Pavón's closest lieutenant. Canseco Botello, *Historia de Matamoros*, 23–24; Paredes Manzano, *Homenaje a los fundadores de la heroica, leal e invicta Matamoros en el sesquicentenraio de su nuevo nombre*, 64; Krauze, *Mexico*, 85.

35. Weber, *The Mexican Frontier*, 22; Green, *The Mexican Republic*, 3–4; MAA 16:5, 24 septiembre 1814; MAA 9:76, 17 abril 1824; MAA 14:128–29, 25 febrero 1825; MAA 21:51–52, 7 enero 1830; MAA 16:132, 1823; MAA 16:139, 4 marzo 1823.

36. MAA 16:4–5, 4 marzo 1823; MAA 21:197, 8 agosto 1830; MAA 21:196, 5 agosto 1830; MAA 21:168–69, 14 septiembre 1830; Reséndez, "National Identity on a Shifting Border," 691–92; Hinojosa, *A Borderlands Town in Transition*, 37–38; Herrera Pérez, *Monografía de Reynosa*, 56–57.

37. AHM-COL 1:15, 21 enero 1819; AHM-PRE 2:1, 21 enero 1832; Rodríguez O., "From Royal Subject to Republican Citizen," 40; Rodríguez O., "The Constitution of 1824 and the Formation of the Mexican State," 80–81; Rodríguez O., "Introduction," 6; Weber, *The Mexican Frontier*, 22. Gutiérrez describes a similar shift in the meaning of *calidad* (social status) from denoting race to indicating nationality after Mexican independence. Gutiérrez, *When Jesus Came, the Corn Mothers Went Away*, 190–94.

38. AHM-PRE 1:1, 10 septiembre 1825.

39. Ibid.; AHM-PRE 1:6, 10 junio 1826.

40. De la Teja, *San Antonio de Béxar*, 44; Lomnitz, "Modes of Citizenship in Mexico," 305–7; Guardino, *Peasants, Politics, and the Formation of Mexico's National State*, 91, 100; Sahlins, *Boundaries*, 146; AHM-PRE 1:16, 14 diciembre 1828; AHM-COL 1:19, 8 diciembre 1822.

41. Weber, *The Mexican Frontier*, 103, 175–76; Juan N. Almonte quoted in Reséndez, "National Identity on a Shifting Border," 4; Green, *The Mexican Republic*, 60–64; *El Ancla*, 8 junio 1838.

42. Zorrilla, Miró Flaquer, and Herrera Pérez, *Tamaulipas: Una historia compartida I*, 125–26; Meyer, Sherman, and Deeds, *The Course of Mexican History*, 283–84.

43. Reséndez, *Changing National Identities at the Frontier*, 124–45; Casas, *Married to a Daughter of the Land*, 49–112; AHM-PRE 1:17, 12 febrero 1828; *La Gaceta del Gobierno de Tamaulipas*, 8 diciembre 1842; Cuéllar, *De Matamoros a México con sus gobernantes*, 32.

44. Weber, *The Taos Trappers*, 176–91; Ewers, "Introduction," 2–11, 18; Kearney and Knopp, *Boom and Bust*, 40; Muller, "Introduction," xxxiv; AHM-PRE 6:3, 9 marzo 1841; AHM-PRE 6:9, 22 enero 1841; *La Gaceta del Gobierno de Tamaulipas*, 8 diciembre 1842.

45. Weber, *The Mexican Frontier*, 122; Reséndez, "National Identity on a Shifting Border," 694.

46. Rodríguez O., "Down from Colonialism," 11–23; Meyer, Sherman, and Deeds, *The Course of Mexican History*, 282; Graf, "The Economic History of the Lower Rio Grande Valley," 51–52, 131; Weber, *The Mexican Frontier*, 149.

47. Meyer, Sherman, and Deeds, *The Course of Mexican History*, 282; Graf, "The Economic History of the Lower Rio Grande Valley," 551; Weber, *The Mexican Frontier*, 52, 148.

48. Graf, "The Economic History of the Lower Rio Grande Valley," 53–55.

49. MAA 16:192, 21 marzo 1824; MAA 21:23, 28 abril 1830; Weber, *The Mexican Frontier*, 151; Graf, "The Economic History of the Lower Rio Grande Valley," 52, 110–11, 117.

50. AHM-JUS 1:18, 14 septiembre 1823; Hammett, *The Empresario*, 8, 52, 54; Castillo Crimm, *De León*, 67; MAA 9:141, 16 agosto 1824; MAA 10:99, 12 mayo 1825; MAA 14:57, 24 mayo 1825; MAA 14:90, 18 noviembre 1825; MAA 9:126, 26 enero 1824; AHM-JUS 1:18, 14 septiembre 1823; Graf, "The Economic History of the Lower Rio Grande Valley," 53; MAA 9:105–7, 16 diciembre 1824; MAA 21:23, 28 abril 1830; MAA 16:187, 8 abril 1824; MAA 16:181, 3 abril 1824; MAA 16:192, 21 marzo 1824; AHM-JUD 2:39, 7 septiembre 1831; AHM-JUS 1:1, 3 febrero 1806; Scott, *Weapons of the Weak*, 129; Weber, *The Mexican Frontier*, 149–53.

51. Zorrilla, Miró Flaquer, and Herrera Pérez, *Tamaulipas: Textos de su historia*, 1:210–15; *La Gaceta del Gobierno de Tamaulipas*, 21 abril 1842; Weber, *The Mexican Frontier*, 122, 146, 150–51.

52. Graf, "The Economic History of the Lower Rio Grande Valley," table 4, chap. 2.

53. Examples in the MAA include *El Argos de Matamoros*; *El Demócrata*; *Mercurio del Puerto de Matamoros*; *La Gaceta del Gobierno de Tamaulipas*; *El Restaurador de Tamaulipas*; *El Telescopio de Tamaulipas*; *Atalaya*; *La Columna de la Constitución Federal de la República Mexicana*; *El Telégrafo*; Graf, "The Economic History of the Lower Rio Grande Valley," 131–33.

54. Reséndez, *Changing National Identities at the Frontier*, 123, 148.

55. Weber, *The Mexican Frontier*, 39, 124–25; Rodríguez, "Down from Colonialism," 11–17; Nugent, "Are We Not [Civilized] Men?," 218; Vázquez, "La supuesta república del Río Grande," 49–80.

56. MAA 14:125, 4 febrero 1825; MAA 22:142–43, 17 noviembre 1835; MAA 22:131–32, 8 diciembre 1835; MAA 26:144–48, 4 enero 1836; MAA 26:149, 21 enero 1836; MAA 23:53–54, 28 diciembre 1835; MAA 14:31, 21 julio 1825; MAA 10:121, 17 abril 1823; Graf, "The Economic History of the Lower Rio Grande Valley," 133n69; Canseco Botello, *Historia de Matamoros*, 26; Horgan, *Great River*, 492–93.

57. MAA 22:27–28, 16 junio 1830.

58. DHL 62–64, letter from Lucas Fernández, 23 Marzo 1824, letter from Juan

José Galán, 1 Septiembre 1826, letter from José Lázaro Benavides, 3 Marzo 1827; Hinojosa, *A Borderlands Town in Transition*, 44; MAA 10:108, 21 agosto 1823; MAA 10:106, 24 junio 1823; MAA 23:53–54, 28 diciembre 1835; MAA 10:115, 13 febrero 1823; MAA 10:121, 17 abril 1823.

59. MAA 16:133, 31 enero 1823; MAA 16:141, 1 abril 1823; DHL 70, letter from Manuel Lafuente, 2 enero 1835.

60. DHL 63, Anastacio Bustamante, 2 Marzo 1827; MAA 10:121, 17 abril 1823; MAA 16:140, 9 marzo 1823; MAA 9:67, 16 enero 1824; MAA 12:118–19, 8 junio 1825; AHM-PRE 1:2, 31 mayo 1825.

61. Weber, *The Mexican Frontier*, 153–55; MAA 9:116, 4 marzo 1824; MAA 9:174, 17 marzo 1824.

62. Wright, "Popular and Official Religiosity," 508–9; Wilcox, "Laredo during the Texas Republic," 89–92; Wilkinson, *Laredo and the Rio Grande Frontier*, 135; AHM-PRE 4:6, 22 junio 1836, 15 julio 1836; MAA 22:131–32, 8 diciembre 1835; MAA 26:58, 21 junio 1836; MAA 26:185–86, 14 julio 1836; MAA 26:150, 21 enero 1836; MAA 26:152–53, 25 enero 1836; MAA 26:174, 7 abril 1836.

63. Weber, *The Mexican Frontier*, 110; AHM-PRE 4:6, 27 mayo 1836; AHM-PRE 4:3, 14 enero 1836; MAA 21:194–95, 8 julio 1830; MAA 29:20–21, 13 agosto 1838; MAA 21:86–87, 8 julio 1830; MAA 29:183–84, 13 diciembre 1839; MAA 27:85, 10 octubre 1838; MAA 29:56–57, 8 febrero 1838; MAA 26:14–15, 7 diciembre 1836; MAA 21:86–87, 8 julio 1830; MAA 21:132–35, 16 julio 1830; MAA 29:38–39, 16 enero 1838; MAA 21:92, 3 julio 1830; MAA 22:39–41, 5 julio 1830; MAA 21:82–84, 17 junio 1830; MAA 27:77, 1 septiembre 1837; MAA 27:90, 12 octubre 1838; MAA 27:84, 22 octubre 1838; MAA 21:93–94, 21 agosto 1830; MAA 16:141, 1 abril 1823; AHM-PRE 2:14, 2 junio 1833.

64. MAA 21:189–90, 2 agosto 1830; MAA 21:186–87, 3 agosto 1830; MAA 27:20–23, n.d.; MAA 29:195–96, 1 mayo 1839; AHM-PRE 2:4, 7 junio 1832; AHM-JUS 2:3, 29 octubre 1832.

65. AHM-PRE 4:7, 2 marzo 1836; MAA 26:14, 7 diciembre 1836; MAA 27:92, 25 noviembre 1838, 10 octubre 1838; MAA 29:184, 13 diciembre 1839; MAA 26:167–70, 2 marzo 1836; MAA 26:163–64, 27 febrero 1836; Bacilio Benavides's letter appeared in *Mercurio del Puerto de Matamoros*, 24 marzo 1836.

66. MAA 26:163–64, 27 febrero 1836; MAA 26:167–70, 2 marzo 1836; MAA 26:187, 29 julio 1836.

67. MAA 26:171, 24 marzo 1836; Wilcox, "Laredo during the Texas Republic," 96–97; Wilkinson, *Laredo and the Rio Grande Frontier*, 145–47.

68. Weber, *The Mexican Frontier*, 118–19; Sahlins, *Boundaries*, 111–13.

69. MAA 26:161, 27 febrero 1836; MAA 26:165–66, 2 marzo 1836; MAA 26:174–75, 7 abril 1836; MAA 26:144–48, 4 enero 1836; AHM-PRE 4:6, 28 enero 1836.

70. Hinojosa, *A Borderlands Town in Transition*, 50, 52–53; AHM-PRE 4:20, 11 febrero 1837 (quote), 20 febrero 1837, 4 marzo 1837, 22 marzo 1837; *Eco del Norte de Tamaulipas*, 1 septiembre 1845; AHM-PRE 6:10, 13 abril 1841; AHM-PRE 6:17, 6 enero 1842; MAA 26:180, 8 julio 1836; MAA 29:85–86, 24 febrero 1838; MAA 29:20–21, 13 agosto 1838; MAA 26:14, 7 diciembre 1836; MAA 27:92, 25 noviembre 1838; MAA 25:68–71, 25 mayo 1837; MAA 27:9–11, 2 diciembre 1836. AHM-PRE 4:6,

4 junio 1836; MAA 26:74, 4 marzo 1836; MAA 26:60–70, 26 marzo 1836; AHM-PRE 4:6, 21 julio 1836.

71. MAA 26:180, 8 julio 1836; MAA 26:30–31, 11 octubre 1836; MAA 26:10, 17 noviembre 1836; MAA 26:157, 6 febrero 1836; MAA 26:30–31, 11 octubre 1836; MAA 22:146, 20 octubre 1836; MAA 22:135, 16 enero 1836; AHM-PRE 4:20, 6 junio 1837; Weber, *The Mexican Frontier*, 110–12.

72. AHM-PRE 4:6, 15 julio 1836; Hinojosa, *A Borderlands Town in Transition*, 50; Graf, "The Economic History of the Lower Rio Grande Valley," 122–23; Vigness, "Indian Raids on the Lower Rio Grande," 21; Ramón quoted in Wilcox, "Laredo during the Texas Republic," 92–93.

73. Graf, "The Economic History of the Lower Rio Grande Valley," 122–23, 125–29, 136.

74. *Eco del Norte de Tamaulipas*, 1 septiembre 1845; AHM-PRE 6:10, Mariano Arista, 13 abril 1841; AHM-PRE 6:17, 6 enero 1842; Wilcox, "Laredo during the Texas Republic," 98; *Eco del Norte de Tamaulipas*, 23 mayo 1844 (quote).

75. Lattimore, "The Frontier in History," 470; Weber, *The Mexican Frontier*, 240 (quote); Sahlins, *Boundaries*, 107–8, 140.

76. Vázquez, "The Texas Question in Mexican Politics," 313; Zorrilla, Miró Flaquer, and Herrera Pérez, *Tamaulipas: Una historia compartida I*, 111–13; De la Torre, *Historia general de Tamaulipas*, 143–44; Herrera Pérez, *Monografía de Reynosa*, 59; Fernández de Castro, "Comercio y contrabando en la frontera noreste," 24; Hinojosa, *A Borderlands Town in Transition*, 53; Zorrilla, Miró Flaquer, and Herrera Pérez, *Tamaulipas: Una historia compartida I*, 113; DeLay, *War of a Thousand Deserts*, 152, 165–93; Reséndez, *Changing National Identities at the Frontier*, 171–96; Gallegos, "Last Drop of My Blood," 92–93.

77. Calvert and De León, *The History of Texas*, 63; Zorrilla, Miró Flaquer, and Herrera Pérez, *Tamaulipas: Textos de su historia*, 1:210–15; Zorrilla, Miró Flaquer, and Herrera Pérez, *Tamaulipas: Una historia compartida I*, 107–11; Hinojosa, *A Borderlands Town in Transition*, 53; Vigness, "Indian Raids on the Lower Rio Grande," 22–23; Gallegos, "Last Drop of My Blood," 95–98.

78. *Mercurio del Puerto de Matamoros*, 5 agosto 1836, quoted in DeLay, *War of a Thousand Deserts*, 174, 179–81; Gallegos, "Last Drop of My Blood," 88, 103–4, 110–13.

79. Vázquez argues that the federalist insurgents were split in their support for Texas. The group led by Canales recognized independent Texas, another sought to restore the federation and thereby reacquire Texas for Mexico, while a third group believed that Texas needed to be taken by force. Vázquez, "La supuesta república del Río Grande," 52–53. 61–62. Zorrilla, Miró Flaquer, and Herrera Pérez, *Tamaulipas: Una historia compartida I*, 113–15; Vázquez, "The Texas Question in Mexican Politics," 328–30; DeLay, *War of a Thousand Deserts*, 179 (quote), 182; Gallegos, "Last Drop of My Blood," 123, 127–28. Canales's fame as an Indian fighter and continued influence would help him secure future military appointments in the villas. AHM-PRE 6:14, 5 febrero 1842.

80. Vázquez, "The Texas Question in Mexican Politics," 330; DeLay, *War of a Thousand Deserts*, 142–43.

4. *Bandidos* or Citizens?

1. White, *"It's Your Misfortune and None of My Own,"* 59–61, 74–75.

2. Mikesell, "Comparative Studies in Frontier History," 65–66; Faragher et al., *Out of Many*, 39, 56; Nugent, "Are We Not [Civilized] Men?," 219; Nugent, *Spent Cartridges of Revolution*, 50.

3. Wilson and Donnan, *Border Identities*, 7–9.

4. Marcum, "Fort Brown, Texas," 52; White, *"It's Your Misfortune and None of My Own,"* 182.

5. Horsman, *Race and Manifest Destiny*, 219–21; Merk and Bannister, *Manifest Destiny and Mission in American History*, 24–33; Hietala, *Manifest Design*, 111–12, 255–56; White, *"It's Your Misfortune and None of My Own,"* 74.

6. Horsman, *Race and Manifest Destiny*, 236–37; Gutiérrez, *Walls and Mirrors*, 15.

7. Hietala, *Manifest Design*, 10–54; Merk and Bannister, *Manifest Destiny and Mission in American History*, 29–31; White, *"It's Your Misfortune and None of My Own,"* 74; Horsman, *Race and Manifest Destiny*, 241; Limerick, *The Legacy of Conquest*, 232–33.

8. De León, *The Tejano Community*, 13–15; Montejano, *Anglos and Mexicans in the Making of Texas*, 26–34.

9. Horgan, *Great River*, 589–600; Calvert and De León, *The History of Texas*, 91–95; Webb, *The Texas Rangers*, 71–77; De León and Stewart, *Tejanos and the Numbers Game*, 90–91; Singletary, *The Mexican War*, 18–19; Johannsen, *To the Halls of the Montezumas*, 185; McCutchan, *Mier Expedition Diary*, 16–72.

10. De León and Stewart, *Tejanos and the Numbers Game*, 92–93; Eisenhower, *So Far from God*, 17–26.

11. Reséndez, *Changing National Identities at the Frontier*, 93–123.

12. *American Flag*, 26 September 1846; Chapman, *News from Brownsville*, 44, 104; Horsman, *Race and Manifest Destiny*, 208–20.

13. Horsman, *Race and Manifest Destiny*, 213, 230–31; Johannsen, *To the Halls of the Montezumas*, 12–23, 167, 260–65.

14. Grant, *Memoirs and Selected Letters: Personal Memoirs of U.S. Grant*, 50; Singletary, *The Mexican War* 11–13; Eisenhower, *So Far From God*, 64–66; Merk and Bannister, *Manifest Destiny and Mission in American History*, 87–88; Hine and Faragher, *The American West*, 204–5 (Polk quote); Limerick, *The Legacy of Conquest*, 232; Thompson, "Historical Survey," 34–36; Engstrand, Griswold del Castillo, and Poniatowska, *Culture y Cultura*, 20; Roa Bárcena, *Recuerdos de la invasión norte-americana*, 5–7.

15. Eisenhower, *So Far from God*, 77–85, 100; Bauer, *The Mexican War*, 46–63; Singletary, *The Mexican War*, 28–32; Thompson, "Historical Survey," 38–39; Horgan, *Great River*, 701; Kendall, *Dispatches from the Mexican War*, 50, 60; Grant, *Memoirs and Selected Letters: Personal Memoirs of U.S. Grant*, 71.

16. Montejano, *Anglos and Mexicans in the Making of Texas*, 37–38; Zorrilla, Miró Flaquer, and Herrera Pérez, "Presencia del ayuntamiento de Matamoros durante la intervención norteamericana de 1847," 618–20; Chapman, *News from Brownsville*, xix–xxi, 14n30, 15n31; *American Flag*, 30 December 1847, 3 January 1848, 2 February 1848, quoted in Chapman, *News from Brownsville*, 355–57; *Daily Delta*, 29 August 1848, quoted in Chapman, *News from Brownsville*, 361–62.

17. *Republic of the Rio Grande and Friend of the People*, 6 June 1846; Horgan, *Great River*, 703–4; Eisenhower, *So Far from God*, 100–101; Kearney and Knopp, *Boom and Bust*, 65; Zorrilla, Miró Flaquer, and Herrera Pérez, *Tamaulipas: Historia compartida I*, 171; Graf, "The Economic History of the Lower Rio Grande Valley," 208–9.

18. Singletary, *The Mexican War*, 32–33; Eisenhower, *So Far from God*, 100–102; Johannsen, *To the Halls of the Montezumas*, 34–35; G. Smith and Judah, *Chronicles of the Gringos*, 322–23; Horgan, *Great River*, 702–3; Curtis, *Mexico Under Fire*, 1, 19; Graf, "The Economic History of the Lower Rio Grande Valley," 170–71.

19. Singletary, *The Mexican War*, 145; Curtis, *Mexico Under Fire*, 19–20; Horgan, *Great River*, 707; F. Smith, *The Mexican War Journal of Captain Franklin Smith*, 4–7; G. Smith and Judah, *Chronicles of the Gringos*, 286–87 (first quote); Johannsen, *To the Halls of the Montezumas*, 35 (second quote).

20. Johannsen, *To the Halls of the Montezumas*, 38 (second quote); Horgan, *Great River*, 703; Eisenhower, *So Far from God*, 103 (first quote); Dana, *Monterrey Is Ours!*, 74; Edwards, *A Campaign in New Mexico*, 155–56. Grant, *Memoirs and Selected Letters: Personal Memoirs of U.S. Grant*, 918.

21. Sahlins, *Boundaries*, 165–66; Ramos, *Beyond the Alamo*, 133–65.

22. F. Smith, *The Mexican War Journal of Captain Franklin Smith*, 21–23, 41–42, 51, 132–34, 166–67, 174, 191–99, 204, 223–24n46, 231n85, 250n13, 250–51n14; Kearney and Knopp, *Boom and Bust*, 59; Thompson, "A Nineteenth Century History of Cameron County, Texas," 45; Marcum, "Fort Brown, Texas," 91; *Diccionario Porrúa*, 473, 520, 744; F. Smith, *The Mexican War Journal of Captain Franklin Smith*, 199; Webb, *The Texas Rangers*, 96–98; Eisenhower, *So Far from God*, 106; McCutchan, *Mier Expedition Diary*, 36–37n5, 53, 65n1, 72–73, 82–83, 91; Dilworth, *The March to Monterrey*, 11, 23–24, 28–33, 39, 91n2; Eisenhower, *So Far from God*, 52, 63, 71n, 103–6; G. Smith and Judah, *Chronicles of the Gringos*, 74; Kendall, *Dispatches from the Mexican War*, 47, 63, 68, 70–74, 235; Johannsen, *To the Halls of the Montezumas*, 36–37; Webb, *The Texas Rangers*, 96–100.

23. Johannsen, *To the Halls of the Montezumas*, 34 (quote); Horgan, *Great River*, 71; F. Smith, *The Mexican War Journal of Captain Franklin Smith*, 223n46; *Diccionario Porrúa*, 473.

24. Herrera Pérez, *Monografía de Reynosa*, 64–65; F. Smith, *The Mexican War Journal of Captain Franklin Smith*, 51.

25. AHR-PRE 1:6, 15 enero 1847, 15 abril 1847; *El Defensor de Tamaulipas*, 16 septiembre 1847, quoted in Dávila y Rivera Saldaña, *Matamoros en la guerra con los Estados Unidos*, 33–35.

26. Paredes Manzano, *La Casa Mata y fortificaciones de la heroica Matamoros, Tamaulipas*, 26; Horgan, *Great River*, 712; Kearney and Knopp, *Boom and Bust*, 61; Graf, "The Economic History of the Lower Rio Grande Valley," 153–55, 168–69, 201–2; Eisenhower, *So Far from God*, 107; Hinojosa, *A Borderlands Town in Transition*, 56; G. Smith and Judah, *Chronicles of the Gringos*, 307; Dana, *Monterrey Is Ours!*, 82; *American Flag*, 7 October 1846; Grant, *Memoirs and Selected Letters: Personal Memoirs of U.S. Grant*, 72–73.

27. Calvert and De León, *The History of Texas*, 96; Singletary, *The Mexican War*, 160–61; Eisenhower, *So Far from God*, 363; Bauer, *The Mexican War*, 384; Griswold

del Castillo, *Treaty of Guadalupe Hidalgo*, 62–63, 189–90 (quote); Almaguer, *Racial Fault Lines*, 23.

28. Hinojosa, *A Borderlands Town in Transition*, 59; Calderón, "Mexican Politics in the American Era," 240–42; Wright, "Popular and Official Religiosity," 401.

29. Paredes Manzano, *La Casa Mata y fortificaciones de la heroica Matamoros, Tamaulipas*, 28–29; Herrera Pérez, *Monografía de Reynosa*, 66–67; Rivera Saldaña, "Tamaulipas a un año de la guerra México-Estados Unidos," 70; Mora-Torres, *The Making of the Mexican Border*, 27–28.

30. The 1850 census grouped the population of Cameron, Starr, and Webb Counties together. Graf, "The Economic History of the Lower Rio Grande Valley," 213; Thompson, "A Nineteenth Century History of Cameron County, Texas," 67, 72; Hinojosa, *A Borderlands Town in Transition*, 65.

31. Kearney and Knopp, *Border Cuates*, 71–86; Arreola, *Tejano South Texas*, 68–79.

32. Thompson, "A Nineteenth Century History of Cameron County, Texas," 61, 74; Marcum, "Fort Brown, Texas," i, 39, 50–55; Collins, *Texas Devils*, 100–101.

33. Hinojosa, *A Borderlands Town in Transition*, 64–65; Thompson, "A Nineteenth Century History of Cameron County, Texas," 32; Marcum, "Fort Brown, Texas," 47–58; Montejano, *Anglos and Mexicans in the Making of Texas*, 41–49.

34. Thompson, "A Nineteenth Century History of Cameron County, Texas," 39; Graf, "The Economic History of the Lower Rio Grande Valley," 198–99, 229, 247n55, 307; Montejano, *Anglos and Mexicans in the Making of Texas*, 41–47.

35. Montejano, *Anglos and Mexicans in the Making of Texas*, 42–43; Kearney and Knopp, *Border Cuates*, 77–80; Graf, "The Economic History of the Lower Rio Grande Valley," 255–63. La Habitación (opposite Reynosa) became known as Edinburg in 1852, and eventually as Hidalgo in 1876. Originally known as Chapin in 1908, Edinburg obtained its present name in 1911. Stambaugh and Stambaugh, *The Lower Rio Grande Valley of Texas*, 96.

36. Chapman, *News from Brownsville*, 102; Graf, "The Economic History of the Lower Rio Grande Valley," 227–38; Goldfinch and Canales, *Juan N. Cortina*, 35–37; Douglas, "Juan Cortina," 18–21; Kearney and Knopp, *Boom and Bust*, 67–70; Marcum, "Fort Brown, Texas," 46; Stambaugh and Stambaugh, *The Lower Rio Grande Valley of Texas*, 89–92.

37. Olmsted, *Journey through Texas*, 152; Montejano, *Anglos and Mexicans in the Making of Texas*, 17–20, 41–42; Thompson, "A Nineteenth Century History of Cameron County, Texas," 39–40; Graf, "The Economic History of the Lower Rio Grande Valley," 221–22, 349–51, 359–63.

38. Chapman, *News from Brownsville*, 107; Graf, "The Economic History of the Lower Rio Grande Valley," 273–75; Fernández de Castro, "Comercio y contrabando en la frontera noreste," 24–26; Cerutti and González Quiroga, "Guerra y comercio en torno al Río Bravo," 219–25.

39. Vigness, *The Revolutionary Decades*, 111; Thompson, "A Nineteenth Century History of Cameron County, Texas," 40; Graf, "The Economic History of the Lower Rio Grande Valley," 286–87; Fernández de Castro, "Comercio y contrabando en la frontera noreste," 24–25.

40. Graf, "The Economic History of the Lower Rio Grande Valley," 262, 273–74, 286–89 (quote), 307–11; Marcum, "Fort Brown, Texas," 67–69; Montejano, *Anglos and Mexicans in the Making of Texas*, 47; Cerutti and González Quiroga, "Guerra y comercio en torno al Río Bravo," 219–25, 235–37; Mora-Torres, *The Making of the Mexican Border*, 32–34.

41. Graf, "The Economic History of the Lower Rio Grande Valley," 273, 292–302; Marcum, "Fort Brown, Texas," 67–70.

42. Montejano, *Anglos and Mexicans in the Making of Texas*, 42–43; Graf, "The Economic History of the Lower Rio Grande Valley," 255–63, 346–50; Cerutti and González Quiroga, "Guerra y comercio en torno al Río Bravo," 220; Domenech, *Missionary Adventures in Texas and Mexico*, 267–68 (first quote), 327 (second quote); Horgan, *Great River*, 790–91; Marcum, "Fort Brown, Texas," 68; Mora-Torres, *The Making of the Mexican Border*, 32; Lattimore, "The Frontier in History," 470; Sahlins, *Boundaries*, 129, 140–41; Paredes, *Folklore and Culture on the Texas-Mexican Border*, 24–26.

43. Three other villas became paired with American towns with Spanish-language names: Laredo–Nuevo Laredo, Mier–Roma, and Guerrero (originally known as Revilla)–Zapata. Kearney and Knopp, *Border Cuates*, 74–80; Thompson, *A Wild and Vivid Land*, 34–35; McAllen Amberson, McAllen, and McAllen, *I Would Rather Sleep in Texas*, 112. Major Jacob Brown was killed defending the fort in an early battle of the U.S.-Mexican War. Ewen Cameron (a filibuster captured during the Mier Expedition), James Harper Starr (a secretary of treasury for the Texas Republic), and James A. Webb (a district judge in Corpus Christi) never lived in the counties named after them. Marcum, "Fort Brown, Texas," 33–36; Chapman, *News from Brownsville*, 136n9; Calderón, "Mexican Politics in the American Era," 246–47n33; Stambaugh and Stambaugh, *The Lower Rio Grande Valley of Texas*, 88–90; Fulmore, *The History and Geography of Texas as Told in County Names*, 93–95, 171, 206; Green, *A History of Webb County*, 27.

44. Robertson, *Wild Horse Desert*, 87; McAllen Amberson, McAllen, and McAllen, *I Would Rather Sleep in Texas*, 130. After leading insurrections against the Spanish crown and the Mexican national government, respectively, Hidalgo and Zapata (coincidentally) fell victim to beheadings. Fulmore, *The History and Geography of Texas as Told in County Names*, 14–15, 172; Thompson, "Historical Survey," 44; Gallegos, "'Last Drop of My Blood' Col. Antonio Zapata," 94–150.

45. Alonzo, *Tejano Legacy*, 171–81, 257, 265; Montejano, *Anglos and Mexicans in the Making of Texas*, 50–74; Haas, *Conquests and Historical Identities in California*, 63–68; Monroy, *Thrown among Strangers*, 199–205; González, *Refusing the Favor*, 89–92; Montoya, *Translating Property*, 78–120.

46. De León and Stewart, *Tejanos and the Numbers Game*, 12; Alonzo, *Tejano Legacy*, 97. Table 8 is based on a random subsample of census data.

47. Montejano, *Anglos and Mexicans in the Making of Texas*, 34–37, 43–47; Kearney and Knopp, *Boom and Bust*, 65, 70–77; Graf, "The Economic History of the Lower Rio Grande Valley," 247n55.

48. Calderón, "Mexican Politics in the American Era," 212–33, 248–51; Hinojosa, *A Borderlands Town in Transition*, 71–72; Montejano, *Anglos and Mexicans in the Making of Texas*, 36, 40; Wright, "Popular and Official Religiosity," 556.

49. Montejano, *Anglos and Mexicans in the Making of Texas*, 36–37, 41; Kearney and Knopp, *Border Cuates*, 65; Wright, "Popular and Official Religiosity," 565, 621; Matovina, *Tejano Religion and Ethnicity*, 57; Dysart, "Mexican Women in San Antonio," 369–71; Reséndez, *Changing National Identities at the Frontier*, 124–45; Goldfinch and Canales, *Juan N. Cortina*, 27; Calderón, "Mexican Politics in the American Era," 228–30; Casas, *Married to a Daughter of the Land*, 49–76; González, *Refusing the Favor*, 72–74, 113–15; Benton-Cohen, *Borderline Americans*, 36–38.

50. BCCP; Thompson, "A Nineteenth Century History of Cameron County, Texas," 28–32; Matovina, *Tejano Religion and Ethnicity*, 37–38; Stambaugh, *History of Hidalgo County Elected Officials*, 3–6; *Ranchero*, 11 August 1860; Stambaugh and Stambaugh, *The Lower Rio Grande Valley of Texas*, 104; Goldfinch and Canales, *Juan N. Cortina*, 39; Douglas, "Juan Cortina," 8; De León, *The Tejano Community*, 38, 101–2. On tejano constables, see *Daily Ranchero*, 18 December 1866, 20 January 1867.

51. Chatfield, *The Twin Cities (Brownsville, Texas; Matamoros, Mexico) of the Border and the Country of the Lower Rio Grande*, 14 (first quote); Domenech, *Missionary Adventures in Texas and Mexico*, 228 (second quote).

52. Domenech, *Missionary Adventures in Texas and Mexico*, 228 (quote); BCCP 19 April 1850, 25 May 1860, 19 April 1850, 9 September 1850, 5 October 1850; *Daily Ranchero*, 26 September 1866, 24 October 1866, 28 October 1866, 25 November 1866, 16 January 1867, 7 December 1866, 16 December 1866, 18 December 1866, 16 January 1867; Hinojosa, *A Borderlands Town in Transition*, 70.

53. Pitt, *The Decline of the Californios*, 130–47, 249–76.

54. Viqueira Albán, *Propriety and Permissiveness in Bourbon Mexico*, xv–xxii, 6, 16–26, 67–68, 204; Camarillo, *Chicanos in a Changing Society*, 16, 60–62; Pitt, *The Decline of the Californios*, 197–98.

55. *Daily Ranchero*, 17 January 1867; Faragher, *Women and Men on the Overland Trail*, 57, 78–79; Chapman, *News from Brownsville*, 25 (quote).

56. Chapman, *News from Brownsville*, 25, 39, 109; Vielé, *"Following the Drum,"* 154–55; Montgomery, *Eagle Pass, or, Life on the Border*, 56.

57. Vielé, *"Following the Drum,"* 155; De León, *The Tejano Community*, 3–4; Weber, *The Spanish Frontier in North America*, 323; Wright, "Popular and Official Religiosity," 424; Jones, *Los paisanos*, 74; Dysart, "Mexican Women in San Antonio," 367 (first quote); Williams, *With the Border Ruffians*, 177 (second quote); Domenech, *Missionary Adventures in Texas and Mexico*, 39.

58. Eisenhower, *So Far from God*, 54–56; Dana, *Monterrey Is Ours!*, 105, 144; Dilworth, *The March to Monterrey*, 101n5; De León, *They Called Them Greasers*, 38; Domenech, *Missionary Adventures in Texas and Mexico*, 272; Weber, "'Scarce More Than Apes,'" 303.

59. BCCP 19 April 1850, 27 July 1851 (quotes); Hinojosa, *A Borderlands Town in Transition*, 70; Thompson, *Warm Weather and Bad Whiskey*, 19; Wilkinson, *Laredo and the Rio Grande Frontier*, 244; Calderón, "Mexican Politics in the American Era," 447n41.

60. De León, *They Called Them Greasers*, 69 (first quote), 124n19; *Daily Ranchero*, 23 September 1865, 9 January 1867, 27 November 1867, 8 June 1867; De León, *The Tejano Community*, 184–85; Lord, *The Fremantle Diary*, 11 (second quote); Cama-

rillo, *Chicanos in a Changing Society*, 16, 60–62; Pitt, *The Decline of the Californios*, 197–98.

61. Tijerina, *Tejano Empire*, 102–5; González, "Social Life in Cameron, Starr, and Zapata Counties," 53–54; Matovina, *Tejano Religion and Ethnicity*, 21–22, 53; F. Smith, *The Mexican War Journal of Captain Franklin Smith*, 112–14; Horgan, *Great River*, 796–97.

62. Chapman, *News from Brownsville*, 38, 75, 357; *Daily Ranchero*, 15 August 1865 (quote), 19 August 1865, 26 August 1865, 20 February 1867, 22 February 1867, 2 February 1868, 19 March 1868, 25 September 1867; De León, *The Tejano Community*, 174; Matovina, *Tejano Religion and Ethnicity*, 38; Vielé, *"Following the Drum,"* 106–7; *Rio Grande Courier*, 20 February 1867.

63. Domenech, *Missionary Adventures in Texas and Mexico*, 277–78, 288–89; Tijerina, *Tejano Empire*, 102–6; Villarreal, *The Mexican-American Vaqueros of the King Ranch*, 22; González, "Social Life in Cameron, Starr, and Zapata Counties," 53; Peña, *The Texas-Mexican Conjunto*, 47; Vielé, *"Following the Drum,"* 106–7.

64. Martin, *Governance and Society in Colonial Mexico*, 91, 98, 121, 133, 173, 192–95; De León, *They Called Them Greasers*, 37; De León, *The Tejano Community*, 172–73; *Daily Ranchero*, 7 October 1866; Lord, *The Fremantle Diary*, 14–15; Chapman, *News from Brownsville*, 53, 59, 210.

65. Dilworth, *The March to Monterrey*, 61; G. Smith and Judah, *Chronicles of the Gringos*, 312–13; F. Smith, *The Mexican War Journal of Captain Franklin Smith*, 112–14 (first quote); De León, *They Called Them Greasers*, 9, 44–45; Hinojosa, *A Borderlands Town in Transition*, 65; Dana, *Monterrey Is Ours!*, 91 (second quote).

66. De León, *They Called Them Greasers*, 45 (first quote); Matovina, *Tejano Religion and Ethnicity*, 55 (second quote); Dysart, "Mexican Women in San Antonio," 367 (third quote); *American Flag*, 26 September 1846.

67. González, "Social Life in Cameron, Starr, and Zapata Counties," 53–54; Dana, *Monterrey Is Ours!*, 95; *Fort Brown Flag/La Bandera*, 4 September 1863 (first quote); *American Flag*, 26 September 1846 (second quote); De León, *They Called Them Greasers*, 37 (third quote), 45; Matovina, *Tejano Religion and Ethnicity*, 40, 122n21.

68. Matovina, *Tejano Religion and Ethnicity*, 55 (first quote); De León, *They Called Them Greasers*, 44–45; Dysart, "Mexican Women in San Antonio," 367; *El Bejareño*, 7 febrero 1855; *Daily Ranchero*, 26 February 1868 (second quote), 11 February 1868 (third quote), 9 April 1868 (fourth quote), 6 March 1868; Hinojosa, *A Borderlands Town in Transition*, 70; Calderón, "Mexican Politics in the American Era," 389, 401–2; BCCP 25 May 1850; Wilkinson, *Laredo and the Rio Grande Frontier*, 244; Chatfield, *The Twin Cities (Brownsville, Texas; Matamoros, Mexico) of the Border and the Country of the Lower Rio Grande*, 26.

69. BCCP 1850, 25 May 1850 (quote); De León, *The Tejano Community*, 172–74; Calderón, "Mexican Politics in the American Era," 447–48; Thompson, *Warm Weather and Bad Whiskey*, 19, 33–39; Crews, "Reconstruction in Brownsville, Texas," 28; Hinojosa, *A Borderlands Town in Transition*, 70; Matovina, *Tejano Religion and Ethnicity*, 55–56; BCCP 10 August 1850, 27 July 1851, 19 August 1851, 15 January 1859; McAllen Amberson, McAllen, and McAllen, *I Would Rather Sleep in Texas*,

309, 590n57; Chatfield, *The Twin Cities (Brownsville, Texas; Matamoros, Mexico) of the Border and the Country of the Lower Rio Grande*, 25; De León, *They Called Them Greasers*, 45; *Daily Ranchero*, 9 April 1868.

70. *Fort Brown Flag*, 4 September 1863; *Daily Ranchero*, 9 April 1868; Chatfield, *The Twin Cities (Brownsville, Texas; Matamoros, Mexico) of the Border and the Country of the Lower Rio Grande*, 26; Matovina, *Tejano Religion and Ethnicity*, 56; Kelley, *Race Rebels*, 3, 45–48.

71. Reséndez, *Changing National Identities at the Frontier*, 228. The five newspapers were the *American Flag* (later known as the *Brownsville Flag* and *Fort Brown Flag*), *Ranchero* (also known as the *Corpus Christi Ranchero*, the *Daily Ranchero/El Ranchero Diario*, and the *Daily Ranchero and Republican*), *Nueces Valley*, *Corpus Christi Star*, and the *Weekly Gazette*. José de Alba was the sole publisher (briefly in 1846) of the *Corpus Christi Gazette*. De León, *Apuntes Tejanos*, 103–40; Chatfield, *The Twin Cities (Brownsville, Texas; Matamoros, Mexico) of the Border and the Country of the Lower Rio Grande*, 24–25. On Spanish-language newspapers along the Texas border (which appeared in the mid-1880s), see Young, *Catarino Garza's Revolution on the Texas-Mexico Border*.

72. *Fort Brown Flag/La Bandera*, 4 September 1863; *Daily Ranchero*, 2 February 1868, 29 May 1867. On poor laborers and "pelados," see *Journal*, 13 July 1864; *Daily Ranchero*, 17 January 1867, 8 November 1865, 13 November 1866, 24 November 1866, 27 November 1866. For positive portrayals of wealthy Mexicans, see *Daily Ranchero*, 15 January 1867, 16 January 1867, 19 February 1867.

73. *Daily Ranchero*, 9 April 1868 (first three quotes), 26 March 1868, 3 May 1868 (fourth quote), 27 September 1866 (seventh quote), 19 January 1867; *Ranchero*, 11 August 1860, 25 February 1860; *Daily Ranchero*, 28 October 1866 (fifth quote), 13 June 1867 (sixth quote), 24 August 1867 (eighth quote). For similar humor in New Mexico, see Mitchell, *Coyote Nation*, 6, 85, 153.

74. *Fort Brown Flag*, 13 June 1861, quoted in *Ranchero*, 22 June 1861 (first set of quotes); *Daily Ranchero*, 26 February 1868, 16 August 1867 (final quote); De León, *They Called Them Greasers*, 70; Monroy, *Thrown among Strangers*, 208–19; Camarillo, *Chicanos in a Changing Society*, 18–22; González, *Refusing the Favor*, 112–13; White, *"It's Your Misfortune and None of My Own,"* 334–37; Rosenbaum, *Mexicano Resistance in the Southwest*, 53–67. On Mexican's criminalization in the twentieth century, see Escobar, *Race, Police, and the Making of a Political Identity*, 1–20, 104–31.

75. Weber, "'Scarce More Than Apes,'" 295–307; *American Flag*, 26 September 1846; Montgomery, *Eagle Pass, or, Life on the Border*, 56.

76. Haas, *Conquests and Historical Identities in California*, 43; Flores, "The Good Life the Hard Way," 118–26; *Daily Ranchero*, 14 May 1867 (first quote), 9 May 1867, 2 July 1867 (second quote), 29 May 1867 (third quote), 16 August 1867; *American Flag*, 26 September 1846; *Ranchero*, 7 April 1860, 31 December 1859, 25 August 1860, 22 September 1860, 17 September 1863; *Fort Brown Flag*, 13 June 1861, quoted in *Ranchero*, 22 June 1861 (fourth quote).

77. GDK, Gilbert D. Kingsbury, 16 August 1858; *Daily Delta*, 23 July 1850, quoted in Chapman, *News from Brownsville*, 375–76; De León, *They Called Them Greasers*, 72 (*Harper's Weekly* quote).

78. *New Orleans Times*, quoted in *Daily Ranchero*, 5 January 1866; *Daily Ranchero*, 13 February 1867.

79. On liquor's popularity in the United States and in Mexico's northern borderlands, see Reséndez, *Changing National Identities at the Frontier*, 110–14; and Olmsted, *Journey through Texas*, 159; *Daily Ranchero*, 30 October 1866, 31 October 1866, 1 November 1866, 2 November 1866. A newspaper survey of arrests on drunkenness charges yielded 40 Mexicans (72.7 percent), 10 European Americans (18.2 percent), and 5 African Americans (9.1 percent). *Daily Ranchero*, 27 September 1866 through 19 January 1867; Chapman, *News from Brownsville*, 178, 188 (first quote); *Daily Ranchero*, 7 April 1868, 1 May 1866; Domenech, *Missionary Adventures in Texas and Mexico*, 226 (second quote); Lord, *The Fremantle Diary*, 15 (third quotes).

80. *Daily Ranchero*, 5 April 1866, 18 January 1867, 19 January 1867; Domenech, *Missionary Adventures in Texas and Mexico*, 226, 239; *Daily Delta*, 20 August 1850, quoted in Chapman, *News from Brownsville*, 162, 178 (last quote), 376–77.

81. Olmsted, *Journey through Texas*, 164; De León, *They Called Them Greasers*, 80, 90–91 (quote); Collins, *Texas Devils*, 56–57; Chatfield, *The Twin Cities (Brownsville, Texas; Matamoros, Mexico) of the Border and the Country of the Lower Rio Grande*, 14; Chapman, *News from Brownsville*, 186, 368–76; Pitt, *The Decline of the Californios*, 167–73; Monroy, *Thrown among Strangers*, 214–19; Limerick, *The Legacy of Conquest*, 241–42; White, *"It's Your Misfortune and None of My Own,"* 334–35.

82. De León, *They Called Them Greasers*, 73 (first quote), 90; *Ranchero*, 17 September 1863; *Daily True Delta*, 18 May 1852, quoted in Chapman, *News from Brownsville*, 390–91 (second quote).

83. *Daily Delta*, 11 October 1850, quoted in Chapman, *News from Brownsville*, 186 (first quote), 379–80 (second quote); Webb, *The Texas Rangers*, 96, 100; De León, *They Called Them Greasers*, 88; Paredes, *"With His Pistol in His Hand,"* 23–32.

84. Olmsted, *Journey through Texas*, 159 (first quote); Domenech, *Missionary Adventures in Texas and Mexico*, 237–38 (second and third quotes).

85. De León, *They Called Them Greasers*, 125n39.

86. On adult males as the vast majority of criminals, see Courtwright, *Violent Land*, 9–11; and Gómez, "Race, Colonialism, and Criminal Law," 1149. Census figures are for the total Mexican population (Mexican Texans and Mexican nationals). Estimates based on tables in Calvert and De León, *The History of Texas*, 156; Zamora, *The World of the Mexican Worker in Texas*, 211; and De León and Stewart, *Tejanos and the Numbers Game*, 12. *Crockett Printer*, quoted in *Ranchero*, October 6, 1860; Crouch, *Dance of Freedom*, 160–62; Pitt, *The Decline of the Californios*, 256.

87. Verdicts and convictions for Cameron County (1848–61) and Webb County (1848–76). Cameron County yielded 60.9 percent and Webb County delivered 50.7 percent guilty findings. CCDCM 1016155, 1016160, 1016156; WCDCM 1017260; *Daily Ranchero*, 22 May 1866, 28 September 1866, 9 November 1866, 7 December 1866.

88. CCDCM 1016155, 1016160, 1016156; WCDCM 1017260. Total jurors for Cameron County were 1,682 (1848–61) and for Webb County (1848–76) 1,559. Gómez, "Race, Colonialism, and Criminal Law," 1129–1202; Ramos, *Beyond the Alamo*, 192–94.

89. Paschal, *Digest of the Laws of Texas*, 673–80; CCDCM 1016155, 1016160; Kerber, *No Constitutional Right to be Ladies*, 128–32; Bosniak, "Citizenship Denationalized," 463–79.

90. CCDCM 1016155, 1016160, 1016156; Thompson, "A Nineteenth Century History of Cameron County, Texas," 28; CCMR 1016185; WCDCM 1017260; Calderón, "Mexican Politics in the American Era," 1029. I identified tejano elected officials by first identifying all Spanish-language surnames, then eliminating the names of Spanish immigrants.

91. These figures also differ markedly from those found by Laura Gómez for San Miguel County, New Mexico, where Mexicans filled the majority of law-enforcement positions. Gómez, "Race, Colonialism, and Criminal Law," 1171–75; CCDCM 1016155, 1016160; WCDCM 1017260; De León, *The Tejano Community*, 35–38, 99; Thompson, "A Nineteenth Century History of Cameron County, Texas," 28–32; Anders, *Boss Rule in South Texas*, 17–18; Chatfield, *The Twin Cities (Brownsville, Texas; Matamoros, Mexico) of the Border and the Country of the Lower Rio Grande*, 25–26.

92. *Daily Ranchero*, 26 September 1866, 26 October 1866, 22 November 1866, 2 December 1866, 18 January 1867.

93. *Daily Ranchero*, 30 September 1866 (headlines quote), 5 October 1866 (first quote), 7 October 1866, 24 November 1866, 26 September 1866, 27 September 1866, 29 September 1866 (second quote).

94. *Daily Ranchero*, 23 October 1866 (first quote), 16 April 1867, 1 December 1866, 25 November 1866 (second quote).

95. CCDCM 1016161, cases 590–94, *Texas v. JW Hunter et als.*, 23 November 1866; *Daily Ranchero*, 16 April 1867, 1 December 1866, 25 November 1866 (quote).

96. *Daily Ranchero*, 25 November 1866, 7 December 1866.

97. Olmsted, *Journey through Texas*, 200–202, 323–28, 338–39; AHD Valentín Cano to Joaquín I. De Castillo, 15 July 1853, exp. 6-16-102; De León, *The Tejano Community*, 15, 28, 1; Scott, *Weapons of the Weak*, 28–35.

98. *Daily Ranchero*, 27 September 1866, 24 November 1866, 27 January 1867. On Mexicans fleeing into Texas to escape conscription, see Herrera Pérez, *El norte de Tamaulipas y la conformación de la frontera México-Estados Unidos*, 104–5. For suspects fleeing across the river prior to arrest, see *Daily Ranchero*, 25 December 1866, 28 April 1867, 2 July 1867. For escaped prisoners crossing the Rio Grande, see *Daily Ranchero*, 8 April 1866, 23 February 1867, 25 February 1868. For deserters fleeing across the river, see *Daily Ranchero*, 7 November 1866, 29 May 1866, 21 May 1863, 2 July 1863. For river drownings see *Daily Ranchero*, 30 September 1865, 11 November 1866, 2 December 1866, 17 January 1867.

99. Vielé, *"Following the Drum,"* 165–68; *Ranchero*, 30 October 1860, 3 November 1860, 10 November 1860; *Daily Ranchero*, 8 April 1866, 9 June 1866, 4 October 1866, 8 November 1866, 9 November 1866, 1 December 1866, 24 January 1867, 25 January 1867, 27 January 1867, 12 February 1867, 13 February 1867, 17 February 1867, 23 February 1867, 26 February 1868, 20 February 1868, 6 March 1868; CCDCM 1016155, 25 September 1857 (first quote); Domenech, *Missionary Adventures in Texas and Mexico*, 232 (second quote); Vielé, *"Following the Drum,"* 167–68; *Daily Delta*, 23 July 1850, quoted in Chapman, *News from Brownsville*, 371–72;

CCDCM 1016155, case 2014, *Texas v. Peter Nichols*, 24 May 1853, case 423, *Texas v. David Ward*, 23 November 1860; CCDCM 1016161, case 629, *Texas v. Henry Middleton*, 1 April 1867, case 755, *Texas v. Rudolph Krause*, 12 September 1868.

100. Major William H. Emory, "Report of the United States and Mexican Boundary Survey," quoted in Marcum, "Fort Brown, Texas," 44–49; *Daily Ranchero*, 10 June 1866, 11 February 1868, 25 February 1868; *El Ranchero Diario*, 12 junio 1866.

101. For extraditions from the United States to Mexico, see *Daily Ranchero*, 29 December 1866, 5 January 1867, 2 February 1867, 29 June 1867, 11 February 1868. For extraditions from Mexico to the United States, see *Daily Ranchero*, 16 January 1867, 2 July 1867, 25 February 1868, 27 May 1868, 11 January 1867, 8 March 1867, 15 March 1868 (quote).

102. *Ranchero*, 29 October 1859, 5 November 1859, 21 January 1860, 28 January 1860, 25 February 1860, 30 March 1860, 5 May 1860, 8 June 1861, 18 December 1862, 8 January 1863, 5 October 1866, 13 October 1866, 20 November 1866, 25 November 1866, 20 January 1867, 24 January 1867, 6 June 1866; *Daily Ranchero*, 1 December 1866, 27 February 1867, 1 March 1867; Webb, *The Texas Rangers*, 181–82; Chatfield, *The Twin Cities (Brownsville, Texas; Matamoros, Mexico) of the Border and the Country of the Lower Rio Grande*, 25; Thompson, *Warm Weather and Bad Whiskey*, 22–25.

5. Divorcées, Rancheros, and Peons

1. *Daily Ranchero*, 13 June 1867.

2. Zavaleta, *The Twin Cities (Brownsville, Texas; Matamoros, Mexico) of the Border and the Country of the Lower Rio Grande*, 162; De León and Stewart, *Tejanos and the Numbers Game*, 12; BCCP book A, 1; Montejano, *Anglos and Mexicans in the Making of Texas*, 16, 20, 356; Chatfield, *The Twin Cities (Brownsville, Texas; Matamoros, Mexico) of the Border and the Country of the Lower Rio Grande*, 12–13; USCP (Cameron, Starr, and Webb) 1850; CCDCM 1016156, 6 November 1866, 1016161, case 700, *Texas v. Francisco Ruiz et al.*, 17 April 1868. Dougherty's children also intermarried with local families. ICCB María Concepción Dougherty, 23 December 1850; ICCM Mariano Treviño and María Concepción Dougherty, 17 July 1887; ICCD Marcela García de Dougherty, 19 November 1869. In 1872, Dougherty represented María Josefa Cavazos in a land dispute over her part of the Espíritu Santo grant. *Daily Ranchero*, 14 August 1872; Kearney and Knopp, *Boom and Bust*, 51–54, 69, 89–91.

3. I did not find any information on Canute de la Paz in vital statistics and census records.

4. Tejanos in Webb and Zapata Counties were better represented on juries than in other border counties.

5. Alonzo, *Tejano Legacy*, 158; Montejano, *Anglos and Mexicans in the Making of Texas*, 43–47.

6. Goldfinch and Canales, *Juan N. Cortina*, 35–39; Graf, "The Economic History of the Lower Rio Grande Valley," 235–55.

7. Montejano, *Anglos and Mexicans in the Making of Texas*, 50–53, 59–74; Alonzo, *Tejano Legacy*, 146–48, 158–59, 176–78, 266–67, 332n33, 332n34.

8. Alonzo, *Tejano Legacy*, 174–75.

9. Ibid., 161–81, 190–91, 227–58, 265–70; Montejano, *Anglos and Mexicans in the Making of Texas*, 42–43, 70–73.

10. Hinojosa, *A Borderlands Town in Transition*, 70; BCCP 16; *Daily Ranchero*, 19 April 1867, 18 September 1867; Taylor, *An American-Mexican Frontier*, 148–49; Kerber, *No Constitutional Right to be Ladies*, 78.

11. Gonzalez, "Social Life in Cameron, Starr, and Zapata Counties," 49–52; Taylor, *An American-Mexican Frontier*, 116–17; Montejano, *Anglos and Mexicans in the Making of Texas*, 76–80. Mora-Torres, *The Making of the Mexican Border*, 27–28.

12. Among the few artisans to serve on juries were Juan Pecina and Nicholas Chano, well known among *americanos*. *Daily Ranchero*, 28 September 1866, 17 January 1867, 9 January 1867, 7 October 1866; CCDCM 1016160, 18 May 1860, 8 December 1860; *Ranchero*, 22 October 1859; Chatfield, *The Twin Cities (Brownsville, Texas; Matamoros, Mexico) of the Border and the Country of the Lower Rio Grande*, 29. For literacy rates, see De León and Stewart, *Tejanos and the Numbers Game*, 35–38.

13. Throughout Texas, agricultural jobs decreased (21.3 percent), professional positions increased (9.1 percent), and jobs in trade or transportation increased (6.3 percent). In *tejano* settlement regions, agricultural positions increased (1 percent), professional jobs sharply decreased (14.4 percent), and trade or transportation positions decreased (8.7 percent). Stewart and De León, *Not Room Enough*, 21–26.

14. Stewart and De León, *Not Room Enough*, 27–31.

15. Mora-Torres, *The Making of the Mexican Border*, 7–8, 22, 27–28, 62; Rivera Saldaña, "Tamaulipas a un año de la guerra México-Estados Unidos," 69–70; Wilkinson, *Laredo and the Rio Grande Frontier*, 238; González Quiroga, "Los inicios de la migración laboral mexicana a Texas," 205–6; Montejano, *Anglos and Mexicans in the Making of Texas*, 77; Thompson, *Vaqueros in Blue and Gray*, 7.

16. González Quiroga, "Los inicios de la migración laboral mexicana a Texas," 203–4, 214–15; Mora-Torres, *The Making of the Mexican Border*, 28; Montejano, *Anglos and Mexicans in the Making of Texas*, 78; Taylor, *An American-Mexican Frontier*, 116. To calculate the dollar equivalent, I used the average exchange rate (0.961 peso per dollar) for the years 1840–49 as found in EHM 810.

17. González Quiroga, "Los inicios de la migración laboral mexicana a Texas," 206–10, 215.

18. De León and Stewart, *Tejanos and the Numbers Game*, 21–22; Martínez, *Border Boom Town*, 13–14; Mora-Torres, *The Making of the Mexican Border*, 31.

19. RCI 401–2.

20. Chatfield, *The Twin Cities (Brownsville, Texas; Matamoros, Mexico) of the Border and the Country of the Lower Rio Grande*, 12; Schwartz, *Across the Rio to Freedom*, 16, 24–54; Olmsted, *Journey through Texas*, 323–34; Kelley, "Mexico in His Head," 709 (quote), 712–16; Franklin and Schweninger, *Runaway Slaves*, 26, 115–16.

21. Taylor, *An American-Mexican Frontier*, 33 (first and second quotes); Tyler, "Fugitive Slaves in Mexico," 6, 10–12; Scott, *Weapons of the Weak*, 28–30; Baud and Van Schendel, "Toward a Comparative History," 216; Mora-Torres, *The Making of the Mexican Border*, 23; Franklin and Schweninger, *Runaway Slaves*, 91.

22. Commercial agriculture did not develop until the late nineteenth century.

Graf, "The Economic History of the Lower Rio Grande Valley," 435–51; Montejano, *Anglos and Mexicans in the Making of Texas*, 76–79.

23. Taylor, *An American-Mexican Frontier*, 100–101, 117, 147–54; González Quiroga, "Los inicios de la migración laboral mexicana a Texas," 211; González, "Social Life in Cameron, Starr, and Zapata Counties," 50.

24. Taylor, *An American-Mexican Frontier*, 116–17, 147; González, "Social Life in Cameron, Starr, and Zapata Counties," 49–50; Montejano, *Anglos and Mexicans in the Making of Texas*, 79–80 (quote).

25. Montejano, *Anglos and Mexicans in the Making of Texas*, 79–82.

26. Taylor, *An American-Mexican Frontier*, 148–56; Foley, *The White Scourge*, 25.

27. González Quiroga, "Los inicios de la migración laboral mexicana a Texas," 203–4; Montejano, *Anglos and Mexicans in the Making of Texas*, 82; Taylor, *An American-Mexican Frontier*, 100–105; De León, *The Tejano Community*, 60–62 (quote).

28. González Quiroga, "Los inicios de la migración laboral mexicana a Texas," 211–13.

29. *Daily Ranchero*, 27 September 1866.

30. Ibid., 7 November 1866, 10 January 1867.

31. Ibid., 18 June 1867, 25 June 1867.

32. CCMR 1016185, 16 September 1848; CCDCM 1016155, case 485, *Clay v. Clay*, 25 July 1856.

33. In 1851, Cameron County convicted and hung Howard Slaughter and two Mexicans (names unknown) for murder (victims unnamed). *Daily Delta*, 9 July 1850, 10 June 1851, 12 June 1850, cited in Chapman, *News from Brownsville*, 370–71, 390; *Daily Cosmopolitan*, 5 November 1863.

34. *Daily Ranchero*, 6 November 1866, 26 April 1867, 18 June 1867, 25 June 1867.

35. *Daily Ranchero*, 3 October 1866, 5 February 1867; Gammel, *Laws of Texas*, 3:169.

36. *Daily Delta*, 12 June 1850, cited in Chapman, *News from Brownsville*, 371; *Daily Ranchero*, 13 June 1867; CCDCM 1016161. On prison escapes, see *Daily Ranchero*, 12 February 1867, 20 February 1868, 26 February 1868, 6 March 1868; 8 April 1866, 1 December 1866; CCDCM 1016161, case 1217, *Texas v. Gutiérrez*, 11 August 1875, 14 August 1875, 19 August 1875, 29 August 1875, 21 August 1875; CCDCM 1016161, 15 May 1875, Grand Jury Report; HCDCM 1017252, 13 March 1868; CCDCM 1016161, case 1276, *Texas v. Glavecke*, 24 August 1876, 25 February 1878; and HCDCM 1017257, case 91, *Texas v. Estapa*, 20 September 1877, 18 September 1878, 16 April 1885.

37. Villas del norte officials sentenced one convicted rapist to four years of presidio service, but he served less than a year before being released on appeal. AHM-JUD 5:22, 5 agosto 1834; Gammel, *Laws of Texas*, 3:221; CCDCM 1016156, case 564, *Texas v. Torres*, 17 November 1866, 21 November 1866, 22 November 1866, 1 December 1866; CCDCM 1016158, case 2403, *Texas v. Flores*, 17 September 1894. On hanging of African American Union soldiers, see *Daily Ranchero*, 30 July 1865.

38. HCDCM 1017257, case 91, *Texas v. Cora High*, 20 September 1877; CCDCM 1016161, case 1412, *Texas v. Lucinda Cordero*, 6 March 1878; Gammel, *Laws of Texas*,

3:222; CCDCM 1016161, case 705, *Texas v. Vega*, 5 September 1868; SPCDCM 1013259, *Texas v. Martínez*, 6 March 1874.

39. D'Emilio and Freedman, *Intimate Matters*, 38–49.

40. Arrom, *The Women of Mexico City*, 56; Lavrin, "Sexuality in Colonial Mexico," 61–63; Sinclair, "Seduction and the Myth of the Ideal Woman," 35–42; Larson, "Women Understand So Little, They Call My Good Nature 'Deceit,'" 382–93; Donovan, "Gender Inequality and Criminal Seduction," 66–67; VanderVelde, "The Legal Ways of Seduction," 821, 891; D'Emilio and Freedman, *Intimate Matters*, 68; Haag, *Consent*, 6–9.

41. If the defendant in a seduction case was married, the court charged him with adultery. The punishment was a two-to-five-year penitentiary sentence or a fine not to exceed five thousand dollars. Paschal, *A Digest of the Laws of Texas*, 472. According to Haag, states that allowed civil damages did not permit criminal charges. Haag, *Consent*, 10, 188–89n21; VanderVelde, "The Legal Ways of Seduction," 886–88; Donovan, "Gender Inequality and Criminal Seduction," 67; Larson, "Women Understand So Little, They Call My Good Nature 'Deceit,'" 388n54.

42. Lavrin, "Sexuality in Colonial Mexico," 61; CCDCM 1016156, case 611, *Texas v. Vargas*, 29 November 1866, case 600, 31 November 1866; CCDCM 1016158, case 2546, *Texas v. Guillén*, 26 September 1895; CCMR 1016187, 13 August 1903.

43. *Daily Ranchero*, 14 February 1867.

44. Ibid., 13 October 1866, 28 May 1867, 30 April 1867, 17 November 1866, 8 June 1867, 2 November 1866; CCDCM 1016161, case 714, *Texas v. Echarete*, 15 September 1868; Gammel, *Laws of Texas*, 3:221. The newspaper failed to identify the first names of Mrs. Ramírez and Mrs. Echarete.

45. Cott, *Public Vows*, 1–8; Pascoe, *What Comes Naturally*, 2, 22–24; Foley, *White Scourge*, 208. According to Menchaca, afromestizos were legally prohibited from marrying whites. Menchaca, "Anti-miscegenation History of the American Southwest," 284–89.

46. Enstam, "Women and the Law"; Cott, *Public Vows*, 52–55; Montoya, *Translating Property*, 56–57.

47. Enstam, "Women and the Law"; Clinton, *The Other Civil War*, 8; Stuntz, *Hers, His, and Theirs*, 138–39, 153–58; Montoya, *Translating Property*, 57, 76; Casas, *Married to a Daughter of the Land*, 117, 142; Chávez-García, *Negotiating Conquest*, 126–27.

48. Castañeda, *Our Catholic Heritage in Texas*, 7:24–26, 112–15; Matovina, *Tejano Religion and Ethnicity*, 41–43, 60; Juárez, "La Iglesia Católica y el Chicano en Sud Tejas," 222–23, 244.

49. Castañeda, *Our Catholic Heritage in Texas*, 113, 208–10; CCMR 1016185, 28 October 1849; Wright, "Popular and Official Religiosity," 576–77, 604–21, 646–48.

50. Matovina, *Tejano Religion and Ethnicity*, 43, 67–68, 88–91; Juárez, "La Iglesia Católica y el Chicano en Sud Tejas," 220, 228–30 (first quote); Bayard, *Lone-Star Vanguard*, 55–57; Wright, "Popular and Official Religiosity," 609; Domenech, *Missionary Adventures in Texas and Mexico*, 11.

51. Juárez, "La Iglesia Católica y el Chicano en Sud Tejas," 226, 234–42; Wright, "Popular and Official Religiosity," 578.

52. Phelan, *A History of Early Methodism in Texas*, 307–8; Red, *A History of the Presbyterian Church in Texas*, 87–89; Chapman, *News from Brownsville*, 93–97, 111–12, 130, 304n31; Chatfield, *The Twin Cities (Brownsville, Texas; Matamoros, Mexico) of the Border and the Country of the Lower Rio Grande*, 8–9; Brown, *The Episcopal Church in Texas*, 68–71; Vielé, *"Following the Drum,"* 109, 161–64; Montgomery, *Eagle Pass, or, Life on the Border*, 148–49, 168–70; Rankin, *Texas in 1850*, 194–95.

53. Chapman, *News from Brownsville*, 130, 145n24; Phelan, *A History of Early Methodism in Texas*, 324, 437; Red, *A History of the Presbyterian Church in Texas*, 87, 181–93; Brown, *The Episcopal Church in Texas*, 169–71; Ruiz, *From Out of the Shadows*, 33–50; Wright, "Popular and Official Religiosity," 230n15, 238–47; Nail, *The First Hundred Years of the Southwest Texas Conference of the Methodist Church*, 121–22; Náñez, "History of the Rio Grande Conference of the United Methodist Church," 42–54.

54. Brown, *The Episcopal Church in Texas*, 69–71; Rankin, *Texas in 1850*, 177 (Baker quote); De León, *They Called Them Greasers*, 17 (Addison quote); McMillin, "Anglo Methodist Missionaries and Mexicans in the Southwest and Mexico," 24–30, 51–78.

55. CCMR 1016185, 1 October 1850; SAP-I, Guillermo F. Alexander and Carlota Dovalina, 30 August 1852; CCMR 1016185, 28 May 1850, 24; Chapman, *News from Brownsville*, 168–72, 370–71; Matovina, *Tejano Religion and Ethnicity*, 57–58, 60–62; sap-ii, Adolfo Staacke and Alejandra Pérez, 31 March 1867.

56. SAP-I, SAP-II; 16 September 1848 through 5 July 1860, CCMR 1016185; Wright, "Popular and Official Religiosity," 577; SAP-II, 39, 201, 205. On marriage impediments, see Wright, "Church Marriage Regulations," in SAP-I, 307–11.

57. Notable examples of such strategic marriages include John Young and Salome Ballí in Cameron County, Henry Clay Davis and Hilaria de la Garza in Starr County, and Hamilton Bee and María Andrea Martínez in Webb County. Cameron County's interethnic marriages during the first four years of American rule included thirteen between americanos and tejanas as well as thirteen involving spouses of mixed ancestry. CCMR 1016185; Dysart, "Mexican Women in San Antonio," 369–70; USCP (Cameron, Starr, Webb) 1850; Montejano, *Anglos and Mexicans in the Making of Texas*, 41; Wright, "Popular and Official Religiosity," 560; *Daily Ranchero*, 1 February 1868; Casas, *Married to a Daughter of the Land*, 49–76; González, *Refusing the Favor*, 71–74, 113.

58. Various scholars, including Downing de De Juana, identify Jackson as Nathaniel, but the U.S. census identifies him as Mathew Jackson. USCP (Hidalgo) 1860; Downing de De Juana, "Intermarriage in Hidalgo County," 59–61, 76–77, 99; Alonzo, *Tejano Legacy*, 164; David Mycue, "Jackson Ranch Church," *Valley Town Crier*, 21 January 1987, 28 January 1987; Isbell, "Jackson Ranch Church," 3–5; Carroll, *Homesteads Ungovernable*, 68–70; Foley, *The White Scourge*, 208.

59. CCMR 1016186; Downing de De Juana, "Intermarriage in Hidalgo County," 107–8, 119; Benton-Cohen, *Borderline Americans*, 159–61.

60. CCMR 1016186. The 618 marriages occurred between 8 May 1883 and 6 June 1887.

61. Basch, *Framing American Divorce*, 50–53; Larson, "A History of Divorce in

Texas," 33 (first quote); Enstam, "Women and the Law" (second quote); Pruitt, "'But a Mournful Remedy,'" 16–19. A spouse could obtain an annulment if her partner was impotent. I found no records of annulment in the border counties' civil and ecclesiastical records.

62. Texas (Republic), *Laws of the Republic of Texas*, 2:483–86.

63. Divorce lawsuits in twentieth-century Puerto Rico also led to speedier and more reliable results. Findlay, *Imposing Decency*, 124; Arrom, *The Women of Mexico City*, 208–10. Divorce cases were found in CCDCM, HCDCM, WCDCM, SCDCM, and ZCDCM. Additional information appeared in *Daily Ranchero*, and *Ranchero*.

64. Texas (Republic), *Laws of the Republic of Texas*, 2:483–84; Paschal, *A Digest of the Laws of Texas*, 566–68; Larson, "A History of Divorce in Texas," 33–35; Basch, *Framing American Divorce*, 105; *Daily Ranchero*, 4 April 1867; CCDCM 1016156, 5 June 1867.

65. SCDCM 1017266, case 276, *Malleth v. Malleth*, 20 September 1880; Texas (Republic), *Laws of the Republic of Texas*, 2:484 (quotes, emphasis added); Carroll, *Homesteads Ungovernable*, 144–45; Pruitt, "'But a Mournful Remedy,'" 19; Enstam, "Women and the Law."

66. CCDCM 1016155, case 672, *Ghalson v. Ghalson*, 3 May 1862.

67. Larson, "A History of Divorce in Texas," 36–38; CCDCM 1016155, *Ghalson v. Ghalson*, case 672, 3 May 1862; *Cuellar v. Cuellar*, *Ranchero*, 12 May 1860; Paschal, *A Digest of the Laws of Texas*, 566; AHM-JUS 3:7, 1 mayo 1835, *C. Eulogio Peres v. su muger* (wife's name not given).

68. Larson, "A History of Divorce in Texas," 35–36; Chávez-García, *Negotiating Conquest*, 117. On desertion rates, see Ford, "Women, Marriage, and Divorce in California," 120–22; Riley, *Building and Breaking Families*, 118–19; Riley, *Divorce*, 87; Pruitt, "'But a Mournful Remedy,'" 58–59; and Basch, *Framing American Divorce*, 104, 215n10.

69. HCDCM 1017257, case 162, *Fernández v. Fernández*, 10 October 1893; Downing de De Juana, "Intermarriage in Hidalgo County," 123. For another example of a woman divorcing, reclaiming her maiden name, and later remarrying, see CCDCM 1016161, *García Brooks v. Brooks*, 10 December 1875; and CCMR 1016186, Francisco Benito and Francisca García, 16 August 1876, D518.

70. CCDCM 1016161, case 835, *Ximénez v. Ximénez*, 30 March 1868; *Daily Ranchero*, 1 April 1868.

71. Halem, *Divorce Reform*, 21–28, 61; Blake, *The Road to Reno*, 122, 128–29; Larson, "A History of Divorce in Texas," 11–13, 41–44. For other divorce trends in Texas, see Carroll, *Homesteads Ungovernable*, 140; Pruitt, "'But a Mournful Remedy,'" 31–78; and Hartog, *Man and Wife in America*, 14. Among the factors that increased the divorce rate are the passage of states' divorce legislation, the emergence of the modern companionate family, greater economic opportunities for women, the stress of the Civil War, increasing mobility of the population, the influence of the growing women's rights movement, increasing marriage rates, and greater expectations for marriage. Riley, *Building and Breaking Families in the American West*, 113–14; May, *Great Expectations*, 6–7; Basch, *Framing American Divorce*, 128–29; Cott, *Public Vows*, 49–55; Griswold, *Family and Divorce in California*, 2. For

the Mendiola case, see SAP-I, Pablo José Mendiola and Doña Maria de las Nieves Salinas, entry 531, 13 February 1830; WCDCM 1017260, case 3, *Mendiola v. Mendiola*, 2 November 1857; and SAP-II Carlos Salinas and Paula Mendiola, entry 33, 25 July 1859, Santiago Mendiola and Paula González, entry 71, 30 April 1862, Edward Frederick Hall and Carolina Mendiola, entry 228, 20 April 1868.

72. Francisco Abrego immigrated in 1893 and filed for divorce from Isabel Valdez Abrego in 1896. Both spouses later remarried. CCDCM 1016158, 5 February 1896, *Francisco Abrego v. Isabel Valdez Abrego*, USCP (Cameron) 1900; CCMR; *Ranchero*, 12 May 1860; MPR (Guerrero) *Marriages*, Felipe Cuellar and Antonia Díaz, 19 August 1852, Manuel María Sanmiguel and Josefa Cuellar, 28 November 1874; MPR (Guerrero) *Baptisms*, María Antonia Díaz, 28 May 1836, Felipe Cuellar, 30 May 1823, José Fernando Cuellar, 8 June 1856, María Tomasa Cuellar, 1 January 1858, María Carolina (*hija natural*) Díaz, 20 March 1863; MPR (Guerrero) *Deaths*, Fernando Cuellar, 10 June 1856, María Tomasa Cuellar, 27 March 1859; USCP (Zapata) 1860. On church services in Carrizo, see Lott and Martínez, *The Kingdom of Zapata*, 71. For a fascinating discussion of the "geography of remarriage," see Hartog, *Man and Wife in America*, 20–23, 31–33, 242–86. The number of couples who married in Mexico and later divorced in the counties under study is unknown because the border counties' divorce records do not indicate where the marriage took place.

73. Paschal, *A Digest of the Laws of Texas*, 778; Gammel, *Laws of Texas*, 3:486; Arrom, *The Women of Mexico City*, 209–10. Texas judges occasionally split the court expenses or asked the winning party to pay the costs if the losing party was impoverished. For an example, see CCDCM 1016155, case 612, *Leo v. Leo*, 25 April 1860, 14 May 1860.

74. Courts usually followed the "tender years" principle by awarding mothers custody of infant children. Riley, *Divorce*, 83–84; Paschal, *A Digest of the Laws of Texas*, 775; CCDCM 1016161, case 958, *Somerville v. Molina de Somerville*, 27 October 1870; CCDCM 1016161, case 1071, *Soria v. Soria*, 10 April 1874; CCDCM 1016155, case 3003, *Rodríguez v. López*, 15 November 1861.

75. Gammel, *Laws of Texas*, 3:485; Larson, "A History of Divorce in Texas," 39–40; Paulsen, "Remember the Alamo[ny]!," 8–15; *Daily Ranchero*, 20 December 1866; CAT *Marriages*, Frederick Schreck and Adela Chano, 29 November 1865; CCDCM 1016161, case 912, *Schreck v. Schreck*, 3 September 1869; CCMR 1016185, John C. Mix and Adela Chano, 21 March 1870; USCP (Cameron) 1870. On the difficulty of enforcing alimony judgments, see Chused, *Private Acts in Public Places*, 147–48; Basch, *Framing American Divorce*, 113–14; Riley, *Divorce*, 53, 82–83, 90; Ford, "Women, Marriage, and Divorce in California," 112; and Chávez-García, *Negotiating Conquest*, 99–100.

76. Gammel, *Laws of Texas*, 3:77–78; Texas (Republic), *Laws of the Republic of Texas*, 2:483–86; Paschal, *A Digest of the Laws of Texas*, 775–76. According to Carroll, Texas courts "almost always awarded a divorcing woman her community share and all of her separate property," even in cases when the wife had committed adultery. Carroll, *Homesteads Ungovernable*, 138. My research did not confirm Carroll's findings. B. F. Donaldson, for example, obtained sole control over the couple's community property after his divorce from Refugia Garza Girón. CCDCM 1016155,

case 3001, *Donaldson v. Garza Girón*, 17 May 1855; CCDCM 1016162, *Rodriguez v. Barbosa*, 5 October 1888; USCP (Cameron) 1900; Calderón, "Mexican Politics in the American Era," 1008; De León and Stewart, *Tejanos and the Numbers Game*, 80–81.

77. Basch, *Framing American Divorce*, 215n6; Larson, "History of Divorce in Texas," 43. After receiving custody of the couple's children, Luisa and José, Antonio Malleth moved in with his mother. SCDCM 1017266, case 276, *Malleth v. Malleth*, 20 September 1880; USCP (Starr) 1880. For similar examples, see CCDCM 1016158, *Longoria v. Longoria*, 24 February 1897; USCP (Cameron) 1900; WCDCM 1017263, *Gonzales v. Gonzales*, 17 March 1898; and USCP (Webb) 1900.

78. De León and Stewart, *Tejanos and the Numbers Game*, 12; Basch, *Framing American Divorce*, 20. Among tejano litigants were four individuals with mixed Mexican Anglo or Mexican and European immigrant ancestry.

79. M. Smith, *Breaking the Bonds*, 44–75; Basch, *Framing American Divorce*, 97–140; Riley, *Divorce*, 55–59, 90; Griswold, *Family and Divorce in California*, 30–31; Ford, "Women, Marriage, and Divorce in California," 235–38, 244.

80. Several states prohibited remarriage for adulterous spouses, but Texas had no remarriage prohibitions. Basch, *Framing American Divorce*, 104, 134, 216n16; Riley, *Divorce*, 126; Paschal, *A Digest of the Laws of Texas*, 566–68; WCDCM 1017260, case 53, *Texas v. Pedro Maquersas and Martina Rodrigues*, 27 June 1867, case 59, *Texas v. Alvino Ramires and Estefana Martines*, December 1870. CCDCM 1016162, *Garza v. Garza*, 13 November 1889; Young, *Catarino Garza's Revolution on the Texas-Mexico Border*, 39, 54. On the importance of marriage and remarriage in the nineteenth century, see Hartog, *Man and Wife in America*, 284; Halem, *Divorce Reform*, 31–33; and Blake, *The Road to Reno*, 137–39. On pseudoremarriages, see Basch, *Framing American Divorce*, 105; CCDCM 1016162, *Fischer v. Fischer*, 9 October 1888, *Escamilla de Torres v. Torres*, 23 November 1889; and USCP (Cameron) 1870, 1880. The total number of remarriages after divorce is difficult to determine because of the abundance of common names (e.g., María Villarreal, Juan Garza) and because subsequent marriages might have occurred in a distant county or in Mexico. Unlike religious marriage records, civil marriage documents do not list the names of the spouses' parents, so each spouse's name is the only information that can be used to track remarriages.

81. CCMR 1016185, 18 May 1851; Paschal, *A Digest of the Laws of Texas*, 567–68; CCDCM 1016155, case 512, *Llosas v. Llosas*, 23 July 1856, 21 March 1857, case 547, *Llosas v. Llosas*, 5 March 1857; CAT *Baptisms*, Alexo Llosas and Cayetano Llosas, 3 February 1857; CCDCM 1016160, case 547, *Llosas v. Llosas*, 27 March 1857.

82. CCDCM 1016160, spring 1857, List of Jurors, 333; CAT *Deaths*, Cayetano Llosas, 20 May 1857; CCDCM 1016155, case 547, *Llosas v. Llosas*, 24 September 1857, 26 September 1857, 1 October 1857, 2 October 1857, 16 April 1858; CCDCM 1016155, case 597, *Tentovert & Teatjo v. Llosas*, 15 April 1858.

83. CCDCM 1016155, case 547, *Llosas v. Llosas*, 5 May 1858, 7 May 1858; CCDCM 1016160, case 597, *Tentovert & Teatjo v. Llosas*, 7 May 1858.

84. CAT *Deaths*, María Loreto Joaquina de la Brena, 26 October 1858; CCPM 1016175, 4 December 1858, B553; 6 December 1858, B558; CCDCM 1016160, case

373, *Texas v. Pedro Llosas*, 21 April 1859, 26 April 1859, 7 May 1860, 26 November 1860, 13 November 1861, case 416, *Texas v. Juan Llosas*, 10 May 1860, 26 November 1860, case 412, *Texas v. Juan Llosas*, 27 November 1860, 15 November 1861.

6. Contested Citizenship

1. *American Flag* Extra, 1 October 1859; Goldfinch and Canales, *Juan N. Cortina*, 5, 42–43; Chatfield, *The Twin Cities (Brownsville, Texas; Matamoros, Mexico) of the Border and the Country of the Lower Rio Grande*, 23; Thompson, *Cortina*, 11–12, 39.

2. DSF 70–72, Juan Nepomuceno Cortinas to the inhabitants of the state of Texas, 30 September 1859 (quote); Thompson, *Cortina*, 12, 46; Young, *Catarino Garza's Revolution on the Texas-Mexico Border*, 111–17.

3. *American Flag*, 26 November 1859; DSF 19–20, Stephen Powers, et al., to James Buchanan, president of the United States, 2 October 1859; DSF 20–23, Henry Webb, et al., to Hardin R. Runnels, governor of the state of Texas, 2 October 1859.

4. Anderson, *Imagined Communities*, 5–6.

5. Alonzo, *Tejano Legacy*, 147–48; Montejano, *Anglos and Mexicans in the Making of Texas*, 43–47; DSF 65, W. P. Reyburn to F. A. Hatch, 21 November 1859; Goldfinch and Canales, *Juan N. Cortina*, 17–41; Thompson, *Cortina*, 28–32, 37–38.

6. Montejano, *Anglos and Mexicans in the Making of Texas*, 32–33; Goldfinch and Canales, *Juan N. Cortina*, 46–48; Douglas, "Juan Cortina," 56; De León, *The Tejano Community*, 18; TFT 13, S. P. Heintzelman to Colonel Lee, 1 March 1860; Webb, *The Texas Rangers*, 192.

7. *Ranchero*, 22 October 1859, 24 December 1859; ICP 18, 72; Thompson, *Juan Cortina and the Texas-Mexico Frontier*, 101–2; Thompson, *Cortina*, 11, 39, 48–49, 52–57, 82–85; Salinas, *Indians of the Rio Grande Delta*, 62–63; Montejano, *Anglos and Mexicans in the Making of Texas*, 36; GDK 117, "Texas, The Rio Grande Valley, Cortina" (quote).

8. Thompson, *Juan Cortina and the Texas-Mexico Frontier*, 23; DSF 71, 79–82 (quotes); Calderón, "Mexican Politics in the American Era," 265–77; Alonzo, *Tejano Legacy*, 259–70.

9. *American Flag*, November 26, 1859; DSF 81 (quotes); Goldfinch and Canales, *Juan N. Cortina*, 42–43.

10. *American Flag*, 26 November 1859; DSF 82.

11. *American Flag*, 26 November 1859; DSF 71–72 (second quote), 80 (first quote).

12. Sahlins, *Boundaries*, 164–66.

13. DSF 74–76, Mr. Lathan and others to the president, 30 November 1859; DSF 34–35, Stephen Powers to the president, 18 October 1859; *American Flag* Extra, 1 October 1859; *American Flag*, 26 November 1859.

14. *American Flag* Extra, 1 October 1859; DSF 31–32, 47–50, 78–79, 92–96; *American Flag*, 26 November 1859; DSF 128–29, Charles Stillman to Messrs. Taylor and Navarro, 14 January 1860.

15. DSF 136–37, General Winfield Scott to secretary of war, 19 March 1860,; ICP 76; DSF 19–20, "The people of Brownsville to the President," 2 October 1859 (emphasis added); DSF 20–23, Henry Webb and others to Hardin R. Runnels, 2 October 1859; Haynes quoted in Thompson, *Vaqueros in Blue and Gray*, 86; Thompson, *Mexican Texans in the Union Army*, 13–14.

16. ICP 72; Thompson, *Juan Cortina and the Texas-Mexico Frontier*, 14, 102; TTF 4, S. P. Heintzelman to Colonel Lee, 1 March 1860; Montejano, *Anglos and Mexicans in the Making of Texas*, 36; Goldfinch and Canales, *Juan N. Cortina*, 6.

17. DSF 5, D. E. Twiggs to General Scott, 13 January 1859; DSF 11, John Hemphill and Matt. Ward to Hon. John B. Ford, 21 March 1859; DSF 12–14, F. W. Latham, F. Cummings, et al., to Hon. John B. Ford, 9 March 1859; DSF 14–15, D. E. Twiggs to General Scott, 28 March 1859.

18. F. F. Fenn to *San Antonio Ledger and Texan*–Extra, 4 December 1859, reprinted in DSF 84–85; "Cortinas, the Leader, and His Character," *Picayune*, 10 October 1859, reprinted in DSF 39–40.

19. *Ranchero*, 11 February 1860 (first quote), 24 December 1859 (second quote); DSF 43, 93, 138 (third quote); Sahlins, *Boundaries*, 165.

20. *Picayune*, 10 October 1859, reprinted in DSF 39–40; Israel Bigelow to the *American Flag* editors, 23 October 1859, reprinted in DSF 47–48.

21. *San Antonio Ledger and Texan*–Extra, 4 December 1859, reprinted in DSF 84–85; "Report of the grand jury on the disturbances of the country," November 1859, DSF 39–40, 43, 94, 109; *Picayune*, 10 October 1859, reprinted in DSF 39–40.

22. *Ranchero*, 12 November 1859, 2; Thompson, *Cortina*, 56 (first quote); Israel Bigelow to the *American Flag* editors, 1 November 1859, reprinted in DSF 48–49.

23. GDK 39–42, Kingsbury to Mr. Editor, 29 December 1859; DSF 83; *Ranchero*, 12 November 1859, 25 November 1859 (second quote); DSF 49–50 (first quote). On the Yaqui uprisings, see Hu-DeHart, *Yaqui Resistance and Survival*. For the Yucatán's Caste War, see Joseph, "The United States, Feuding Elites, and Rural Revolt in Yucatán," 188–89; and De León, *They Called Them Greasers*, 83–84. On the Yaqui and Apache threats, see *New York Times*, "Arizona and Sonora—No. 111," 5 February 1859, "News by Telegraph," 20 July 1859.

24. *Ranchero*, 25 November 1859, 2; Domenech, *Missionary Adventures in Texas and Mexico*, 238–39; De León, *They Called Them Greasers*, 84.

25. Taylor, *An American-Mexican Frontier*, 230–34; Horsman, *Race and Manifest Destiny*, 236–40; Haney López, *White by Law*, 7–26; Haas, *Conquests and Historical Identities in California*, 10, 126, 166.

26. *Ranchero*, 19 May 1860; Lowe, *Immigrant Acts*, 8; Mitchell, *Coyote Nation*, 122–73; Gómez, *Manifest Destinies*, 81–115; Benton-Cohen, *Borderline Americans*, 30–31, 196–97.

27. *Ranchero*, 17 March 1860 (first quote; emphasis added), 8 June 1861, 29 June 1861, 6 July 1861, 17 November 1860 (second and third quotes).

28. Almaguer, *Racial Fault Lines*, 45–46; Montejano, *Anglos and Mexicans in the Making of Texas*, 35–37; Jacobson, *Whiteness of a Different Color*, 8–9, 20–21, 142, 205–6; Benton-Cohen, *Borderline Americans*, 30–31, 46–47, 144–45; Horsman, *Race and Manifest Destiny*, 301; White, "Race Relations in the American West," 400–401; Gordon, *The Great Arizona Orphan Abduction*, 76–77, 103–5.

29. DSF 70.

30. *American Flag*, 26 November 1859; DSF 72 (third quote), 78 (first and second quotes).

31. Wilkinson, *Laredo and the Rio Grande Frontier*, 370–71; Calderón, "Mexican Politics in the American Era," 423–56; Thompson, *Warm Weather and Bad Whiskey*, 66–67; Kearney and Knopp, *Boom and Bust*, 33, 81; Thompson, "A Nineteenth Century History of Cameron County, Texas," 32–37; García, "Don Francisco Yturria," 17–27; Kearney and Knopp, *Border Cuates*, 141–45; Chatfield, *The Twin Cities (Brownsville, Texas; Matamoros, Mexico) of the Border and the Country of the Lower Rio Grande*, 14 (quote).

32. Thompson, "A Nineteenth Century History of Cameron County, Texas," 38; Domenech, *Missionary Adventures in Texas and Mexico*, 241–42 (first, second, and fourth quotes); Chatfield, *The Twin Cities (Brownsville, Texas; Matamoros, Mexico) of the Border and the Country of the Lower Rio Grande*, 14 (third quote).

33. DSF 123; Kearney and Knopp, *Boom and Bust*, 108; Chatfield, *The Twin Cities (Brownsville, Texas; Matamoros, Mexico) of the Border and the Country of the Lower Rio Grande*, 15; GDK 23–25, Kingsbury to Sister Maria, 16 August 1858; Thompson, "A Nineteenth Century History of Cameron County, Texas," 80–81; GDK 110, Kingsbury, "Texas, The Rio Grande Valley, Cortina"; Goldfinch and Canales, *Juan N. Cortina*, 38–39.

34. *Daily True Delta*, 20 August 1850, reprinted in Chapman, *News from Brownsville*, 377 (first quote); Taylor, *An American-Mexican Frontier*, 234; *Ranchero*, 6 October 1860, 22 June 1861; Chatfield, *The Twin Cities (Brownsville, Texas; Matamoros, Mexico) of the Border and the Country of the Lower Rio Grande*, 14 (second and third quotes).

35. Thompson, "A Nineteenth Century History of Cameron County, Texas," 38, 118; De León, *They Called Them Greasers*, 58; Young, *Catarino Garza's Revolution on the Texas-Mexico Border*, 32–33.

36. GDK 23–25, Kingsbury to Sister Maria, 16 August 1858; *Ranchero*, 6 October 1860 (first quote to sixth), 10 August, 1861; *American Flag* quoted in *Ranchero*, 3 September 1863 (last quote).

37. *Daily Ranchero*, 23 November 1869, 25 November 1869, 27 November 1869, 30 November 1869, 23 April, 1870; *Ranchero*, 25 August 1860, 6 October 1860, 6 July 1861 (quote), 10 November 1860; De León, *The Tejano Community*, 35–36; De León and Stewart, *Tejanos and the Numbers Game*, 12; De León, *They Called Them Greasers*, 58–59.

38. Kearney and Knopp, *Border Cuates*, 141; Montejano, *Anglos and Mexicans in the Making of Texas*, 37; Alonzo, *Tejano Legacy*, 111; Calderón, "Mexican Politics in the American Era," 26–29.

39. *Daily Ranchero*, 12 March 1868, 17 March 1868, 21 March 1868, 18 March 1868; Chapman, *News from Brownsville*, 95–98, 130; Mitchell, *Coyote Nation*, 29–30; Mora, *Border Dilemmas*, 144–49.

40. *American Flag*, 5 July 1848, reprinted in Chapman, *News from Brownsville*, 361, 137; *Ranchero*, 29 June 1861, 7 July 1860; *Daily Ranchero*, 4 July 1865 (quote), 29 June 1867, 6 July 1867, 23 November 1866, 25 November 1866, 15 February 1867, 21

February 1867; Chatfield, *The Twin Cities (Brownsville, Texas; Matamoros, Mexico) of the Border and the Country of the Lower Rio Grande*, 13–14.

41. Chapman, *News from Brownsville*, 130, 152, 173–75; Chatfield, *The Twin Cities (Brownsville, Texas; Matamoros, Mexico) of the Border and the Country of the Lower Rio Grande*, 10, 18.

42. Chapman, *News from Brownsville*, 102, 172, 179–80, 187, 201–3, 260–64; Calderón, "Mexican Politics in the American Era," 956–57; Rankin, *Twenty Years among the Mexicans*, 58; Alonzo, *Tejano Legacy*, 126–27.

43. Chapman, *News from Brownsville*, 130, 139, 145, 172, 180, 190, 201, 260; Red, *A History of the Presbyterian Church in Texas*, 87; Rankin, *Twenty Years among the Mexicans*, 37–38, 57–58; Rayburn, "Introduction," vii; San Miguel, *"Let All of Them Take Heed,"* 9; *American Flag*, 15 May 1852; Calderón, "Mexican Politics in the American Era," 636–41.

44. Chatfield, *The Twin Cities (Brownsville, Texas; Matamoros, Mexico) of the Border and the Country of the Lower Rio Grande*, 10–11, 17–18; Crews, "Reconstruction in Brownsville, Texas," 23–24; Hinojosa, *A Borderlands Town in Transition*, 88–89; Calderón, "Mexican Politics in the American Era," 630–33; González, "Social Life in Cameron, Starr, and Zapata Counties," 69–74; San Miguel, *"Let All of Them Take Heed,"* 10.

45. Hinojosa, *A Borderlands Town in Transition*, 62, 88–89; Crews, "Reconstruction in Brownsville, Texas," 24–25; HDC 329–31, Typescript notes from Commissioner's Court of Cameron County; González, "Social Life in Cameron, Starr, and Zapata Counties," 78–79; Calderón, "Mexican Politics in the American Era," 630–31; San Miguel, *"Let All of Them Take Heed,"* 12–13.

46. Calderón, "Mexican Politics in the American Era," 645–69; De León and Stewart, *Tejanos and the Numbers Game*, 85–86; Chatfield, *The Twin Cities (Brownsville, Texas; Matamoros, Mexico) of the Border and the Country of the Lower Rio Grande*, 16–17; González, "Social Life in Cameron, Starr, and Zapata Counties," 69–82.

47. De León, *They Called Them Greasers*, 49–62; DSF 41–44, W. G. Hale to Hon. J. B. Floyd, 7 November 1859; DSF 35, Loomis L. Langdon to President James Buchanan, 18 October 1859.

48. De León, *They Called Them Greasers*, 59; *New York Times*, 28 August 1880; Paschal, *A Digest of the Laws of Texas*, 615–16.

49. Chatfield, *The Twin Cities (Brownsville, Texas; Matamoros, Mexico) of the Border and the Country of the Lower Rio Grande*, 29 (emphasis added); TFT 122 (second quote).

50. TBT 145.

51. Sahlins, *Boundaries*, 167.

52. Irby, *Backdoor at Bagdad*, 1–10; Thompson and Jones, *Civil War and Revolution on the Rio Grande Frontier*, 40–43; Hinojosa, *A Borderlands Town in Transition*, 87; Calvert and León, *The History of Texas*, 123; Graf, "The Economic History of the Lower Rio Grande Valley," 489–91, 577; *Daily Ranchero*, 15 June 1867.

53. Thompson, *Mexican Texans in the Union Army*, 3, 43. Thompson, *Vaqueros in Blue and Gray*, 26–27, 56–57, 92–93, 123.

54. De León, *They Called Them Greasers*, 49–52; Kelley, "'Mexico in His Head,'" 714; Thompson, *Mexican Texans in the Union Army*, viii.

55. Thompson, *Warm Weather and Bad Whiskey*, 22; Thompson, *Civil War and Revolution on the Rio Grande Frontier*, 31, 34–35; Lott and Martínez, *The Kingdom of Zapata*, 43.

56. *Ranchero*, 27 April 1861, 8 June 1861 (quote); De León, *They Called Them Greasers*, 55–56; Thompson, *Mexican Texans in the Union Army*, 3; Thompson, *Vaqueros in Blue and Gray*, 15–17; Thompson, *Civil War and Revolution on the Rio Grande Frontier*, 35–36.

57. Thompson, *Vaqueros in Blue and Gray*, 16, (fourth quote), 18–19 (third quote); *Ranchero*, 18 May 1861 (first and second quotes); Thompson, *Mexican Texans in the Union Army*, 8, 17.

58. Thompson, *Cortina*, 97–98; *Ranchero*, 27 April 1861 (quote).

59. Hinojosa, *A Borderlands Town in Transition*, 82–86; Thompson, *Civil War and Revolution on the Rio Grande Frontier*, 36–39, 46–48; Thompson, *Mexican Texans in the Union Army*, 1–5, 9; Thompson, *Vaqueros in Blue and Gray*, 49; Thompson, *Warm Weather and Bad Whiskey*, 22–24.

60. Several scholars argue that tejano soldiers did not understand the ideological motivations for the Civil War. Thompson, *Mexican Texans in the Union Army*, 8, 17; De León, *Mexican Americans in Texas*, 47; Hinojosa, *A Borderlands Town in Transition*, 83.

61. De León, *They Called Them Greasers*, 49–50 (quote); Olmsted, *Journey through Texas*, 106, 163, 256–59, 271–72, 331–34, 456; Downing de De Juana, "Intermarriage in Hidalgo County," 59–61, 99.

62. Tyler, "Fugitive Slaves in Mexico," 7; *Ranchero*, 8 June 1861; Vielé, *"Following the Drum*," 156–58.

63. RG94, Col. John L. Haynes to Col. E. J. Davis, 11 March 1864, George Treviño et al. to Col. Juan L. Haynes, 26 February 1864; Thompson, *Vaqueros in Blue and Gray*, 6, 47, 90–91, 121–22.

64. Quoted in Thompson, *Vaqueros in Blue and Gray*, 44–45.

65. RG94, Capt. A. J. Vidal to Lieut. H. Clamp, 30 May 1864; Thompson, *Mexican Texans in the Union Army*, 27; Thompson, *Vaqueros in Blue and Gray*, 90–92; Thompson, *Civil War and Revolution on the Rio Grande Frontier*, 56–59, 70–73, 80.

66. Davis had been a district attorney and judge for the Twelfth Judicial District in Brownsville, while Haynes had been a county clerk and state legislator from Starr County. Thompson, *Vaqueros in Blue and Gray*, 52, 81–83; Thompson, *Mexican Texans in the Union Army*, 10–18.

67. WR 4:152, A. Buchel to Samuel Boyer Davis, 5 December 1861; McIntyre quoted in Thompson, *Mexican Texans in the Union Army*, 25; Taylor, *An American-Mexican Frontier*, 46.

68. WR 34, pt. 2, 288, Edmund J. Davis to Edward Ord, 10 February 1864; Løvenskiold quoted in Thompson, *Vaqueros in Blue and Gray*, 46.

69. *Corpus Christi Ranchero*, 23 April 1863 (quotes); Thompson, *Vaqueros in Blue and Gray*, 56; Sahlins, *Boundaries*, 165.

70. RG94, Santos Cadena to G. W. Paschal, 19 May 1864; Thompson, *Mexican Texans in the Union Army*, 27, 32; Thompson, *Vaqueros in Blue and Gray*, 77–78 (Vidal quote), 94–95.

71. Thompson, *Vaqueros in Blue and Gray*, 89–92.

72. Ibid., 58–59; *American Flag* quoted in *Ranchero*, 3 September 1863 (first and third quotes), 13 August 1863 (second quote).

73. H. P. Bee to Edmund P. Turner, 27 April 1863, WR, Series I, 15:1056–57 (emphasis added); RG94, George Treviño et al. to Col. Juan L. Haynes, 26 February 1864.

74. Campbell, *Grass-Roots Reconstruction in Texas*, 198–99, 221–22, 226–27; Thompson, *Mexican Texans in the Union Army*, 36–38; *Daily Ranchero*, 23 November 1869, 23 April 1870.

75. Campbell, *Grass-Roots Reconstruction in Texas*, 18; De León, *They Called Them Greasers*, 56; *Daily Ranchero*, 2 July 1867.

76. Meyer, Sherman, and Deeds, *The Course of Mexican History*, 334–48; Thompson, *Cortina*, 120–99.

77. Paredes, *A Texas-Mexican Cancionero*, 24–25, 49–51; Paredes, "Folklore e historia: Dos Cantares de la frontera norte," 216–20; *Daily Ranchero*, 5 May 1870, 7 May 1870.

78. Paredes, *A Texas-Mexican Cancionero*, 24–25, 52–53; Paredes, "Folklore e historia: Dos cantares de la frontera norte," 216–19.

79. Ramos, *Beyond the Alamo*, 182–85, 190; Alonzo, *Tejano Legacy*, 85–89; TFT ii–iii (first quote), 13 (second quote), 32, 56; TBT 82, 261 (third quote); De León, *They Called Them Greasers*, 59–60.

80. TBT 145, 149.

81. TFT 5–6, 9.

82. ICP 41; TFT 5–9 (quotes), 34.

83. TFT xi, 51.

84. TBT 83 (Ord quote), 130–31 (Clous quote), 144–45; Hogue, "Between Race and Nation," 59–69.

85. TFT x (second quote), 56; De León, *They Called Them Greasers*, 60 (first quote).

86. ICP 16–20, 24–37; Rachel St. John, "Divided Ranges," 128–34.

87. TBT 36, 144–45; TFT i–xvii, 54–55; ICP 17–20.

88. ICP 12; TBT 131; TFT vii (quote), 11–13, 29, 120; Young, *Catarino Garza's Revolution on the Texas-Mexico Border*, 136–41.

89. TFT 7–13 (McNally quote), 23–25 (Steele quote), 32 (Ord quote).

90. TFT 40, 56–57.

91. TFT 10, 23–25, 57; Hogue, "Between Race and Nation," 60–61, 81.

92. *Daily Ranchero*, 23 November 1869, 25 November 1869.

93. Ibid., 25 November 1869, 30 November 1869, 4 December 1869.

94. Bukowczyk et al., *Permeable Border*, 5–6, 91–92.

95. Young, *Catarino Garza's Revolution on the Texas-Mexico Border*, 57–97.

96. Carrigan and Webb, "The Lynching of Persons of Mexican Origin or Descent in the United States," 413–15; Young, *Catarino Garza's Revolution on the Texas-Mexico Border*, 155–78.

97. Young, *Catarino Garza's Revolution on the Texas-Mexico Border*, 165–66, 177–90.

98. Reséndez, *Changing National Identities at the Frontier*, 2–3.

99. Gómez, *Manifest Destinies*, 51–52; Menchaca, *Recovering History, Constructing Race*, 62–66.

100. Thompson, *Mexican Texans in the Union Army*, 5–7.

101. Gellner, *Nations and Nationalisms*, 12–13; Reséndez, *Changing National Identities at the Frontier*, 2–3, 270–71; Sahlins, *Boundaries*, 165–66.

Conclusion

1. Thompson, *Juan Cortina and the Texas-Mexico Frontier*, 29–48, 67–73.

2. TFT 152; Thompson, *Cortina*, 200–47; Thompson, *Juan Cortina and the Texas-Mexico Frontier*, 71–72, 87–93.

3. Paredes, *A Texas-Mexican Cancionero*, 22–23, 47–48.

4. Ibid., 47–48; Thompson, *Cortina*, 245–47; M. Smith and Bakker, *Citizenship across Borders*, 78, 167–68.

5. Gilroy, *"There Ain't No Black in the Union Jack,"* 33.

6. Sánchez, *Becoming Mexican American*, 87–107; Arreola, *Tejano South Texas*, 198–99; Ruiz, *From Out of the Shadows*, 50.

7. Davis, *Magical Urbanism*, 52–54; Chavez, *The Latino Threat*, 23–43, 152–76; Ngai, *Impossible Subjects*, 58–71; Young, *Catarino Garza's Revolution on the Texas-Mexico Border*, 136; M. Smith and Bakker, *Citizenship across Borders*, 27–41, 45–78.

8. Johnson, *Revolution in Texas*, 188, 194; Olivas, "Hernandez v. Texas: A Litigation History," 209–22; Foley, *The White Scourge*, 132, 179; Montejano, *Anglos and Mexicans in the Making of Texas*, 130–31, 143, 251, 279. Several scholars have referred to American society's views of Mexicans as "perpetual foreigners," the term used by Mora to aptly describe their status. Mora, *Border Dilemmas*, 280–82; Fregoso, *Mexicana Encounters*, 127.

9. Johnson, *Revolution in Texas*, 71–143, 171–75; Gutiérrez, *Walls and Mirrors*, 154–55; Thompson, *Cortina*, 2, 251; Young, "Deconstructing 'La Raza,'" 227–38, 257–59.

10. Paredes, *Folklore and Culture on the Texas-Mexican Border*, 24; Andreas, *Border Games*, 3–14, 22–29; Montejano, *Anglos and Mexicans in the Making of Texas*, 42–44; Mora-Torres, *The Making of the Mexican Border*, 32–36, 62–63. See "King Ranch" on the Handbook of Texas Online website, http://www.tshaonline.org (accessed 24 October 2009).

11. Solomon Moore, "Border Proves No Obstacle for Mexican Cartels," *New York Times*, 2 February 2009; Randal C. Archibold, "As U.S. Tightens Mexico Border, Smugglers Are Taking to the Sea," *New York Times*, 18 July 2009; Richard Marosi, "Arrest Drop as Border Traffic Slows," *Los Angeles Times*, 8 March 2009; N. C. Aizenman, "Despite Economy, Illegal Immigrants Unlikely to Leave U.S.," *Washington Post*, 14 January 2009; Julia Preston, "Mexican Data Say Migration to U.S. Has Plummeted," *New York Times*, 15 May 2009; Sacha Feinman, "A New Danger Awaits in the Desert," *Los Angeles Times*, 19 July 2009.

12. Gutiérrez, "Citizens, Noncitizens, and the Shell Game of Immigration Policy Reform," 71–75; Lee Nichols, "How to Turn Purple to Blue," *Austin Chronicle*, 6 February 2009.

Bibliography

Archival Sources

ACM   Amon Carter Museum, Fort Worth, Tex.

AEM   Archivo Eclesiástico de Matamoros, Catedral de Matamoros, Tamaulipas. Cited by book no.
       BAU   Libro de Bautismos

AGI   Archivo General de las Indias, Seville, Spain.

AGN   Archivo General de la Nación, Mexico City.

AHD   Archivo Histórico Diplomático, Secretaría de Relaciones Exteriores de México, Mexico City.

AHM   Archivo Histórico de Matamoros, Casa Mata, Matamoros, Tamaulipas. Cited by [box no.]:[expediente no.].
       COL   Colonial
       JUD   Judicial
       JUS   Justicia
       PRE   Presidencia

AMR   Archivo Municipal de Reynosa, Reynosa, Tamaulipas. Cited by box no.
       PRE   Presidencia
       JUZ   Juzgado

BCCP   City Council Proceedings, City of Brownsville. Book A, Minute Book From 1866 to 1878, Brownsville, Tex.

CAT   Catholic Archives of Texas, Austin.
       ICCB   Immaculate Conception Church, Brownsville, Tex. Baptisms, vols. 1–7 (1849–1920).
       ICCD   Immaculate Conception Church, Brownsville, Tex. Deaths, vols. 1–8 (1852–1978).
       ICCM   Immaculate Conception Church, Brownsville, Tex. Marriages (1849–1913).

CCDCM   Cameron County District Court Minutes (1849–1906), Microfilm reels 1016155, 1016156, 1016157, 1016158, 1016160, 1016161, 1016162.

CCMR   Cameron County Marriage Records (1848–1905). Microfilm reels 1016185, 1016186, 1016187.

CCPM   Cameron County Probate Minutes (1848–58). Microfilm reel 1016175.

GDK   G. D. Kingsbury Papers, Box 2R72, Center for American History (University of Texas at Austin), Austin, Tex.

HCDCM   Hidalgo County District Court Minutes (1853–98). Microfilm reel 1017257.

HCMR   Hidalgo County Marriage Records (1852–88). Microfilm reel 1017253.

HDC   Harbert Davenport Collection, Texas State Archives, Austin, Tex. Box no. 2–23/212.

IR   "Informe del Rey Nuestro Señor en su Último Consejo de un días, cerca de las Misiones del Seno Mexicano, 1749." DeGolyer Library, Southern Methodist University, Dallas, Tex.

LA   Laredo Archives, St. Mary's University, San Antonio, Tex. Cited by [folder no.]:[document no.].

LBC   Libros de Bautismos de Camargo, Photocopies at Rio Grande Valley Historical Collection, University of Texas, Pan American, Edinburg, Tex.

MAA   Matamoros Ayuntamiento Archives, Newberry Library, Chicago, Ill. Cited by [volume]:[page no.].

NA   National Archives, Washington, D.C.

RBR   Reynosa Baptismal Records, photocopies at Rio Grande Valley Special Collections, University of Texas, Pan American, Edinburg, Tex.

RG94   Regimental Papers of the Second Regiment. National Archives, Washington, D.C. Record group 94.

SCDCM   Starr County District Court Minutes (1848–86). Microfilm reel 1017266.

SCMR   Starr County Marriage Records (1858–93). Microfilm reel 1016452.

SPCDCM San Patricio County District Court Minutes (1848–86). Microfilm reel 1013259.

WCDCM   Webb County District Court Minutes (1851–1902). Microfilm reels 1017260, 1017261, 1017262, 1017263.

WCMR   Webb County Marriage Records (1852–1902). Microfilm reels 1017221, 1017223.

ZCDCM   Zapata County District Court Minutes (1851–94). Microfilm reels 1017260, 1017261, 1017262.

ZCMR   Zapata County Marriage Records (1874–1928). Microfilm reel 1016432.

Periodicals

American Flag (Brownsville, Tex., and Matamoros, Tamaulipas), 1847–59.
American Star (Mexico City), 1847.
Atalaya (Tampico, Tamaulipas).
Austin Chronicle (Austin, Tex.).
Caller (Corpus Christi, Tex.).
Corpus Christi Gazette (Corpus Christi, Tex.), 1846.
Corpus Christi Star (Corpus Christi, Tex.).
Daily Cosmopolitan (Brownsville, Tex.), 1863.
Daily Delta (New Orleans, La.).

Daily True Delta (New Orleans, La.).
El Águila del Norte (Matamoros, Tamaulipas).
El Ancla (Matamoros, Tamaulipas).
El Argos de Matamoros (Matamoros, Tamaulipas).
El Bejareño (San Antonio, Tex.), 1855.
El Defensor de Tamaulipas (Ciudad Victoria, Tamaulipas).
El Demócrata (Matamoros, Tamaulipas).
El Látigo de Tejas (Matamoros, Tamaulipas).
El Restaurador de Tamaulipas (Ciudad Victoria, Tamaulipas).
El Telégrafo (Ciudad de México).
El Telescopio de Tamaulipas (Ciudad Victoria, Tamaulipas).
Eco del Norte de Tamaulipas (Matamoros, Tamaulipas)
Fort Brown Flag/La Bandera (Brownsville, Tex.), 1863.
Journal (Brownsville, Tex.), 1864.
La Columna de la Constitución Federal de la República Mexicana (Mexico City).
La Diana de Matamoros (Matamoros, Tamaulipas).
La Gaceta del Gobierno de Tamaulipas (Tampico, Tamaulipas).
Los Angeles Times (Los Angeles, Calif.), 2000–12.
Mercurio del Puerto de Matamoros (Matamoros, Tamaulipas).
New Orleans Times (New Orleans, La.).
New York Times (New York City, N.Y.), 1846–1900, 2000–12.
Nueces Valley (Corpus Christi, Tex.), 1857.
Picayune (New Orleans, La.).
Ranchero (Brownsville, Tex., and Corpus Christi, Tex.), 1859–63. Name and place
 of publication changed to *The Daily Ranchero/El Ranchero Diario* (Brownsville,
 Tex., and Matamoros, Tamaulipas), 1865–70; *The Daily Ranchero and
 Republican* (Brownsville, Tex.), 1871–72.
Republic of the Rio Grande, and Friend of the People (Matamoros, Tamaulipas),
 1846.
Rio Grande Courier (Brownsville, Tex.), 1867.
San Antonio Ledger and Texan (San Antonio, Tex.).
Tejano Community (Brownsville, Tex., and Matamoros, Tamaulipas), 1863–76.
Valley Town Crier (McAllen, Tex.).
Washington Post (Washington, D.C.), 2000–2012.
Weekly Gazette (Brownsville, Tex.).

Published Primary Sources

CCBR   *Camargo Church Baptism Records*, book 1: 1764–1864. Corpus Christi,
       Tex.: Spanish American Genealogical Association, 1989.

DG   *Documentos para la genealogía: Archivos de Laredo*. Translated by Robert
       D. Wood, S.M. San Antonio, Tex.: St. Mary's University, 2000. Cited by
       page no.

DFT   42nd Congress, 3rd Session, no. 39, "Depredations on the Frontiers of
       Texas." Vol. 7, 1872–73, serial no. 1565. Washington, D.C.: Government
       Printing Office, 1873.

DHL   *Documents for the History of Laredo: Archivos de Laredo*. Translated by
       Robert D. Wood, S.M. San Antonio, Tex.: St. Mary's University, 1999.
       Cited by [page no.]:[folder no.]:[document no.].

DRI   *Documentos referentes a los indios: Archivos de Laredo.* Translated by Robert D. Wood, S.M. San Antonio, Tex.: St. Mary's University, 1998.

DSF   36th Congress, 1st session, no. 52, "Difficulties on Southwestern Frontier." Vol. 7, 1859–60, serial no. 1050. Washington, D.C.: Thomas H. Ford, Printer, 1860.

EGF   Tienda de Cuervo, José, and Vicente Santa María. *Estado general de las fundaciones hechas por D. José de Escandón en la colonia del Nuevo Santander, costa del Seno Mexicano: Documentos originales que contienen la inspección de la provincial efectuada por el capitán de dragones don José Tienda de Cuervo, el informe del mismo al virrey y un apéndice con la relación histórica del Nuevo Santander.* 2 vols. Mexico City: Tall. Graf. de la Nación, 1929.

EHM   Instituto Nacional de Estadística, Geografía e Informática (Mexico). *Estadísticas históricas de México.* Mexico City: Instituto Nacional de Estadística, Geografía e Informática, Instituto Nacional de Antropología e Historia, SEP, 1985.

Gammel, H. P. N. *Laws of Texas 1822–1897.* Vol. 3. Austin: The Gammel Company, 1898.

HM   *Archivos de Laredo: The History of Mexico 1809–1845 in the Laredo Archives.* Translated by Robert D. Wood, S.M. San Antonio, Tex.: St. Mary's University, 2000.

ICP   México, Comisión Pesquisidora de la Frontera del Noroeste. *Informe general de la Comisión Pesquisidora de la Frontera del Noroeste, al ejecutivo de la unión: En cumplimiento del artículo 3. De la ley de 30 de septiembre de 1872.* Mexico City: Impr. del "Eco de Ambos Mundos," 1874.

IMC   *Archivos de Laredo: Index to the Municipal Correspondence, 1825–1845, and Verbal Arbitrations and Decisions, 1832–1842.* Translated by Robert D. Wood, S.M. San Antonio, Tex.: St. Mary's University, 2000. Cited by [page no.]:[folder no.]:[document no.].

MPR   Spanish American Genealogical Association, Mexican Parish Records, 1751–1880. (Database online.) Provo, Utah: Generations Network, 1999.

Paschal, George W. *A Digest of the Laws of Texas, Containing Laws in Force and the Repealed Laws on Which Rights Rest.* Galveston, Tex.: S. S. Nichols, 1866.

RCI   México, *Reports of the Committee of Investigation Sent in 1873 by the Mexican Government to the Frontier of Texas.* New York: Baker and Godwin Printers, 1875.

SAP-I   Brown, Angel Sepulveda, and Gloria Villa Cadena. *San Agustin Parish of Laredo: Abstracts of Marriage Book I, 1790–1857.* Saltillo, Mexico: Gráficas Canepa, 1989.

SAP-II   Brown, Angel Sepulveda, and Gloria Villa Cadena. *San Agustin Parish of Laredo: Abstracts of Marriage Book II, 1858–1881.* Saltillo, Mexico: Gráficas Canepa, 1993.

TBT   45th Congress, 2nd session, no. 64, "Texas Border Troubles." *House Miscellaneous Documents,* serial 1820.

Texas (Republic), *Laws of the Republic of Texas, Passed at the Session of the Fifth Congress.* Vol. 2. Houston: Telegraph Power Press, 1841.

TFT   44th Congress, 1st Session, no. 343, "Texas Frontier Troubles." Vol. 2, 1876–77, serial no. 1709. Washington, D.C.: Government Printing Office, 1877.

TTF   36th Congress, 1st session, no. 81, "Troubles on Texas Frontier." Vol. 12, 1859–60, serial no. 1056. Washington, D.C.: Thomas H. Ford, Printer, 1860.

USCP (Cameron) U.S. Census of Population, Cameron County, 1860, 1870, 1880, 1900.

USCP (Cameron, Starr, and Webb) U.S. Census of Population, Cameron, Starr, and Webb Counties, 1850.

USCP (Hidalgo) U.S. Census of Population, Hidalgo County, 1860, 1870, 1880, 1900.

USCP (Starr) U.S. Census of Population, Starr County, 1860, 1870, 1880, 1900.

USCP (Webb) U.S. Census of Population, Webb County, 1860, 1870, 1880, 1900.

USCP (Zapata) U.S. Census of Population, Zapata County, 1860, 1870, 1880, 1900.

WR   War of Rebellion: Official Records of the Union and Confederate Armies, series 1, vols. 4, 15, 34.

Secondary Sources

Adelman, Jeremy, and Stephen Aron. "From Borderlands to Borders: Empires, Nation-States, and the Peoples in Between in North American History." *American Historical Review* 104:3 (June 1999): 814–41.

Alessio Robles, Vito. *Coahuila y Texas en la época colonial*. Mexico City: Editorial Porrúa, 1978.

Almaguer, Tomás. *Racial Fault Lines: The Historical Origins of White Supremacy in California*. Berkeley: University of California Press, 1994.

Alonso, Ana María. *Thread of Blood: Colonialism, Revolution, and Gender on Mexico's Northern Frontier*. Tucson: University of Arizona Press, 1995.

Alonzo, Armando C. *Tejano Legacy: Rancheros and Settlers in South Texas, 1734–1900*. Albuquerque: University of New Mexico Press, 1998.

Anders, Evan. *Boss Rule in South Texas: The Progressive Era*. Austin: University of Texas Press, 1979.

Anderson, Benedict. *Imagined Communities: Reflections on the Origin and Spread of Nationalism*. New York: Verso, 1991.

Andreas, Peter. *Border Games: Policing the U.S.-Mexico Divide*. Ithaca: Cornell University Press, 2000.

Archer, Christon I. "'La Causa Buena': The Counterinsurgency and the Ten Years' War." In *The Independence of Mexico and the Creation of the New Nation*. Edited by Jaime E. Rodriguez O. Los Angeles: UCLA Latin American Center Publications, 1989.

Arreola, Daniel D. *Tejano South Texas: A Mexican American Cultural Province*. Austin: University of Texas Press, 2002.

Arrom, Silvia M. "Changes in the Mexican Family Law in the Nineteenth Century: The Civil Codes of 1870 and 1884." *Journal of Family History* 10:3 (fall 1985): 305–17.

———. *The Women of Mexico City, 1790–1857*. Stanford: Stanford University Press, 1987.

Barr, Juliana. *Peace Came in the Form of a Woman: Indians and Spaniards in the Texas Borderlands*. Chapel Hill: University of North Carolina Press, 2007.

Basch, Norma. *Framing American Divorce: From the Revolutionary Generation to the Victorians*. Berkeley: University of California Press, 1999.

Baud, Michael, and Willem Van Schendel. "Toward a Comparative History of Borderlands." *Journal of World History* 8:2 (fall 1997): 211–42.

Bauer, K. Jack. *The Mexican War, 1846–1848*. New York: Macmillan, 1974.

Bayard, Ralph Francis. *Lone-Star Vanguard: The Catholic Re-occupation of Texas (1838–1848)*. St. Louis: Vincentian Press, 1945.

Berlandier, Jean Louis. *Journey to Mexico during the Years 1826 to 1834*. 2 vols. Austin: Texas State Historical Association, 1980.

Benton-Cohen, Katherine. *Borderline Americans: Racial Division and Labor War in the Arizona Borderlands*. Cambridge: Harvard University Press, 2009.

Blackhawk, Ned. *Violence over the Land: Indians and Empires in the Early American West*. Cambridge: Harvard University Press, 2006.

Blake, Nelson Manfred. *The Road to Reno: A History of Divorce in the United States*. New York: Macmillan, 1962.

Bolton, Herbert E. *Wider Horizons in American History*. New York: D. Appleton-Century Company, 1939, 1967.

Bosniak, Linda. "Citizenship Denationalized." *Indiana Journal of Global Studies* 7 (1999–2000): 447–509.

Boyer, Richard. "Women, *La Mala Vida*, and the Politics of Marriage." In *Sexuality and Marriage in Colonial Latin America*. Edited by Asunción Lavrin. Lincoln: University of Nebraska Press, 1989.

Brooks, James F. *Captives and Cousins: Slavery, Kinship, and Community in the Southwest Borderlands*. Chapel Hill: University of North Carolina Press, 2002.

Brown, Lawrence L. *The Episcopal Church in Texas, 1838–1874*. Austin: Church Historical Society, 1963.

Bukowczyk, John J., Nora Faires, David R. Smith, and Randy William Widdis. *Permeable Border: The Great Lakes Basin as Transnational Region, 1650–1990*. Pittsburgh: University of Pittsburgh Press, 2005.

Calderón, Roberto R. "Mexican Politics in the American Era, 1846–1900: Laredo, Texas." PhD diss., University of California, Los Angeles, 1993.

Calvert, Robert A., and Arnoldo De León. *The History of Texas*. Arlington Heights, Ill.: Harlan Davidson, 1990.

Camarillo, Albert. *Chicanos in a Changing Society: From Mexican Pueblos to American Barrios in Santa Barbara and Southern California, 1848–1930*. Cambridge: Harvard University Press, 1979.

Campbell, Randolph B. *Grass-Roots Reconstruction in Texas, 1865–1880*. Baton Rouge: Louisiana State University Press, 1997.

Campbell, T. N. "Coahuiltecans and Their Neighbors." In *Handbook of North American Indians*. Vol. 10. Edited by William C. Sturtevant. Washington, D.C.: Smithsonian Institution, 1984.

Canseco Botello, José Raúl. *Historia de Matamoros*. 2nd ed. Matamoros, Tamaulipas: Tipográficos de Litográfica Jardín, 1981.

Carrigan, William D., and Clive Webb. "The Lynching of Persons of Mexican Origin or Descent in the United States, 1848 to 1928." *Journal of Social History* 37:2 (winter 2003): 411–38.

Carroll, Mark M. *Homesteads Ungovernable: Families, Sex, Race, and the Law in Frontier Texas, 1823–1860*. Austin: University of Texas Press, 2001.

Casas, María Raquél. *Married to a Daughter of the Land: Spanish-Mexican Women and Interethnic Marriage in California, 1820–1880.* Reno: University of Nevada Press, 2007.

Castañeda, Antonia I. "Presidarias y Pobladoras: Spanish-Mexican Women in Frontier Monterey, California, 1770–1821." PhD diss., Stanford University, 1990.

Castañeda, Carlos E. *Our Catholic Heritage in Texas, 1519–1936.* Vol. 7: *The Church in Texas since Independence, 1836–1950.* Austin: Von Boeckmann-Jones, 1958.

Castañeda, Carmen. *Violación, estupro y sexualidad 1790–1821.* Guadalajara, Jalisco: Editorial Hexágono, 1989.

Castillo Crimm, Ana Carolina. *De León: A Tejano Family History.* Austin: University of Texas Press, 2003.

Cerutti, Mario, and Miguel González Quiroga. "Guerra y comercio en torno al Río Bravo (1855–1867): Línea fronteriza, espacio económico común." *Historia Mexicana* 40:2 (1991): 217–97.

Chapman, Helen. *News from Brownsville: Helen Chapman's Letters from the Texas Military Frontier, 1848–1852.* Edited by Caleb Coker. Austin: Texas State Historical Association, 1992.

Chatfield, W. H. *The Twin Cities (Brownsville, Texas; Matamoros, Mexico) of the Border and the Country of the Lower Rio Grande.* New Orleans: E. P. Brandao, 1893; repr., Brownsville, Tex.: Brownsville Historical Association, 1991.

Chavez, Leo R. *The Latino Threat: Constructing Immigrants, Citizens, and the Nation.* Stanford: Stanford University Press, 2008.

Chávez-García, Miroslava, *Negotiating Conquest: Gender and Power in California, 1770s to 1880s.* Tucson: University of Arizona Press, 2004.

Chused, Richard H. *Private Acts in Public Places: A Social History of Divorce in the Formative Era of American Family Law.* Philadelphia: University of Pennsylvania Press, 1994.

Clinton, Catherine. *The Other Civil War: American Women in the Nineteenth Century.* New York: Hill and Wang, 1984.

Collins, Michael L. *Texas Devils: Rangers and Regulars on the Lower Rio Grande, 1846–1861.* Norman: University of Oklahoma Press, 2008.

Corrigan, Philip, and Derek Sayer. *The Great Arch.* Oxford: Blackwell, 1985.

Cotera, María Eugenia. *Native Speakers: Ella Deloria, Zora Neale Hurston, Jovita González, and the Poetics of Culture.* Austin: University of Texas Press, 2008.

Cott, Nancy. *Public Vows: A History of Marriage and the Nation.* Cambridge: Harvard University Press, 2000.

Courtwright, David T. *Violent Land: Single Men and Social Disorder from the Frontier to the Inner City.* Cambridge: Harvard University Press, 1996.

Crews, James Robert. "Reconstruction in Brownsville, Texas." MA thesis, Texas Tech University, 1969.

Crouch, Barry A. *The Dance of Freedom: Texas African Americans during Reconstruction.* Austin: University of Texas Press, 2007.

Cruz, Gilbert R. *Let There Be Towns: Spanish Municipal Origins in the American Southwest, 1610–1810.* College Station: Texas A&M Press, 1988.

Cuéllar, Andrés F. *De Matamoros a México con sus gobernantes.* Matamoros: Arte Gráfico, 1996.

Cummins, Light Townsend. "Church Courts, Marriage Breakdown, and Separation in Spanish Louisiana, West Florida, and Texas, 1763–1836." *Journal of Texas Catholic History and Culture* 4 (1993): 97–114.

Curtis, Samuel Ryan. *Mexico Under Fire: Being the Diary of Samuel Ryan Curtis, 3rd Ohio Volunteer Regiment, during the American Military Occupation of Northern Mexico, 1846–1847.* Edited by Joseph E. Chance. Fort Worth: Texas Christian University Press, 1994.

Dana, Napoleon Jackson Tecumseh. *Monterrey Is Ours! The Mexican War Letters of Lieutenant Dana, 1845–1847.* Edited by Robert H. Ferrell. Lexington: University Press of Kentucky, 1990.

Dávila, Rosaura Alicia, and Oscar Rivera Saldaña, eds. *Matamoros en la guerra con los Estados Unidos.* Matamoros, Tamaulipas: Sociedad de Historia, 1996.

Davis, Mike. *Magical Urbanism: Latinos Reinvent the U.S. City.* New York: Verso, 2000.

D'Emilio, John, and Estelle B. Freedman. *Intimate Matters: A History of Sexuality in America.* 2nd ed. Chicago: University of Chicago Press, 1997.

De la Teja, Jesús. *San Antonio de Béxar: A Community on New Spain's Northern Frontier.* Albuquerque: University of New Mexico Press, 1995.

De la Torre. *Historia general de Tamaulipas.* 2nd ed. Ciudad Victoria, Tamaulipas: Instituto de Investigaciones Históricas, 1986.

DeLay, Brian. *War of a Thousand Deserts: Indian Raids and the U.S.-Mexican War.* New Haven: Yale University Press, 2008.

De León, Arnoldo. *Apuntes tejanos.* Ann Arbor, Mich.: Published for the Texas State Historical Association by University Microfilms International, 1978.

———. *Mexican Americans in Texas: A Brief History.* Arlington Heights, Ill.: Harlan Davidson, 1993.

———. *The Tejano Community, 1836–1900.* Albuquerque: University of New Mexico Press, 1982.

———. *They Called Them Greasers: Anglo Attitudes toward Mexicans in Texas, 1821–1900.* Austin: University of Texas Press, 1983.

De León, Arnoldo, and Kenneth L. Stewart. *Tejanos and the Numbers Game: A Socio-Historical Interpretation from the Federal Censuses, 1850–1900.* Albuquerque: University of New Mexico Press, 1989.

Diccionario Porrúa de historia, biografía y geografía de México. 5a ed. corr. y aum., con un suplemento (5th ed., corrected and expanded, with a supplement). Mexico City: Editorial Porrúa, 1986.

Dilworth, Rankin. *The March to Monterrey: The Diary of Lt. Rankin Dilworth, U.S. Army: A Narrative of Troop Movements and Observations on Daily Life with General Zachary Taylor's Army during the Invasion of Mexico.* Edited by Lawrence R. Clayton and Joseph E. Chance. El Paso: Texas Western Press, 1996.

Domenech, Emmanuel H. D. *Missionary Adventures in Texas and Mexico: A Personal Narrative of Six Years' Sojourn in Those Regions.* London: Longman, Brown, Green, Longmans, and Roberts, 1858.

Donovan, Brian. "Gender Inequality and Criminal Seduction: Prosecuting Sexual Coercion in the Early-20th Century." *Law and Social Inquiry* 30:1 (winter 2005): 61–88.

Douglas, James R. "Juan Cortina: El Caudillo de la Frontera." MA thesis, University of Texas, Austin, 1987.

Downing de De Juana, Ana Cristina. "Intermarriage in Hidalgo County, 1860–1900." MA thesis, University of Texas, Pan American, 1998.

Dysart, Jane. "Mexican Women in San Antonio, 1830–1860: The Assimilation Process." *Western Historical Quarterly* 7 (October 1976): 365–75.

Edwards, Frank S. *A Campaign in New Mexico.* Ann Arbor: UMI, 1966.

Eisenhower, John S. D. *So Far from God: The U.S. War with Mexico 1846–1848*. New York: Random House, 1989.

Engstrand, Iris, Richard Griswold del Castillo, and Elena Poniatowska. *Culture y Cultura: Consequences of the U.S.-Mexican War, 1846–1848*. Los Angeles: Autry Museum of Western Heritage, 1998.

Enstam, Elizabeth York. "Women and the Law." *The Handbook of Texas Online*. Article title can be searched for at www.tshaonline.org.

Escobar, Edward J. *Race, Police, and the Making of a Political Identity: Mexican Americans and the Los Angeles Police Department, 1900–1945*. Berkeley: University of California Press, 1999.

Ewers, John C. "Introduction." In *The Indians of Texas in 1830*, by Jean Louis Berlandier. Washington, D.C.: Smithsonian Institution Press, 1969.

Faragher, John Mack. *Women and Men on the Overland Trail*. New Haven: Yale University Press, 1979.

Faragher, John Mack, Mari Jo Buhle, Daniel Czitrom, and Susan H. Armitage. *Out of Many: A History of the American People*. 3rd ed. Upper Saddle River, N.J.: Prentice Hall, 2000.

Fernández de Castro, Patricia. "Comercio y contrabando en la frontera noreste, 1861–1865." *Frontera Norte* 6:11 (January–June 1994): 23–33.

Findlay, Eileen J. Suárez. *Imposing Decency: The Politics of Sexuality and Race in Puerto Rico, 1870–1920*. Durham: Duke University Press, 1999.

Flores, María Eva. "The Good Life the Hard Way: The Mexican American Community of Fort Stockton, Texas." PhD diss., Arizona State University, 2000.

Foley, Neil. *The White Scourge: Mexicans, Blacks, and Poor Whites in Texas Cotton Culture*. Berkeley: University of California Press, 1997.

Ford, Bonnie L. "Women, Marriage, and Divorce in California." PhD diss., University of California, Davis, 1985.

Frank, Ross. *From Settler to Citizen: New Mexican Economic Development and the Creation of Vecino Society, 1750–1820*. Berkeley: University of California Press, 2000.

Franklin, John Hope, and Loren Schweninger. *Runaway Slaves: Rebels on the Plantation*. New York: Oxford University Press, 1999.

Fregoso, Rosa Linda. *Mexicana Encounters: The Making of Social Identities on the Borderlands*. Berkeley: University of California Press, 2003.

Fulmore, Z. T. *The History and Geography of Texas as Told in County Names*. Austin: Steck, 1935.

Gallegos, Juan José. "'Last Drop of My Blood.' Col. Antonio Zapata: A Life and Times on México's Río Grande Frontier, 1797–1840." MA thesis, University of Houston, 2005.

García, Lilia Marisa. "Don Francisco Yturria: The Beginnings of a South Texas Entrepreneur, 1830–1870." MA thesis, Southern Methodist University, Dallas, 1993.

Gellner, E. *Nations and Nationalisms*. Ithaca: Cornell University Press, 1983.

Gerhard, Peter. *The Northern Frontier of New Spain*. Rev. ed. Norman: University of Oklahoma Press, 1993.

Gilroy, Paul. *"There Ain't No Black in the Union Jack": The Cultural Politics of Race and Nation*. Chicago: University of Chicago Press, 1987.

Goldfinch, Charles William, and José Tomás Canales. *Juan N. Cortina: Two Interpretations (The Mexican American)*. New York: Arno Press, 1974.

Gómez, Laura E. *Manifest Destinies: The Making of the Mexican American Race.* New York: New York University Press, 2007.

———. "Race, Colonialism, and Criminal Law: Mexicans and the American Criminal Justice System in Territorial New Mexico." *Law and Society Review* 34:4 (2000): 1129–202.

González, Deena J. *Refusing the Favor: The Spanish-Mexican Women of Santa Fe, 1820–1880.* New York: Oxford University Press, 1999.

González, Jovita. "Social Life in Cameron, Starr, and Zapata Counties." MA thesis, University of Texas, Austin, 1954.

González Quiroga, Miguel A. "Los inicios de la migración laboral mexicana a Texas, 1850–1880." In *Mexicanos y norteamericanos en un espacio común.* Tijuana: El Colegio de la Frontera Norte, 1996.

———. "Trabajadores mexicanos en Texas (1850–1865): Los carreteros y el transporte de carga." *Siglo XIX* 3:9 (1994): 51–81.

Gordon, Linda. *The Great Arizona Orphan Abduction.* Cambridge: Harvard University Press, 1999.

Graf, Leroy P. "The Economic History of the Lower Rio Grande Valley, 1820–1875." PhD diss., Harvard University, 1942.

Grant, Ulysses S. *Memoirs and Selected Letters: Personal Memoirs of U.S. Grant, Selected Letters 1839–1865.* New York: Library of America, 1990.

Green, Stanley C. *A History of Webb County.* Laredo, Tex.: Border Studies Center, 1992.

———. *The Mexican Republic: The First Decade 1823–1832.* Pittsburgh: University of Pittsburgh Press, 1987.

Green, Thomas J. *Journal of the Texian Expedition against Mier.* Austin, Tex.: Steck, 1935.

Griswold, Robert L. *Family and Divorce in California, 1850–1890: Victorian Illusions and Everyday Realities.* Albany: State University of New York Press, 1982.

Griswold del Castillo, Richard. *The Treaty of Guadalupe Hidalgo: A Legacy of Conflict.* Norman: University of Oklahoma Press, 1990.

Guardino, Peter F. *Peasants, Politics, and the Formation of Mexico's National State: Guerrero, 1800–1857.* Stanford: Stanford University Press, 1996.

Gudeman, Stephen, and Stuart B. Schwartz. "Cleansing Original Sin: Godparenthood and the Baptism of Slaves in Eighteenth-Century Bahia." In *Kinship Ideology and Practice in Latin America.* Edited by Raymond T. Smith. Chapel Hill: University of North Carolina Press, 1984.

Gutiérrez, David G. "Citizens, Noncitizens, and the Shell Game of Immigration Policy Reform: A Response to Dan Tichenor." *Labor: Studies in Working-Class History of the Americas* 5:2 (summer 2008): 71–75.

———. "Claims and Prospects." In Virginia Scharff, James P. Ronda, John M. Faragher, David G. Gutiérrez, Kathleen Underwood, and María E. Montoya, "Claims and Prospects of Western History: A Roundtable." *Western Historical Quarterly* 31:1 (spring 2000): 25–46.

———. "Migration, Emergent Ethnicity, and the 'Third Space': The Shifting Politics of Nationalism in Greater Mexico." *Journal of American History* 86:2 (September 1999): 481–517.

———. *Walls and Mirrors: Mexican Americans, Mexican Immigrants, and the Politics of Ethnicity.* Berkeley: University of California Press, 1995.

Gutiérrez, Ramón A. "Unraveling America's Hispanic Past: Internal Stratification and Class Boundaries." *Aztlán* 17:1 (spring 1986): 79–101.

——. *When Jesus Came, the Corn Mothers Went Away: Marriage, Sexuality, and Power in New Mexico, 1500–1846*. Stanford: Stanford University Press, 1991.

Gutiérrez, Ramón A., and Elliott Young. "Transnationalizing Borderlands History." *Western Historical Quarterly* 41:1 (spring 2010): 27–53.

Haag, Pamela. *Consent: Sexual Rights and the Transformation of American Liberalism*. Ithaca: Cornell University Press, 1999.

Haas, Lisbeth. *Conquests and Historical Identities in California*. Berkeley: University of California Press, 1995.

Halem, Lynne Carol. *Divorce Reform: Changing Legal and Social Perspectives*. New York: Free Press, 1980.

Hall, Stuart. "Cultural Identity and Diaspora." In *Identity: Community, Culture, Difference*. Edited by Jonathan Rutherford. London: Lawrence and Wishart, 1990.

Hall, Stuart, and Paul Du Gay, eds. *Questions of Cultural Identity*. London: Sage Publications, 1996.

Hämäläinen, Pekka. *The Comanche Empire*. New Haven: Yale University Press, 2008.

Hämäläinen, Pekka, and Samuel Truett. "On Borderlands." *Journal of American History* 98:2 (September 2011): 338–61.

Hammett, A. B. J. *The Empresario: Don Martin De Leon*. Waco: Texian Press, 1973.

Haney López, Ian. *White by Law: The Legal Construction of Race*. 10th ed. New York: New York University Press, 2006.

Harris, Charles H. *A Mexican Family Empire: The Latifundio of the Sánchez Navarros, 1765–1867*. Austin: University of Texas Press, 1975.

Hartog, Hendrik. *Man and Wife in America: A History*. Cambridge: Harvard University Press, 2000.

Heidenreich, Linda. *"This Land Was Mexican Once": Histories of Resistance from Northern California*. Austin: University of Texas Press, 2007.

Herrera Pérez, Octavio. "Del señorío a la posrevolución: Evolución histórica de una hacienda en el noreste de México. El caso de la Sauteña." *Historia Mexicana* 43:1 (1993): 5–76.

——. *El norte de Tamaulipas y la conformación de la frontera México–Estados Unidos, 1835–1855*. Ciudad Victoria: El Colegio de Tamaulipas, 2003.

——. *Monografía de Reynosa*. Ciudad Victoria: Instituto Tamaulipeco de Cultura, 1989.

Hietala, Thomas R. *Manifest Design: Anxious Aggrandizement in Late Jacksonian America*. Ithaca: Cornell University Press, 1985.

Hill, Lawrence F. *José de Escandón and the Founding of Nuevo Santander: A Study in Spanish Colonization*. Columbus: Ohio State University Press, 1926.

Hine, Robert V., and John Mack Faragher. *The American West: A New Interpretive History*. New Haven: Yale University Press, 2000.

Hinojosa, Gilberto M. *A Borderlands Town in Transition: Laredo, 1755–1870*. College Station: Texas A&M Press, 1983.

Hogue, Michel. "Between Race and Nation: The Creation of a Métis Borderland on the Northern Plains." In Johnson and Graybill, eds., *Bridging National Borders in North America*.

Horgan, Paul. *Great River: The Rio Grande in North American History*. 2 vols. New York: Holt, Rinehart, and Wilson, 1954.

Horsman, Reginald. *Race and Manifest Destiny: The Origins of American Racial Anglo-Saxonism*. Cambridge: Harvard University Press, 1981.

Hu-DeHart, Evelyn. *Yaqui Resistance and Survival: The Struggle for Land and Autonomy, 1821–1920*. Madison: University of Wisconsin Press, 1984.

Hunefeldt, Christine. *Liberalism in the Bedroom: Quarrelling Spouses in Nineteenth-Century Lima*. University Park: Pennsylvania State University Press, 2000.

Irby, James A. *Backdoor at Bagdad: The Civil War on the Rio Grande*. El Paso: Texas Western Press, 1977.

Isbell, Frances W. "Jackson Ranch Church." Typescript located at Museum of South Texas History, Hidalgo County Historical Commission, Edinburg, Tex., December 1982.

Jackson, Robert H. *Race, Caste, and Status:Indians in Colonial Spanish America*. Albuquerque: University of New Mexico Press, 1999.

Jacobson, Matthew Frye. *Whiteness of a Different Color: European Immigration and the Alchemy of Race*. Cambridge: Harvard University Press, 1998.

Jarratt, Rie. *Gutiérrez de Lara, Mexican Texan: The Story of a Creole Hero*. In *The Mexican Experience in Texas*. Edited by Carlos Cortés. New York: Arno Press, 1976.

Johannsen, Robert W. *To the Halls of the Montezumas: The Mexican War in the American Imagination*. New York: Oxford University Press, 1985.

John, Elizabeth A. H. "Independent Indians and the San Antonio Community." In *Tejano Origins in Eighteenth-Century San Antonio*. Edited by Gerald E. Poyo and Gilberto M. Hinojosa. Austin: University of Texas Press, 1991.

———. *Storms Brewed in Other Men's Worlds: The Confrontation of Indians, Spanish, and French in the Southwest, 1540–1795*. College Station: Texas A&M University Press, 1975.

Johnson, Benjamin Heber. *Revolution in Texas: How a Forgotten Rebellion and Its Bloody Suppression Turned Mexicans into Americans*. New Haven: Yale University Press, 2003.

Johnson, Benjamin H., and Andrew R. Graybill, eds. *Bridging National Borders in North America: Transnational and Comparative Histories*. Durham: Duke University Press, 2010.

———. "Introduction: Borders and Their Historians in North America." In Johnson and Graybill, eds., *Bridging National Borders in North America*.

Jones, Oakah L., Jr. *Los paisanos*. Norman: University of Oklahoma Press, 1979.

Joseph, Gilbert M. "The United States, Feuding Elites, and Rural Revolt in Yucatán, 1836–1915." In *Rural Revolt in Mexico: U.S. Intervention and the Domain of Subaltern Politics*. Edited by Daniel Nugent. Durham: Duke University Press, 1998.

Joseph, Gilbert M., and Daniel Nugent, eds. *Everyday Forms of State Formation: Revolution and the Negotiation of Rule in Modern Mexico*. Durham: Duke University Press, 1994.

Juárez, José Roberto. "La Iglesia Católica y el Chicano en Sud Tejas, 1836–1911." *Aztlán: Chicano Journal of the Social Sciences and the Arts* 4:2 (fall 1973): 217–55.

Katz, Friedrich. "Labor Conditions on Haciendas in Porfirian Mexico: Some Trends and Tendencies." *Hispanic American Historical Review* 54:1 (February 1974): 1–47.

Kearney, Milo, and Antony Knopp. *Boom and Bust: The Historical Cycles of Matamoros and Brownsville*. Austin: Eakin Press, 1991.

———. *Border Cuates: A History of the U.S.-Mexican Twin Cities*. Austin: Eakin Press, 1995.

Kelley, Robin D. G. *Race Rebels: Culture, Politics, and the Black Working Class*. New York: Free Press, 1996.

Kelley, Sean. "'Mexico in His Head': Slavery and the Texas-Mexico Border, 1810–1860." *Journal of Social History* 37:3 (spring 2004): 709–23.

Kendall, George Wilkins. *Dispatches from the Mexican War*. Edited by Lawrence Delbert Cress. Norman: University of Oklahoma Press, 1999.

Kerber, Linda. *No Constitutional Right to be Ladies: Women and the Obligations of Citizenship*. New York: Hill and Wang, 1998.

Krauze, Enrique. *Mexico: Biography of Power, A History of Modern Mexico, 1810–1996*. New York: HarperPerennial, 1997.

Larson, Jane E. "Women Understand So Little, They Call My Good Nature 'Deceit': A Feminist Rethinking of Seduction." *Columbia Law Review* 93:2 (March 1993): 374–472.

Larson, Wendy. "A History of Divorce in Texas." MA thesis, Texas A&M University, College Station, 1986.

Lattimore, Owen. "The Frontier in History." In *Studies in Frontier History: Collected Papers 1928–1958*. Edited by Owen Lattimore. London: Oxford University Press, 1962.

Lavrin, Asunción. "Sexuality in Colonial Mexico: A Church Dilemma." In *Sexuality and Marriage in Colonial Latin America*. Edited by Asunción Lavrin. Lincoln: University of Nebraska Press, 1989.

LeCompte, Janet. "The Independent Women of Hispanic New Mexico, 1821–1846." *Western Historical Quarterly* 22 (January 1981): 17–35.

León, Nicolás. *Las castas del México colonial o Nueva España: Noticias etno-antropológicas*. Mexico City: Talleres gráficos del Museo Nacional de Arqueología, Historia y Etnografía, 1924.

Limerick, Patricia N. *The Legacy of Conquest: The Unbroken Past of the American West*. New York: W. W. Norton, 1987.

Lockhart, James. *The Nahuas after the Conquest: A Social and Cultural History of the Indians of Central Mexico, Sixteenth through Eighteenth Centuries*. Stanford: Stanford University Press, 1992.

Lockhart, James, and Stuart B. Schwartz. *Early Latin America: A History of Colonial Spanish America and Brazil*. New York: Cambridge University Press, 1983.

Lomnitz, Claudio. "Modes of Citizenship in Mexico." In *Alternative Modernities*. Edited by Dilip Parameshwar Gaonkar. Durham: Duke University Press, 2001.

Lord, Walter, ed. *The Fremantle Diary: Being the Journal of Lieutenant Colonel James Arthur Lyon Frmantle, Coldstream Guards, on His Three Months in the Southern States*. London: Andre Deutsch, 1956.

Lott, Virgil N., and Mercurio Martínez. *The Kingdom of Zapata*. Austin: Eakin Press, 1953.

Lowe, Lisa. *Immigrant Acts: On Asian American Cultural Politics*. Durham: Duke University Press, 1996.

Marcum, Richard T. "Fort Brown, Texas: The History of a Border Post." PhD diss., Texas Technical College, Lubbock, 1964.

Marshall, T. H., and Tom Bottomore. *Citizenship and Social Class*. Concord, Mass.: Pluto Press, 1992.

Martin, Cheryl E. *Governance and Society in Colonial Mexico*. Stanford: Stanford University Press, 1996.

Martin, Patricia Preciado. *Songs My Mother Sang to Me: An Oral History of Mexican American Women*. Tucson: University of Arizona Press, 1992.

Martínez, Oscar J. *Border Boom Town: Ciudad Juárez since 1848*. Austin: University of Texas Press, 1975.

Marzahl, Peter. *Town in the Empire: Government, Politics, and Society in Seventeenth-Century Popayá.* Austin: University of Texas, Institute of Latin American Studies, 1978.

Matovina, Timothy M. *Tejano Religion and Ethnicity: San Antonio, 1821–1860.* Austin: University of Texas Press, 1995.

May, Elaine Tyler. *Great Expectations: Marriage and Divorce in Post-Victorian America.* Chicago: University of Chicago Press, 1980.

McAlister, L. N. "Social Structure and Social Change in New Spain." *Hispanic American Historical Review* 63 (August 1963): 349–70.

McAllen Amberson, Mary Margaret, James A. McAllen, and Margaret H. McAllen. *I Would Rather Sleep in Texas: A History of the Lower Rio Grande Valley and the People of the Santa Anita Land Grant.* Austin: Texas State Historical Association, 2003.

McCutchan, Joseph D. *Mier Expedition Diary: A Texan Prisoner's Account.* Edited by Joseph Milton Nance. Austin: University of Texas Press, 1978.

McMillin, James. "Anglo Methodist Missionaries and Mexicans in the Southwest and Mexico, 1836–1910." MA thesis, Southern Methodist University, Dallas, 1994.

Meade, Joaquín. *Etimologías toponímicas indígenas del Estado de Tamaulipas.* Ciudad Victoria, Tamaulipas: Universidad Autónoma de Tamaulipas, 1977.

Meeks, Eric V. *Border Citizens: The Making of Indians, Mexicans, and Anglos in Arizona.* Austin: University of Texas Press, 2007.

Menchaca, Martha. "The Anti-miscegenation History of the American Southwest, 1837 to 1970: Transforming Racial Ideology into Law." *Cultural Dynamics* 20:3 (2008): 279–318.

———. *Recovering History, Constructing Race: The Indian, Black, and White Roots of Mexican Americans.* Austin: University of Texas Press, 2001.

Merk, Frederick, and Lois Bannister. *Manifest Destiny and Mission in American History: A Reinterpretation.* New York: Knopf, 1963.

Meyer, Michael C., William L. Sherman, and Susan M. Deeds, eds. *The Course of Mexican History.* 8th ed. New York: Oxford University Press, 2007.

Mikesell, Marvin W. "Comparative Studies in Frontier History." *Annals of the Association of American Geographers* 50:1 (March 1960): 62–74.

Miller, Hubert J. *José de Escandón: Colonizer of Nuevo Santander.* Edinburg, Tex.: New Santander Press, 1980.

Milligan, James Clark. "José Bernardo Gutiérrez de Lara, Mexican Frontiersman 1811–1841." PhD diss., Texas Tech University, Lubbock, 1975.

Mitchell, Pablo. *Coyote Nation: Sexuality, Race, and Conquest in Modernizing New Mexico, 1880–1920.* Chicago: University of Chicago Press, 2005.

Monroy, Douglas. *Thrown among Strangers: The Making of Mexican Culture in Frontier California.* Berkeley: University of California Press, 1990.

Montejano, David. *Anglos and Mexicans in the Making of Texas, 1836–1986.* Austin: University of Texas Press, 1987.

Montgomery, Cora [Jane Maria McManus Cazneau]. *Eagle Pass, or, Life on the Border.* New York: G. P. Putnam and Co., 1852; repr., Austin: Pemberton Press, 1966.

Montoya, María E. *Translating Property: The Maxwell Land Grant and the Conflict over Land in the American West, 1840–1900.* Berkeley: University of California Press, 2002; repr., Lawrence: University Press of Kansas, 2005.

Mora, Anthony. *Border Dilemmas: Racial and National Uncertainties in New Mexico, 1848–1912.* Durham: Duke University Press, 2011.

Mora-Torres, Juan. *The Making of the Mexican Border: The State, Capitalism, and Society in Nuevo León, 1848–1910.* Austin: University of Texas Press, 2001.

Mörner, Magnus. *Race Mixture in the History of Latin America.* Boston: Little, Brown, 1967.

Muller, C. H. "Introduction." In *Journey to Mexico during the Years 1826 to 1834.* Edited by Jean Louis Berlandier. Austin: Texas State Historical Association, 1980.

Myres, Sandra L. "The Ranching Frontier: Spanish Institutional Backgrounds of the Plains Cattle Industry." In *New Spain's Far Northern Frontier: Essays on Spain in the American West, 1540–1821.* Edited by David J. Weber. Albuquerque: University of New Mexico Press, 1979.

———. *The Ranch in Spanish Texas, 1691–1800.* El Paso: Texas Western Press, University of Texas, 1969.

Nail, Olin Webster. *The First Hundred Years of the Southwest Texas Conference of the Methodist Church, 1858–1958.* San Antonio, Tex.: Methodist Church, 1958.

Náñez, Alfredo. "History of the Rio Grande Conference of the United Methodist Church." MA thesis, Southern Methodist University, Dallas, 1980.

Newcomb, William W. *The Indians of Texas: From Prehistoric to Modern Times.* Austin: University of Texas Press, 1961.

Ngai, Mae M. *Impossible Subjects: Illegal Aliens and the Making of Modern America.* Princeton: Princeton University Press, 2004.

Nizza da Silva, María Beatriz. "Divorce in Colonial Brazil: The Case of São Paulo." In *Sexuality and Marriage in Colonial Latin America.* Edited by Asunción Lavrin. Lincoln: University of Nebraska Press, 1989.

Nugent, Daniel. "'Are We Not [Civilized] Men?' The Formation and Devolution of Community in Northern Mexico." *Journal of Historical Sociology* 2:3 (September 1989): 206–39.

———. *Spent Cartridges of Revolution: An Anthropological History of Namiquipa, Chihuahua.* Chicago: University of Chicago Press, 1993.

Olivas, Michael A. "Hernandez v. Texas: A Litigation History." In *Colored Men and Hombres Aquí: Hernandez v. Texas and the Emergence of Mexican American Lawyering.* Edited by Michael A. Olivas. Houston: Arte Público Press, 2006.

Olmsted, Frederick Law. *Journey through Texas: A Saddletrip on the Southwestern Frontier.* Edited by James Howard. Austin: Von Boeckmann-Jones Press, 1962.

Omi, Michael, and Howard Winant. *Racial Formation in the United States: From the 1960s to the 1980s.* New York: Routledge and Kegan Paul, 1987.

Osante, Patricia. *Orígenes del Nuevo Santander, 1748–1772.* Mexico City: Universidad Nacional Autónoma de México, 1997.

Paredes, Américo. *Folklore and Culture on the Texas-Mexican Border.* Edited and with an introduction by Richard Bauman. Austin: Center for Mexican American Studies, University of Texas at Austin, 1993.

———. "Folklore e historia: Dos Cantares de la frontera del norte." In *25 Estudios de Folklore.* Vol. 4. Edited by Fernando Anaya Monroy. Mexico City: Instituto de Investigaciones Estéticas, Universidad Autónoma de México, 1971.

———. *A Texas-Mexican Cancionero: Folksongs of the Lower Border.* Urbana: University of Illinois Press, 1976.

———. *"With His Pistol in His Hand": A Border Ballad and Its Hero.* Austin: University of Texas Press, 1958.

Paredes Manzano, Eliseo. *Homenaje a los fundadores de la heroica, leal e invicta Matamoros en el sesquicentenario de su nuevo nombre.* Matamoros, Tamaulipas, 1976.

———. *La Casa Mata y fortificaciones de la heroica Matamoros, Tamaulipas.* Matamoros, Tamaulipas, 1974.

Pascoe, Peggy. *What Comes Naturally: Miscegenation Law and the Making of Race in America.* New York: Oxford University Press, 2009.

Paulsen, James W. "Remember the Alamo[ny]! The Unique Texas Ban on Permanent Alimony and the Development of Community Property Law." *Law and Contemporary Problems* 56:2 (spring 1993): 8–70.

Peña, Manuel H. *The Texas-Mexican Conjunto: History of a Working-Class Music.* Austin: University of Texas Press, 1985.

Phelan, Macum. *A History of Early Methodism in Texas, 1817–1866.* Nashville: Cokesbury Press, 1924.

Pitt, Leonard. *The Decline of the Californios: A Social History of the Spanish-Speaking Californians, 1846–1900.* With a new foreword by Ramón A. Gutiérrez. Berkeley: University of California Press, 1998.

Poyo, Gerald E. "Immigrants and Integration in Late Eighteenth-Century Béxar." In Poyo and Hinojosa, eds., *Tejano Origins in Eighteenth-Century San Antonio.*

Poyo, Gerald E., and Gilberto M. Hinojosa, eds. *Tejano Origins in Eighteenth-Century San Antonio.* Austin: University of Texas Press, 1991.

Prieto, Alejandro. *Historia, geografía y estadística del Estado de Tamaulipas.* Mexico City: Librería Manuel Porrúa,1975.

Pruitt, Francelle LeNaee. "'But a Mournful Remedy': Divorce in Two Texas Counties." MA thesis, University of North Texas, Denton, 1999.

Ramos, Raúl A. *Beyond the Alamo: Forging Mexican Ethnicity in San Antonio, 1821–1861.* Chapel Hill: University of North Carolina Press, 2008.

Rankin, Melinda. *Texas in 1850.* Waco, Tex.: Texian Press, 1966.

———. *Twenty Years among the Mexicans: A Narrative of Missionary Labor.* Cincinnati, Ohio: Central Book Concern, 1881.

Rayburn, John C. "Introduction." In Rankin, *Texas in 1850.*

Red, William Stuart. *A History of the Presbyterian Church in Texas.* Austin: Steck, 1936.

Rendón de la Garza, Clemente. *Bicentenario de Nuestra Señora del Refugio de los Esteros.* Matamoros, Tamaulipas: Obsipado de Matamoros, 1994.

Reséndez, Andrés. *Changing National Identities at the Frontier: Texas and New Mexico, 1800–1850.* New York: Cambridge University Press, 2004.

———. "National Identity on a Shifting Border: Texas and New Mexico in the Age of Transition, 1821–1848." *Journal of American History* 86:2 (September 1999): 688–709.

Reyes, Barbara O. *Private Women, Public Lives: Gender and the Missions of the Californias.* Austin: University of Texas Press, 2009.

Riley, Glenda. *Building and Breaking Families in the American West.* Albuquerque: University of New Mexico Press, 1996.

———. *Divorce: An American Tradition.* New York: Oxford University Press, 1991.

Rivera Saldaña, Oscar. *Frontera heroica: Tomo I colonización del noreste de México (1748–1821).* Matamoros, Tamaulipas: Impresiones y Publicaciones, 1984.

———. "Tamaulipas a un año de la guerra México-Estados Unidos: Reseña del informe de gobierno de Jesús Cárdenas, 1849." In Dávila and Rivera Saldaña, eds., *Matamoros en la guerra con los Estados Unidos.*

Roa Bárcena, José María. *Recuerdos de la invasión norte-americana, 1846–1848.* México: J. Buxó, 1883.

Robertson, Brian. *Wild Horse Desert: The Heritage of South Texas.* Edinburg, Tex.: New Santander Press, 1985.

Rodríguez O., Jaime E. "The Constitution of 1824 and the Formation of the Mexican State." In *The Evolution of the Mexican Political System.* Edited by Jaime E. Rodríguez O. Wilmington: Scholarly Resources, 1993.

———. "Down from Colonialism: Mexico's Nineteenth-Century Crisis." In *The Mexican and Mexican American Experience in the 19th Century.* Edited by Jaime E. Rodríguez O. Tempe, Ariz.: Bilingual Press, 1989.

———. "From Royal Subject to Republican Citizen." In *The Independence of Mexico and the Creation of the New Nation.* Edited by Jaime E. Rodriguez O. Los Angeles: UCLA Latin American Center Publications, 1989.

———. "Introduction." In *The Evolution of the Mexican Political System.* Edited by Jaime E. Rodríguez O. Wilmington: Scholarly Resources, 1993.

Rodríguez S., Eugenia. "Civilizing Domestic Life in the Central Valley of Costa Rica, 1750–1850." In *Hidden Histories of Gender and the State in Latin America.* Edited by Elizabeth Dore and Maxine Molyneux. Durham: Duke University Press, 2000.

Rosenbaum, Robert J. *Mexicano Resistance in the Southwest: "The Sacred Right of Self-Preservation."* Austin: University of Texas Press, 1981.

Ruiz, Vicki L. *From Out of the Shadows: Mexican Women in Twentieth-Century America.* New York: Oxford University Press, 1998.

Sahlins, Peter. *Boundaries: The Making of France and Spain in the Pyrenees.* Berkeley: University of California Press, 1989.

Saldívar, Ramón. *The Borderlands of Culture: Américo Paredes and the Transnational Imaginary.* Durham: Duke University Press, 2006.

Salinas, Martín. *Indians of the Rio Grande Delta: Their Role in the History of Southern Texas and Northeastern Mexico.* Austin: University of Texas Press, 1990.

Sánchez, George J. *Becoming Mexican American: Ethnicity, Culture, and Identity in Chicano Los Angeles, 1900–1945.* New York: Oxford University Press, 1993.

San Miguel, Guadalupe. *"Let All of Them Take Heed": Mexican Americans and the Campaign for Educational Equality in Texas, 1910–1981.* Austin: University of Texas Press, 1987.

Schwartz, Rosalie. *Across the Rio to Freedom: U.S. Negroes in Mexico.* El Paso: Texas Western Press, 1975.

Scott, Florence Johnson. *Historical Heritage of the Lower Rio Grande: A Historical Record of Spanish Exploration, Subjugation and Colonization of the Lower Rio Grande Valley and the Activities of José Escandón, Count of Sierra Gorda together with the Development of Towns and Ranchos under Spanish, Mexican, and Texas Sovereignties 1747–1848.* Rev. ed. Waco, Tex.: Texian Press, 1966.

———. "Spanish Colonization of the Lower Rio Grande, 1747–1767." In *Essays in Mexican History.* Edited by Thomas E. Cotner and Carlos E. Castañeda. Austin: University of Texas Press, 1958.

Scott, James. *Weapons of the Weak: Everyday Forms of Peasant Resistance.* New Haven: Yale University Press, 1986.

Seed, Patricia. *To Love, Honor, and Obey in Colonial Mexico: Conflicts over Marriage Choice, 1574–1821.* Stanford: Stanford University Press, 1988.

Simmons, Marc. *Little Lion of the Southwest.* Chicago: Sage Books, 1973.

Singletary, Otis A. *The Mexican War*. Chicago: University of Chicago Press, 1960.

Sinclair, M. B. W. "Seduction and the Myth of the Ideal Woman." *Law and Inequality* 5 (1997–1998): 33–102.

Smith, Franklin. *The Mexican War Journal of Captain Franklin Smith*. Edited by Joseph E. Chance. Jackson: University of Mississippi Press, 1991.

Smith, George Winston, and Charles Judah, eds. *Chronicles of the Gringos: The U.S. Army in the Mexican War, 1846–1848, Accounts of Eyewitnesses and Combatants*. Albuquerque: University of New Mexico Press, 1968.

Smith, Merril D. *Breaking the Bonds: Marital Discord in Pennsylvania, 1730–1830*. New York: New York University Press, 1991.

Smith, Michael Peter, and Matt Bakker. *Citizenship across Borders: The Political Transnationalism of El Migrante*. Ithaca: Cornell University Press, 2008.

Smith, Rogers M. *Civic Ideals: Conflicting Visions of Citizenship in U.S. History*. New Haven: Yale University Press, 1997.

Stambaugh, J. Lee. *History of Hidalgo County Elected Officials from 1852 to 1963*. Austin: Pharr Press, 1963.

Stambaugh, J. Lee, and Lillian J. Stambaugh. *The Lower Rio Grande Valley of Texas*. Austin: San Felipe Press, 1974.

Stern, Steve J. *The Secret History of Gender: Women, Men, and Power in Late Colonial Mexico*. Chapel Hill: University of North Carolina Press, 1995.

Stets, Jan E., and Peter J. Burke. "Identity Theory and Social Identity Theory." *Social Psychology Quarterly* 63:3 (September 2000): 224–37.

Stewart, Kenneth L., and Arnoldo De León. *Not Room Enough: Mexican, Anglos, and Socio-Economic Change in Texas, 1850–1900*. Albuquerque: University of New Mexico Press, 1993.

St. John, Rachel. "Divided Ranges: Trans-border Ranches and the Creation of National Spaces along the Western U.S.-Mexico Border." In Johnson and Graybill, eds., *Bridging National Borders in North America*.

Stuntz, Jean A. *Hers, His, and Theirs: Community Property Law in Spain and Early Texas*. Lubbock: Texas Tech University Press, 2005.

Taylor, Paul S. *An American-Mexican Frontier: Nueces County, Texas*. Chapel Hill: University of North Carolina Press, 1934.

TePaske, John Jay. "The Financial Disintegration of the Royal Government of Mexico during the Epoch of Independence." In *The Independence of Mexico and the Creation of the New Nation*. Edited by Jaime E. Rodriguez O. Los Angeles: UCLA Latin American Center Publications, 1989.

Thompson, James Heaven. "A Nineteenth Century History of Cameron County, Texas." MA thesis, University of Texas, Austin, 1965.

Thompson, Jerry D. *Cortina: Defending the Mexican Name in Texas*. College Station: Texas A&M University Press, 2007.

———. "Historical Survey." In *A Shared Experience*. Austin: Texas Historical Commission, 1991.

———. *Juan Cortina and the Texas-Mexico Frontier, 1859–1877*. El Paso: Texas Western Press, 1994.

———. *Mexican Texans in the Union Army*. El Paso: Texas Western Press, 1986.

———. *Vaqueros in Blue and Gray*. Austin: Presidial Press, 1977.

———. *Warm Weather and Bad Whiskey: The 1886 Laredo Election Riot*. El Paso: Texas Western Press, 1991.

———. *A Wild and Vivid Land: An Illustrated History of the South Texas Border*. Austin: Texas State Historical Association, 1997.

Thompson, Jerry D., and Lawrence T. Jones III. *Civil War and Revolution on the Rio Grande Frontier: A Narrative and Photographic History.* Austin: Texas State Historical Association, 2004.

Tijerina, Andrés. *Tejanos and Texas under the Mexican Flag, 1821–1836.* College Station: Texas A&M Press University, 1994.

———. *Tejano Empire: Life on the South Texas Ranchos.* College Station: Texas A&M Press University, 1998.

Truett, Samuel. *Fugitive Landscapes: The Forgotten History of the U.S.-Mexico Borderlands.* New Haven: Yale University Press, 2006.

Truett, Samuel, and Elliott Young, eds. *Continental Crossroads: Remapping U.S.-Mexico Borderlands History.* Durham: Duke University Press, 2004.

———. "Introduction: Making Transnational History: Nations, Regions, and Borderlands." In Truett and Young, eds., *Continental Crossroads.*

Twinam, Ann. "Honor, Sexuality, and Illegitimacy in Colonial Spanish America." In *Sexuality and Marriage in Colonial Latin America.* Edited by Asunción Lavrin. Lincoln: University of Nebraska Press, 1989.

Tyler, Ronnie C. "Fugitive Slaves in Mexico." *Journal of Negro History* 57:1 (January 1972): 1–12.

Valdés, Carlos Manuel. *La gente del mezquite: Los nómadas del noreste en la colonia.* Mexico City: Centro de Investigaciones y Estudios Superiores en Antropología Social, 1995.

VanderVelde, Lea. "The Legal Ways of Seduction." *Stanford Law Review* 48:4 (April 1996): 817–901.

Van Young, Eric. *Hacienda and Market in Eighteenth-Century Mexico: The Rural Economy of the Guadalajara Region, 1675–1820.* Berkeley: University of California Press, 1981.

———. *The Other Rebellion: Popular Violence, Ideology, and the Mexican Struggle for Independence, 1810–1821.* Stanford: Stanford University Press, 2001.

Vázquez, Josefina Zoraida. "The Texas Question in Mexican Politics, 1836–1845." *Southwestern Historical Quarterly* 89:3 (January 1986): 309–44.

———. "La supuesta república del Río Grande." *Historia Mexicana* 36:1 (July–September 1986): 49–80.

Vidaurreta Tjarks, Alicia. "Comparative Demographic Analysis of Texas, 1777–1793." In *New Spain's Far Northern Frontier: Essays on Spain in the American West, 1540–1821.* Edited by David J. Weber. Dallas: Southern Methodist University Press, 1979.

Vielé, Teresa (Griffin). *"Following the Drum": A Glimpse of Frontier Life.* New York: Rudd and Carleton, 1858; repr., Lincoln: University of Nebraska Press, 1984.

Vigness, David M. "Indian Raids on the Lower Rio Grande, 1836–1837." *Southwestern Historical Quarterly* 59 (July 1955): 14–23.

———, ed. and trans. "Nuevo Santander in 1795: A Provincial Inspection by Felix Calleja." *Southwestern Historical Quarterly* 75 (April 1972): 461–506.

———. *The Revolutionary Decades, 1810–1836.* Austin: Steck-Vaughn, 1965.

Villarreal, Roberto M. "The Mexican-American Vaqueros of the King Ranch: A Social History." MA thesis, Texas A&I University, 1972.

Viqueira Albán, Juan Pedro. *Propriety and Permissiveness in Bourbon Mexico.* Translated by Sonya Lipsett-Rivera and Sergio Rivera Ayala. Wilmington, Del.: Scholarly Resources, 1999.

Webb, Walter Prescott. *The Texas Rangers: A Century of Frontier Defense.* Boston: Houghton Mifflin, 1935.

Weber, David J. *Bárbaros: Spaniards and Their Savages in the Age of Enlightenment.* New Haven: Yale University Press, 2005.

——. *The Mexican Frontier, 1821–1846: The American Southwest under Mexico.* Albuquerque: University of New Mexico Press, 1982.

——. "'Scarce More Than Apes': Historical Roots of Anglo-American Stereotypes of Mexicans." In *New Spain's Far Northern Frontier: Essays on Spain in the American West, 1540–1821.* Edited by David J. Weber. Albuquerque: University of New Mexico Press, 1979.

——. *The Spanish Frontier in North America.* New Haven: Yale University Press, 1992.

——. *The Taos Trappers: The Fur Trade in the Far Southwest, 1540–1846.* Norman: University of Oklahoma Press, 2005.

White, Richard. *"It's Your Misfortune and None of My Own": A New History of the American West.* Norman: University of Oklahoma Press, 1991.

——. "Race Relations in the American West." *American Quarterly* 38:3 (1986): 396–416.

Wilcox, Seb S. "Laredo during the Texas Republic." *Southwestern Historical Quarterly* 42:2 (October 1938): 83–107.

Wilson, Thomas M., and Hastings Donnan, eds. *Border Identities: Nation and State at International Frontiers.* Cambridge: Cambridge University Press, 1998.

Wilkinson, J. B. *Laredo and the Rio Grande Frontier.* Austin: Jenkins, 1975.

Williams, R. H. *With the Border Ruffians: Memories of the Far West, 1852–1868.* Edited by E. W. Williams. London: J. Murray, 1907.

Wood, Robert D. *Life in Laredo: A Documentary History from the Laredo Archives.* Denton: University of North Texas Press, 2004.

Wright, Robert E. "Popular and Official Religiosity: A Theoretical Analysis and a Case Study of Laredo-Nuevo Laredo, 1755–1857." PhD diss., Graduate Theological Union, Berkeley, Calif., 1992.

Wunder, John R., and Pekka Hämäläinen. "Of Lethal Places and Lethal Essays." *American Historical Review* 104:4 (October 1999): 1229–34.

Young, Elliott. *Catarino Garza's Revolution on the Texas-Mexico Border.* Durham: Duke University Press, 2004.

——. "Deconstructing 'La Raza': Identifying the 'Gente Decente' of Laredo, 1904–1911." *Southwestern Historical Quarterly* 98:2 (October 1994): 227–59.

Zamora, Emilio. *The World of the Mexican Worker in Texas.* College Station: Texas A&M University Press, 1993.

Zavala, Silvio. "The Frontiers of Hispanic America." In *New Spain's Far Northern Frontier: Essays on Spain in the American West, 1540–1821.* Edited by David J. Weber. Dallas: Southern Methodist University Press, 1979.

——. *Los esclavos indios en Nueva España.* Mexico City: El Colegio Nacional, 1967.

Zavaleta, Antonio N. "'The Twin Cities': A Historical Synthesis of the Socio-Economic Interdependence of the Brownsville-Matamoros Border Community." In *Studies in Brownsville History.* Edited by Milo Kearney. Brownsville, Tex.: Pan American University at Brownsville, 1986.

Zorrilla, Juan Fidel. *El poder colonial en Nuevo Santander.* Mexico City: Librería Manuel Porrúa, 1976.

——. *Estudio de la legislación en Tamaulipas.* 2a ed., aum. y corregida (2nd ed., expanded and revised). Ciudad Victoria, Tamaulipas: Universidad Autónoma de Tamaulipas, Instituto de Investigaciones Históricas, 1980.

——. *Historia de Tamaulipas: Síntesis.* Mexico City: Editorial Jus, 1977.

———. *Tamaulipas—Tamaholipa*. Ciudad Victoria, Tamaulipas: Universidad Autónoma de Tamaulipas, 1973.

Zorrilla, Juan Fidel, Maribel Miró Flaquer, and Octavio Herrera Pérez. "Presencia del ayuntamiento de Matamoros durante la intervención norteamericana de 1847." In *México en Guerra (1846–1848)*. Edited by Laura Herrera Serna. Mexico City: Consejo Nacional para la Cultura y las Artes, 1997.

———, eds. *Tamaulipas: Textos de su historia, 1810–1921*. Vol. 1. Mexico City: Instituto de Investigaciones Dr. José María Luis Mora, 1990.

———. *Tamaulipas: Una historia compartida I, 1810–1921*. Ciudad Victoria, Tamaulipas: Universidad Autónoma de Tamaulipas, 1993.

Index

Page numbers in italics indicate figures.

OMAR S. VALERIO-JIMÉNEZ IS AN ASSOCIATE PROFESSOR
IN THE DEPARTMENT OF HISTORY AT THE
UNIVERSITY OF IOWA.

Library of Congress Cataloging-in-Publication Data
Valerio-Jiménez, Omar S. (Omar Santiago)
River of hope : forging identity and nation in
the Rio Grande borderlands / Omar S. Valerio-Jiménez.
p. cm.
Includes bibliographical references and index.
ISBN 978-0-8223-5171-9 (cloth : alk. paper)
ISBN 978-0-8223-5185-6 (pbk. : alk. paper)
1. Group identity—Texas—Lower Rio Grande Valley.
2. Group identity—Mexican-American Border Region.
3. Citizenship—Political aspects—United States.
4. Citizenship—Political aspects—Mexico.
5. Lower Rio Grande Valley (Tex.)—History.
6. Mexican-American Border Region—History. I. Title.
HM753.V33 2012
305.8009764'4—dc23
2012011638